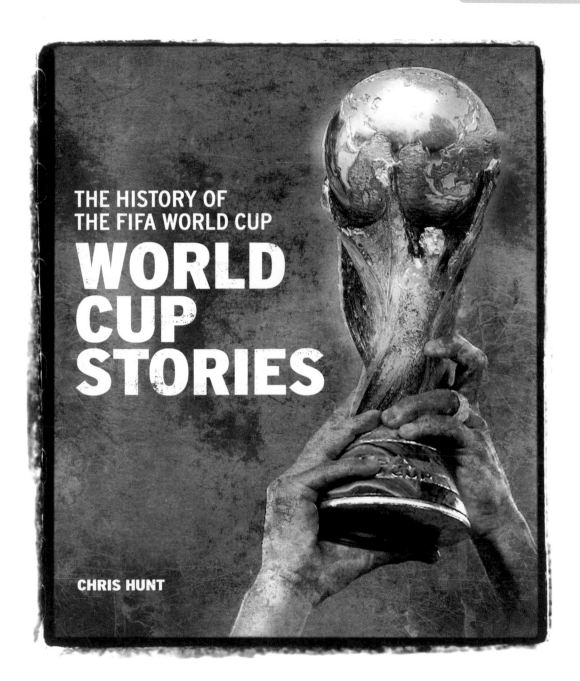

THE HISTORY OF
THE FIFA WORLD CUP

WORLD CUP STORIES

CHRIS HUNT

interact publishing

First published in 2006 by Interact Publishing Limited

Interact Publishing
PO Box 239
Football Yearbook
Ware SG9 9WX
www.footballyearbook.co.uk

© Interact Publishing Limited
Published by arrangement with the BBC. The BBC logo is a registered trademark of the
British Broadcasting Corporation and is used under licence. BBC logo © BBC 1996

A 'MILE AWAY CLUB' PRODUCTION
Text & design © Chris Hunt: www.ChrisHunt.biz
Designed by David Houghton

BBC Series Producer: Tom Ware
Photographs © Getty Images and © Popperfoto.com
Fact Checking: Nick Gibbs, Frank Gilbert, John Glover, Sara Hunt and Paul Robson
Design Production: Cambridge Publishers Ltd
Printed and bound by The Bath Press.

ISBN 0 95498 192 8

CONTENTS

THE ORIGINS

OF THE WORLD CUP

There really is no bigger sporting event than the World Cup. Every football fan dreams of lifting that incomparable trophy, just 14 inches tall and made from 18-carat solid gold. While it's a prize that few people get to lay their hands on, we all grow up reading of the daring deeds of the men that have won it, football legends like Pelé and Moore, Maradona and Beckenbauer, Garrincha and Rossi; of the beautiful Brazilian team of 1970, of England's wingless wonders of 1966, the rainbow warriors of France in 1998. We discover how matches can turn on a single instant of exquisite skill, how a football legend can be built in just one moment of instinctive brilliance, how dreams can be shattered by the consequences of a single missed penalty or mistimed tackle. We learn that although the World Cup can be won in just 90 minutes, it leaves memories that will last forever.

It's an experience that is shared by billions of people around the world every four years, guaranteeing a collective outpouring of emotion like nothing else on the planet. When Brazil and Germany took to the pitch of the Yokohama International Stadium in Japan for the 2002 World Cup final, 1.1 billion viewers were watching, the match screened in 213 countries – virtually every nation in the world. Despite the non-prime time broadcasting hours in Europe and the Americas, the tournament pulled a cumulative audience of 28.8 billion. With less problematic screening times the audience for 1998 World Cup in France was even larger, 37 billion viewers watching the tournament's 64 games, with a worldwide television audience of 1.3 billion tuning in for the final between France and Brazil.

No other sporting occasion can inspire the same kind of passionate commitment. The Olympics doesn't even come close. The highest viewed event at the 2004 Olympic Games in Athens was the opening ceremony,

The 2002 World Cup final in Japan – watched by 69,000 fans in the stadium and 1.1 billion TV viewers around the world.

which attracted a worldwide audience of 127 million, while its blue riband event, the men's 100m sprint final, racked up viewing figures of 87 million. Not even close to the average audience of 314.1 million viewers per match at the 2002 World Cup. But the power of football is not in its statistics. That can be left for the American sports. Football is really defined by the passions it inspires in fans the world over, by the emotions that it can stir. The World Cup is about exhilaration and anticipation, the thrill of the goal, the fantastical dreams of unobtainable success, the outlandish stories behind those great moments of glorious victory and noble defeat.

Ever since the first competition was staged in Uruguay in 1930, it has grown in popularity and prestige. But that's not to say the World Cup has been without its problems. Indeed, the origins of the tournament were so wrapped up in politics that it took 26 years for the idea of a world football championship to become a reality. The origins of the competition can be traced back to the formation of the *Fédération Internationale de Football Association*, or FIFA as it would become better known, during a three-day congress in Paris in May 1904. Football was growing in popularity around the world, and many of the emerging European football nations wanted some kind of loose affiliation with the British game that they so admired. They felt through a unifying body like FIFA, they could tempt England's governing body of the sport, known simply as the Football Association, out of their attitude of arrogant isolationism, to play a part in further developing the world game. A global governing body was also deemed to be the way to ensure that each country could only be represented by just one association, thus guarding

Previous pages: the crowd at Montevideo's Centenary Stadium watch the first ever World Cup final between Argentina and Uruguay.

1er CAMPEONATO MUNDIAL DE FOOTBALL

URUGUAY 1930

SOLER y Cª

The French team wave Uruguayan flags onboard their ship in Montevideo.

against internal splits and divisions within the sport, and it could encourage the creation of individual associations in emerging football territories, whilst maintaining a consistency in the rules of the game.

The Football Association had initially been approached by CAW Hirschmann, secretary of the Dutch football association. On May 8, 1902, he wrote to FA secretary Frederick Wall, asking for advice from the English about setting up such a world body. The Football Association took two months to respond, but all they were offering was to discuss the idea at the next meeting in a further two months. The next correspondence from the English put the discussions back until their meeting the following June, over a year since the first suggestion. With the Dutch unable to elicit a response from the FA, French journalist Robert Guérin of the *Union des Societés Françaises de Sports Athlétiques,* twice went to London, first to meet with Wall, and then FA president Lord Kinnaird. He suggested a football federation of European nations. The FA remained uninterested, responding that they "could not see the advantages" of such an organisation. At that time the English Football Association had been in existence for over 40 year and they remained uninterested in the needs of the emerging nations. Guérin described the whole process as like "slicing water with a knife".

Guérin decided to persevere without the English, and called a meeting for May 21-23, 1904. Attended by representatives from France, Belgium, Denmark, Holland, Spain, Sweden and Switzerland, and with an understanding that the Germans would also sign up to any agreement reached, FIFA was formed and 28-year-old Robert Guérin installed as its first president. At the inaugural meeting, FIFA composed a statute, consisting of ten articles, by which they would govern the world game. In Article Nine was the skeleton of an idea for a world football tournament: "The International Federation is the only organisation with the right to organise an international competition", it noted. A year later, at the second FIFA Congress in Paris, the idea was fleshed out to a full vision for a 16-team tournament. It was agreed the competition should

The opening ceremony of 1930 World Cup at the Centenary Stadium in Montevideo, Uruguay.

take place the following year, scheduled to coincide with the 1906 FIFA Congress in Berne, Switzerland. It had been thought that the tournament could be a great financial success, but initially FIFA struggled to encourage their associations to commit the necessary time and money that could make the competition a reality and eventually the idea had to be shelved.

Despite this initial setback, there was still a growing desire for a competition that enabled nations to test their footballing prowess. The first opportunity had come at the Olympic Games of 1896, but since the teams taking part came from Denmark, Athens and Izmir, it could hardly be seen as a genuine international tournament. At the Olympics of 1900 and 1904 a major football tournament was deemed too ambitious for the International Olympic Committee and it was represented merely as a demonstration sport, but at the 1908 Olympics in London the game was finally accepted, the Football Association staging a competition that was duly won by England, who beat Denmark 2-0 in the final. Four years later in Stockholm, FIFA took control of the organisation of the Olympic football tournament, which was again won by England.

The idea of a world football championship was dealt a hefty blow by the onset of the Great War in 1914. After the war, the British nations and their allies refused to play against any country with whom they had been at war, extending their boycott to any country who even played competitive games against their former enemies. As a consequence of this decision, the four British football associations withdrew from FIFA in 1919. They did not rejoin until 1924.

At their 1924 congress, FIFA again agreed to assume responsibility for the Olympic football tournament, "on condition that it took place in accordance with the regulations of FIFA". If it did so, FIFA would recognise it as the official world football championship. But the level of competitiveness at the 1924 Paris Olympics also ignited a debate about professionalism at a time when the Olympics was still a strictly amateur event. The British associations and Denmark refused to send teams in protest at FIFA's refusal to adopt a fixed definition for 'amateurism'. The problem resurfaced once again in the run up to the 1928 Amsterdam Olympics, when FIFA acknowledged a definition of amateurism that allowed for 'broken time' payments to players to compensate for loss of earnings and other expenses, but the exact amount of remuneration was left up to the individual associations. This led to cries of 'shamateurism' from the British, who believed that a player should be either 'amateur' or 'professional'. On February 17, 1928, all four British nations withdrew from FIFA, a split that would not be reconciled, however amicable their relationship with FIFA remained, until after World War II. William Pickford, vice-president of both the Football Association and FIFA, told CAW Hirschman, "We have nothing against FIFA, but our people here prefer to manage their own affairs in their own way, and not be entangled in too many regulations."

Even without the British teams, the Olympic football tournaments proved a great success, and in 1924 over 60,000 spectators attended the final between Uruguay and Switzerland. In the early years of the 20th Century, it had been the European nations that had dominated the sport, but by the mid-Twenties, South American football had grown in strength and stature. Uruguay followed up their 1924 Olympic victory by retaining the title in 1928, after beating neighbours Argentina in a replay. Such was the growth of interest in football on the South American continent that an international tournament had long since come into being in the region. Starting life as an unofficial championship between Argentina, Uruguay and Chile in 1910, the Copa América had developed into an annual opportunity for the major South American football nations to test themselves against each other. It resulted in an improvement in standards and gave the continent a selection of teams that could compete at the highest level, as demonstrated by Uruguay's Olympic successes.

FIFA president Jules Rimet had watched developments with a growing interest. A long-time advocate of a world championship, Rimet now sensed an opportunity to get this project off the ground, finally resolving the thorny question of 'shamateurism'. By separating a FIFA world championship from the Olympic football tournament, there would no longer be any need to maintain a pretense of amateurism. The World Cup could be a truly professional event.

A FIFA commission had been put together in 1927 to once again examine the creation of an international football competition. FIFA vice-president Hugo Meisl's recommendation was for a competition of European nations, while Henri Delaunay, the man who much later would become the founding father of the European Championship, vigorously argued for a world tournament. The recommendations struck a chord with FIFA's Executive Committee, and at the 1928 congress in Amsterdam, FIFA voted in favour of Henri Delaunay's recommendations. An organising committee was established to plan for a 1930 world championship that was open to all players, whether professional or amateur.

The thorny issue of how such a tournament should be funded hadn't been resolved. At the Barcelona Congress of May 1929 it was decided that FIFA would earmark ten per cent of the gross revenues for itself, while all costs, risks and losses incurred, should be borne by the host association. On hearing this, Holland, Hungary, Italy, Sweden and Spain all withdrew their candidature, leaving Uruguay as the one nation still prepared to finance the entire cost of the tournament. Not only were they prepared to pay all travel and accommodation expenses of the visiting teams, they promised to build a huge new stadium in Montevideo suitable of staging such a prestigious tournament. The government of Uruguay, desperate for international recognition, had made it clear that it was prepared to underwrite the costs of staging the event, as the World Cup would coincide with the centenary of Uruguayan independence.

Several European nations had already made clear that they would not take part if a South American country was chosen, and this would ultimately cause problems throughout the early World Cup tournaments,

July 5, 1930: Jules Rimet hands over the World Cup to Dr Raul Jude of the Uruguayan FA after arriving in Montevideo before the start of the first tournament.

as the South Americans would later return Europe's lack of courtesy by shunning the 1934 and 1938 tournaments in Italy and France. Although few European associations planned to send teams to the 1930 World Cup, Uruguay remained the unanimous choice of the FIFA congress.

When the tournament was first agreed upon, FIFA had decided that a trophy would be needed to mark the event. The first World Cup trophy, The Goddess Of Victory, was made of solid silver and gold plate by French sculptor Abel Lafleur. Based on one of the great surviving masterpieces of Greek sculpture, Winged Victory of Samothrace – also called Nike of Samothrace, and now housed in the Louvre in Paris – the trophy would be renamed the Jules Rimet Cup in 1946, having survived World War II hidden in a shoebox under the bed of Dr Ottorino Barassi, the Italian vice-president of FIFA. As it had been written into World Cup rules that the trophy would be retained by the first team to win it three times, it passed permanently into the hands of Brazil in 1970, although it was stolen in 1983 and never recovered. In 1971 FIFA commissioned a new solid gold trophy, designed by Italian artist Silvio Gazzaniga. This time it would simply be called the World Cup and it will stay forever the property of FIFA, although it is loaned out every four years to the winners. It remains the most fiercely contested prize in sport.

THE FIRST WORLD CUP

Entry to the first World Cup was by invitation only, but although many of the leading European nations decided not to travel to Uruguay, the Jules Rimet Trophy proved to be a prize worth fighting for.

A t daybreak on Saturday June 21, 1930, in the small harbour town of Villefranche-sur-Mer, four miles east of Nice on the French Riviera, Jules Rimet boarded the Italian luxury liner, SS Conte Verde. As he stepped aboard, carrying the twelve-and-a half-inch solid silver and gold-plated World Cup trophy in his baggage, the 56-year-old president of FIFA couldn't resist a farewell cry of *"Vive la France"*. After a lifetime's work, Rimet was setting sail for Uruguay for the first World Football Championship.

Awarded the tournament at FIFA's 1929 congress in Barcelona, there were sound reasons why 1930 was the right time for Uruguay to host the World Cup. Not only were they the holders of the Olympic title, but 1930 marked the centenary of the country's independence, Uruguay's first constitution having been adopted on July 18, 1830. The decision hadn't been popular with the European nations. Coming as it did just eight months after the Wall Street Crash, they weren't comfortable with the expense and travelling time that a tournament in South America would entail. Ultimately, after much manoeuvring by Jules Rimet, the only European nations to sign on for the tournament were Belgium, France, Romania and Yugoslavia, none of which could really be regarded as powerhouses of European football. Of the 41 countries that boasted FIFA membership in 1930, only 13 contested the inaugural tournament, with nine from the Americas: Argentina, Bolivia, Brazil, Chile, Mexico, Paraguay, Peru, USA, and hosts Uruguay.

When Jules Rimet and the French delegation set sail for South America, his fellow passengers included all

Belgian referee John Langenus looks on as Uruguay's captain José Nasazzi (left) shakes hands with Argentina's Manuel Ferreira before the 1930 World Cup final in Montevideo, Uruguay.

A colour postcard of the Centenary Stadium, Montevideo, the venue for the the first World Cup final in 1930.

four of the European football teams taking part and John Langenus, who would go on to become the referee of the first World Cup final. The Conte Verde was a palatial 18,000-ton liner regularly sailing the route between Genoa in Italy, where the Belgian and Romanian teams had boarded, and Buenos Aires in Argentina, stopping off at ports along the way. A one-time holder of the South American speed record, the ship could carry 2,400 passengers in absolute luxury.

The teams had attempted to keep themselves fit during the two-week voyage, training on the boat while at sea. "It was a really tough trip because in those days the only way you could get to Montevideo was by boat," French player Edmond Delfour would recall. "Caudron, who was the coach back then, said to me, 'You've got to keep the players busy on the boat, keep them in shape'. And so I became their fitness coach on the trip. It was a superb voyage. We had a match one day above the swimming pool. Etienne Mattler overdid it and fell in the pool."

After eight days at sea, the Conte Verde picked up the Brazilian squad in Río de Janeiro, before arriving in Montevideo, Uruguay, on July 4, five hours later than scheduled but welcomed by an ecstatic crowd. On docking Rimet was invited to meet the Uruguayan head of state, President Campistegui.

For the European nations, the entire trip would take up at least two months, which meant some teams struggled to find players who could commit that amount of time to the competition. Romania had entered on the personal instructions of King Carol, who also selected the squad. He gave the players three months off from their jobs with guarantees that they would be re-employed, having put extreme pressure on their employers. But not every country had such a powerful benefactor. "The French Federation had great difficulty putting a team together," inside-left Lucien Laurent would recall. "Several of the players who were contacted were forced to decline because their bosses didn't want them to leave for two months." Laurent, his brother Jean, Etienne Mattler and André Maschinot all played for Peugeot Sochaux, subsidised by the Peugeot factory where they worked. The players were given time off for the World Cup, but were not paid while they were away, and as amateurs they received only basic expenses from the *Fédération Française de Football.*

Because of the limited entry, the original concept of a straight knock-out tournament of 16 invited teams had to be abandoned in favour of a group phase, followed by a knock-out section. With 13 finalists, the teams were split into four uneven pools, one containing four teams, the rest with three teams in each. The draw itself didn't take place until all the sides had actually arrived in Uruguay.

The very first World Cup matches took place at 3pm on July 13, 1930. The opening game between Mexico and France was not played as planned at the *Estadio Centenário* in Montevideo – the newly built Centenary Stadium would not be finished until several days into tournament – but at the much smaller Pocitos Stadium in the same city. Elsewhere in Montevideo, the USA's game with Belgium at *Estadio Parque Central* kicked off at the same time. The 1930 tournament remains the only World Cup where all the matches were played in just one city.

Despite snow on the day of the first game, France took the initiative, their first goal – and the World Cup's – coming in the 19th minute. "Thépot, our keeper, launched the ball long for Augustin Chantrel, who in turn found Libérati on the wing," recalled Lucien Laurent before his death in 2005. "He then played a cut-back cross to me – the cut-back is football's deadliest weapon – and I volleyed it first time into the top corner. When I scored I just felt a simple joy, the joy of a goalscorer with his teammates. At the time it never occurred to me that it was the first goal in World Cup history."

FIFA president Jules Rimet disembarks from the SS Conte Verde after arriving in Montevideo for the first World Cup final.

At full-time France had secured a comfortable 4-1 win, made all the more impressive when considering they had played the majority of the match with just ten men, an injury to the French keeper removing him from the pitch after 24 minutes, to be replaced between the posts by left-half Chantrel.

Although all of the seeded teams in the tournament were from the Americas, France were the European side most likely to win the tournament. However, any such ambitions came grinding to a halt in their very next match, a controversial encounter with Argentina. Laurent certainly remembers the impact that one particular Argentine made in the game. "I remember Monti, the central-defender. They said he was tough and we should try to upset him, but maybe that's what he really wanted to happen."

A ferocious hardman, Luís Monti was one of the toughest players of his day. While playing in a friendly against Chelsea for Boca Juniors, he had reputedly approached a Chelsea player, held out his hand to greet him, and when the Chelsea man reciprocated, kicked him. Against France, Luís Monti stamped his authority on the game from the start, inflicting such a nasty injury on Laurent in the 10th minute that it would make him a virtual passenger for the rest of the game. A magnificent display by the French keeper remained the only thing between France and defeat until nine minutes from time, when Monti took a free-kick from the edge of the penalty area. The French were caught by surprise, still arranging their defensive wall when the ball sailed past the unsighted Thépot and into the net. With the South Americans leading 1-0 and less than ten minutes to go, the French attacked, but with Marcel Langiller bearing down on goal, Brazilian referee Almeido Rego blew the whistle for full-time – with six minutes still left on the clock. Argentine fans invaded the pitch in celebration, but the French appealed to the referee.

Overleaf: Uruguay's Jose Nasazzi and Argentina's Manuel Ferreira lead their teams out for the first ever World Cup Final.

LCO FOOTBALL MONTEVIDEO.

WE EXTEND OUR SINCERE CONGRATULATIONS TO YOUR TEAM ON ITS

WONDERFUL VICTORY AND FOR THE COMPLETE SUCCESS OF THE GREAT

VENTURE UNDERTAKEN BY YOUR ASSOCIATION STOP WITH EXPRESSIONS

OF PROFOUND ESTEEM.

Uraquay 4 Argentina 2

1:0 PABLO DORADO (URU) 12', 1:1 CARLOS PEUCELLE (ARG) 20', 1:2 GUILLERMO STÁBILE (ARG) 38',
2:2 PEDRO CEA (URU) 58', 3:2 SANTOS IRIARTE (URU) 68', 4:2 HECTOR CASTRO (URU) 89'

Such was the furore that, after mounted police had cleared fans from the pitch, the referee was forced to call the players from the dressing room to complete the final six minutes. By that stage the French had lost their momentum and the game ended 1-0. Playing their subsequent game without the injured Laurent, they lost to Chile and were on their way back to France.

Argentina qualified for the semi-finals, defeating Mexico and Chile. Their match with Mexico boasted three penalties (one successful) and a hat-trick from young striker Guillermo Stàbile. He scored two more against Chile and would end the campaign as the tournament's highest scorer.

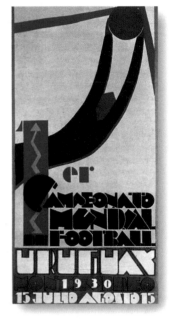

Yugoslavia headed Pool Two, the only European entrants to make it to the semi-finals. Uruguay's first game was against Peru and it saw the long awaited opening of the Centenary Stadium, 70,000 fans watching Uruguay win 1-0. This was in steep contrast to the crowd of 300 who passed through the turnstiles for the previous Pool Three game between Peru and Romania at Pocitos, the stadium of club side Peñarol. Uruguay didn't concede a single goal in qualifying, despatching Peru and Romania.

In Pool Four USA registered impressive 3-0 victories over Belgium and Paraguay. Bertram Patenaude scored at least twice against the South Americans, but remains at the centre of one of the great statistical discrepancies in World Cup history. To this day some sources list him as having scored a hat-trick in the game, the first in World Cup history. Other sources attribute the disputed goal to captain Thomas Florie, while some records indicate that it was an own goal by Gonzáles. Coached by Scottish-born Bob Millar and aided by Glaswegian trainer Jack Coll of Brooklyn Wanderers, the USA were a powerful team who had been nicknamed the 'shot-putters' during the tournament; they defended hard and attacked with pace, using just three forwards at a time when five was the norm. Fielding a side that featured six British immigrants, they were found wanting in the semi-finals, Argentina beating them 6-1 in front of a crowd of 80,000 at the Centenary Stadium.

Although the US coach had claimed that the Argentines didn't worry him and that he was more concerned with the final, he hadn't taken into account the rough and ruthless nature of his opposition and the game didn't pass without incident. American centre-half Raphael Tracy had his leg broken after just ten minutes, keeper Jim Douglas was badly injured and left-half Andy Auld was kicked in the face. According to the official World Cup report written by US team manager Wilfred Cummings, the dirty tricks didn't stop at fouling. "Andy Auld had his lip ripped wide open and one of the players from across *La Platte River* had knocked the smelling salts out of trainer Coll's hand and into Andy's eyes, temporarily blinding one of the outstanding 'little stars' of the World's Series."

In front of a capacity crowd of 93,000 at the Centenary Stadium Uruguay started their semi-final showdown with Yugoslavia slowly, falling behind after just four minutes. The lead was short-lived, however, Pedro Cea scoring one and Pelegrin Anselmo two for the South Americans to make it 3-1 before the interval, although in the build-up to the Uruguayans' third goal the ball had appeared to go out of play, only to be kicked discreetly back on to the pitch by a uniformed policeman. Iriarte made it 4-1 with half an hour still to play, and Cea completed an extraordinary hat-trick, with goals in the 67th and 72nd minutes.

Uruguay and Argentina would face each other in the final on July 30. The two teams had met in the Olympic final two years earlier in Amsterdam. Uruguay, who had also been Olympic champions in 1924, ran out 2-1 winners in that encounter. This created a fierce rivalry between the two teams, and there was a fervent interest in the match in both countries. Ten boats were chartered to bring fans from Buenos Aires, seen off by a large crowd chanting *"Argentina si, Uruguay no! Victory or death!"* Such was the clamour to get to the final that fans had crowded into

Opposite: (top) The Uruguay team line up after winning the 1930 World Cup final; (centre) Uruguayan keeper Enrique Ballestrero fails to save Carlos Peucelle's shot as Argentina level the scores in the final at 2-2.

the centre of the city demanding that extra boats were laid on. But not everyone who found transportation managed to get to the match. "One of the ships carrying Argentinian supporters couldn't cross the River Plate due to intense fog," recalls Argentine forward Francisco Varallo. On arrival at Montevideo docks, armed police searched the fans for weapons. There were further searches at the Centenary Stadium, where the atmosphere was so volatile that even the referee, Belgium's John Langenus, had refused to officiate until assurances were given about his safety.

In the first World Cup final, it was the players that had the most significant say in team selection and tactics. Before the match, the Uruguayans opted for stamina over style and dropped the injured Anselmo for their one-armed centre-forward, Hector 'Manco' Castro. Argentina, meanwhile, recalled Francisco Varallo, who had missed the semi-final through injury. "On the morning of the game I tried some shots in a henhouse near our hotel in Santa Lucia and my knee responded pretty well, so the most experienced team-mates decided that I should be in the line-up," recalls Varallo. "In those days the oldest players took the decisions. We had a manager, but he wasn't important."

The teams salute the crowd at the Centenary Stadium, Montevideo, before the start of the first World Cup final.

The match didn't even kick off without incident. FIFA's competition rules hadn't anticipated that each team might want to use their own ball. A pre-match row ensued. "The Uruguayans wanted to use their bigger ball and we were expecting to play with ours," says Varallo, nicknamed *'El Canonito'* (the Little Canon) because of his powerful shot. "A coin thrown into the air decided that it would be our ball and we could have won the match – I hit the post when we were leading 2-1 – but, as they were losing, they disrespected the promise and used their ball in the second half. That's when the party started for them."

For all the hard-tackling reputations of the Argentine team they failed to rise to the occasion, hardman Luís Monti having an uncharacteristically quiet game. Varallo would later claim that Monti had been in a state of panic in the dressing room, threatening to not play as a result of death threats. Argentina were unable to take their chances and Uruguay proved too strong. On top after 12 minutes through Pablo Dorado, Uruguay were stunned when Carlos Peucelle equalised, Argentina then taking the lead in the 37th through Stàbile. Uruguay rallied after the break and were soon ahead – Pedro Cea equalising in the 57th minute, and Santos Iriarte snatching a third ten minutes later. Argentina were unlucky when Varallo had a shot dramatically cleared off the line, and their ill fortune was compounded a minute before the end when Hector Castro made it 4-2 with a long range shot.

Uruguayans celebrated at the final whistle, but the intimidating atmosphere had left Argentine fans having to escape the stadium as best they could. "My father was in the stands and had to leave the stadium disguised with a Uruguayan flag as the Uruguayans were trying to find Argentines to punch," recalls Varallo.

It was perhaps fitting that the tournament's first hosts should also end up as its first winners. Jules Rimet presented the World Cup trophy to Dr Raul Jude from the Uruguayan football federation. Montevideo celebrated with a spontaneous street party, motor horns sounding and ships sirens wailing. The following day was declared a national holiday and each member of the winning team was gifted a house. In Buenos Aires scenes couldn't have been more different, as thousands of despondent Argentines returned from Montevideo by boat. An angry mob stoned the Uruguayan Consulate and the two football associations broke off relations with each other.

The first *Campeonato Mundial de Football* had proved an unquestionable success and showed the potential for such a tournament in the future. If it could whip up this kind of intense passion, the World Cup would be a prize worth playing for.

Uruguay score in the World Cup final.

GROUP 1

July 13: Pocitos, Montevideo
France 4 - 1 Mexico

July 15: Central Park, Montevideo
Argentina 1 - 0 France

July 16: Central Park, Montevideo
Chile 3 - 0 Mexico

July 19: Centenary Stadium, Montevideo
Chile 1 - 0 France

July 19: Centenary Stadium, Montevideo
Argentina 6 - 3 Mexico

July 22: Centenary Stadium, Montevideo
Argentina 3 - 1 Chile

	P	W	D	L	F	A	Pts
Argentina	3	3	0	0	10	4	6
Chile	3	2	0	1	5	3	4
France	3	1	0	2	4	3	2
Mexico	3	0	0	3	4	13	0

GROUP 2

July 14: Central Park, Montevideo
Yugoslavia 2 - 1 Brazil

July 17: Central Park, Montevideo
Yugoslavia 4 - 0 Bolivia

July 20: Centenary Stadium, Montevideo
Brazil 4 - 0 Bolivia

	P	W	D	L	F	A	Pts
Yugoslavia	2	2	0	0	6	1	4
Brazil	2	1	0	1	5	2	2
Bolivia	2	0	0	2	0	8	0

GROUP 3

July 14: Pocitos, Montevideo
Romania 3 - 1 Peru

July 18: Centenary Stadium, Montevideo
Uruguay 1 - 0 Peru

July 22: Centenary Stadium, Montevideo
Uruguay 4 - 0 Romania

	P	W	D	L	F	A	Pts
Uruguay	2	2	0	0	5	0	4
Romania	2	1	0	1	3	5	2
Peru	2	0	0	2	1	4	0

GROUP 4

July 13: Central Park, Montevideo
USA 3 - 0 Belgium

July 17: Central Park, Montevideo
USA 3 - 0 Paraguay

July 20: Centenary Stadium, Montevideo
Paraguay 1 - 0 Belgium

	P	W	D	L	F	A	Pts
USA	2	2	0	0	6	0	4
Paraguay	2	1	0	1	1	3	2
Belgium	2	0	0	2	0	4	0

SEMI-FINALS

July 26: Centenary Stadium, Montevideo
Argentina 6 - 1 USA

July 27: Centenary Stadium, Montevideo
Uruguay 6 - 1 Yugoslavia

THE FINAL

URUGUAY	(1) 4
ARGENTINA	(2) 2

DATE Wednesday July 30, 1930
ATTENDANCE 93,000
VENUE Centenary Stadium, Montevideo

```
                 Ballestrero

         Nasazzi          Mascheroni

     Andrade      Fernandez      Gestido

   Dorado  Scarone   Castro   Cea   Iriarte


     Evaristo, M    Stàbile    Peucelle
          Ferreira          Varallo

       Suárez      Monti    Evaristo, J
        Paternóster        Della Torre

                  Botasso
```

URUGUAY
COACH: ALBERTO SUPPICCI

BALLESTRERO

NASAZZI

MASCHERONI

ANDRADE

GESTIDO

FERNÁNDEZ

SCARONE

CEA ⚽
Goal: 57 mins

DORADO ⚽
Goal: 12 mins

CASTRO ⚽
Goal: 89 mins

IRIARTE ⚽
Goal: 68 mins

ARGENTINA
COACH: AUGUSTO ROUQUETTE

BOTASSO

DELLA TORRE

PATERNÓSTER5

EVARISTO, J

MONTI

SUÁREZ

VARALLO

FERREIRA

PEUCELLE ⚽
Goal: 20 mins

STÀBILE ⚽
Goal: 37 mins

EVARISTO, M

REFEREE: Langenus (Belgium)

The Uruguayan team celebrate after winning the first ever World Cup final.

TOP SCORERS 8 goals: Guillermo Stàbile (Argentina) **5 goals:** Pedro Cea (Uruguay)
4 goals: Guillermo Subiabre (Chile)

FASTEST GOAL 1 minute: Adalbert Desu (Romania v Peru)

TOTAL GOALS 70 **AVERAGE GOALS** 3.88 per game

MUSSOLINI'S WORLD CUP

When Itay were awarded the 1934 World Cup, Benito Mussolini saw it as the perfect opportunity to showcase the progress made by his Fascist regime, but nothing other than victory for the *azzurri* would be tolerated by *Il Duce*.

The Italians were awarded the second World Cup at the FIFA Congress in Stockholm on October 9, 1932, the association's Executive Committee taking the decision without the need for a full vote of the congress. FIFA membership had risen to 51 and with 32 countries expressing an interest in taking part in the competition, a qualifying phase would be necessary. FIFA insisted that Italy go through the qualification process, the only time the hosts would have to do so in World Cup history. Uruguay and some of the South American nations were not among the entrants. Piqued by the refusal of many European countries to attend the tournament four years earlier, Uruguay opted not to travel to Italy and remain the only reigning champions not to defend their title. Yet again all of the British nations, still at odds with FIFA after their disagreement about the definition of 'amateurism' before the 1928 Olympics, refused to enter the competition.

Italy's Fascist dictator Benito Mussolini was delighted to get the opportunity to stage the first European based World Cup. Realistically it had been one of the only countries capable of staging and financing a multi-city tournament on such a scale. Under Mussolini's Fascist regime, the country had embarked on an unprecedented programme of construction, putting sporting facilities and stadia at the top of the agenda. Fascist sports buildings were to be works of beauty and expressions of athletic culture, a signpost to the Italian youth to indicate the importance of athleticism. By 1932 there were enough large, showpiece stadia for Italy to successfully bid for the World Cup.

The Italian team carry their coach Vittorio Pozzo as they celebrate victory in the 1934 World Cup final in Rome.

The German team give the Nazi salute before their World Cup quarter-final with Sweden at the San Siro.

Mussolini had led Italy from 1922, creating a Fascist regime through the use of state terror and propaganda, gradually dismantling the country's democratic system and taking total control of the media. He planned to use the World Cup as a propaganda tool to showcase his regime, its achievements and its creative potential. He wanted to stage an event that would not only be the envy of the world, but with an Italian victory, one that would consolidate a strong nationalist feeling at home.

The first politician to understand football's power to unite a country, Mussolini personally took control of the organisation of the 1934 World Cup. Although he demanded victory, if the well-trained and disciplined *azzurri* failed to deliver the ultimate prize, at least there would be diplomatic benefits to be gained from the tournament. Even the decision to pay competing countries in lire, rather than dollars or sterling, was seized upon by the regime as an example of an increase in Italian national standing. *La Nazione* newspaper told its readers that it was a sign of "official recognition that Italian currency offers a greater confidence than that of other foreign currencies".

When FIFA General Secretary Ivo Schricker visited Rome in the run up to the tournament it was widely reported that he had been impressed with the preparations, declaring the World Cup "a prize that Italy merited", and thanking the country for the way it had been organised "without giving a thought for the benefits or costs involved". And such was Mussolini's desire to spread the word of his regime's successes, that foreign tourists were actively encouraged to come to Italy to support their teams, the Italian football federation – the *Federazione Italiana Giuoco del Calcio* – subsidised travel from abroad by 70 per cent, while internal travel was heavily discounted for those travelling between host cities.

As a further sign of the regime's progressive organisation of the World Cup, match tickets were elegantly designed and printed in the hope they would become souvenirs that travelling fans would show off at home. Collectable commemorative stamps were printed and a competition to design a promotional poster was won by the Futurist artist FT Marinetti, a long-time disciple of the Fascist regime.

Such was Mussolini's control of the organisation of the 1934 World Cup that, during the tournament, Jules Rimet is said to have felt that Mussolini was acting more like the president of FIFA than he was. "Physically you can see it in the cup," argues historian Pierre Lanfranchi. "The World Cup given by FIFA was the Jules Rimet Cup, but the cup offered by Mussolini – the *Coppa Del Duce* – was six times bigger, and Mussolini was not prepared to offer this cup to anyone except Italy."

Mussolini was also determined to turn the competition to his advantage wherever he could. Some claim this included handpicking the referees, although he didn't go as far as training the team himself, he left that to Italy's longest serving football coach, Vittorio Pozzo. "Pozzo is very interesting as in many ways he reflected the nature of fascism through the team, through his leadership," explains Simon Martin, author of *Football And Fascism: The National Game Under Mussolini*. "He was the leader, the *capo del capi* – the main man, so to speak. What he said went."

The Brazilian team before their last match of the World Cup against Spain.

"He was an authoritarian," says journalist Brian Glanville. "He used to say to me, 'Kind but with a firm hand, if I let them make mistakes I lose my control'. There's no doubt in my mind he was not a Fascist, though he did profit from the tenor of the time."

Although Pozzo would later claim that he had been instructed to pick only Fascist Party members for the team in 1934, he welcomed the support of top officials from the regime as it allowed him the control to introduce a more professional approach to the national team. The Fascist regime had for many years set great store in athleticism and there had been a significant growth in sporting participation in schools, colleges and universities. The first indications of this came at the 1928 Amsterdam Olympics, where the Italian football team came home with the bronze medal. Although there was no football competition at the 1932 Los Angeles Olympics – a result of the ongoing battle between FIFA and the International Olympic Committee – the Italian Olympic team finished second in the overall medals table. For Pozzo, this new and serious attitude to sport allowed him to impose militaristic schedules and closed training camps as a part of his strategy. He was even allowed to recruit Luís Monti, Raimundo Orsi and Enrique Guaita, three Argentinian *oriundi* – foreign players of Italian extraction – who were playing their club football in the Italian league.

Unlike the 1930 tournament in Uruguay that had been staged solely in Montevideo, eight venues across Italy played host to the matches in 1934. Brazil, Argentina, USA and Egypt were the only non-European countries in the final 16 and all were making the long journey home after just one game, although the US had played one extra pre-tournament qualifier against Mexico in Rome. The Americans had made a late application and, unfairly for the Mexicans who had qualified once already, FIFA insisted that the two teams play-off against each other. The Mexicans made an 8,000 mile round trip without even playing in the finals proper. To avoid a quick exit for any of the major nations, FIFA allowed eight countries to be seeded: Argentina, Austria, Brazil, Czechoslovakia, Germany, Holland, Hungary and Italy.

The 1934 World Cup final, staged at the Stadio Nazionale del Partiti Nazionale Fascista in Rome.

By the start of the competition the football grounds were decorated with the imagery of the Fascists. Even the first round draw had been dressed for the occasion, Mussolini's *Coppa del Duce* used as a symbolic centrepiece, flanked by a squad of armed blackshirts. Many arriving teams paid their respects to Mussolini, some sending telegrams of congratulation and admiration, while the Argentine squad visited *Il Duce's* village of birth, laying a wreath of Italian and Argentine colours at the tomb of his family.

On May 27, all eight Round One matches kicked-off simultaneously, in Genoa, Turin, Florence, Milan, Trieste, Rome, Naples and Bologna. Favourites Italy began their campaign at the *Stadio Nazionale del Partito Nazionale Fascista*, or the PNF Stadium, the central showcase for the tournament in Rome. Mussolini was among the paying crowd, sending a message to the Italian people that the Fascists had ended the immoral system of complementary tickets.

The Italian team had been well prepared, Pozzo having taken the squad to a mountain retreat near Lake Maggiore six weeks before the tournament. On the pitch Pozzo had built his team's play around the Italian *metodo* style, a formation adapted from the classic 2-3-5 pyramid system, as played by the Austrians in the so-called 'Danubian School' of football (otherwise known as the 'Vienna School'). This style had emerged from the Scottish short-passing game brought to central Europe by Englishman Jimmy Hogan. By 1934 the Austrians, under national coach Hugo Meisl, had perfected the style, making the Austrian 'Wunderteam' the strongest side in Europe.

Lacking the players to perform the vital attacking centre-half role, Pozzo adapted the formation, withdrawing the two inside-forwards to just in front of the midfield, creating a 2-3-2-3 formation. This allowed for a stronger defence and effective counter-attacking. In their first game Italy registered a comfortable 7-1 victory, Angelo Schiavio netting a hat-trick against the USA, the last goal being scored by Italy's most gifted forward, Giuseppe Meazza, whose name would later be given to the San Siro stadium in Milan. The USA's goal came courtesy of Aldo T 'Buff' Donelli, an American of Italian descent, who would later become a successful American Football coach.

The Italian team in their first game had featured two of their squad's three Argentinian-born players. One of whom, Luís Monti, had played in their previous World Cup final, but after receiving death threats from Argentine fans that blamed him for the final defeat, he had moved to Italy to play for Juventus. He wasn't the only one. Many of the Argentine stars had moved to the European leagues after the first World Cup, and not one member of their 1930 team lined up for them against Sweden in Bologna. Twice the Argentinians led before a late goal from Kroon sent the Swedes through 3-2.

The Spanish had qualified for the finals by beating Portugal, and their preparations had included contracting English league side Sunderland to travel to Spain for a series of matches. Spain drew two and lost one, but it helped toughen the side up for their first World Cup. Their opponents Brazil were barely in the game in Genoa before the Spanish had taken control, leading 2-0 by the break. The Brazilians pulled one back through Leônidas, who had been dubbed 'The Rubber Man' by the European press because of the array of tricks he could perform, but their fate was sealed by Langara's second goal of the match. The tournament had been an unhappy experience for several members of the Brazilian squad. On the 12-day sea voyage to Italy, their black players had not been allowed to mix with the other passengers or to train.

France took a shock lead against the second-favourites Austria in Turin, and though the scores were levelled by centre-forward Matthias Sindelar, known as *'Der Paperiener'* – 'the Man Of Paper' – because of his frail build, it wasn't until extra-time that Austria's superiority showed. It took a blatantly offside strike from Anton Schall to unsettle the French, before Josef Bican decided the match for the Austrians. A late penalty for the French was nothing more than a consolation.

Italy's Giuseppe Meazza is helped from the field after injury in the first of their two quarter-final matches with Spain.

Germany arrived at the tournament in fine form, with a team playing the 'WM' formation evolved by Herbert Chapman at Arsenal. They hadn't lost a game in the previous 16 months, but nevertheless were portrayed in the Italian press as one of the competition's weaker teams, largely because at this point in history Mussolini was still threatening Chancellor Hitler with war if Germany invaded Austria. In their first game, the Germans turned around a 2-1 half-time deficit to beat Belgium 5-2 in Florence, the victory owing much to the performance of their captain Fritz Szepan and a hat-trick in less than 20 minutes from centre-forward Edmund Conen.

The Dutch had qualified for the finals comfortably from a group containing Belgium and the Irish Free State, but despite their seeding, they crashed out of the competition 3-2 to Switzerland in Milan. In Naples Egypt, who had put 11 goals past Palestine to become the first African World Cup challengers, went out of the competition. Ten years earlier they had shocked world football with a 3-0 win over the Hungarians at the Olympics, but in this repeat meeting they were defeated 4-2.

In Trieste highly-fancied Czechoslovakia struggled past Romania. Dobai had given the Romanians the lead shortly before the break but the Czechs possessed a formidable forward pairing of Antonin Puc and Oldrich Nejedly, who both scored to line-up a meeting with the Swiss.

Italy 2 Czechoslovakia 1

0:1 ANTONIN PUC (CZH) 71', 1:1 RAIMONDO ORSI (ITA) 81', 2:1 ANGELO SCHIAVIO (ITA) 95'

CAMPIONATI MONDIALI DI CALCIO

F.I.G.C.
F.I.F.A.

ITALIA

MAGGIO GIUGNO 1934 XII

In Round Two, effectively the quarter-finals, the Czechs struggled against the Swiss outsiders, falling behind to an early Kielholz goal before Svoboda levelled the tie soon after. Sobotka put the Czechs ahead early in the second half, but Switzerland hit back and once again it needed Nejedly to find the target seven minutes from time to decide the see-saw match and put Czechoslovakia through to the semi-finals.

Germany and Austria disposed of Sweden and Hungary respectively, but the most remarkable tie of the round saw Italy triumph over Spain in Florence in a replay, the first encounter having finished 1-1, with extra-time not even able to separate the sides. Italy's equalising goal had caused controversy, finding the net after a challenge by Schiavio had impeded Spanish keeper Zamora, just one of a series of rough challenges on the player that went unpunished by Belgian referee Louis Baert. Initially the referee had ruled for a foul and disallowed the goal, before a crowd of pushing and shoving Italian players persuaded him to change his mind. In the second half he would disallow a Spanish goal for offside, despite the fact that Ramón de Lafuente had beaten four opponents by himself before putting the ball in the net.

For the following day's replay, injuries resulted in the Spanish making seven changes, including the outstanding Zamora. The Italians, meanwhile, replaced four players, including wing-half Pizziola because he had broken a leg. The referee was also replaced, Rene Mercet coming in for Baert, but Mercet's performance was no better. He dubiously disallowed two Spanish goals as offside and was subsequently suspended by the Swiss FA for his performance. It was another close encounter settled in favour of the hosts by prolific Inter Milan marksman Meazza.

There was little respite for Vittorio Pozzo's side and just 48 hours later, having now moved on to Milan's San Siro stadium, they took on Austria's 'Wunderteam' in the semi-finals. On a sticky, rain-soaked pitch that didn't suit Austria's neat passing football, the Italians triumphed as Luís Monti marked Austrian star striker Matthias Sindelar out of the game. A first-half goal from Argentine-born winger Guaita was enough to take Italy through to their fourth game in eight days. There were many who felt that Italy's success had little to do with their improved tactics and training techniques. Players from other teams complained about Mussolini's handpicked referees, and after the semi-final the Austrians were convinced that their game had been fixed. "They were little crooks, they used to cheat a little, no they used to cheat a lot," said Austrian striker, Josef Bican. "The referee even played for them. When I passed the ball out to the right wing one of our players, Cicek, ran for it and the referee headed it back to the Italians. It was unbelievable."

The Czechs progressed through the other semi-final in Rome with a 3-1 victory over the Germans. Nejedly took centre stage once again, netting a hat-trick. The poor performance of Dresden keeper Willi Kress had not helped the Germans, while their team had also been weakened by the absence of defender Rudi Gramlich, a leather trader by profession, who had been forced to return home to assist his Jewish employers who were feeling the effects of Nazi-inspired boycotts. The encounter was witnessed by just 13,000 people, some 30,000 less than at the Italy-Austria match. Four days later Germany did at least salvage some pride by winning the inaugural third-place play-off over Austria, despite missing Sigi Haringer, who had been left out of the team by disciplinarian coach Otto Nerz for eating an orange on a station platform.

Despite all the protests Italy had made it through to the World Cup final at Mussolini's showcase stadium in Rome, where the stage was set for the perfect Fascist finale. And for the first time a World Cup final would be transmitted live on the radio. "I think the final in many ways is most memorable for the crowd scenes," says historian Simon Martin. "It was equated in the press to a Fascist rally rather than a World Cup final. As Mussolini entered the stadium there were 55,000 Italians waving white handkerchiefs and

Opposite: (bottom) Italy's World Cup winners; (top) Czechoslovakia take the lead as Italian keeper Giampiero Combi is beaten; (centre left) Italy prepare for extra-time; (centre right) Vittorio Pozzo celebrates as Raimondo Orsi scores Italy's first goal to force the match into extra-time.

Detail of a postcard setting Italy's world champions against a backdrop of the Stadio del PNF in Rome. General Vaccaro, president of the Federazione Italiana Giuoco del Calcio, is second from right.

screaming *'Duce, Duce'*!" It was the kind of support that had, earlier in the tournament, caused Mussolini to wonder "how can Italy not be champions". But the *azzurri* still had to win one more game and there was a sizeable Czech minority in the crowd too, the visitors having taken full advantage of the subsidised travel offered by the Italian authorities.

The Czechs were a strong side who played in a similar way to the Austrians, pushing the ball around the pitch with style, while the Italians defended well and attacked with pace. One thing they did have in common was that goalkeepers captained both teams. Despite the inclusion of tough-tackling hardman Luís Monti, it was Czechoslovakia who scored first, Antonin Puc firing them ahead in the 71st minute despite having just returned to the field after a bout of cramp.

The Czechs kept the pressure up, Frantisek Svoboda hitting the post. But with eight minutes remaining Italy broke through and equalised through Raimondo Orsi, who ran through the Czech defence and dummied a shot with his left-foot, shooting instead with the outside of the right and curling the ball freakishly past the Czech keeper who appeared to have it covered. It looked like a fluke, and although afterwards Orsi insisted he could repeat the shot on demand, when asked to try the next day for the assembled press, he missed every one of his 20 attempts.

In extra-time, Italian coach Pozzo struggled to have his instructions heard over the noise of the crowd, but eventually managed to persuade winger Guaita to keep switching positions with centre-forward Angelo Schiavio, as they had done on occasion earlier in the competition. The ploy worked and Schiavio scored his fourth goal of the competition, rounding a defender and beating the keeper with a shot that crept into the net under the crossbar. Mussolini's dream had been fulfilled. Not even Nejedly, the tournament's top-scorer, could save the Czechs.

On behalf of the team, captain Giampiero Combi received the World Cup trophy from *Il Duce,* but the players were also presented with the *Coppa del Duce*, a signed photograph of Mussolini, and a gold medal in recognition of their conquest of the football world in the name of Mussolini and Fascism. The national anthems of both nations had been observed at the end of the match, and the players had acknowledged the Fascist hierarchy in the stand. Finally the celebrations could begin. But questions still remained about the way Italy had secured their victory. They had undoubtedly been a success at home, with all the advantages that Mussolini's regime had to offer, but the big question ahead for Pozzo's team was could they repeat the success on foreign soil in four years time.

FIRST ROUND

May 27: PNF Stadium, Rome
Italy **7 - 1** USA

May 27: Littorio Stadium, Trieste
Czechoslovakia **2 - 1** Romania

May 27: Giovanni Berta Stadium, Florence
Germany **5 - 2** Belgium

May 27: Mussolini Stadium, Turin
Austria **3 - 2** France
(aet)

May 27: Luigi Ferraris Stadium, Genoa
Spain **3 - 1** Brazil

May 27: San Siro Stadium, Milan
Switzerland **3 - 2** Holland

May 27: Littoriale Stadium, Bologna
Sweden **3 - 2** Argentina

May 27: Ascarelli Stadium, Naples
Hungary **4 - 2** Egypt

SECOND ROUND

May 31: San Siro Stadium, Milan
Germany **2 - 1** Sweden

May 31: Littoriale Stadium, Bologna
Austria **2 - 1** Hungary

May 31: Giovanni Berta Stadium, Florence
Italy **1 - 1** Spain
(aet)

June 1: Giovanni Berta Stadium, Florence
Italy **1 - 0** Spain
(replay)

May 31: Mussolini Stadium, Turin
Czechoslovakia **3 - 2** Switzerland

SEMI-FINALS

June 3: PNF Stadium, Rome
Czechoslovakia **3 - 1** Germany

June 3: San Siro Stadium, Milan
Italy **1 - 0** Austria

THIRD-PLACE PLAY-OFF

June 7: Asarelli Stadium, Naples
Germany **3 - 2** Austria

Czech goalkeeper Planicka leaps to catch the ball in the final.

THE FINAL

ITALY	(0) **2**
CZECHOSLOVAKIA	(0) **1**

(AET; 1-1 AT 90 MINS)

DATE Sunday June 10, 1934
ATTENDANCE 55,000
VENUE PNF Stadium, Rome

ITALY
COACH: VITTORIO POZZO

COMBI
MONZEGLIO
ALLEMANDI
FERRARIS
MONTI
BERTOLINI
MEAZZA
FERRARI
GUAITA
SCHIAVIO ⚽
Goal: 95 mins
ORSI ⚽
Goal: 81 mins

CZECHOSLOVAKIA
COACH: CORNEL PETRU

PLÁNICKA
ZENISEK
CTYROKY
KOSTÁLEK
CAMBAL
KRCIL
SVOBODA
NEJEDLY
JUNEK
SOBOTKA
PUC ⚽
Goal: 71 mins

REFEREE: Eklind (Sweden)

Referee Ecklind of Sweden with linesman Birlem of Germany and Ivancics of Hungary give the Fascist salute prior to World Cup final.

TOP GOALSCORERS 5 goals: Oldrich Nejedly (Czechoslovakia) **4 goals:** Angelo Schiavio (Italy), Edmund Conen (Germany)

FASTEST GOAL 30 seconds: Ernst Lehner (Germany v Austria)

TOTAL GOALS 70 **AVERAGE GOALS** 4.12 per game

THE CLOUDS OF WAR

With Nazi salutes on the pitch, anti-fascist protests on the terraces, and Austria's withdrawal due to annexation by Germany, the 1938 World Cup finals was the last great international sporting event before the onset of war.

Despite the gathering clouds of war, the 1938 World Cup took place in France, a nod of thanks to FIFA president Jules Rimet. Although circumstances conspired to ensure that the tournament was not truly representative of the best nations in world football at that time, the Italians at least proved the 1938 World Cup could boast one of the great teams in football history. If there had been questions about the validity of Italy's World Cup victory in their home country four years earlier, the 1938 tournament proved that this time the Italian team were unquestionably worthy World Cup winners. With only two survivors from the 1934 team, Giuseppe Meazza and Giovanni Ferrari, Vittorio Pozzo's new side was peppered with the stars of the successful Italian gold medal-winning team from the 1936 Berlin Olympics, most noticeably the full-backs Piero Rava and Alfredo Foni. It also had the undeniable talents of Silvio Piola, a prolific goalscorer of great strength and skill.

Italy weren't the only team boasting a fantastic world-class striker, Brazilian Leônidas emerging as the outstanding individual of the tournament. While it would be impossible to argue with Italy's eventual triumph, thanks largely to their outstanding mix of tactical astuteness and pragmatic defending, Leônidas could feel at least a little hard done by that he ended without even the chance to prove himself in the latter stages of the competition. Yet Italy's all-round mix of resilience and flair was enough for a second consecutive triumph and confirmed Vittorio Pozzo as the foremost coach of his era.

The Italy team celebrate with the World Cup trophy. Standing from left: Amadeo Biavati, coach Vittorio Pozzo holding the trophy, Silvio Piola, Giovanni Ferrari and Gino Colaussi. Front row: Ugo Locatelli, Giuseppe Meazza, Alfredo Foni, Pietro Serantoni, Aldo Olivieri, Pietro Rava and Michele Andreolo.

France had been awarded the World Cup by 19 votes to four at the 1936 FIFA Congress in Berlin. Argentina had viewed themselves as favourites to host the competition, believing that the venue would alternate between South America and Europe. But the world had changed in four years and there were no longer such certainties. Europe was hovering on the edge of conflict and when FIFA awarded the tournament to France, it was a diplomatic decision to ensure that this World Cup would not be used for the same propaganda purposes as the 1934 competition, entrusting the tournament to the pioneers of the competition, Jules Rimet, Henri Delaunay and the *Fédération Française de Football*. If they needed any further warning about the misuse of major sporting events for political ends, the proof was all around them. The decisive FIFA Congress was taking place at the Berlin Olympics, just a couple of days before the end of that showcase for Hitler's National Socialist regime.

The German team execute the Nazi salute before the start of their World Cup match against Switzerland, while the swastika flag flies above them.

The decision was badly received in South America. Argentina prevaricated about whether to take part in the competition, before finally withdrawing their application, a decision that provoked a riot outside their football federation's offices in Buenos Aires. The tournament would also be without Uruguay, still irked by the European boycott of the 1930 World Cup. The fact that Brazil were the only South American side to take part in the competition, and that Japan withdrew, opened the door for two countries who would be making their first – and last – appearances at the finals: Cuba and the Dutch East Indies.

The unstable political landscape of Europe cast a long shadow over the tournament. In the midst of civil war, Spain had pulled out before the qualification process had begun. Austria had qualified for the tournament after beating Latvia, but had to withdraw after the country was annexed by Germany in the *Anschluss* of March 1938. Hitler's Nazi regime had incorporated Austria into a 'Greater Germany' and several of the country's best players were co-opted into the German side, while others refused, most notably star striker Matthias Sindelar, who would die a year later in mysterious circumstances, a note on his Gestapo file reporting him as a "social democrat and a Jews' friend". Austria's place in the finals was offered to England, but even a personal plea to the FA's Stanley Rous by FIFA secretary Ivo Schricker failed to hold any sway, all of the British nations ignoring the World Cup once again. Austria's place remained unfilled and just 15 teams contested the third World Cup, using the same knockout format that had been used in 1934.

Italy arrived in France as the reigning world champions, but after the triumph of 1934 their hoped-for international recognition had failed to materialise. In their first match after the World Cup they had lost to England in a particularly fierce bout dubbed 'The Battle of Highbury', hardman Luís Monti breaking his foot in a challenge with Ted Drake. The match had been billed in England as 'the real World Cup final', while so important was it to Mussolini, that he had reportedly offered each player an Alfa Romeo car to win. The England team was relatively inexperienced at international level – no player had more than ten caps – but their victory reassured them that regardless of titles, they were still the world's leading football nation. But the result left the Italians with something still to prove. "The 1938 World Cup was in many ways the opportunity for the Italian team, and the regime, to prove not only that they were the best team in the world but also that the tournament in 1934 hadn't been corrupt," says historian Simon Martin.

In this tournament, however, the reception for the champions would be completely different. Anti-Fascist protests and rallies were growing in intensity all over Europe, and France was no exception. Throughout the tournament exiled Italian communists made sure the *azzurri* didn't get a warm welcome, a large crowd of French and Italian anti-Fascists angrily greeting the team's arrival at Marseille. "We were also Italians like them but they had left Italy," says Piero Rava. "Their argument shouldn't have been with us."

The Germans would receive a similarly hostile reaction on June 4 when the tournament kicked off at the Parc des Princes stadium in Paris. At one point French fans would even go as far as throwing broken bottles. As the Germans stood to attention giving the Nazi salute before the game, the Swiss kept their arms resolutely by their sides – unlike Stanley Matthews and the England team, who had willingly proffered the Nazi salute as a courtesy to their hosts before a game in Berlin exactly three weeks earlier. For the Swiss it was a gesture that was out of the question. When the two teams had played in Zurich the previous year, home fans had thrown rotten fruit at the travelling German supporters and tried to destroy every swastika flag they could find.

In the months leading up to the tournament German manager Josef 'Sepp' Herberger had taken full control of the national team from Otto Nerz, but to a certain extent his hands were tied regarding team selection, as to placate a political diktat, he had to pick a team made up almost evenly of Germans and Austrians. The team to face Switzerland in the opening World Cup game featured five Austrian players and six Germans, but it was not enough to break down a strong Swiss team coached by Austrian Karl Rappan and employing the famed 'Swiss Bolt' formation, one of the first systems to employ what would become known much later as a sweeper. The game finished 1-1 after extra-time. Five days later in the replay, the Swiss fell two goals behind, but despite playing much of the game with only ten fit men after an injury to Aebi, they shocked the so called 'Greater Germany' with three second-half goals to win 4-2. Sepp Herberger's team were on their way home and it would be another 16 years until he could once again lead a German side in the World Cup finals.

Pre-match entertainment: Leônidas talks to fans before Brazil's third place play-off game.

All the remaining Round One games were played the following day. In Toulouse, Cuba drew 3-3 with Romania and then caused a sensation four days later by winning the replay 2-1. Czechoslovakia beat Holland with three goals in extra-time in Le Havre, while at *Stade Colombes* in Paris, France knocked out Belgium 3-1, their side featuring two veterans from the 1930 and 1934 campaigns, captain Etiénne Mattler and inside-left Edmund Delfour. Sweden were given a bye through to the quarter-finals due to the absence of Austria, while in Reims Hungary proved to be too powerful an opponent for the Dutch East Indies, beating them 6-0 and leaving them as the only country in World Cup history to have played just one game in the finals.

Despite Vittorio Pozzo's belief that he had a much more skilful team than four years earlier, the Italians needed a Silvio Piola goal in extra-time to win their opening match against unfancied Norway. With an

Italy 4 Hungary 2

1:0 GINO COLAUSSI (ITA) 6', 1:1 PAL TITKOS (HUN) 8', 2:1 SILVIO PIOLA (ITA) 16', 3:1
GINO COLAUSSI (ITA) 35', 3:2 GYORGY SAROSI (HUN) 70', 4:2 SILVIO PIOLA (ITA) 82'.

estimated 10,000 Italian political exiles among the crowd, they faced a hostile reception, particularly during the team's Fascist salute while lining up before the game. To prove a point to the antagonistic mob, Pozzo insisted his team do the salute twice. "At the salute, as predicted, we were greeted by a solemn and deafening barrage of whistles and insults," Pozzo would later recall. "We had just put our hands down when the demonstration started again. Straight away: 'Team be ready. Salute'. And we raised our hands again, to confirm we had no fear. Having won the battle of intimidation, we played."

After the match Pozzo was questioned by General Vacarro, the President of the Italian football federation, as to why he had played the ageing Monzeglio in defence rather than Alfredo Foni, one of the young stars of Italy's Olympic team. It transpired that it was on instructions emanating from Mussolini's residence, as Monzeglio would often spend time coaching *Il Duce* and his sons. Vacarro ensured that this was the last political interference in team selection.

The game of the first round, and arguably the best of any World Cup, saw Brazil facing Poland in Strasbourg on June 5. The 6-5 winning score-line was thanks mainly to Leônidas, a player famed for his use of the bicycle kick. According to one Brazilian reporter, Leônidas was "simply amazing. He was our stick of dynamite. He did the impossible. Each time he touched the ball there was an electric current of enthusiasm through the crowd." Scoring one of his goals barefoot, he hit the shot after his boot had come off in the mud. "The shot, strong and unexpected, left everyone in Strasbourg's small stadium open-mouthed. People were stunned," wrote another Brazilian journalist, who even recorded shouts of, "Bravo, bravo" from Europe's jaded football press. After 90 minutes the game was level at 4-4, but three minutes into extra-time Leônidas scored his second goal of the game to put Brazil ahead. He completed his hat-trick in the 104th minute,

although many records incorrectly indicate that he scored four times. Such was the exceptional nature of the Brazilian's performance in this astonishing match, that it is often overlooked that just minutes later Polish striker Ernest Wilimowski did, in fact, score four goals, the first player to do so in a World Cup game.

Following their sensational attacking play in Round One, Brazil showed an uglier side to their game in the quarter-final clash with Czechoslovakia. A brawl and the sending-off of three players blighted the match, which ended 1-1 and left the sensational Czech striker Oldrich Nejedly with a broken leg. For the replay, Brazil made nine changes, leaving only keeper Walter and their prolific striker Leônidas in the line-up from the first game. Brazil won the tamer replay 2-1 through goals from Leônidas and Roberto.

Italy faced hosts France at *Stade Colombes* in their quarter-final. Since both teams normally played in blue Italy were forced to change, but instead of wearing their usual away colour of white, Mussolini ordered them to play in black shirts. "We were told to put on black shirts, the Fascist symbol," explains Italian defender Piero Rava. "This was done to provoke the anti-Fascists." This would be the one and only time the Italian football team would play in the black shirts of Mussolini, the hostility binding the team together to achieve a 3-1 victory. Piola added two more goals to his tally and captain Giuseppe Meazza dominated in midfield.

Hungary also made it through to the semi-finals with an impressive 2-0 victory over Switzerland, while

Opposite: (above) The 1938 World Cup final. (centre left) Italian players embrace after victory in the final. (centre right) Captain Giuseppe Meazza receives the Jules Rimet trophy. (bottom) The Italian squad pose with Mussolini during a reception at the Palazzo Venezia in Rome on July 1, 1938. (overleaf) Hungarian goalkeeper Antal Szabó tries to stop a shot from Italian forward Giovanni Ferrari.

La Gazzetta dello Sport

Apoteosi dello sport feciale nello stadio di Parigi

STREPITOSA VITTORIA DELLA SQUADRA ITALIANA NEL CAMPIONATO MONDIALE DI CALCIO

Gli azzurri, splendenti di slancio e di stile, partono all'offensiva al segnale dell'... in fanzzuna prontamente i cnnleattaccchi magiaresi e trionfano nella luce d'un c... ragixdrole

Italia-Ungheria: 4-2 (3-1)

Sweden smashed eight goals past Cuba, causing French journalist Emmanuel Gambardella to pack up his typewriter and announce, "Up to five goals is journalism, after that it becomes statistics."

In the semi-finals Brazil faced Italy in Marseille, but in a display of supreme over-confidence, Brazil coach Adhemar Pimenta decided to rest the tournament's top goalscorer for the final, going into the match without Leônidas. Italy gained the advantage immediately, Gino Colaussi scoring shortly after half-time. Meazza added a penalty on the hour, Brazil managing only a consolation goal three minutes from time through Romeu. The Black Diamond, as Leônidas was nicknamed, may have missed the semi-final, but

after scoring another two goals in Brazil's 4-2 win in the third-place play-off game against Sweden, he finished up as the highest goalscorer of the 1938 World Cup. "Leônidas was the guy who first did the bicycle kick in Brazil," recalls 1950 World Cup finalist Friaça, who played alongside the Black Diamond later in his career. "He was a fantastic player. He had a presence, an exceptional presence. He was very fast and he would run all 90 minutes." Leônidas would return home the most famous man in Brazil, inspiring a brand of cigarettes and causing confectionary company Lacta to launch the *Diamante Negro* chocolate bar, Brazil's second best-selling chocolate and still available in ten countries around the world.

In the other semi-final Hungary, despite having conceded in the first minute, were able to celebrate the 80th birthday of their monarch, King Gustav V, with a 5-1 win. The attacking partnership of Gyula Zsengellér and Gyorgy Sárosi was perhaps the most thrilling in the tournament, proving devastating against Sweden.

On June 19, Italy and Hungary contested the 1938 World Cup final. For Pozzo this match was finally a chance to prove that his defending champions deserved their title. His side was much the stronger of the two teams and boasted the prolific Lazio centre-forward Piola in attack.

Hungary had some tremendous individual talents in their side, and Gyula Zsengellér's scoring rate in the tournament was a match for anyone, but they lacked the drive and determination that would propel the Italians to their second world title. Colaussi opened the scoring for Italy when he collected a Piola cross in the sixth minute and prodded home past Szabó from close range. Titkos immediately equalised, but Hungarian hopes were dashed when Piola scored on 16 minutes, picking up a pass from Meazza to lash the ball high into the net. Colaussi added a third before half-time to put Italy in total control.

Although the Hungarians made a game of it in the second half, the *azzurri* finished the game in style, and although a goal from Gyorgy Sárosi reduced the lead, Piola struck again with eight minutes remaining to seal an outstanding victory. They were in a class of their own. Despite the political furore that had dogged their tournament, for the Italian players victory away from home was a sweet triumph. "An incredible joy," recalls Piero Rava. "I was only 20 years old at the time and had never seen anything like it before."

Moulding two different World Cup winning teams earned Pozzo a place in the game's history books, and to this day no other manager has matched this remarkable achievement. For Mussolini, being seen with the winning squad was another chance to prove the regime's success. However, there would soon be a real test of Fascist supremacy. Shortly after the tournament Europe was at war and the world would be a very different place by the time it next saw the *Coupe du Monde*.

Alfredo Foni in action in the final.

FIRST ROUND

June 4: Parc des Princes, Paris
Switzerland **1 - 1** Germany
(aet)

June 9: Parc des Princes, Paris
Switzerland **4 - 2** Germany
(replay)

June 5: Chapou Stadium, Toulouse
Cuba **3 - 3** Romania
(aet)

June 9: Chapou Stadium, Toulouse
Cuba **2 - 1** Romania
(replay)

June 5: Stade Vélodrome Municipal, Reims
Hungary **6 - 0** Dutch E. Indies

June 5: Stade Colombes, Paris
France **3 - 1** Belgium

June 5: Stade de la Cavée Verte, Le Havre
Czechoslovakia **3 - 0** Holland
(aet)

June 5: Stade de La Meinau, Strasbourg
Brazil **6 - 5** Poland
(aet)

June 5: Stade Velodrome, Marseilles
Italy **2 - 1** Norway
(aet)

Game not played
Sweden **w / o** Austria

QUARTER-FINALS

June 12: Stade du Fort Carré, Antibes
Sweden **8 - 0** Cuba

June 12: Stade Victor Boucquey, Lille
Hungary **2 - 0** Switzerland

June 12: Stade Colombes, Paris
Italy **3 - 1** France

June 12: Parc de Lescure, Bordeaux
Brazil **1 - 1** Czechoslovakia
(aet)

June 14: Parc de Lescure, Bordeaux
Brazil **2 - 1** Czechoslovakia
(replay)

SEMI-FINALS

June 16: Stade Vélódrome, Marseilles
Italy **2 - 1** Brazil

June 16: Parc des Princes, Paris
Hungary **5 - 1** Sweden

THIRD-PLACE PLAY-OFF

June 19: Parc de Lescure, Bordeaux
Brazil **4 - 2** Sweden

THE FINAL

ITALY	(3)	**4**
HUNGARY	(1)	**2**

DATE Sunday June 19, 1938
ATTENDANCE 45,000
VENUE Stade Olympique de Colombes, Paris

Olivieri
Foni — Rava
Serantoni — Andreolo — Locatelli
Meazza — Ferrari
Biavati — Piola — Colaussi
Titkos — Sárosi — Sas
Zsengellér — Vincze
Lázár — Szücs — Szalay
Biró — Polgar
Szabó

ITALY
COACH: VITTORIO POZZO

OLIVIERI
FONI
RAVA
SERANTONI
ANDREOLO
LOCATELLI
MEAZZA
FERRARI
BIAVATI
PIOLA ⚽ ⚽
Goal: 16 mins, 85 mins
COLAUSSI ⚽ ⚽
Goal: 6 mins, 35 mins

HUNGARY
COACH: KAROLY DIETZ

SZABÓ
POLGAR
BIRÓ
SZALAY
SZÜCS
LÁZÁR
VINCZE
ZSENGELLÉR
SAS
SÁROSI ⚽
Goal: 70 mins
TITKOS ⚽
Goal: 8 mins

REFEREE: Capdeville (France)

Giuseppe Meazza (left) shakes hands with Hungarian captain Gyorgy Sárosi before the final.

TOP GOALSCORERS 7 goals: Leónidas (Brazil) **5 goals:** Gyorgy Sárosi, Gyula Zsengellér (Hungary), Silvio Piola (Italy)

FASTEST GOAL 35 seconds: Arne Nyberg (Sweden v Hungary)

TOTAL GOALS 84 AVERAGE GOALS 4.67 per match

THE FATEFUL FINAL

Nothing was more important to Brazil than winning the World Cup at home. The world's biggest stadium was built to showcase the triumph, but defeat cast a shadow over the country that has never quite lifted.

The 12-year gap between tournaments caused by the Second World War meant the 1950 World Cup wouldn't be the easiest competition to stage. Brazil felt that they were ready for the challenge of hosting a spectacle capable of moving forward the world game, but they had waited a long time to get their World Cup. On the opening day of the 1938 World Cup in Paris, FIFA had met to discuss the venue for the 1942 tournament. Both Brazil and Germany had been in contention, but because of the precarious political situation in Europe, it had been decided to postpone a decision until the next FIFA Congress. Although FIFA maintained their Zurich offices throughout the war, their next congress did not take place until July 1946. With much of Europe still suffering from the ravaging effects of the war, it was decided that the 1950 World Cup tournament should take place in Brazil. It was perfect timing for the young republic, eager to make a mark on the international stage. By the time of the tournament Brazil were the reigning South American champions, having beaten Paraguay 7-0 in the Copa América play-off the previous May, and the country was demonstrating a fanatical interest in the sport of football.

"In Europe the most significant dates of the 20th Century are the dates of the World Wars," says Alex Bellos, author of *Futebol: The Brazilian Way Of Life*. "Brazil has never really been in the wars. It doesn't really have any significant dates like that. The dates when Brazil feels most like a nation are the World Cup, so it divides its history into World Cups."

Uruguay forward Juan Alberto Schiaffino shoots past Brazilian goalkeeper Moacir Barbosa to tie the score at 1-1 during the 1950 World Cup final at the Maracanã in Río de Janeiro.

As a nation Brazil had great potential. This vast, multi-cultural country had huge natural resources. But it also had serious problems, not least with poverty. Football was the great unifier of Brazilian life and the vehicle through which the government of the day hoped to move the nation forward and show the world what it was capable of.

Sports writer João Maximo was 15 years old in 1950 and he remembers the importance of staging the tournament to the Brazilian people. "The World Cup created a mood of nationalism that was very curious, that we don't really get any more. At the time winning the World Cup was the way to find out whether Brazil was or wasn't a great nation… it's where the union of nation and football began. Football wasn't just the sport of the country, it was the country itself."

The eyes of the world would be on Brazil like never before and they were determined to impress. The concrete manifestation of their ambition was the decision to build a new stadium to host the World Cup. The Maracanã stadium in Río would not just be the biggest stadium Brazil had ever seen, it would be the biggest in the world. "The very construction of the stadium was a status symbol for the Brazilian citizen because it was a huge project," says Maximo. "A stadium built for 200,000 people – that was ten per cent of the population of Río de Janeiro, capital of the republic."

Ultimately its cost would be more than financial. Brazil would invest so much in this cup, yet come away with nothing. But for Brazil, hosting the World Cup was the opportunity to test the strength of their nation.

"This was the great opportunity for Brazil to prove itself," explains Alex Bellos. "It was much more than just having a sporting event. It was the greatest event that it had ever had, and possibly has ever had. There was this desire to say, 'Look, we are a great nation – we have a great future, and football is the way that we're going to prove it to you'. They weren't happy just to put on some event. They built the world's biggest stadium. The stadium was really about proving themselves as a serious nation – as a big nation, as a nation with a great future."

The world's biggest stadium had hitherto been Glasgow's Hampden Park, but with an official capacity of 183,000 the Maracanã outstripped its rival by 43,000, although an amazing 199,854 would squeeze into the stadium for the World Cup final itself.

The construction of the Maracanã started in 1948, employing some 10,000 labourers. Although it wasn't fully completed in time for the competition's opening game on June 24, 1950, it had already staged its inaugural match two weeks earlier, when future 1958 and 1962 Brazilian World Cup winner Didi scored the stadium's first goal in a game between junior representative sides from Río and São Paulo.

"The Brazilians are a very exaggerative race," says Alex Bellos. "They have this obsession about always being the biggest and the best in the world. They wanted to prove there was a man-made monument that somehow reflected their own stature. Río de Janeiro is an outstanding city. It has Sugar Loaf Mountain, it has the Christ statue, it has Copacabana beach, so if you're going to create something man-made that can live in the same city, it's got to have some kind of extravagance – and the Maracanã certainly did."

Of the 73 FIFA member countries, only 31 entered the qualifying phase of the tournament. This close to the war, Germany and Japan were not invited to take part, although the West Germans had been willing to send a team if asked. Having resurrected the *Deutscher Fussball Bund* at the beginning of 1950, they were still excluded from international competition. Switzerland campaigned hard for their readmission to FIFA, citing "the unifying mission of sport", but they were not officially welcomed back into world football until two months after the 1950 World Cup final.

Opposite: (top) Play goes on at the beginning of the 1950 World Cup finals, with the gigantic Maracanã still under construction. (bottom) Crowds storm barriers and force their way into the unfinished stadium via the back of the stands to watch the opening game of the tournament. The crowd trouble was due to the official entrances not being ready.

The draw for the finals appeared lop-sided, the opening round consisting of two groups of four teams, one of three and one of just two sides. Ecuador, Peru and Argentina were among the many teams to pull out before the qualifiers, enabling Uruguay, Paraguay, Bolivia and Chile to reach the finals without having kicked a ball. Scotland and Turkey, meanwhile, withdrew after booking their places, the Scots unprepared to attend the World Cup as group runners-up to England.

To plug some gaps, FIFA extended invitations to France and Portugal, both of whom had been eliminated in qualification – Portugal declined and France, after initially accepting, withdrew from Pool Four having discovered how much travelling would be involved between games. India too refused to take their place in Pool Three, according to some reports because FIFA insisted they wore boots in the finals.

In 1950 a format was adopted that has never been used before or since, replacing the knockout phase with a 'Final Pool' of four teams who would play each other, the team topping the group finishing the competition as World Cup winners.

When the tournament finally kicked-off on June 24, 1950, the chaotic preparations and uneven qualification process were forgotten in the face of some excellent football and arguably the greatest clash the World Cup has ever seen. In Pool One, Brazil and highly-fancied outsiders Yugoslavia immediately turned on the style. The host nation, playing the tournament in white, had a wonderfully entertaining line-up, boasting a trio of attackers – Ademir, Jair and Zizinho – who ranked among the finest in the world. They played skilful, inventive football and were the favourites to lift the trophy for the first time. Composer Lamartine Babo had even written 'March Of The Brazilian Team', a populist number that urged fans to 'cheer with faith in our hearts, let's cheer to be champions'.

Although not fully finished for the opening game of the tournament, 81,000 fans still made it to the Maracanã to witness the 21-gun salute, firework display, and the release of 5,000 pigeons. The hosts made light work of their first opponents, thrashing Mexico 4-0, with Ademir scoring twice. The game proved an inauspicious start to the World Cup career of Mexican goalkeeper Antonio Carbajal, who was playing in the first of his five consecutive tournaments.

Yugoslavia kept pace with a convincing victory over Switzerland, maintaining their stunning form with a 4-1 win over Mexico. Switzerland surprisingly held Brazil 2-2 at the Pacaembu Stadium in São Paulo, but coach Flavio Costa had made three midfield changes for the game by selecting a trio of São Paulo players to please local fans, a common practice in Brazil. The decision very nearly backfired as his side's performance didn't match the expectations of the 42,000 fans. He was barracked as he left the stadium.

When the two group leaders met in the Maracanã in front of 142,429 spectators, the hosts had to win to progress to the final pool, but they kicked-off the game with a one-man advantage after Yugoslav star player, inside-right Rajko Mitic, had injured himself on the stairs walking on to pitch. "They had raised the ground level in the corridors by the changing rooms because it had rained and there was a lot of water," recalls Brazilian radio commentator Luiz Mendes. "They put a plank on top of it, so the players wouldn't get their feet wet, but he was really tall and he ended up hitting his head and ripped the skin."

Badly shaken, Mitic only returned to the pitch with his head heavily bandaged later in the game, by which time Ademir's third minute opening goal had already put Brazil in front. With Mitic back on the pitch, Yugoslavia fought back. "They had the better of our team at the end of the first half," remembers Mendes, "but we had Moacir Barbosa in goal, who was the best Brazilian goalkeeper of all time. It was Barbosa who saved the team."

The match-winner came courtesy of an outstanding solo effort from Zizinho, ensuring the hosts a 2-0 victory and safe passage to the Final Pool. "Brazil won 2-0 and it was a memorable game," says Mendes.

"That game really should have been the final game." With only one team to go through, it was harsh on the talented Yugoslavs who went home early.

England had arrived in Brazil as the main attraction in Pool Two. The English Football Association had consistently refused to enter previous tournaments, and after years of arrogant isolationism, the self-professed inventors of the game were taking part in their very first World Cup. The team may have lost star players Frank Swift and Tommy Lawton since the war, but their side still boasted Billy Wright, Tom Finney and Stan Mortensen. Although with the English Football Association's convoluted selection process, you could never be sure who would be playing. Walter Winterbottom was the manager and in charge of coaching the team and driving the tactics, but team selection was in the hands of the FA's International Selection Committee, of which Winterbottom was just one member. "He didn't select the teams then, the board of selectors did," says journalist Brian Glanville. "It was a ridiculous situation."

"As players we didn't really know how they made the team selection," recalls Tom Finney. "From what we could gather from the press the selection committee used to meet and select who they felt should play, or make suggestions to Walter that certain changes should be made to a team. But this was only hearsay and what we read about in the press."

For Tom Finney, taking part in the World Cup was a new experience. "It was strange but quite exciting as you were playing against the best teams in the world," he says. "It was the first time England took part in the World Cup and I think it's fair to say that we were an unknown quantity. Some places really fancied England to be the favourites. We'd never seen the Brazilians play before and we were taken to watch their opening game. We were fascinated by the skill that they showed. My own opinion was that they were the favourites and not us."

Arriving in the country just two or three days before the beginning of the tournament, the England team had done little in the way of specialist preparation. They even based themselves in a run-of-the-mill tourist hotel on Copacabana beach that had been recommended to them by Arsenal, who had once used it for an end of season tour rather than as a serious training camp.

The team had trained together for just four days before leaving England and now they had failed to acclimatise themselves to the harsh conditions that playing in Brazil would entail. "The thought of hanging around at the end of the season waiting for 'cup time' to come around was in my view rather a waste of time," defender Alf Ramsey would later recall. "I would have preferred to have gone to Brazil, got accustomed to the conditions, had a series of trial matches under the conditions we should have to face – and of course, overcome."

Even Walter Winterbottom had noticed the reservations of his great England team. "The players are worried about the atmosphere they'll be playing in," he noted, "scared to death of supporters when, if you'd been there before, you realised it was simply crowds having fun!"

"We weren't really well prepared," says Finney. "We did a bit of training in Brazil but not a lot. I think our preparation wasn't anywhere near as good as the Brazilians, for instance, who went away for three or four weeks."

The England players struggled to cope with Río's thin air in their opening Pool Two game at the Maracanã. Their opponents Chile were a country with only one full-time professional footballer, George Robledo, who played in the English first division for Newcastle United, but still England made hard work of the

Uruguay forward Julio Perez is thwarted by Bolivian goalkeeper Guttiérrez in Belo Horizonte. Uruguay win the match 8-0.

South American part-timers. Goals from Stan Mortensen and Wilf Mannion either side of the interval secured a 2-0 win. "For the first time in my life, I felt tired long before the end of the game," captain Billy Wright would later observe.

The United States should have proved even easier opponents – after all, this was a team beaten 9-0 by Italy in a World Cup warm-up game. But on the rutted pitch of the tiny Mineiro Stadium in Belo Horizonte, 300 miles north of Río, England suffered one of the most embarrassing defeats in their history.

England had expected the game to be a walkover. Arthur Drewry, the FA's sole selector travelling with the squad, decided against recalling 35-year-old Stanley Matthews, who had arrived late in Brazil. But the USA had already shown they were capable of springing a surprise or two. They may have lost their opening game 3-1 to Spain, but they had been leading 1-0 until three late goals saved the day for the Spanish. Against England, and in front of just over 10,000 fans, they pulled off one of the biggest surprises in world football.

Coached by Scotsman Bill Jeffrey of Penn State, the US team contained three foreign-born players, including their one full-time professional, captain Eddie McIlvenny, a Scot who had been on the books of Wrexham and Manchester United before moving to America. The underdogs weathered England's opening onslaught in the game's first half hour, before breaking out of their own half for a 38th minute goal, Haitian-born Joseph 'Larry' Gaetjens nodding a Walter Bahr cross past Bert Williams in the England net.

US goalkeeper Frank Borghi kept the retaliation at bay with an acrobatic display between the posts. Billy Wright would later note, "the feeble finishing of our forwards who time and time again tore the ponderous American defence wide open only to fail lamentably with their finishing". England thought they had

England's Alf Ramsey watches as goalkeeper Bert Williams is beaten by a header from Joseph Gaetjens. The USA beat England 1-0 in Belo Horizonte.

equalised when a Jimmy Mullen header appeared to cross the US goal line, but the referee denied the appeal. The defeat was a major shock for the English.

"To lose was really something extraordinary," says Tom Finney, "but it was one of those games that we just weren't going to win. I think we hit the woodwork on three or four occasions. They got one chance and took it. We got lambasted in the press. We were not really expecting to lose to a team like America, because they were looked on as non-entities – we proved that by playing them three years later in New York, when we beat them by six goals to three."

"People tried to blame Arthur Drewry, who was the sole selector," explains Brian Glanville. "He confirmed the same team that had beaten Chile 2-0 in Río. Afterwards people were saying how fatuous not to put in the great Stanley Matthews, who was always being snubbed by England although he was the greatest player of his generation and one of the greatest players the world's ever seen. But if you look at that England team, it was absolutely full of talent. They should have crushed the Americans but on the day they just didn't and they couldn't. Maybe tactically Walter Winterbottom got it a bit wrong, but with players so experienced, with such tremendous reputations, you would have thought they could have got it right themselves."

Going into their final Pool Two game at the Maracanã, the English could still scrape through to a play-off game if they beat Spain. They made four changes to the team, calling up a not fully fit Stanley Matthews and prolific Newcastle United centre-forward Jackie Milburn for their first games of the tournament. Tottenham's Eddie Baily and Bill Eckersley of Blackburn Rovers were also called-up to the team, both making their international debuts.

The changes appeared to work for England who gave a mesmerising display. They should have taken a first-half lead when Jackie Milburn's perfectly good 12th minute goal was ruled offside by Italian referee Giovanni Galeati, but after Zarra headed Spain into the lead in the 48th minute, the Spanish pulled all their men behind the ball to keep hold of their slender lead. The goal inspired Spanish radio commentator Matías Prats to famously announce, "Zarra – the best head in Europe after Churchill!" In Spain the game still counts as the nation's most famous victory. England had arrived at the tournament as one of the favourites, but they left the Maracanã pitch to the jeers of the Brazilian fans who had expected more from Winterbottom's famous team.

English football had been isolated from international competition and its team was out of step with the kind of preparation that was needed to succeed in a major modern tournament. "I think it's true to say we had our heads in the sand," says Tom Finney. "We didn't realise just how good these other sides were… and the conditions took their toll really."

In the three-nation Pool Three, holders Italy, Sweden and Paraguay squared up to each other. The Italians arrived in Brazil undefeated in their World Cup history. Having not competed in 1930, they were winners in 1934 and 1938, but without double World Cup winning coach Vittorio Pozzo (also coach of Italy's Olympic champions of 1936), they weren't the same side. After the misery and hardship of the war football was one of the few collective activities that could still be celebrated in Italy, but new coach Lajos Czeizler had been dealt a mighty blow in May 1949 when 18 members of the all-conquering Torino team, including ten Italian internationals, were killed as their plane crashed into Superga Basilica on the hills overlooking Turin.

"Not only did this destroy any chance that Italy had of winning a third consecutive World Cup in 1950," suggests historian Simon Martin, "but it also contributed to the need for a more defensive style of play because of the dearth of players that Italy had at the time. There was a need to make the best of the resources available."

In the short term Italy were still reigning world champions and had to field a team in Brazil. The memory of the disaster caused the squad to travel to Río by boat and they didn't arrive in time for adequate preparation, losing their first game 3-2 to a Sweden side coached by Englishman, George Raynor. It had been Raynor who had helped the Scandinavians win the 1948 Olympic football title, and Sweden's 2-2 draw with Paraguay in the next match was enough to clinch the top spot of Pool Three, Italy's 2-0 win over Paraguay a mere consolation.

WORLD CUP STORIES

FRIAÇA

For Brazil's goalscorer, the 1954 World Cup final was an experience to forget.

"Brazil had everything to be World Cup winners. Vasco gave 12 players to the national team and it was a really good team. You had to work hard to have a national team like the one we had. The Vasco team was always winning and I was always taking part in scoring goals, until one day I was called up and I found myself at that World Cup.

"We stayed in São Januário before the final. We would chat with each other but we weren't talking about defeat, we were just chatting and having fun. I got up in the morning as normal, I was always happy and calm, with lots of confidence that I was going to play well and that we would beat Uruguay. But life's like that. God didn't want us to win.

"I scored Brazil's goal in the final – it was really good and I felt very proud because of the reaction of the fans. It was an enormous thing. You didn't see one empty space and everyone was shouting. We weren't used to that sort of thing. After the goal I had a mental blank. I played, but I don't really know how I played. I completely blanked out. I don't remember Uruguay's goals.

"After the defeat I went to my sister's house. I don't know how I got there. The Mayor of Teresópolis found me underneath a jackfruit tree, completely out of it. He took me to my sister's house to lie down and after five or six days my sister took me home. After this I wasn't 100 per cent back to normal. I was kind of inside my own head for six or seven days. Time passes and I was playing again. It took me about a year before everything got back to normal. I had just been out of it. I was so stuck in my thoughts that I disappeared. I thought that I hadn't been as useful to my team as I should have been."

In the absurd two-team Pool Four it seemed that fate was smiling on Uruguay. They had already qualified for the finals without playing a single game, and after the draw was made, the withdrawal of France meant they would only have to face the inexperienced Bolivia. They made it to the deciding final pool with a comfortable 8-0 victory.

In advance of the tournament, Brazil coach Flavio Costa had seen the main threat as coming from Europe. Brazil hadn't actually played against a European team since 1938, but they had faced Uruguay 17 times in same period, winning eight and losing five. "The President of the Brazilian football federation called the press together to tell them the games that would be played in the final group," recalls commentator Luiz Mendes. "He asked if anyone objected to this order of games. I put my hand up and said, 'You should play Uruguay first'. A few months before, in the Copa Río Branco, we played Uruguay and they won. They beat us 4-3 in São Paulo, and then lost to us 3-2 and 1-0 in Río. So it was a team who were neck and neck with us. People laughed, but the Uruguayans are dangerous in final games because they create a whole new soul. They're courageous."

Without the drama of the knockout format, the final pool of the 1950 World Cup finals could have been an anti-climax if one team had clinched the title before the games had concluded. The results, however, added to the drama, teeing up the most thrilling climax to any World Cup. The hosts looked to be the favourites when the pool kicked off, destroying Sweden 7-1 with some of the finest attacking football ever seen at the time. The mercurial Ademir scored four goals in a bravura display, his understanding with Jair and Zizinho reaching its peak. In their next game all three strikers hit the net, helping the hosts to dispatch Spain 6-1. Danger man Ademir even managed to score twice, despite being marked throughout the game by two Spanish defenders.

In a physical encounter, the 'sky blues' of Uruguay were held 2-2 by Spain, but a narrow victory over the amateurs of Sweden was enough to retain a small chance of causing an upset. The final group match, between Brazil and Uruguay, would decide the winners of the World Cup – Uruguay needed to beat the favourites to triumph, while Brazil needed only a draw to win the trophy. It looked a foregone conclusion, Brazil having played the better football and having the advantage of a home crowd in the Maracanã.

The high expectations brought pressures and distractions for the Brazil squad. The week before the final, they had transferred their base from a quiet out-of-town hotel to the São Januário Stadium in the city. Their new, easily accessible base proved to be a magnet for the great and the good of Río, including a steady flow of politicians campaigning for the October elections. Even on the morning of the game the players passed the time shaking hands and signing autographs.

In Brazil, the result of the 1950 World Cup final wasn't so much hoped for as expected. The day before the game, São Paulo's *Gazeta Esportivo* ran the front-page headline 'Tomorrow we will beat Uruguay'. In Río, early editions of *O Mundo* carried a picture of the Brazil team under the words: 'These are the world champions'. It was a game that no one who was there would ever forget.

"The game would start at three o'clock," recalls João Luis Alberqueque, an 11-year-old fan blessed with a prime position in the second row behind the goal. "We got there at ten in the morning but the time went by because the whole stadium was full after one hour or so. And there was this festivity thing. Nobody was nervous. Everyone told this 11-year-old boy – the newspapers, the radio, my family, the guy who came to my house to sell milk – that Brazil is already the world champion."

Overleaf: (top) Uruguay's Schubert Gambetta reaches for the ball at the end of the final. (bottom left) Cover of a magazine celebrating Uruguay's success. (bottom centre) Obdulio Varela receives the trophy from Jules Rimet. (bottom right) Scorers for Uruguay, Ghiggia (2nd right) and Schiaffino (3rd right) are in the front row.

IV CAMPEONATO
MUNDIAL DE
FUTEBOL

TAÇA JULES RIMET

URUGUAY
CAMPEON

ALBUM
GOLES Y DOBLES
EXTRA

JUNHO DE 1950
BRAS...

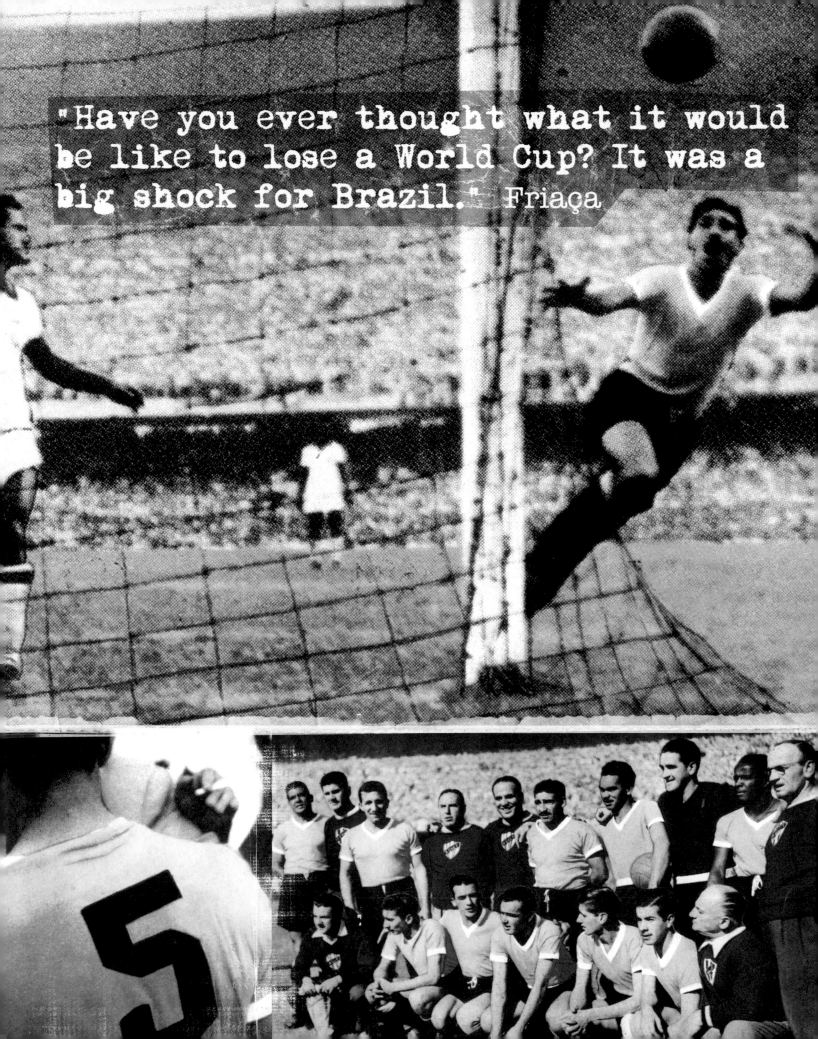

"Have you ever thought what it would be like to lose a World Cup? It was a big shock for Brazil." Friaça

"When I left for the Maracanã Stadium I was going through a city where there was already a carnival atmosphere," recalls commentator Luiz Mendes. "It was contagious. I caught the bug. I felt that optimism. I even forgot about the Copa Río Branco of a month before. I was absolutely convinced that Brazil would win this game."

Their opponents were not so confident of victory. According to their winger Alcides Ghiggia, the night before the final several members of the Uruguayan delegation returned home with the assumption that the team had no chance of winning, while Julio Pérez unashamedly admits to having wet himself while lining-up for the national anthem.

"I remember that the Uruguayans were a tough team," says João Maximo. "They had a player called Juan Schiaffino who was a genius, you know he was an equal to our three musketeers – maybe not Zizinho, who was the greatest player that Brazil had at the time, but Schiaffino was an incredible player."

Despite needing only a draw, Brazil's dynamic frontline trio of Ademir, Zizinho and Jair piled the pressure on. The Uruguayan defence weathered the storm, surviving a goalless first half. But just two minutes after the break Friaça scored for Brazil. In front of a partisan home crowd, in the highest attended football match of all time, the goal was met by the loudest roar in sporting history, the stadium erupting in celebration. "When the ball went into the net three journalists jumped on top of me and almost suffocated me," remembers Friaça. "I was on the ground and these journalists, they hugged me. All the fans were cheering, and I just sort of lost myself."

Luiz Mendes: "The public went wild. Everyone was already celebrating the victory. People were throwing ribbons, confetti, shouting 'Brazil! Champions!'"

With Brazil ahead, coach Flavio Costa sent instructions for Jair to drop back into defence, but the forward didn't get the message. With just a draw good enough to bring them the Jules Rimet cup, Brazil continued to attack as they had throughout the tournament. In the 66th minute, however, Uruguay right-winger Ghiggia beat Bigode down the flank and crossed for Schiaffino to sweep in an equaliser.

The Brazilians continued to press for goals, but Uruguay captain Obdulio Varela drove his team to counter-attack. On the break Ghiggia again dribbled past Bigode, exactly as he had done before, but instead of crossing, this time he shot towards the near post. Barbosa was caught off guard and the ball hit the back of the net. It was a goal that became one of the most significant events in Brazilian history. The Maracanã, citadel of football and celebration of all of Brazil's international aspirations, was transformed into an unbearable burden.

"The fans should have screamed, shouted," recalls fan João Luis Alberqueque. "But the whole stadium was absolutely quiet." Commentating on the match for Rádio Globo, Luiz Mendes was caught by surprise. "GOOOOL do Uruguay," he uttered. "Gol do Uruguay? Gol do Uruguay!" He repeated himself another six times in disbelief.

Many years later, Ghiggia would say, "Only three people have, with just one motion, silenced the Maracanã: Frank Sinatra, Pope John Paul II and me."

Luiz Mendes: "When Uruguay scored it was like a great stab in the back to all the public who were present on that day in the Maracanã stadium. There was a deathly silence, something really stunning and moving. It was the first time I ever heard silence. It was a silence of wails and tears, because the women were crying and at that moment, in that atmosphere, the tears of the women could be heard throughout that huge stadium which was made just for that World Cup."

Opposite: The 1950 World Cup final. (top left) Uruguay keeper Roque Máspoli throws his arms around coach Juan Lopez. (top right) Uruguayan radio commentator Nobel Valentini congratulates Juan Alberto Schiaffino. (bottom) Chaotic scenes at the final whistle, with Uruguay defender Schubert Gambetta forcing his way through a crowd of photographers and journalists as he leaves the field.

Uruguay 2 Brazil 1

0:1 FRIAÇA (BRA) 47', 1:1 JUAN SCHIAFFINO (URU) 66', 2:1 ALCIDES GHIGGIA (URU) 79'.

IV CAMPEONATO MUNDIAL DE FUTEBOL

· TAÇA JULES RIMET ·

Little more than ten minutes later English referee George Reader called time on the game and the unthinkable had happened. For the Brazil side the shock of losing the 'fateful final' had a profound impact. "Have you ever thought what it would be like to lose a World Cup?" asks Friaça. "I remember the goal that I scored but after that, I just have a mental blank… I switched off. I used to say that I was on autopilot but that's not true, I just don't remember. I think it was just a big shock for Brazil. We had a complete team, each one better than the next. You're never going to think that this is going to happen, that you're going to lose to Uruguay. But they scored two goals, we just scored one."

"I'll take that loss to my grave," Jair would say afterward. "And then I'll ask God why we gave away the greatest opportunity to win a World Cup."

Uruguay had achieved the impossible and the supporters could hardly believe what they had witnessed. In the most dramatic circumstances, Brazil had failed to lift the World Cup. Contemporary newspaper reports indicate that in Uruguay three fans died of excitement listening to the radio, while in Río a 58-year-old man collapsed in his home.

"The game ended and I just sat there," says João Maximo. "Two friends were sat with me and, not knowing what would happen in the future, they said, 'We are never going to win the World Cup'. The goal was heard by the silence of 200,000 people and the goal divided Brazil into before and after. We stopped thinking that we were the best in the world. Never again would we think the game was won the night before. We started to respect adversaries in a way that we didn't on that afternoon. Ghiggia's goal was almost like a punch in the face. We had to wake up from that dream, which like every dream is unreal: us as champions of the world, us holding the cup, us drinking champagne from the cup. This moment divides Brazil."

Writing in the *Journal dos Sports* the day after the final, José Lins do Rego reported on the depth of the despair. "I saw people leave the Maracanã with their heads hung low, tears in their eyes, speechless, as if they were returning from the funeral of a loved father. I saw a nation defeated – more than that – one without hope. That hurt my heart. All the vibrancy of the first minutes reduced to the ashes of an extinguished fire. And suddenly a greater disappointment, it stuck in my head that we really were a luckless people, a nation deprived of the great joys of victory, always pursued by bad luck, by the meanness of destiny."

The loss fed Brazil's natural superstition as they looked for a reason for this national tragedy. "In the recriminations after the game it wasn't Uruguay's fault for being the better team," says Alex Bellos, "it was somehow Brazil's fault for not really having the moral fibre for winning, for failing at the final hurdle, as if maybe it was natural for Brazilians to fail at the final hurdle."

It was the black players who took the blame. They were accused of not having enough commitment to the match because they weren't patriotic enough. Among those singled out was the goalkeeper Barbosa, who was made a scapegoat for the defeat. "Barbosa was really marked by the defeat," says Friaça. "He suffered a lot, but it wasn't his fault. Everyone used to say, 'Barbosa's the guy that lost the cup', but to me he was the best goalkeeper I ever saw in my career."

Although journalists had voted Barbosa the best keeper of the tournament, his international career was over. He only played one more time for Brazil and later he would work as a cleaner at the Maracanã stadium. Never allowed to forget the 'fateful final', he was shunned by his country and when he visited the Brazil training camp in 1993, he was turned away by a superstitious squad in case any of his bad luck rubbed off.

For Brazil, the defeat to Uruguay would continue to haunt the nation for many years to come. "In 1950 we became obsessed with the idea that Brazil would only be a great country on the day that it won the World Cup," concludes João Maximo. Brazil had lost the one thing they thought could make their country great, and losing it only made them want it more.

POOL 1

June 24: Maracanã Stadium, Rio de Janeiro
Brazil **4 - 0** Mexico

June 25: Sete de Setembro Stadium, Belo Horizonte
Yugoslavia **3 - 0** Switzerland

June 29: Beira-Rio Stadium, Pôrto Alegre
Yugoslavia **4 - 1** Mexico

June 28: Pacaembu Stadium, São Paulo
Brazil **2 - 2** Switzerland

July 1: Maracanã Stadium, Rio de Janeiro
Brazil **2 - 0** Yugoslavia

July 2: Beira-Rio Stadium, Pôrto Alegre
Switzerland **2 - 1** Mexico

	P	W	D	L	F	A	Pts
Brazil	3	2	1	0	8	2	5
Yugoslavia	3	2	0	1	7	3	4
Switzerland	3	1	1	1	4	6	3
Mexico	3	0	0	3	2	10	0

POOL 2

June 25: Brito Stadium, Curitiba
Spain **3 - 1** USA

June 25: Maracanã Stadium, Rio de Janeiro
England **2 - 0** Chile

June 29: Mineiro Stadium, Belo Horizonte
USA **1 - 0** England

June 29: Maracanã Stadium, Rio de Janeiro
Spain **2 - 0** Chile

July 2: Maracanã Stadium, Rio de Janeiro
Spain **1 - 0** England

July 2: Ilha do Retiro Stadium, Recife
Chile **5 - 2** USA

	P	W	D	L	F	A	Pts
Spain	3	3	0	0	6	1	6
England	3	1	0	2	2	2	2
Chile	3	1	0	2	5	6	2
USA	3	1	0	2	4	8	2

POOL 3

June 25: Pacaembu Stadium, São Paulo
Sweden **3 - 2** Italy

June 29: Brito Stadium, Curitiba
Sweden **2 - 2** Paraguay

July 2: Pacaembu, São Paulo
Italy **2 - 0** Paraguay

	P	W	D	L	F	A	Pts
Sweden	2	1	1	0	5	4	3
Italy	2	1	0	1	4	3	2
Paraguay	2	0	1	1	2	4	1

POOL 4

July 2: Mineiro Stadium, Belo Horizonte
Uruguay **8 - 0** Bolivia

	P	W	D	L	F	A	Pts
Uruguay	1	1	0	0	8	0	2
Bolivia	1	0	0	1	0	8	0

FINAL POOL

July 9: Pacaebu Stadium, São Paulo
Uruguay **2 - 2** Spain

July 9: Maracanã Stadium, Rio de Janeiro
Brazil **7 - 1** Sweden

July 13: Pacaembu Stadium, São Paulo
Uruguay **3 - 2** Sweden

July 13: Maracana Stadium, Rio de Janeiro
Brazil **6 - 1** Spain

July 16: Pacaembu Stadium, São Paulo
Sweden **3 - 1** Spain

July 16: Maracanã Stadium, Rio de Janeiro
Uruguay **2 - 1** Brazil*

The last game of the Final Pool decided the tournament and is regarded as the 1950 World Cup final (see panel).

	P	W	D	L	F	A	Pts
Uruguay	3	2	1	0	7	5	5
Brazil	3	2	0	1	14	4	4
Sweden	3	1	0	2	6	11	2
Spain	3	0	1	2	4	11	1

THE FINAL

URUGUAY	(0) **2**
BRAZIL	(0) **1**

DATE Sunday July 16, 1950
ATTENDANCE 199,854
VENUE Estadio Maracana, Rio de Janeiro

Máspoli

Gonzáles, M   Tejera

Gambetta   Varela   Andrade

Ghiggia Peréz Miguez Schiaffino Morán

Chico   Ademir Menezes   Friaça

Jair   Zizinho

Bigode   Danilo Alvim   Bauer

Juvenal   Augusto

Barbosa

URUGUAY
COACH: JUAN LOPEZ

MÁSPOLI

GONZÁLES M

ANDRADE

TEJERA

VARELA

GAMBETTA

PERÉZ

SCHIAFFINO ⚽
Goal: 66 mins

GHIGGIA ⚽
Goal: 79 mins

MIGUEZ

MORÁN

BRAZIL
COACH: FLAVIO COSTA

BARBOSA

AUGUSTO

JUVENAL

BAUER

DANILO ALVIM

BIGODE

ZIZINHO

JAIR

FRIAÇA ⚽
Goal: 47 mins

ADEMIR MENEZES

CHICO

REFEREE: Reader (England)

Augusto (left) of Brazil and Uruguay's Obdulio Varela exchange pennants before kick off.

TOP GOALSCORERS 9 goals: Ademir Menezes (Brazil) **5 goals:** Juan Schiaffino (Uruguay), Estanislao Basora (Spain)

FASTEST GOAL 2 minutes: Alfredo (Brazil v Switzerland)

TOTAL GOALS: 88 **AVERAGE GOAL** 4.00 per game

THE MIRACLE OF BERNE

For a nation consumed by guilt and ashamed of any show of nationalism, the 1954 World Cup was a football miracle that gave West Germans a real sense of pride for the first time since the war

Although it came nearly ten years after the end of World War II, Switzerland was a logical choice to host Europe's first post-war tournament, and not simply because the neutral Swiss had escaped the devastation sustained across the continent. FIFA's headquarters were situated in Zurich and 1954 represented the 50th anniversary of its formation. The Swiss had been granted the tournament at FIFA's first post-war congress in 1946, and spent eight years building new stadia for the occasion. The finished grounds had limited capacities and were not really up to the organisational requirements of such a tournament, nevertheless the competition proved a financial success. This was a tournament seen by a privileged few in flickering black and white television pictures for the first time, but it also produced some of the most colourful attacking football in World Cup history, 140 goals shared between 16 teams at an average of over five per game.

For the first time since the war West Germany had been allowed to enter the tournament. Banned from international football after the war and with pitiful resources, the Germans struggled for re-acceptance and recognition as they attempted to rebuild their country. Divided after the war into East and West, the nation was consumed by poverty and guilt – any sense of nationalism had been deeply buried and football was well down the agenda. It was down to one man that they even had what they could call a national team. That man was Josef 'Sepp' Herberger. "Herberger was a great idealist," says German commentator Rudi Michael. "He was fanatically inspired by the reconstruction of his football team."

West Germany captain Fritz Walter (left) shakes hands with beaten rival, Hungary's Ferenc Puskás, after the World Cup final.

West German miracle makers: Fritz Walter, Anton Turek, Horst Eckel, Helmut Rahn, Ottmar Walter, Werner Liebrich, Josef Posipal, Hans Schäfer, Werner Kohlmeyer, Karl Mai and Max Morlock. (right) Manager Josef 'Sepp' Herberger

Although not a believer in Nazi ideology, Herberger had been picked as national team trainer by the Nazi sports authorities and had coached the team from 1938, Germany continuing to play international fixtures through the early war years until 1942. He had joined the Nazi party in May 1933, effectively as a means of career advancement, but it gave him a certain influence that he used to keep his team alive during the war.

"They would get jobs, not too dangerous, postings not too dangerous, so that they would be kept together," explains German football journalist Markus Brauckmann. "And he had a master plan that this team would make it in Europe."

After the war, the denazification committee in Herberger's town eventually cleared him by classifying him as a *Mitlaüfer*, a follower who joined Nazi organisations but did not actively collaborate. The German football federation had to admit he was still the best-qualified person to coach the national team and he was able to continue with his job, first tracking down as many of his star players as he could find.

Herberger's captain was Fritz Walter, the unquestioned star of German football. His skill and creativity as a goal scoring midfielder was unrivalled. Herberger had successfully kept Walter from the frontline until the final stages of the war, when the Russians imprisoned him. A guard recognised him as one of the stars of Germany's 5-3 defeat of Hungary in Budapest in 1942 and spared him the dreaded fate of being sent to Siberia.

"Fritz Walter was the number one for us and he was also the team captain," says Horst Eckel, German right-half and Kaiserslautern team-mate of both of the Walter brothers, Fritz and Ottmar. "He was the long arm of Sepp Herberger and when Fritz Walter played well, we all played well."

But his war experiences had left him scarred. Since catching malaria he found it particularly difficult playing in hot conditions. It was well known that the worse the weather, the better Fritz played. 'Fritz Walter weather', as it would become known in Germany, would play a big part in the outcome of the 1954 World Cup.

The qualifying rounds featured the highest number of nations yet, starting with 38 entries, although Poland and China later withdrew. Poland's withdrawal meant that favourites Hungary progressed to the finals without having to play a game. England and Scotland came through the British Home Nations group, while France qualified scoring 20 goals in four games against the Republic of Ireland and Luxembourg.

Sweden and Spain failed to qualify, the latter being beaten in a play-off by Turkey who automatically became seeds in Spain's place, a ruling that was to have particular significance for West Germany as the competition unfolded. One unsolved mystery surrounding the game involves the non-appearance of Ladislav Kubala, a lethal finisher who had become a vital component of the Spanish side the previous year. Ten minutes before the start of the play-off game at the Olympic Stadium in Rome, a man claiming to be a FIFA executive brandished a letter questioning Kubala's right to play for Spain, given that he had previously played international football for both Hungary and Czechoslovakia. Kubala pulled out of the tie and without him Spain struggled to a 2-2 draw, Turkey qualifying for the finals by the drawing of lots. The next day, however, FIFA denied that they had sent an official to the game and said that they had no objection with Kubala playing for Spain.

Almost inevitably FIFA experimented with the tournament rules once more, reverting to a complicated pool phase featuring 16 teams divided into four groups, with two seeded sides in each group who would not play each other – to avoid undue fatigue was the reason offered. In the knockout phase the four group winners progressed to one half of the draw, with the four runners-up in the other half, which meant the final would definitely be contested between a group winner and a group runner-up. The system was open to exploitation and, as the competition progressed, the West Germans did just that.

It was no surprise to find that Hungary, coached by Gusztáv Sebes, were favourites to win the tournament. This was the era of the 'Magical Magyars'. Two years previously they had been crowned Olympic champions and now their players were at the peak of their powers. The line-up was packed with world-class players, including the 'Galloping Major' Ferenc Puskás, striker Sándor Kocsis (dubbed 'The Man With The Golden Head'), midfield dynamo Josef Bozsik, and deep-lying centre-forward Nandor Hidegkuti. This was the core of the side that destroyed English pretentions to superiority a year earlier when they had shocked the football world by winning 6-3 at Wembley. England's rigid tactics were no match for the new football revolution from the East.

When the first World Cup had taken place in Uruguay in 1930, England, supremely confident of its role in world football, had simply refused to take part. It was an attitude of arrogant isolation. Not entering the World Cup until 1950, England were so confident they gave themselves no time to prepare and flew to Brazil just a couple of days before their first game. Their early exit at the group stages of that tournament had included a shock defeat by the amateurs of the USA, but the result hardly registered with a nation still gloriously wrapped up in itself. England were happy playing the way they had always played: physical, rather than tactical. Training was based on making sure that the players were fit, and for some it often meant that they didn't see the ball more than once or twice a week. The attitude was that if you didn't have the ball in training during the week, you'd be hungry for it on Saturday. "We had stamina and endurance capacities in our make up, so we could run all day," recalls Bobby Robson, a 20-year-old Fulham winger at the time.

"England were looked upon as a decent side but the Hungarians showed us up. We were no longer the best in the world."
Tom Finney

No one was complaining, because despite the tactical limitations of the players, it was a very effective style that left England invincible on home soil. They'd never been beaten at home by a continental side, but in 1953 Hungary took on England at Wembley with a completely different approach to tactics and preparation.

"The Hungarian football team came up with a new playing system, which was a great advantage," explains the team's right-back Jenö Buzánszky. "The so-called 2-3-5 system was invented by the English and was played all over the world at the time. While the centre-forward is up front in the 2-3-5 system, in Hungary Hidegkúti played in a withdrawn role and the half-backs were pushed forward. This was the so-called 4-2-4 formation, and in the end we surprised the world with it.

"The other factor in that era was that great football personalities came together in Hungary, such as Puskás, Hidegkúti, Kocsis, Bozsik and Grosics, who were defining players in this team. To have so many personalities coming together is unusual, even in world terms, and they all had an influence on the structural set-up of the team. Over many years, if not 11, then at least nine players were constant members of a settled team. This meant familiar teamwork and a new system of playing, which changed football history."

The England team were stuck rigidly in a past where the number on your shirt dictated your position on the pitch. But Hungary played a new free-flowing game, interchanging positions at will to disguise the formation, beating opponents with well-crafted wall passes, attacking spaces rather than sticking dogmatically to zonal play. While the rest of the world was playing the English-invented 2-3-5 'pyramid system', England themselves were still using their trusty old WM formation, pioneered by Herbert Chapman's Arsenal in the early Thirties. The WM formation relied on a single man-marking centre-back to shadow the centre-forward, flanked by two wide full-backs to keep the attacking wingers in check. In advance of the game, England had barely registered the dominant form of Hungary and their new flexible formation. Although it was yet to be given a name, it was a prototype of 4-2-4 that had two midfield half-backs helping both the defence and the attack, and a deep-lying centre-forward playing behind two attacking inside-forwards, in effect inverting the 'M' of the WM formation (it is sometimes called the WW formation).

"England played with one centre-half," explains Bobby Robson. "The Hungarians came with two centre-forwards – so the centre-half marked two players. You can't cope with that, you can't mark two players. You can only mark one – and if that one's better than you anyway, you're going to have some problems. But when it's two against one against you, it is a nightmare."

"When we attacked, everyone attacked, and in defence it was the same," Puskás later said. "We were the prototype for Total Football."

A goal up after 60 seconds, the Hungarians left England marking empty spaces and they were 4-2 up by half-time. By the final whistle, even one more consolation goal from England's right-back Alf Ramsey could not distract from a 6-3 defeat. Ramsey would be the man to finally bring change to English football in the following decade. But the lesson was there at Wembley for anyone willing to learn.

"It was the first time we'd lost to a foreign country on English soil," says Bobby Robson. "We weren't the masters of football any more. We were the teachers of the game but the pupils had overtaken us."

England's inability to cope was clear to everyone watching that day. Tom Finney, one of the greatest

Opposite: (top) England v Hungary, November 25, 1953. Captains Ferenc Puskás and Billy Wright lead their teams on to the Wembley pitch before England's historic 6-3 defeat. (bottom) England lose the return fixture in Budapest in May 1954.

England players of his generation, did not play in the game but was watching from the stands, and even the pre-match preparation of the Hungarians was a revelation for the English, who looked on as Puskás juggled with the ball in the centre circle. "It was something entirely different from what we did," recalls Finney. "The Hungarians came out some 20 minutes before the kick-off and did ball work. They did a warming up period

like we normally associate with the teams nowadays. In the English game at that time you came out five minutes before the kick-off and that was the warm-up. You had to start the game whether it was a cold bitter day in December or nice, warm day in August.

"England were looked upon as a fairly decent side but the Hungarians showed up the England team. It was something entirely different that we'd never seen before. I think the majority of players that took part in that game learnt an awful lot from it. We learnt then, of course, that the English game was nowhere near what it was made out to be. We were no longer the best in the world – and a long way from it."

But England heeded none of the warnings. The fluid and flexible style of the Hungarians was years ahead of its time and a precursor to the Total Football of the Dutch in the Seventies. They reconfirmed their superiority when beating England 7-1 in Budapest just three weeks before the 1954 World Cup. "I was unfortunate enough to play in that game," says Finney. "And again we were given a lesson." Hungary were a supremely well-prepared side, but for the World Cup in Switzerland England manager Walter Winterbottom was barely given time to get his squad together in preparation.

While England were being humiliated by Hungary, West Germany had dispensed with any friendly internationals in the months prior to the World Cup, instead concentrating on a thorough training regime. "We went to Munich for training," says Horst Eckel. "That was a hard time but it had an effect later. We certainly weren't the best team, Hungary were, but in terms of conditioning we were the strongest team that played in Switzerland in 1954. We didn't just train once a day, there were four training sessions in one day."

The tournament finally kicked off with a shock on the opening day in Pool One when seeded France lost to a Yugoslavian team fielding ten of their silver medallists from the 1952 Helsinki Olympics. Yugoslavia's 1-1 draw with Brazil three days later meant that both sides progressed, while *Les Bleus* were on their way home.

In Pool Two Hungary hammered nine goals passed South Korea in their opening game in Zurich, Sándor Kocsis scoring three of the 11 goals that would land him the tournament's Golden Boot.

The West Germans began their campaign in distinctly un-Fritz Walter weather, rapidly making a mockery of their non-seeding by beating Turkey 4-1. It was a great start for the unfancied Germans but their next encounter would be against Hungary. The 'Magical Magyars' hadn't been beaten for over four years and were clear favourites to win the tournament. This was the golden generation for Hungarian football, the first footballing powerhouse to emerge from behind the Iron Curtain.

Against such a formidable team the West Germans would need a remarkable performance in Basel. However, Sepp Herberger had hatched a cunning plan. He let Fritz Walter lead the team on to the pitch, but to the shock of the German supporters he had chosen to send out a side of mainly reserves.

Puskás won the toss, setting the tone for the first half. The Hungarians showed no mercy and by half-time they were leading 3-1 with the Germans facing an uphill battle. "When a team hasn't lost a game for four years across the whole world, then one thing is clear," says Horst Eckel. "Against such a team you have to try and pull together and get through it as best you can." But merely pulling together against this Hungary side wasn't enough. It was soon clear that the Germans were completely outclassed. They were thrashed by a humiliating 8-3.

Although no-one had expected Germany to actually beat the Hungarians, so shocking was the extent of the defeat that calls for Herberger's head rang out. "There was a storm of indignation that such a desperate team was fielded by the Germans," says German football historian Harry Valerian. "It was something which made people's blood boil."

German manager Sepp Herberger was unphased. He had exploited the play-off system, electing to send out a side missing eight of his first choice starting line-up. With Hungary unbeaten in four years, he had already written off the game. Herberger was certain his team would beat Turkey, and that South Korea would finish bottom of the group – thus the crucial match would be the group play-off game with Turkey to decide who went through in second place. This rendered the result of their game with Hungary irrelevant.

"That match against Hungary was not at all decisive for us," says centre-forward Ottmar Walter, younger brother of Fritz. "If we had got five, ten or 15 goals, that would not have mattered at all if we had won the other games. The Hungarians, they had an easy time. For us the harmony was lacking as we had never played together in this line-up."

The decisive win did bring with it some negative consequences for Hungary that would affect them through the tournament. "Sadly this match came at a great price," recalls Jenő Buzánszky. "Puskás was kicked, I think deliberately, by a player called Liebrich. He tried to take him out on three occasions and unfortunately the third time he succeeded. Puskás couldn't play in the following two matches."

"Puskás was one of the most famous footballers of the time," says Horst Eckel. "He could do everything – apart from headers, because he wasn't that tall. But he was captain of the team and he led them like Fritz Walter did us. And he could also score lots of goals – he was just an extraordinary footballer."

After the World Cup German journalists and football analysts would construct a theory that Sepp Herberger had decided to rest eight members of his first team for the match because he wanted to lull the Hungarians into a false sense of security, and by finishing second in the group, thus navigate a route to the final avoiding Uruguay and Brazil. Herberger would forever evade giving a straight answer to the question.

In the immediate aftermath of the match it would have taken a brave pundit to advocate any theory that suggested the tactical genius of Herberger. The German coach rode his criticism with a stream of

(top) Jules Rimet opens the World Cup at La Pontaise stadium in Lausanne. (bottom) Officials at the Wankdorf Stadium in Berne measure crowd capacity before the World Cup.

characteristically ambiguous one-liners, which would either baffle or charm the assembled media. But his reputation was partly rehabilitated when Germany thrashed Turkey 7-2 in the Pool Two play-off. His plan had worked and against all the odds they were through to the last eight.

Based at the Belvédère Hotel in Spiez, with views overlooking Lake Thun, Herberger was engendering a feeling of camaraderie within his squad that would become known as the 'Spirit of Spiez'. To fire up the team after the defeat by Hungary he read aloud to the players many of the demeaning telegrams and vitriolic press reports. He extended his team-building to the allocation of hotel rooms, partnering players together in a way that would help their play. Although Fritz Walter might have been a fine captain, as a man he was prone to self-doubt and rather than pair him with his brother, Herberger had his captain sharing a room with the effervescent winger Helmut Rahn.

Rahn had only gone to Switzerland as a substitute, called up at the last moment while on a tour of South America with his club side Rot-Weiss Essen. In many ways his boisterous hijinks and spontaneous manner were ill-matched to Herberger's disciplined management style, but the coach saw something special in the player. Rahn's performance against the Hungarians had been one of the few positives to come out of the thrashing and he would earn a recall for the quarter-finals, helping to shape the remainder of the tournament for the Germans.

In Pool Three Scotland finally made their World Cup debut, but they were a depleted force. Rangers had refused to release any of their players and the Scottish FA went into the tournament on a shoestring budget, sending just a 13-man squad, including two goalkeepers. Unsurprisingly they were soon packing their bags after a 1-0 defeat by Austria and a 7-0 drubbing at the hands of Uruguay, their disillusioned manager Andy Beattie having resigned after the first game. Czechoslovakia also failed to register a point in the group, leaving Uruguay and Austria to progress in the two top spots.

In Pool Four, England topped a group that featured Switzerland, Belgium and Italy. The hosts followed England through to the knockout phase after beating Italy in a play-off. Stanley Matthews was in exceptional form in England's opening game, but his side somehow managed to throw away a 3-1 lead over Belgium, drawing the tie 4-4 after extra-time (which was played even in group games in 1954). England boasted the talents of Billy Wright, Nat Lofthouse and Tom Finney – they should have gone further in the tournament, but came unstuck in the quarter-final game against Uruguay, losing 4-2 with keeper Gil Merrick at fault for three of the goals. In the end the feeling was that their shattering pre-tournament 7-1 defeat at the hands of Hungary, just weeks earlier, had destroyed their confidence.

Switzerland were knocked out of the competition in the quarter-finals by Austria in the highest-scoring match to feature in the World Cup finals, losing a 12-goal thriller to Austria 7-5, despite having led the game 3-0 after 23 minutes.

The West Germans squeezed past Yugoslavia 2-0 in their quarter-final, scoring early on and holding out until a late goal sealed the victory. Back home the team's progress was causing a growing sense of excitement and a huge captive audience was tuning in, listening to radio commentaries from the likes of Herbert Zimmerman, who by the end of the tournament would become, for the Germans, the voice of the World Cup. An ecstatic Germany now knew the final was only one game away. To get there, however, they would have to beat the highly rated Austrians.

Horst Eckel: "We'd gotten more self-confidence in the game against Yugoslavia and said, 'Now we're going to win this game, we want to get to the final now'."

Scoring two goals and setting up two more, Fritz Walter inspired his team into destroying Austria 6-1. "They were completely devastated and we were in the final but I'm convinced it was all down to Sepp Herberger," says Ottmar Walter. "We knew that it was he who had believed it was possible all along, and it was he who had told us how to achieve it."

"Suddenly you win against a team as strong as Austria and we were in the final," says Horst Eckel. "We

Opposite: England's Nat Lofthouse is given a sympathetic pat on the shoulder after 4-2 defeat in the World Cup quarter-final in Basle.

Hungarian forward Sándor Kocsis celebrates as the ball rolls past Uruguayan goalkeeper Roque Gaston Máspoli as defender José Santamaría looks on. Hungary win the semi-final 4-2 in extra-time.

were so happy and everyone said, 'Ah ha, the Germans are strong too'. Only one team didn't understand this and that was Hungary."

Hungary's quarter-final opponents Brazil had also proved themselves guilty of underestimating the opposition in 1954. Their squad had arrived in Switzerland determined to lay the ghost of the 'fateful final' of 1950 to rest. In the aftermath of the defeat at the Maracanã four years earlier, every possible excuse was debated, including the idea that somehow the players had not been patriotic enough. In Brazil, national pride had subsequently become inextricably linked with the fortunes of football. The white shirts that had become tainted by defeat at the Maracanã needed replacing. Rio newspaper *Correio da Manhã* declared that Brazil's first choice white strip had suffered from a "psychological and moral lack of symbolism". With the support of the Brazilian Sports Confederation, the newspaper launched a competition to design a new strip using all the colours of the Brazilian flag: blue, white, green and yellow.

Brazil had travelled to the 1954 World Cup in Switzerland with a new yellow-shirted strip and a new sense of nationalism, forgetting that national pride was no substitute for adequate technical and tactical preparation. "The Brazilian national team arrived in Switzerland singing the national anthem and kissing the flag before walking on to the pitch," says journalist João Maximo. "They had no knowledge at all about what European football was. No coach had gone there to find out how they played."

In their quarter-final against Hungary, Brazil encountered a style of football and a level of commitment that they had never seen before. The game went down in football history for all the wrong reasons. Instead of the classic it promised to be, the match degenerated into hand-to-hand combat, subsequently dubbed 'the Battle of Berne'. The bout was refereed by Englishman Arthur Ellis, a future household name in the Britain through his role officiating on comedy sports programme *It's A Knockout*. Ellis sent off three players, Hungary's Bozsik and Brazil's Humberto Tozzi and Nilton Santos, after trouble broke out over a disputed penalty.

"We beat the Brazilians, with a huge fight in the dressing room at the end," recalls Hungarian keeper, Gyula Grosics. "They arrived in Europe intending to prove that their defeat in the previous final was just a slip-up and that they were still the best in the world."

Newly born Brazilian patriotism was beaten 4-2 as the game degenerated into violence that continued in the changing rooms after the match, embroiling both managers and even the delegations.

If Brazil were to have any success at all in future World Cups they would have to come up with a new way of approaching the competition. "The lack of patriotism in 1950 ended up in a defeat," says João Maximo, "and if a double dose of patriotism didn't work in 1954, what on earth were we going to do?"

Hungary's semi-final against 1950 champions Uruguay was a memorable encounter that put paid to the South Americans' unbeaten record in World Cup history. In a thrilling match that went to extra-time, the Magyars finally won 4-2. The only downside to Hungary's day was that after the match they were asked to go back on to the pitch and salute the home fans who were refusing to leave the ground. The celebrations caused them to miss the train back to their camp. "We only got back to Solothurn by taxi at around five or six in the morning," recalls Jenö Buzánszky. "Three days later it was the final. We couldn't have a rest and this affected us."

On paper the final looked to be a forgone conclusion. West Germany, unseeded, faced the might of Hungary, who had not lost in 31 matches and who had scored 25 goals in four games on their way to the final. But that didn't dampen German enthusiasm, much to the surprise of Hungarian goalkeeper Gyula Grosics. "Three matches earlier we had beaten the Germans 8-3 and, to be honest, after that match I couldn't have imagined that we'd come across the West German team again in the final."

The team's success had caught the imagination of the German people and, for the first time since the war, the country had something to shout about. But if the World Cup was giving German football fans the opportunity to believe in their country once more, behind the Iron Curtain in Hungary, supporting the football team was the only way to show true national pride. "Dictatorship was at its peak in those years in Hungary, and the political system operated under such dreadful circumstances which represented an enormous feeling of being threatened, over and above normal sense of fear," explains Gyula Grosics. "You could not travel from Hungary, and we lived in fear, night and day. In those years sport, and specifically football, kept identity-consciousness alive. There were some 90 minutes at the Olympics in Helsinki when you could sing loudly the national anthem, the prayer of Hungarians. These were the rare occasions when you could cheer and shout 'Hungarians forward'. People who did not live in such circumstances have difficulty understanding what enormous importance a football team had in the political life of a country. We, the football team, were the main break-out point for the Hungarian nation. The weekdays were transformed to holidays by magic thanks to sports, and primarily football."

The World Cup final was played on July 4, 1954, and as the kick-off approached it started to rain – it was true 'Fritz Walter weather'. "Fritz Walter was more or less ineffective on very hot days," says Uli Hesse-Lichtenberger, author of *Tor! The Story Of German Football*. "He was playing at his best in a slight downpour. On the morning of the final the German players went out on to the balcony of their hotel to check the weather. It started raining at around midday and that's when Max Morlock said, 'Now nothing can go wrong'."

Herberger knew that to stand any chance he needed his captain to be on top form so he was delighted, but he also had a secret weapon. He had recruited sports shoemaker Adi Dasler into his backroom team. The founder of Adidas had developed a boot for the Germans that had screw-in studs, enabling the team to change the length of their studs depending on the weather conditions. Short studs for dry conditions, longer ones for Fritz Walter weather. "It only took a few seconds to take out the studs and quickly raise the boots," says Ottmar Walter. "I don't know what studs the Hungarians had on, but before half-time we were already using the higher studs and I'd say that gave us a certain advantage."

The teams lined up in front of 60,000 people at the Wankdorf Stadium in Berne, and back in Germany several million were crowding around their radio sets, hanging on to every word spoken by commentator Herbert Zimmerman. It was to be a game of extraordinary drama – one that would make Zimmerman a household name.

The Germans had got further than they had ever thought possible, but for the Hungarians this was the moment of truth. "Only one team had anything to lose in this match and that was the Hungarian team," says Grosics. "The Germans could only win."

"We were convinced of our ability," says Horst Eckel. "We talked amongst ourselves about the game and we said we are going on to the pitch and we want to become world champions."

Once again Fritz Walter and Puskás went head to head and once again Puskás won the toss. After just six minutes Puskás, who had insisted on playing although not fully fit, went on to make his mark, scoring from a rebound. Two minutes later a setback became a disaster when Czibor scored after a backpass by the German left-back, Werner Kohlmeyer, was not gathered by goalkeeper Turek.

Horst Eckel: "If a goal is scored against you straight away in the sixth minute and then another one in the eighth to go 2-0 down, it's already critical for a team. But we didn't let it get to us, we didn't stick our heads in the sand."

Fritz Walter would need to inspire and encourage the players and at the restart it was Herberger's words that gave him the strength to do so. "I looked at him and he looked at me and at Max Morlock, and then he said, 'Don't worry. Always remember what Sepp keeps saying: 'When the 90 minutes are over, then we'll do the accounts','" explains Ottmar Walter.

Italian forward Benito Lorenzi (right) in action against the Swiss at La Pontaise, Lausanne. Switzerland won 2-1.

As the German captain drove them forward it would only take two minutes for a new entry to appear in those accounts, Max Morlock stabbing home a pass from left-winger Hans Schäfer. A swift German reply saw them gather momentum and they pressed on in search of an equaliser. Cracks were beginning to show in the Hungarian defence as the Germans forced a series of corners, and a mistake by Grosics in the 18th minute allowed winger Helmut Rahn to make it 2-2. 'The Boss', as he was known, would go on to finish the tournament with four goals, but the Hungarian keeper felt that this particular one shouldn't have been allowed. "I came out to try and catch it or parry it away and Schäfer jumped up with me, grabbed me from behind and pulled me to the ground," remembers Grosics. "The referee was standing five metres away so there's no way he couldn't have seen it. Schäfer, 30 years later, admitted that the tactical instruction from Herberger was not to bother with anyone else at corners and free-kicks, just me: to obstruct me in keeping goal."

With a little luck and some stout defending the West Germans continued to contain the Hungarians for

GYULA GROSICS

For Hungary's goalkeeper, defeat in the 1954 World Cup final had frightening consequences.

"When we went to the World Cup, there was no football expert in the world who did not expect the triumph of the Hungarian team. Therefore the politicians of the time had already prepared the celebrations for the day after the match at the Hungarian Embassy in Switzerland. The original plan was that the highest-ranking political leaders would welcome the team at the border in Hegyeshalom and manager Gusztáv Sebes and captain Ferenc Puskás would make the reception speech and reply to the ceremonial congratulations. As the team lost, this idea was thrown away and the speeches

were cancelled. A third-class leadership awaited when we arrived.

"The express train we took from Switzerland to Hungary via Vienna usually does not stop anywhere – it used to go from the border straight to Budapest. In this case, the train was stopped in Tata, where the joint training camp of Hungarian sport was. The railway station, its vicinity, and the training camp itself was closed by the soldiers of State Security Authority (ÁVH), the most dreadful armed forces in Hungary.

"We were driven to the training camp for a dinner which was attended by Mátyás Rákosi, the highest ranking political leader of that time [General Secretary of the Hungarian Communist Party]. Instead of a ceremonial dinner it was more like a funeral feast and I felt that

Hungarian football was being buried. Rákosi wanted to let us know that there would be no consequences as a result of this defeat. Of course, we knew right away that we had to fear.

"My life suffered because of the defeat. At the end of November 1954, without any reason I was ordered from the pitch 15 minutes before a match between Honvéd and Vasas. I lived in a vacuum until the beginning of 1955. Nobody spoke to me and I didn't know what was happening around me. There was an atmosphere of fear. It was as if I didn't even exist.

"In January 1955 I was commanded to a questioning at the Ministry of Defence, where I discovered that the accusation against me was suspicion of espionage. I was told that other people had already been hanged for this in Hungary. This was how a 13-month ÁVH procedure was started against me, with questioning every Monday. I was locked from the outside world. My flat was under constant police surveillance so nobody could visit me. I was not allowed to go to training or play in league matches and I was expelled from the national team.

"These 13 months went by and on December 19, 1955, I was taken to the ÁVH centre in the Ministry of the Interior. The chief of the political group of the ministry told me that the procedure was terminated because of lack of evidence. My case was not closed, only suspended. Two days later I was invited to the Ministry of Sport, where minister Gyula Hegyi told me that I would play in Tatabánya from January 1, 1956. I was puzzled, since I was a registered player of Honvéd. He told me that it was Comrade Rákosi's order that I had to join Tatabánya.

"In August 1956 I was re-admitted to the national team. Márton Bukovi had become manager and he told me that his first move was to go to the Party Centre – what did the Party Centre have to do with my case? – and personally asked for

permission to take me back. I played four away games in the next month. On Tuesday October 23 we were at training camp in Tata when news came via radio that there was a revolutionary atmosphere in Budapest. We tuned to Radio Free Europe and listened to the news as an armed battle started against the occupying Soviet army.

"Life stopped for several months after the Soviet intervention of November 4. It was natural that sport was out of the question. Honvéd were playing some friendlies out of the country and asked if I could travel to Spain because they needed a goalkeeper. After the matches there was a big question facing the whole team: should we go home or stay in the West? We were faced with enormous temptation and offers for some of the major players arrived from England, France, Italy, Germany and Spain. In the meantime we accepted a tour of Brazil, despite the fact that the Hungarian Football Association banned it, saying that we should go home.

"We undertook the trip, but unfortunately only seven of the 15 matches were played. FIFA had agreed with the Hungarian FA and the leading Honvéd players were banned: Puskás, Czibor, Sándor Kocsis and myself. When we came back to Vienna from South America we were faced with a big dilemma. Should we go home or stay?

"We heard terrible news from Hungary at that time, but after a couple of months I went to the Hungarian Embassy, on July 5, 1957, and to their great astonishment I requested documents for returning to Hungary. A police van was waiting for me at the border and I was taken to the ÁVH barracks. Two days later I was taken to Tatabánya and I played on as if nothing had happened. These were my personal consequences of the lost World Cup."

the remainder of the half. "They'd been running around the pitch with their chests swollen with pride and after we came back to 2-2 their heads began to drop a bit," says Horst Eckel.

At the interval the mood in the German dressing room was determined. "In the changing room Toni Turek and Kohlmeyer blamed each other for the second goal," says Eckel. "Herberger just got between them and said, 'What's this? What's the point of this? Do you want to abuse each other or do you want to become world champions?' Then we knew where we were. Herberger knew us, we were on fire now and after this he had no more tactical advice but just said, 'Go out there and become world champions'."

West Germany captain Fritz Walter with the Jules Rimet trophy after winning the World Cup.

Ottmar Walter: "Herberger said to us, 'Men, think very carefully about what you have achieved in the first half, you should watch the Hungarians for a bit, how nervous they are'."

In the second half the Germans faced a barrage of Hungarian attacks but they didn't capitulate: Hidegkuti hit the post, Kocsis the bar, Kohlmeyer cleared off the line and Turek made a succession of great saves. The Hungarians piled on the pressure and minimised Germany's scoring opportunities, the battle continuing without a breakthrough until the 84th minute when an opportunity arose.

"The Hungarians made a mistake," says Horst Eckel. "They headed the ball into the path of Helmut Rahn and that was very often fatal. When Helmut Rahn got the ball 18 metres from the goal he didn't pass any more. That was clear to his team-mates, but the Hungarians had not prepared themselves for this."

"I shouted my head off," says Ottmar Walter. "I shouted, 'Boss, Boss', and he only had to play it across to me and I could have almost have run the ball into the empty goal but then he made a start with it."

Horst Eckel: "He dribbled past the first, the second and shot the ball, as we knew Helmut Rahn would, unstoppably into the far corner of the Hungarian goal. Everything goes so quickly, it is only short moments but they stay with you for your whole life."

Across Germany millions gathered around their radio sets listening in amazement to Herbert Zimmerman's excitable commentary. *Aus dem Hintergrund müsste Rahn schiessen... Rahn schiesst... Tor! Tor! Tor!* ("Rahn should take a deep shot... Rahn shoots. Goal! Goal! Goal!") He paused for eight seconds, as if he were checking that the unbelievable had actually happened, before confirming the goal once more. "Germany lead three to two, five minutes before full-time. Call me mad, call me crazy!" His words have passed into German football legend.

At home Germans were hanging on his every word. But with only seconds to go Puskás broke through the German defence and put the ball in the net. "They'd already started celebrating but if you watch the film again you see I ran into the goal with my arms raised up and waved offside," insists Eckel.

"Only when the referee clearly pointed to the offside did everyone take a deep breath and think, Thank God, that was a close shave," says Ottmar Walter.

It was such a close call that the Hungarians were still arguing with the match officials when the final whistle was blown. As Fritz Walter was awarded the trophy the Hungarians looked on in dismay – the idea

Opposite: (top) Max Morlock scores against Hungary in the World Cup final. (bottom) Sepp Herberger and captain Fritz Walter line up with the West Germany team after the match. (overleaf). Fritz Walter is carried aloft after winning the World Cup at the Wankdorf Stadium in Berne.

West Germany 3 Hungary 2

0:1 FERENC PUSKÁS (HUN) 6', 0:2 ZOLTAN CZIBOR (HUN) 9', 1:2 MAX MORLOCK (GER) 11',
2:2 HELMUT RAHN (GER) 18', HELMUT RAHN (GER) 84'

Sie lesen heute: Fritz Walter mit dem Goldpokal / Seite 4

4. Juli 1954

FRANKFURTER
15 **Nachtausgabe**

Ihr Sieg ist Weltgespräch

Sportbericht

Die Weltsensation des Fußballsports:

Deutschland Weltmeister

Ungarn in Bern im Endspiel vor 60000 Zuschauern 3:2 besiegt

of defeat had never even been contemplated. Their government had long since planned their homecoming victory celebrations, right down to the last detail of who should shake hands with who. "When we stood in front of the grandstand to be awarded our medals and the German anthem began to sound out, I suddenly realised that something had happened that really wasn't in the script," says Grosics.

In 1954 the form book had been discarded in a fascinating see-saw encounter. The Magical Magyars were stunned. Unbeaten in 31 games before the final, afterwards they would remain unbeaten for a further 18 games – but in 1956, when the Soviet Union crushed the Hungarian uprising, most of the team were abroad on club duty and decided to stay in exile. The magnificent Hungarian team of the Fifties broke up, effectively ending its football dominance forever. One of the greatest teams the world had seen was no more.

In West Germany the World Cup victory would become known as *Das Wunder von Bern*, the 'Miracle of Berne', and for Herberger, it would seal his place in German football history. While celebrating on the pitch, the players had no idea of the passions that Herbert Zimmerman had unleashed through his radio broadcasts back home. "Over! Over! Over! The game is over, Germany are world champions!" he had exclaimed at the final whistle. As he did so, millions of Germans ran out on to the streets, famously declaring: "*Wir sind wieder wer*!" ("We are somebody again!").

"We first set foot on German soil in Singen and there were thousands of people there standing right at the station and they wouldn't let the train through," says Eckel.

"They didn't say, '*They* are world champions', the whole crowd said, '*We* are world champions'," says Ottmar Walter, "and of course that was the be all and end all, the whole of Germany were world champions."

For the first time since the war the German people had something to celebrate, something to be proud of. For millions of people, Helmut Rahn's match-winning goal had symbolically ended a much longer ordeal – the dark years of poverty and humiliation suffered in the years after the defeat of Nazi Germany. "The '*us*' feeling for many people in Germany after the war – that was suddenly there again. And that helped us move on," says Eckel.

As well as instilling a new sense of pride, the 1954 World Cup victory marked the beginning of an economic revival in West Germany. Within ten years the country went from bust to boom. As capitalism flourished national productivity reached an unprecedented level – unarguably kick-started by the Miracle of Berne.

POOL 1

June 16: La Pontaise Stadium, Lausanne
Yugoslavia **1 - 0** France

June 16: Les Charmilles, Geneva
Brazil **5 - 0** Mexico

June 19: Les Charmilles, Geneva
France **3 - 2** Mexico

June 19: La Pontaise Stadium, Lausanne
Brazil **1 - 1** Yugoslavia
(aet)

	P	W	D	L	F	A	Pts
Brazil	2	1	1	0	6	1	3
Yugoslavia	2	1	1	0	2	1	3
France	2	1	0	1	3	3	2
Mexico	2	0	0	2	2	8	0

POOL 2

June 17: Sportzplatz Hardturm, Zurich
Hungary **9 - 0** South Korea

June 17: Wankdorf Stadium, Berne
West Germany **4 - 1** Turkey

June 20: St Jakob Stadium, Basle
Hungary **8 - 3** West Germany

June 20: Les Charmilles, Geneva
Turkey **7 - 0** South Korea

	P	W	D	L	F	A	Pts
Hungary	2	2	0	0	17	3	4
West Germany	2	1	0	1	7	9	2
Turkey	2	1	0	1	8	4	2
South Korea	2	0	0	2	0	16	0

PLAY OFF FOR 2ND GROUP PLACE

June 23: Sportzplatz Hardturm, Zurich
West Germany **7 - 2** Turkey

POOL 3

June 16: Sportzplatz Hardturm, Zurich
Austria **1 - 0** Scotland

June 16: Wankdorf Stadium, Berne
Uruguay **2 - 0** Czechoslovakia

June 19: Sportzplatz Hardturm, Zurich
Austria **5 - 0** Czechoslovakia

June 19: St Jakob Stadium, Basle
Uruguay **7 - 0** Scotland

	P	W	D	L	F	A	Pts
Uruguay	2	2	0	0	9	0	4
Austria	2	2	0	0	6	0	4
Czechoslovakia	2	0	0	2	0	7	0
Scotland	2	0	0	2	0	8	0

POOL 4

June 17: St Jakob Stadium, Basle
England **4 - 4** Belgium
(aet)

June 17: La Pontaise Stadium, Lausanne
Switzerland **2 - 1** Italy

June 20: Wankdorf Stadium, Berne
England **2 - 0** Switzerland

June 20: Comunale di Cornaredo, Lugano
Italy **4 - 1** Belgium

	P	W	D	L	F	A	Pts
England	2	1	1	0	6	4	3
Switzerland	2	1	0	1	2	3	2
Italy	2	1	0	1	5	3	2
Belgium	2	0	1	1	5	8	1

PLAY-OFF FOR 2ND GROUP PLACE

June 23: St Jakob Stadium, Basle
Switzerland **4 - 1** Italy

THE FINAL

WEST GERMANY	(2) 3
HUNGARY	(2) 2

DATE Sunday July 4, 1954
ATTENDANCE 60,000
VENUE Wankdorf Stadium, Berne

WEST GERMANY
COACH: SEPP HERBERGER

TUREK
POSIPAL
KOHLMEYER
ECKEL
LIEBRICH
MAI
MORLOCK ⚽
Goal: 11 mins
WALTER, F
RAHN ⚽⚽
Goal: 18 mins, 84 mins
WALTER, O
SCHÄFER

HUNGARY
COACH: GUSZTÁV SEBES

GROSICS
BUZÁNSZKY
LANTOS
BOZSIK
LÓRÁNT
ZAKARIÁS
KOCSIS
PUSKÁS ⚽
Goal: 6 mins
CZIBOR ⚽
Goal: 9 mins
HIDEGKUTI
TÓTH, M

REFEREE: Ling (England)

QUARTER- FINALS

June 26: La Pontaise Stadium, Lausanne
Austria **7 - 5** Switzerland

June 26: St Jakob Stadium, Basle
Uruguay **4 - 2** England

June 27: Les Charmilles, Geneva
West Germany **2 - 0** Yugoslavia

June 27: Wankdorf Stadium, Berne
Hungary **4 - 2** Brazil

SEMI-FINALS

June 30: St Jakob Stadium, Basle
West Germany **6 - 1** Austria

June 30: La Pontaise Stadium, Lausanne
Hungary **4 - 2** Uruguay
(aet)

THIRD-PLACE PLAY-OFF

July 3: Sportzplatz Hardturm, Zurich
Austria **3 - 1** Uruguay

The German team celebrate after winning the World Cup final.

TOP GOALSCORERS 11 goals: Kocsis (Hungary) **6 goals:** Maximilian Morlock (West Germany), Josef Hügi (Switzerland), Erich Probst (Austria)

FASTEST GOAL 2 minutes: Mamat Suat (Turkey v West Germany)

TOTAL GOALS 140 **AVERAGE GOALS** 5.38 per game

THE UNBEATABLE SAMBA KINGS

With the 'fateful final' still a painful memory for every Brazilian, in Pelé and Garrincha the country now had a new generation of stars intent on winning the World Cup in 1958.

The 1958 World Cup will always be remembered for the birth of the 'beautiful game', and for the coming of age of a great football nation that had never won the World Cup. It had been the Uruguayans who had forged a reputation as South America's finest side by twice lifting the trophy, but in 1958 the balance of power shifted. For the first time Brazil became champions of the world. They did so by pioneering a style of play that had football writers the world over delighting at its grace and beauty.

Playing a free-flowing game reminiscent of the Hungarians of the early Fifties, Brazil had perfected their own attack-minded 4-2-4 formation. It was the first time a formation would actually be referred to using a numbering system. They would win the 1958 tournament with two dedicated centre-forwards, Vavá and Pelé, flanked by wingers Garrincha and Zagalo. With four across the back, the system depended on quick-moving outside full-backs who could attack on the overlap, adding strength to the midfield and allowing Brazil to press forward with wild abandon. It was a style that would become known as 'Samba football', or 'football art', but in Sweden in 1958 it was seen in its purest form, Garrincha and Pelé mesmerising with their confident ball play. "Where skill alone counted, Brazil stood alone," reported *The Times*. "The way each daffodil shirt of theirs pulled the ball down out of the sky, tamed it with a touch of the foot, caressed it and stroked it away into an open space was a joy."

It is easy to over-romanticise about Brazil and to think that any team with so much skill, combined with

Vavá is congratulated by Pelé after scoring in the final between Brazil and Sweden. After disappointment in 1950, Brazil had finally won the World Cup.

arguably the greatest ever player, was bound to succeed. But there was nothing inevitable about their success. In the early decades of the World Cup, sides unfamiliar with foreign conditions did not travel well: until this tournament the winners had always been a team from the host continent.

As a nation Brazil were still suffering from the psychological scars inflicted by Uruguay in the Maracanã in 1950. But this time their football team meant business. Taking a more professional approach to the game, they had adapted European tactics and fitness techniques and mixed them up with Brazilian style and skill. They travelled with an unprecedented entourage, even putting their players through a series of bizarre psychological tests to check their suitability to play. Not everybody was impressed.

"In one of the tests there was a horizontal line and a vertical line on a piece of paper, and you had to trace on top of it," recalls defender Nilton Santos. "Suddenly the doctor would hit you between the eyes, saying 'carry on, carry on'."

"In 1958 it was the first time that the Brazilian Football Confederation had put a tactical commission together to prepare the national team," recalls technical coach Paolo Amaral, one of the team put together specifically to help Brazil win the World Cup. "Before this the coach was everything – it was the coach who trained them, it was the coach who chose the players. In 1958 they formed a commission of people to do this. And there was three months of physical, technical and tactical training."

Swedish folk dancers perform during the opening ceremony of the 1958 World Cup.

With a desire to have the squad totally focused, the Brazilian Football Confederation also moved all possible temptations from the paths of the players. "When we arrived at the hotel in Sweden there were two women there, two beautiful women actually," recalls Paolo Amaral. "But the head of the delegation asked the hotel if these girls could stop serving us. They were taken away the following day."

More tangibly useful was the decision to tour Europe in preparation for their World Cup opponents. Never before had a Brazil team been better prepared. As for Pelé, the 17-year-old's talents had been recognised at home, but his selection remained in doubt until the last minute, an injury on a pre-tournament tour of Italy threatening his inclusion in the squad and delaying his involvement until Brazil's third game. Garrincha too would sit out the opening games. Coach Vincente Feola initially left his most gifted dribbler out of the line-up for tactical reasons, fearing the playing style of his first two opponents. "It would be impossible to say to Garrincha, 'You've got to stay put just to mark the left-back'," remembers Amaral. "This would go straight in one ear and out the other. Because Feola wanted someone to mark their left-back, Joel played instead."

The tournament was something of a watershed. Sweden marked the end of the more carefree, attack-minded post-war era of international football. By the following World Cup the sport would be characterised by a ruthlessly defensive attitude, but the 1958 tournament would be remembered for its attacking flair, for Pelé and Garrincha, and for the prodigious Just Fontaine of France and his team-mate, the 1958 European Footballer Of The Year, Raymond Kopa.

Fontaine would become the tournament's highest goalscorer with 13 goals, a record that stands to this day. But going into the competition, like Pelé and Garrincha, he wasn't guaranteed his place in the team until an ankle injury to René Bliard gave him his chance.

Brazil coach Vicente Feola talks through the match with Dino Sani and Didi after one of Brazil's group games.

"Just Fontaine was the best goalscorer of all time and will continue to be so," says Raymond Kopa. "It's true that 'Justo' has always said that he was picked to play, but in reality the guy who was picked was Bliard. He was injured during a match in training, and Justo replaced him. I'm glad he played. He was brilliant. We scored those goals because we were a team that attacked and because Just Fontaine was on top form.

"The main thing about Just Fontaine was that he had one fantastic foot. It's better to have one fantastic foot than two average feet. We worked so well because he was able to read exactly what I planned to do. If I got past the players that were in my way, Just Fontaine knew exactly how to help me out."

Just Fontaine is similarly effusive in his praise of Kopa. "If someone was marking him it was a bit like Stanley Matthews," says Fontaine. "He would dribble because he was made for it. He was small, he had good balance and he was fast and could stop and take off again so quickly. We really complemented each other."

The tournament began without some familiar names as Uruguay and fellow two-time winners Italy both failed to qualify. Despite the complete and utter domination of Spanish football at club level, Real Madrid having won all three European Cups played thus far, Spain also failed to make the cut, edged out by Scotland. For British football 1958 remains a high watermark; in the first competition where they didn't have to play each other to qualify, and for the only time, all four British nations progressed to the finals, although Wales were given a second life. Turkey, Indonesia, Egypt and Sudan had all withdrawn, leaving Israel alone in a group, but for the first time FIFA ruled that no country could qualify for the World Cup finals without

RAYMOND KOPA

After the World Cup the France centre-forward was voted the European Player Of The Year.

"I was born in Noeux-les-Mines, in Pas-de-Calais, of Polish decent. My grandparents came to France around 1924 with my parents, who were 18 years old. My father and brother both worked in the mines and when I was 14 I joined them. I tried to find a job above ground, because at that age I was already showing promise as a footballer. But no one helped me out and from the age of 14 to 17 I drilled the mines at a depth of 612 meters.

"This didn't stop me from improving as a footballer. My strength was dribbling. I was able to get around one player, two players, even three. The final pass was also one of my specialties. It's not just a question of knowing how to get past players, putting them out of position; you also have to know how to finish off. I was a perfectionist. When I signed for Reims, Albert Batteux allowed me to experiment and enabled me to grow up quickly. He gave me faith and strengthened my drive to express myself and to go even further.

"In 1958 I'd been playing for Real Madrid in the European Cup final. I was concerned about the physical form I'd be in by the time I joined the French team in Sweden for the World Cup. At the time we weren't really taken seriously, but we prepared quite intensely and concentrated on all aspects of our game. We even concentrated on female emancipation – you know, at the time Swedish women were to be avoided. I'm laughing but it was quite a serious matter. Some countries went quite far down that road and suffered for it. The Argentinians were a good example of that, but I can assure you that we were very vigilant on that front.

"Preparations went really well and that went a long way in getting our spirits up before the start of the competition. I felt we got an excellent bond going. That was important considering everyone was agreed that we didn't stand a chance. I think the French public thought it was an exploit for us to get as far as we did, but that was purely because we'd been put down so much by the press. I think we actually played to the level we knew we could. I think we could have won it but we were unlucky that we had to face Brazil in the semi-final. Our centre-back Jonquet was injured after 20 minutes and we were down to ten men for the rest of the game. That was a great advantage for Brazil.

"We could hold our heads high, because third isn't bad. Brazil was thought to have the best attack but I was hailed as the best player in the world and Just Fontaine the best striker. We came back from Sweden with the best roll call in the game and I believe we could have come home with the trophy. I remember my homecoming in Madrid. Journalists asked the president of the club what he'd seen during the World Cup and he said that he'd come back with the best player in the world – Raymond Kopa."

Raymond Kopa scores from the penalty spot in the third place play-off game against West Germany.

playing a game, and a draw of all the other group runners up enabled Wales to take on Israel for a place in the finals. They won both games 2-0.

Northern Ireland too had received more than their fair share of luck, beating much-fancied Italy to qualification. The Italians only had themselves to blame: Northern Ireland needed to win the match between the two countries in Belfast to reach the finals, but after the FIFA appointed referee was stranded by bad weather at London airport, the Italians would not accept a replacement match official and refused to play the game as a qualifier. The match went ahead as a 'friendly' and finished 2-2, but when it was replayed the following month, with the correct FIFA official in attendance, Northern Ireland snatched a 2-1 victory and Italy failed to qualify for the first time in their history.

The England team were among the tournament favourites, particularly as they had never lost to any of the nations in their group. But in Sweden they weren't quite the same side who had qualified so convincingly the previous year, the Munich air disaster having ripped the heart out of the England team just four months before the tournament, denying them the talents of such great players as Duncan Edwards, Roger Byrne and Tommy Taylor, a striker with 12 goals in his last eight England games. For a period after the crash, mindful of what had happened to Manchester United, the England football squad travelled to away fixtures in two planes.

"It was a tremendous loss to the game to lose players of that ability and I think that England would have had a much better chance of doing far better than we did," says Tom Finney. "I'd felt up to the Munich crash that we had a great chance of making some impact, but we lost so many key players. I think it affected the mood. We were all terribly sad. I think that we suffered through that in the competition."

For England, who had only entered the competition for the first time in 1950, football in this environment had been a steep learning curve. "We'd learnt a lot from the two previous World Cups," says Finney. "I think Walter Winterbottom had learnt an awful lot and had shown us where we were really not up to standard, with the skill or finesse, of these European and continental sides, particularly the South Americans."

Even with all the lessons that had been learnt, England's preparation was hardly a match for that of the Brazilians. After a gruelling nine-month season, England had been taken on a two-match eastern European tour that took in fixtures with the Soviet Union in Moscow and Yugoslavia in Belgrade. Returning to England, the squad focused on their World Cup opponents. "We probably had about a fortnight training in London," says Finney. "There was nothing really, apart from going through the opposition. The manager would point out who he felt were the key men and who we would have to mark quite closely."

Pool One featured defending champions West Germany, who kicked off the competition fielding four of their World Cup winners: Fritz Walter, Hans Schäfer, Horst Eckel and Helmut Rahn, whose international career had appeared to have stalled between the two tournaments. It was also the match that saw the World Cup debut of Uwe Seeler, who would go on to set a competition record with 21 appearances between 1958 and 1970. In their first game the Germans faced Argentina, a team weakened by their refusal to call up any of their Italian-based star players. Two goals from Rahn and one from Seeler saw the West Germans win 3-1. Subsequent 2-2 draws with both Czechoslovakia and Northern Ireland enabled them to progress top of their group.

"Our tactics have always been to equalise before the other team scores," declared Northern Ireland's Danny Blanchflower before the tournament. The team did a little better than that, but only after its football association backed down on their rule forbidding play on the Sabbath. Their first game saw them sneak a surprise 1-0 victory over Czechoslovakia in Halmstad, thanks to an outstanding performance from goalkeeper Harry Gregg. A second 2-1 victory over the Czechs in a group play-off – goal difference having not made it into the tournament rules by that point – allowed them to progress to the knock-out stages, Peter McParland shining as one of the tournaments leading scorers.

France and Yugoslavia jointly topped Pool Two, sending Scotland and Paraguay home. Just Fontaine scored six goals in three games for the French, including a hat trick in the 7-3 thrashing of the South Americans. "In our group, Paraguay were supposed to be our toughest opponents," remembers Raymond Kopa. "They were considered to be as good, if not better, than Brazil. We were a little worried so we rented a bus to go and see them train. We weren't very impressed by what we saw and that allowed us to go into the match with a lot of determination and without fear."

The exuberant play of the French became known as 'Champagne Football', reflecting the philosophy of their manager, Albert Batteux. A great believer in the beautiful game, what Batteux prized above all was a team that played extravagantly and entertained the crowds. "Everyone thought that we would be going straight home after the first three matches," says Just Fontaine. "In the beginning, during training, there were only three journalists covering us. Then there was an infatuation with the French team and other papers came. The type of game we were playing seemed to appeal to the media, even to the foreign papers because they saw the goals we were scoring and the impressive moves we used. You see, in 1958 it was the beginning of television."

In Pool Three Sweden, as hosts, kicked off the tournament's first game. Englishman George Raynor, who had helped them to Olympic gold in 1948, once again coached the Swedes. At previous World Cup tournaments their chances had been damaged by their strict amateur ethos and their refusal to call up many of their Italian-based stars. Swedish football's acceptance of professionalism meant that in 1958 they could field their strongest team possible, allowing them to finish top of their group. Hungary, however, were not the same force they had been four years previous, the 1956 Soviet invasion forcing many of the Magical Magyars into exile. Only Grosics, Bozsik and Hidegkuti remained from the 1954 finalists, but after a series of disappointing performances they were beaten 2-1 in the play-off with a Welsh team who had drawn all three of their group games.

When the draw for the World Cup had been made, it was apparent that Pool Four was by far the toughest. Brazil and England were among the competition favourites, but the Soviet Union had emerged as a formidable footballing nation. Two years later they would become the first European champions.

For Brazil the tournament had started well – a 3-0 victory against Austria was followed by a 0-0 draw with England, the first goalless scoreline in the history of the World Cup finals. England had drawn their game with the Soviets, Tom Finney equalising from the penalty spot with virtually his last ever kick in a World Cup. Injury would rule him out of the remaining matches. Brazil's third group game was against the Soviet Union, the opponents they feared most. At the height of Cold War propaganda, the Soviet Union, playing in their first World Cup, were seen as pioneers of a new scientific approach to football training and preparation. "They even had computers to prepare themselves," says Brazilian journalist João Maximo. But the history of Brazilian football and the World Cup was about to change forever.

João Maximo: "On the eve of the game Gavril Kachalin, the Russian coach, went to visit Brazil when they were training. It was a courtesy call, and he asked through his interpreter how Brazil were shaping up

Garrincha dribbles past Welsh defender Mel Hopkins during the World Cup quarter-final in Gothenburg.

for the game, and the reply came, 'Tomorrow we're going to play three reserve players'. So the Russian coach went away very happy."

One of the reserves was a player called Zito. The others would become two of the greatest footballers ever known: Garrincha and Pelé. "In a sense that was the defining moment of that World Cup, and possibly of Brazilian football of all time," says author Alex Bellos. "That is the game that Pelé and Garrincha were brought in."

Legend has it that in a bid to have Garrincha and Pelé in the team, their team-mates made a representation of their views to the coach. "It was Didi," says Nilton Santos. "He went to speak to Feola. If he hadn't gone, then it would have been me, or anyone else. Even Joel, who was the right-winger and in Garrincha's position, would have felt embarrassed had he been chosen and Garrincha not. When we were running around the stadium after having won at the final, Joel was right next to Garrincha. The national team at that time was a big family."

Paolo Amaral refutes the suggestion that both players were selected as a result of player-power. "The

story that they went to tell him to play Pelé is a complete lie," he says. "Vincente Feola was a very experienced guy and he won the Paulista championship three times in a row. It's a complete lie but you still hear it right up until today."

Pelé would become the greatest footballer of all time, but it was Garrincha, an irrepressible 25-year-old winger, who had the greatest impact in the game against the Soviet Union. Technical coach Paolo Amaral had been responsible for evaluating Garrincha's first trial some years earlier in Río for his club side Botafogo.

"I had to make a report of this match: 'the player Manuel is technically formidable. He has one small defect that can be quite easily resolved. He dribbles far too much'. This small little defect, I said, could be quite easily resolved, but it was never, ever resolved!"

By 1958 Garrincha had become a folklore hero: the poor Indian with prodigious skill who never left his roots behind. Brazilians loved him. Born Manuel dos Santos, he received his nickname because he was as small as a *garrincha* – a wren! During a duel with a defender during a Botafogo tour of Argentina, he had apparently been the inspiration for one of Latin American football's most popular terrace chant, 'Olé'.

He was no ordinary footballer. His simple intellect and his childlike love of playing for playing's sake would make him the most popular footballer in Brazil, even if his antics could sometimes infuriate his team-mates. In Brazil's last friendly before the 1958 World Cup, Garrincha beat three players and the keeper, but instead of scoring he waited for the defender to run back. Garrincha swerved his body, leaving the defender to grab on to the post to stop himself falling over. Garrincha then walked the ball into the goal, flicked it up and carried it back to the centre spot. The stadium went silent except for the shouts of his team-mates, angry at his irresponsibility.

Brazilian defender Nilton Santos kicks the ball away as Soviet Union forward Alexander Ivanov looks on.

A birth defect that had gone untreated left Garrincha with a left leg that curved outward and a right leg that curved inward, but this interesting physical shape meant that he could change direction incredibly quickly, and with great power and acceleration. This made his dribbling impossible to counter.

When the match against the Soviet Union kicked off in Gothenburg on June 15, Garrincha and Pelé turned on the magic immediately, both hitting the woodwork in the first minute. "These reserves came on and in two minutes had driven the Soviets crazy," says João Maximo. The game's opening, culminating in Vavá's goal, is considered to be the best three minutes of Brazilian football ever. From that point, until their last game together at the World Cup finals of 1966, Brazil never lost when Pelé and Garrincha played together.

In the game against the Soviet Union Garrincha was the lynchpin that provided victory. "We started to win that championship from the moment he went on the pitch," says Nilton Santos.

The game ended 2-0 to Brazil, but the impact of the game was far greater. "The scientific systems of the Soviet Union died a death right there," says Brazilian football commentator Luiz Mendes. "They put the first man in space, but they were not able to mark Garrincha."

The defeat pushed the Soviet Union into a play-off game with England, who had drawn their fixture with

Opposite: Brazil captain Bellini receives a kiss from Miss Brazil, Adalgisa Colombo, as he holds the Jules Rimet trophy.

Austria. Changes were made to the England team and many felt that Manchester United's young star Bobby Charlton should have made his tournament debut.

"I was very much in favour of that," says Tom Finney. "Bobby had made his first flight since the Munich disaster and we were all concerned about how he would feel. I was very upset that Bobby wasn't selected, because I felt he should have been one of the key players in the England side."

"I wasn't disappointed at all," remembers Charlton himself. "The Munich air crash had happened – one minute they were wheeling me on castors and within a few weeks I was being pushed forward as an England player. I had other things on my mind at that time really. I'd played a couple of friendly matches and I don't remember playing that well. I didn't think it was the end of the world and I thought, 'Well, I'm young, I'll get the chance one day'. There was supposedly a furore going on in England because I hadn't been picked. The general public didn't seem to understand and they made a big thing about it. I didn't think much of it at all. I was just glad to be there. Walter Winterbottom was the manager and if he decided that I wasn't the person for that position, I accepted it."

England's Tom Finney, Maurice Setters and Bobby Charlton carry Billy Wright during training for the World Cup.

For Winterbottom, England manager since 1946, it had proved a hugely frustrating tournament. A 1-0 defeat in Gothenburg saw his team exit the competition prematurely once again. "Walter Winterbottom was a fantastic man and a great coach," says Bobby Robson, England's inside-forward at the World Cup in 1958. "I learnt a lot from Walter. He had tremendous knowledge of the game and he could impart that knowledge. He was a great talker of football. He hadn't been a great player but you sometimes don't have to be a great player to be a good manager or a big coach, you just have to understand football."

In the quarter-finals all three of the teams who had progressed through play-offs had the disadvantage of having to now play their second games in three days – and all lost as the big guns started to fire. France ended the Northern Irish resistance with a 4-0 thumping. West Germany sneaked home by a single goal against Yugoslavia, and Sweden put paid to the Soviet Union 2-0. Welsh star John Charles was injured and missed his country's encounter with Brazil. For 70 minutes Wales held on as Garrincha, Didi, Mazzola and Zagalo were thwarted, but it was Pelé who knocked them out of the competition, scoring the first of his 12 World Cup goals.

At 17 Pelé was the youngest footballer to play in a World Cup. He had only become a professional the year before when he left his poor home town for club side Santos, but he was already carving out a reputation for his exceptional all-round ability. He stole the show in Brazil's game against Wales.

"Without a doubt, Brazil's best player on the pitch in that game was Pelé, because he decided the game," says Luiz Mendes. "It was wonderful because it showed the player that he would become. He was just starting out for the Brazilian national team and that was the goal that launched him internationally."

Paolo Amaral: "The speed that he had, the impulse that he had, his shooting ability. He could shoot with his left, with his right, the vision that he had. As soon as he got the ball he already knew what he was going to do with it. He was extraordinary."

JUST FONTAINE

The France striker's 13 goals at the 1958 World Cup remain a tournament record to this day.

"I was born in Marrakesh and that's where I grew up. I started playing football in the streets like all the other kids but my father didn't want me to play because he was afraid I would break my legs. My father was a civil servant so I never lacked anything when growing up, even though there were seven of us. When I started college he banned me from playing, but I told my teachers that my father had said I could play, which was a lie. I finished my school and played sport at the same time because I thought it was my vocation.

"When I was 16 I knew I was going to be a footballer. I just couldn't see myself doing anything else. I played for US Casablanca. We became Moroccan champions and won the North African Cup. Nice were there and signed me in 1953, so my dream came true at 20 years old. I was a good all-round striker and think that if I had been in a club earlier I would have improved quicker and got further than I did.

"I arrived in Nice in July 1953 and I played for them for three years, and we won the French Cup in 1954 and the championship in 1956. Throughout that time I was in the army. Because of the war in Algeria I did 30 months of military service, but I didn't get sent to Algeria because my brother was there and they didn't send people from the same family. In 1956 I was transferred to Stade de Reims.

"I think the success that France had at the World Cup in Sweden was due to there being five or six Reims players on the team, plus Raymond Kopa, who was at Real Madrid but had been trained at Reims. Playing in the same spirit meant that the French team had consistency. We called it 'champagne football' because Reims was in the region of Champagne, and because it was slightly sparkling.

"When we first went to the World Cup we were so unpopular that we only took three shirts with us each for the three group matches. Journalists didn't even expect us to qualify from the group stage. They expected the worst and when we qualified we had to wash our shirts to play the three other matches. Then they were confident.

"I had two pairs of boots – one for dry and one for grass. Two days before the first match, my boots for playing on grass broke. They were totally wrecked. Luckily my substitute, Stéphane Bruey, had the same size feet as me. He lent me his boots and I played six matches in them at the World Cup and I scored my 13 goals wearing those boots. At the end of the tournament I gave them back, but they didn't make him score more goals.

"The French team scored 23 goals in six matches, but let in 12. So really, even the defence was prioritising, giving us good service instead of defending at all costs. When we went home to France there were about 50 people there and three days later it was all over and no-one talked about it any more. No one gave me a medal or anything like that.

"I'm proud of my record, but it's no better than it was in 1958, right after the World Cup. I never thought that it would last but the fact that no one has beaten it since means that people come and see me every four years to ask, 'Why has no-one broken the record?' I have no idea, but I'm not going to give them an incentive! For me I am amazed though. I still get 20 letters a month asking for autographs and it's not just the older generation but young people too. It's flattering really that at 72 I still get fan mail.

"It's the memory of those 13 goals which people remember me for, because I didn't really play that many matches. I didn't play enough really, but people can't say of me that I'd got old, or that I wasn't as fast as I used to be. I finished at 27 and that was it. I played 21 matches with the French team and scored 30 goals with no penalties, so I guess all that stays in people's memories.

"I was champion three times, a finalist in the European Cup, the best striker in the French championship, twice the best striker in the European Cup, and the best striker in the World Cup of 1958. But when I was 26 I fractured my leg. It was a double fracture, tibia and fibula. I tried to come back on January 1, 1960 and it happened again. I couldn't bend my knee so I had to stop. I was 27. It's a shame because I don't think that I had reached my peak. I could have gone so much further, but I can't complain. It was just a very short career."

French forward Just Fontaine tries to dribble past Brazil goalkeeper Gilmar during the semi-final.

Although defending champions West Germany were still in the competition, Sweden and Brazil had emerged as favourites. Sweden underlined their credentials in the semi-finals when they eliminated a German team who were hanging on to a 1-1 draw until the last ten minutes, when the home team scored twice to trigger wild celebrations. It was one of West Germany's darkest World Cup moments. Erich Juskowiak was sent off for kicking and at one point they were reduced to playing with nine men for five minutes when another player had to go off for treatment.

In the other semi-final in Stockholm, Brazil electrified the tournament with a 5-2 defeat of France, who had cruised through their quarter-final and were expected to pose a severe test. For half the match they did, but after losing centre-half Jonquet in a collision with Vavá, France were left with ten men and they were blown away when Pelé netted a hat-trick in 23 unforgettable second-half minutes.

"France-Brazil was the climax of our World Cup since Brazil were considered to be the best team in the world and the favourites to win the World Cup," says Raymond Kopa. "Not a single team had managed to score against them. We were on a high and came to it without fear. I think they were quite scared however. They were only leading 2-1 at half time and we'd been playing with ten men for most of it. It was the first time that the Brazilian goalkeeper had been beaten and, although they had the best players in the world, I can tell you they'd never been as worried as when they played against France that day. I have to admit, they did have some exceptional players, namely Pelé. He played supremely well and was certainly a deciding factor in their victory against us."

Vavá hurdles a French defender during the World Cup semi-final at the Rasunda Stadion in Solna, Stockholm.

Just Fontaine: "I think that the best Brazilian team was the one in 1958, because in 1970 they had great strikers and great midfielders, but their defence wasn't too good and they lost quite a few goals. In 1958 they had a great defence, great midfielders and brilliant strikers – Pelé, Zagalo, Vavá, Zito, Didi. They had a brilliant goalkeeper too, which is rare in Brazilian football. To lose against a team like that wasn't too embarrassing, especially as there were only ten of us."

Brazil finally found themselves competing for the World Cup once again. But they had yet to win it – and to do that they would have to get past Sweden, playing at Stockholm's Rasunda Stadium in front of a partisan crowd of 50,000. For the Brazilians, who put so much stock in the patriotism of their yellow kit, they found themselves with a last minute panic, having to scrape around for a change strip. "There'd been a toss of the coin. The Swedes had won and they were going to play in their national colour," explains trainer Paolo Amaral.

"We had to change and play in blue," says Nilton Santos. "Someone was sent to get new shirts and then stuck the Brazil crest on them. We were already used to playing in the yellow shirts, but whether we win or we lose it's not because of the colour of the shirt. We knew we had a good enough team to win. We trusted ourselves – Vavá scored lots of great goals, and we had Pelé and Garrincha."

Heavy rain and a passionate home crowd suggested that now wasn't the right time or place for South American flair, and when Liedholm fired the hosts ahead after five minutes following a well worked move

Opposite: The 1958 World Cup final. (top) Sweden's Nils Liedholm tries a shot. (bottom left) Pelé jumps for the ball. (centre right) Pelé shakes hands with the King of Sweden. (centre and overleaf) The Brazil team salute the crowd carrying the Sweden flag.

Brazil 5 Sweden 2

0:1 NILS LIEDHOLM (SWE) 4', 1:1 VAVÁ (BRA) 9', 2:1 VAVÁ (BRA) 32', 3:1 PELÉ (BRA) 55', 4:1 MARIO ZAGALO (BRA) 68', 4:2 AGNE SIMONSSON (SWE) 80', 5:2 PELÉ (BRA) 90'.

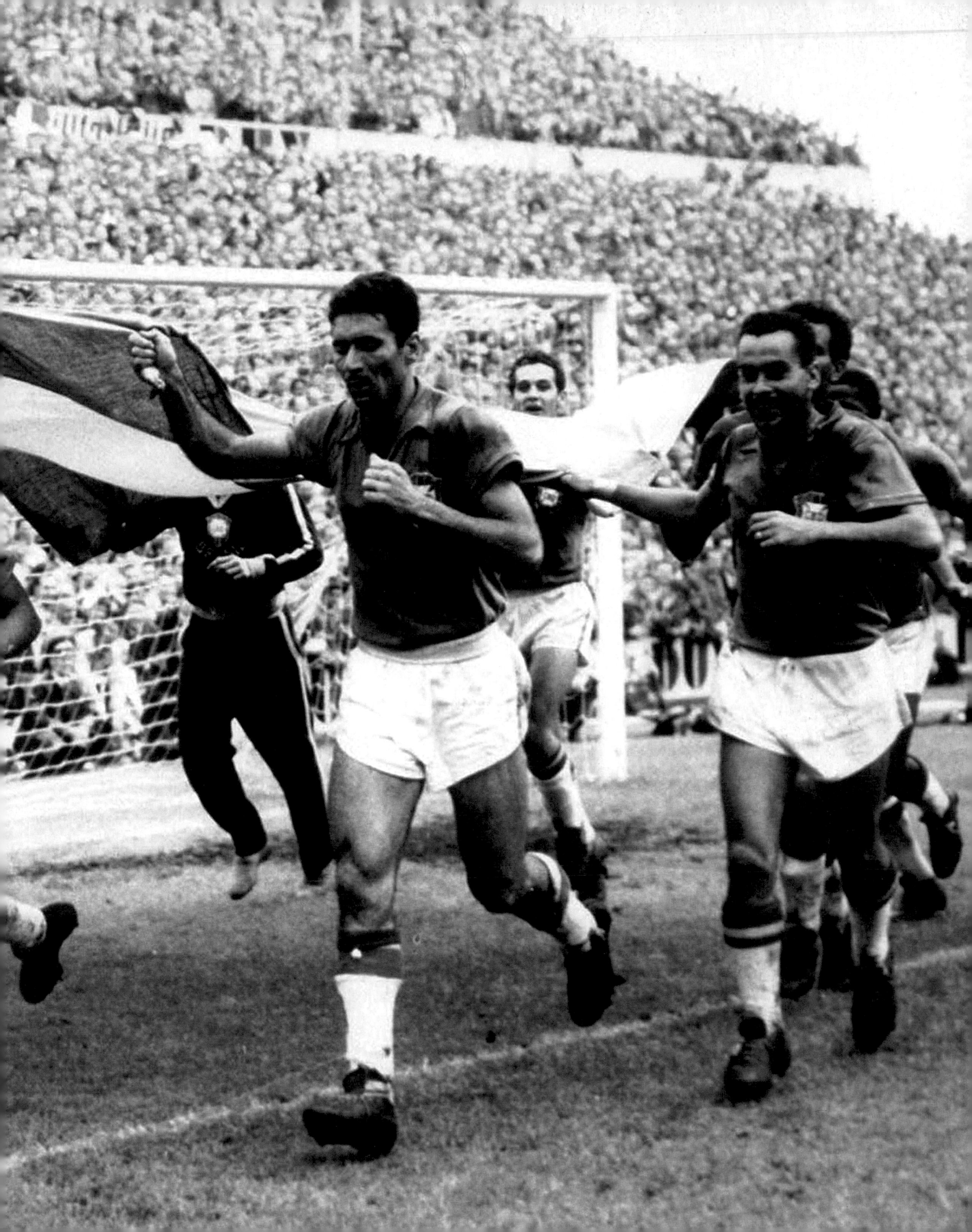

courtesy of Sweden's 'Italian Connection', Brazil were behind for the first time in the tournament. The lead lasted just four minutes until Vavá equalised from Garrincha's cross, then Pelé struck the post and Vavá added a second, firing in from Garrincha in a virtual action replay of the previous goal.

The second half was Pelé's. His first goal in the 55th minute combined individual trickery with a rasping volley. Zagalo made it 4-1 before Simonsson restored some hope for Sweden. But Pelé had the final word, heading home to seal a 5-2 win.

The Brazilians were completely overcome, weeping openly on the pitch. At the request of photographers looking for a better picture of the presentation, Captain Luiz Bellini lifted the Jules Rimet Trophy above his head, inventing the now traditional winners celebration. Then, in one of the most famous moments in World Cup history, they carried the Swedish flag around the ground in a gesture of sportsmanship that brought the crowd to its feet in applause.

Pelé doing his bit for public relations – Sweden fell in love with the Brazilians during the 1958 World Cup.

Brazil's football had wowed Stockholm and left an indelible mark on the game. Garrincha and Pelé came to embody all that was great in the Brazilian game. It was a standard of football that had never been seen before, its flourishes still emulated today.

"I said, 'Brazil, champions of the world at last, champions of the world – today the world is turning itself into Brazil'," recalls commentator Luiz Mendes.

For Nilton Santos, a non-playing squad member at the World Cup in 1950 and an ever-present member of the 1954 Brazil team, it was a dream come true. "You only believe in yourself once you've won. I really thought 'This isn't a dream, I really am a world champion'."

Finally Brazil had the trophy that had eluded them for so long. The team was overcome with emotion, especially Pelé, this child who had been catapulted into the spotlight. "I was just 17 and the King of Sweden stepped out of his throne and came to the middle of the football field to shake my hand," he would later say of the most unforgettable moment of his life. "It all seemed liked a dream."

At home Brazil was organising the party that it felt it had been robbed of in 1950. Every country gets a huge boost of adrenaline and optimism from major sporting victories, but Brazil had tied its flag so firmly to the national football team that this victory was greeted like no other. And this was a changed side. The team who started against Austria had, in Didi, just one black player, but by the time they had won the final, they were fielding three black players and two of mixed race. This was the first fully multi-racial team to win the World Cup.

Flying back to Rio on the Brazilian President's plane, with their own fighter escort, the World Cup winners were greeted by the President and paraded before an adoring public. The fortunes of football and Brazil were beginning to look permanently intertwined.

The World Cup itself had changed and the era of Brazilian dominance was about to begin. In 1958 total gate receipts yielded £620,000 and TV rights cost £103,500 – so much has changed since Brazil's first World Cup triumph, but the fact they have managed to stay ahead of their competition in world football has been an amazing feat. That they have done so without forsaking their unique poetic style is a sporting wonder.

POOL 1

June 8: Malmö Stadium, Malmö
West Germany **3 - 1** Argentina

June 8: Örjans vall, Halmstad
Northern Ireland **1 - 0** Czechoslovakia

June 11: Olympia Stadium, Halsingborg
West Germany **2 - 2** Czechoslovakia

June 11: Örjans vall, Halmstad
Argentina **3 - 1** Northern Ireland

June 15: Malmö Stadium, Malmö
West Germany **2 - 2** Northern Ireland

June 15: Olympia Stadium, Halsingborg
Czechoslovakia **6 - 1** Argentina

	P	W	D	L	F	A	Pts
West Germany	3	1	2	0	7	5	4
Northern Ireland	3	1	1	1	4	5	3
Czechoslovakia	3	1	1	1	8	4	3
Argentina	3	1	0	2	5	10	2

PLAY-OFF FOR 2ND GROUP PLACE

June 17: Malmö Stadium, Malmö
Northern Ireland **2 - 1** Czechoslovakia
(aet)

POOL 2

June 8: Idrottsparken, Norrköping
France **7 - 3** Paraguay

June 8: Arosvallen, Västerås
Yugoslavia **1 - 1** Scotland

June 11: Arosvallen, Västerås
Yugoslavia **3 - 2** France

June 11: Idrottsparken, Norrköping
Paraguay **3 - 2** Scotland

June 15: Eyravallen, Örebro
France **2 - 1** Scotland

June 15: Tunavallen, Eskilstuna
Yugoslavia **3 - 3** Paraguay

	P	W	D	L	F	A	Pts
France	3	2	0	1	11	7	4
Yugoslavia	3	1	2	0	7	6	4
Paraguay	3	1	1	1	9	12	3
Scotland	3	0	1	2	4	6	1

POOL 3

June 8: Råsunda Stadium, Solna
Sweden **3 - 0** Mexico

June 8: Jernvallen, Sandviken
Hungary **1 - 1** Wales

June 11: Råsunda Stadium, Solna
Wales **1 - 1** Mexico

June 12: Råsunda Stadium, Solna
Sweden **2 - 1** Hungary

June 15: Råsunda Stadium, Solna
Sweden **0 - 0** Wales

June 15: Jernvallen, Sandviken
Hungary **4 - 0** Mexico

	P	W	D	L	F	A	Pts
Sweden	3	2	1	0	5	1	5
Wales	3	0	3	0	2	2	3
Hungary	3	1	1	1	6	3	3
Mexico	3	0	1	2	1	8	1

PLAY-OFF FOR 2ND GROUP PLACE

June 17: Råsunda Stadium, Solna
Wales **2 - 1** Hungary

POOL 4

June 8: Nya Ullevi Stadium, Gothenburg
England **2 - 2** Soviet Union

June 8: Rimnersvallen, Uddevalla
Brazil **3 - 0** Austria

June 11: Nya Ullevi Stadium, Gothenburg
England **0 - 0** Brazil

June 11: Ryavallen, Borås
Soviet Union **2 - 0** Austria

June 15: Nya Ullevi Stadium, Gothenburg
Brazil **2 - 0** Soviet Union

June 15: Ryavallen, Borås
England **2 - 2** Austria

	P	W	D	L	F	A	Pts
Brazil	3	2	1	0	5	0	5
Soviet Union	3	1	1	1	4	4	3
England	3	0	3	0	4	4	3
Austria	3	0	1	2	2	7	1

PLAY-OFF FOR 2ND GROUP PLACE

June 17: Nya Ullevi Stadium, Gothenburg
Soviet Union **1 - 0** England

QUARTER-FINALS

June 19: Idrottsparken, Norrköping
France **4 - 0** Northern Ireland

June 19: Malmö Stadium, Malmö
West Germany **1 - 0** Yugoslavia

June 19: Råsunda Stadium, Solna
Sweden **2 - 0** Soviet Union

June 19: Nya Ullevi Stadium, Gothenburg
Brazil **1 - 0** Wales

SEMI-FINALS

June 24: Råsunda Stadium, Solna
Brazil **5 - 2** France

June 24: Nya Ullevi Stadium, Gothenburg
Sweden **3 - 1** West Germany

THIRD-PLACE PLAY-OFF

June 28: Nya Ullevi Stadium, Gothenburg
France **6 - 3** West Germany

THE FINAL

WEST GERMANY	(2) 3
HUNGARY	(2) 2

DATE Sunday June 29, 1958
ATTENDANCE 49,737
VENUE Råsunda Stadium, Solna, Stockholm

Gilmar

Santos, D   Bellini   Orlando   Santos, N

Didi   Zito

Garrincha   Vavá   Pelé   Zagalo

Skoglund   Simonsson   Hamrin

Liedholm   Gren

Parling   Gustavsson   Börjesson

Axbom   Bergmark

Svensson

BRAZIL
COACH: VICENTE FEOLA

GILMAR
SANTOS, D
BELLINI
ORLANDO
SANTOS, N
DIDI
ZITO
GARRINCHA
VAVÁ ⚽⚽
Goal: 9 mins, 32 mins
PELÉ ⚽⚽
Goal: 55 mins, 80 mins
ZAGALO ⚽
Goal: 68 mins

SWEDEN
COACH: GEORGE RAYNOR

SVENSSON
BERGMARK
AXBOM
BÖRJESSON
GUSTAVSSON
PARLING
GREN
LIEDHOLM ⚽
Goal: 4 mins
HAMRIN
SIMONSSON ⚽
Goal: 80 mins
SKOGLUND

REFEREE: Guigue (France)

The Brazil team listen to their national anthem before the World Cup final.

TOP GOALSCORERS 13 goals: Just Fontaine (France) **6 goals:** Pelé (Brazil), Helmut Rahn (West Germany) **5 goals:** Vavá (Brazil), Peter McParland (Northern Ireland)

FASTEST GOAL 90 seconds: Vavá (Brazil v France)

TOTAL GOALS 126 **AVERAGE GOALS** 3.60 per game

ON TOP OF THE WORLD

No single player has influenced the outcome of a World Cup tournament as much as Garrincha did in 1962. It proved that even without Pelé, Brazil were still the best team in the world.

Chile was an unlikely World Cup host. A long thin strip of land only 300 miles wide but stretching 3,000 miles down the western coast of South America to its most southerly tip, it could not rival its easterly neighbour Argentina in size, interest in the game, nor football infrastructure. But along with West Germany and Argentina, Chile formally applied for the role at the 1956 FIFA Congress in Lisbon. West Germany was ruled out as it was decided that the tournament could not be staged in Europe for a third successive time. With their long established football heritage and their larger stadiums, Argentina remained the favourite to host the competition, but through the vigorous campaigning of Carlos Dittborn, president of the *Federación de Fútbol de Chile*, the tournament was awarded to the smaller of the two South American nations. This was despite the devastating earthquake that had caused serious damage and loss of life in the country in May 1960. "We have nothing, that is why we must have the World Cup," pleaded Dittborn after FIFA considered an alternative host. Through his efforts Chile kept the World Cup but Dittborn would die, aged just 38, one month before the opening ceremony.

The 1962 World Cup served up a tournament of extremes, ranging from the appalling 'Battle of Santiago' to the beautiful crafted performances of the sublime Brazilians. The magnificent *Estadio Nacional* in Santiago – the National Stadium – was built especially for the tournament, beautifully set amid the snowcapped mountains of the Andes. Just 11 years later, at the start of Chile's 17-year sufferance of the

In his third World Cup, Brazil's Didi holds the Jules Rimet Cup aloft.

An early bath for the Brazilians: Nilton Santos, Garrincha and Didi look for the soap.

dictatorship of General Augusto Pinochet, the stadium would be used for crimes far more horrific than its architects could have imagined in their worst nightmares. But from May 30 to June 17, 1962, it would serve as an exuberant home to Chilean football ambition.

There were rumblings of discontent during the competition, about inflated hotel prices and the excessive cost of ticketing, but the organisation of the tournament largely proved a credit to Chile. Local interest wavered from ground to ground, however, from disappointingly small attendances of under 6,000 at one extreme, to the crowds of over 60,000 who squeezed into the cauldron of Santiago. It was also apparent to its global television audience that this World Cup was the dawn of defensive football.

A record number of countries took part in qualification, 52 from an initial entry of 57. The finals would host 14 successful qualifiers, plus the hosts and the holders. France were noticeable absentees in 1962, having lost away to Bulgaria in their final qualification game while only needing a draw to progress. Sweden, finalists four years earlier and still coached by George Raynor, failed to make the cut after defeat by Switzerland in a play-off in Berlin. England were the sole qualifiers from the British home countries, while both West Germany and the Soviet Union made it to Chile with 100 per cent qualification records.

The format of the tournament remained largely unaltered, but for the first time goal average was brought in as a means of separating teams with the same amount of points – it eliminated the need for play-offs but unfortunately encouraged the development of defensive football. A more superficial change was the decision to use the term 'Group' rather than 'Pool' to describe the mini-league sections of the competition's opening stage.

For holders Brazil, the 1962 competition was the perfect opportunity to build on their World Cup success. They arrived in Chile with a gifted and experienced team built around their established world champions of four years earlier: Gilmar, Djalma Santos, Nilton Santos, Didi, Vavá, Zagalo, Zito, Pelé and Garrincha were all in the running to add a second World Cup winners' medal to their collection. But there were changes. Mauro, a reserve in 1958, joined the team as centre-half and captain in place of Bellini, while Zozimo replaced Orlando. The most significant change for Brazil was in terms of the coaching position. Vicente Feola was ruled out through illness and was replaced by Aymoré Moreira, brother of Zezé Moreira, coach of the team at the 1954 World Cup.

"The trip to Chile was fantastic," recalls television journalist Luiz Mendes. "I travelled with the national team in the same plane. It felt that every moment it was going to crash above the Andes – it was full of shocks. One air hostess fell and her tray went up in the air and fell all over Didi – he went grey because he was so scared. Everyone got very worried but we arrived peacefully in Chile. There were a few radio journalists at the airport and one asked Zagalo, 'Do you think Brazil are going to win this World Cup?' He said, 'If Brazil do half as much as what this plane has just done, then we're going to win it."

Brazil had every reason to be confident. Pelé, still only 21 years old, was just coming into his prime, while Garrincha, at 28, was an unstoppable force of nature. The previous World Cup had showcased the talents of these supremely gifted players, but it was Pelé who had become the superstar. Whether playing for Santos at home or on European tours, he was the one everybody wanted to see. "Pelé was the first truly professional player that Brazil had," says author, Alex Bellos. "He went to Santos when he was still a teenager, he lived with Santos, he trained himself, he perfected himself, he earned lots of money, he invested the money in business, he became this serious person, he became like the Brazilian establishment."

He became the most famous footballer in the world and Brazil's first truly international star. Garrincha had no such ambitions. It was as if he and Pelé represented two opposing sides of Brazil. "Garrincha was like the last ever amateur player," says Bellos. "He was attached to his home town, he couldn't save any money, he was a fun loving guy and in his playful dribbles he seemed to play just for having fun, while in his life he seemed to just have fun with no thought of the wider consequences."

Garrincha was married with seven children but responsibility was not part of his make-up. This carefree talent had always enjoyed a drink. But drink wasn't his only weakness. "Garrincha was unique," says trainer Paolo Amaral. "A womaniser like him is difficult to find anywhere in the world. When we were travelling through Europe with Botafogo, whenever we arrived at a hotel, the first thing Mané would do would be to ask the receptionist where we go to pay women to have sex. The person would write on a piece of paper the name and address of where to go and then also on the same bit of paper the name and address of the hotel, so he could show it to the taxi driver, who would take him to exactly where the women were. He would do whatever he did with them and then get back by showing the taxi driver the address to come back to."

When the 1962 World Cup finally kicked off, it was apparent that this was a new era for football. By the end of the tournament the average goals scored per game would have fallen from 5.38 in the 1954 World Cup to 2.78 in 1962, signalling a significant turn around in tactical play in just eight years. For all the flair and creativity of their team, even the Brazilians combated the high altitude of Chile by playing a more defensive 4-3-3 system, packing the central midfield and allowing the full backs to attack on the overlap.

The Italians, meanwhile, had long since pioneered a trend for defensive football that became known as *catenaccio* – Italian for 'padlock'. The system used a deep-lying defender, the '*libero*', behind three man-to-man marking full-backs. Free of specific marking duties, the *libero*, or 'free man' (or the 'sweeper' as the English chose to call it), would patrol the centre of defence covering for the other defenders.

Less a tactic for winning games than a means to avoid losing them, *catenaccio* was developed by Nereo Rocco at *Serie A* minnows Triestina as a means of competing in a league dominated by the wealth of the Italian football giants. In 1947 Triestina had finished bottom of the league, but a year later they ended the campaign joint second.

Catenaccio was quickly adopted by other clubs because it relied on the sudden counter-attack that had long been a feature of the Italian game. In the power vacuum created by the Superga air disaster of May 1949, *catenaccio* was a system of play that was well suited to a league stripped of most of its best players and the largest part of its national side. In the mid-Sixties Inter Milan would lift the European Cup with their own particular brand of the formation. Eventually *catenaccio* would become more than a style of play. It became a mentality that would haunt the Italian game, purging it of creativity and adventure. Unfortunately the 1962 World Cup would see plenty of *catenaccio*.

The opening stages of the competition did feature the occasional entertaining match, however, with Group One, based thousands of miles up country in Arica, providing the best football of the early stages. The clash between the Soviet Union and first time qualifiers Colombia was described by *L'Équipe* as "one of the greatest surprises of modern football". Three goals in three minutes gave the Soviets a commanding lead and the game looked over by the 11th minute. The Colombians pulled a goal back ten minutes later through Aceros, but Ponedelnik scored a fourth for the Soviets early in the second-half. Colombia, however, staged a magnificent comeback to secure an amazing 4-4 draw, with Coll, Rada and Klinger all scoring.

Going into their final game Colombia still had the opportunity to progress to the knockout phase if they beat Yugoslavia, but a 5-0 defeat put paid to their ambitions, the Soviets and Yugoslavia qualifying for the quarter-finals at the expense of two-time world champions Uruguay.

After three match days the Chilean press reported there had been 34 serious injuries at the tournament. This largely dismal football showpiece reached its nadir in Group Two with the infamous 'Battle of Santiago' between Italy and hosts Chile. Anti-Italian feeling had been whipped-up in Santiago as a result of the publication of derogatory articles about Chilean life by two Italian journalists. This was in addition to ill-feeling created by Italy's reputation as a poacher of South American players at both domestic and international level. Indeed, their team line-up for the game with Chile included Argentinian Umberto Maschio, and a veteran of Brazil's previous World Cup campaign, José Altafini.

The match, staged in front of a hostile over-capacity crowd in Santiago's National Stadium, quickly descended into violence, which English referee Ken Aston failed to control. He did dismiss the Italian Ferrini for retaliation after just eight minutes, although the player refused to leave the field for a further ten minutes and was eventually removed by FIFA officials and the police. Aston also sent off Ferrini's team-mate David in the second-half, however the referee did nothing when Leonel Sánchez, the son of

Brazil's magical five: Garrincha, Didi, Pelé, Vavá and Zagalo.

a boxer, retaliated to Humberto Maschio's severe foul by breaking the Italian player's nose right in front of a linesman. The disgraceful violence on the field continued and Chile won the game 2-0.

Earlier in the same group Chile had kicked off the tournament with a 3-1 win over Switzerland, while Italy and West Germany had danced cautiously around each other in a cat and mouse battle of *catenaccio,* the Germans playing Schnellinger as the *libero*, Italy countering with Salvadore.

West Germany had arrived in Chile having played only four competitive games in four years, a result of Sepp Herberger's decision not to participate in the first European Nations Cup in 1960. Winning all four of their World Cup qualifiers with Greece and Northern Ireland, Herberger was nevertheless short of talented players and even made an attempt to persuade his 1954 World Cup winning captain to play. Fritz Walter was now 40 years old and had not played serious football in two years, but it didn't stop Herberger suggesting the idea. Walter didn't join the squad, but he made the journey to South America and turned out once for the German reserves in a guest match.

The West Germans managed to beat Switzerland 2-1 in their second game, but the Swiss played with ten men for the whole of the second half after inside-forward Eschmann fractured an ankle before the break. West Germany's 2-0 win over Chile in their final group game allowed both teams to qualify for the second phase and rendered academic the result of Italy's tie with Switzerland the following day.

Nevertheless, the *azzurri* made eight changes to their team and won the match 3-0, thanks in part to an injury to Swiss keeper Charles Elsener. For better or worse, Italy had made their mark on this tournament – and now they were on their way home.

The stars of Group Three were undoubtedly Brazil, favourites to win the tournament with Pelé and Garrincha as their charismatic stars. "Of course Brazil were going to win the World Cup twice," says defender Nilton Santos. "Us guys helped, but those two, they were the real stars."

Their change in formation, playing Zagalo deeper in a more defensive 4-3-3 system, did not instantly produce football as beautiful as the group's surroundings in the seaside resort of Viña del Mar. But although Brazil may not have attacked with the wild abandon of 1958, they immediately returned to their winning ways with a 2-0 win over Mexico, Zagalo putting them ahead after 56 minutes and yet another magnificent solo goal from Pelé sealing the victory 18 minutes from time. Not only did he beat four defenders to score, but he put the ball past Antonio Carbajal, the most experienced keeper in World Cup history, playing in his fourth tournament.

After their next clash with Czechoslovakia, the tournament's ever-growing casualty list would include its biggest star, Pelé, the result of a torn muscle from a groin injury sustained in a pre-tournament friendly. Pelé had refused to declare it because of trainer Paulo Amaral's "don't train, don't play" policy. The injury meant that he would have to watch the rest of the tournament from the stand. But at least Brazil still had Garrincha – and rarely would a single player have such an impact on the outcome of a World Cup tournament.

Luiz Mendes: "The manager went to see Garrincha and said 'Look, Pelé is not able to play. You have to play good enough for you and Pelé too'. Garrincha said 'Yeah, okay, leave it with me, no problem.'"

The Brazilians needn't have worried. "We had other good players," says Nilton Santos. "When Pelé got injured, Amarildo came in – and we carried on winning."

Brazil's final match of the group stage was against a Spanish side coached by the eccentric Helenio

WORLD CUP STORIES

JIMMY ARMFIELD
England's right-back recalls the impact of the World Cup.

"For those of us who grew up after the war I think there was a sort of false security about the strength of English football. We had all the big names but in those days we didn't really look to other countries, it was a narrower vision of life and we thought that everything British was best. It was still only a few years after the war and that did make a difference. The war had an incredible effect on our lives and on football in Britain. We tried to keep football going during the war. Stan Mortensen was in the RAF, and he went down to play for England against Wales – and Wales were short so he played for *them*. That was the scenario during the wartime, where there was a bit of make-do-and-mend.

"After the war everybody was looking for entertainment and football was cheap. It was available to the working man.

I wouldn't say the World Cup was insignificant but it was over there, somewhere far away. Even when we lost to the USA in 1950 there was a song and dance about it for a week and then it was forgotten. That should have been a wake up call, but we just carried on.

"We played quite well in 1962 and we got to the quarter-final. I was really confident we could still win, even though we'd lost several players through injury, but Brazil beat us in Viña del Mar.

"Going to the World Cup in those days was totally different, especially coming home. Four or five of us came back from Chile via New York and we flew to Manchester, while the rest of the team came back to London. All the flights were booked for us, but we made our own way back and looked after our own bags. You wouldn't believe that now."

Opposite: (above) England's Bobby Moore, Maurice Norman, Ron Flowers and captain Johnny Haynes leave the pitch after defeating Argentina in Rancagua. (below) Jimmy Armfield takes the front seat as the England team leave Santiago en route to their training camp at the Braden Copper Company in Coya, 25,000 feet up in the Andes.

Herrera, a revolutionary manager in club football and a well-paid control freak who dominated his sides with a use of man-management techniques that was way ahead of its time. A disciple of *catenaccio*, in the years immediately after the World Cup he would conquer Europe through its use with Inter Milan. Herrera had coached the Italian national team during qualification for the 1962 World Cup, but by the time the tournament came round, he was at the helm of Spain.

Spain should have been contenders under Herrera, as he had at his disposal Alfredo Di Stéfano, one of the greatest footballers to have played the game and a former international striker for both Argentina and Colombia. But although travelling to Chile, Di Stéfano would leave the country having not played a game. Sustaining an injury before his arrival, the opinionated centre-forward had also failed to establish a relationship with his eccentric coach. Herrera subsequently denied that he kept Di Stéfano out of the team, but stories abounded of a training session in Viña del Mar two days before their opening game, where the coach went in particularly hard on a limping Di Stéfano.

Spain boasted other talents, including Luis Suárez, one of the most gifted inside-forwards of his

Referee Ken Aston sends off Italy's Mario David during the 'Battle of Santiago'. An injured Chilean lies on the ground.

generation, and dazzling winger Francisco 'Paco' Gento. Herrera also had 'adopted' talent of outstanding quality. Thanks largely to the pull of Real Madrid's all conquering side of the late Fifties, his Spain team included 40-year-old Hungarian legend Ferenc Puskás and former Uruguayan hardman José Santamaría (a future manager of the Spanish national side in their disappointing campaign in 1982).

With all this experience at their disposal, Spain were expected to be in serious contention, but after defeat by Czechoslovakia and a narrow victory over Mexico, they faced a deciding game with Brazil. Herrera abandoned his experienced players in favour of youth, but despite leading until the 71st minute, they lost the game 2-1 and finished bottom of their group. Two years later, though, they would be crowned European champions.

Brazil had remained unfazed by the loss of their star player, having unearthed Tavares Amarildo, who was quickly dubbed 'the white Pelé'. It was Garrincha, though, who had been Brazil's inspiration in the game against Spain. The father of seven was as productive on the pitch as off it – he didn't just score goals, he created them too, having a hand in both of Amarildo's strikes.

"The game against Spain taught us that it was possible to win the cup without Pelé," says João Maximo.

"Many people thought that without Pelé, Brazil would lose," recalls Paolo Amaral. "But in Pelé's place they had Amarildo. He scored both goals and this gave even the sceptical fan a feeling of real potential."

Brazil topped their group. The Czechs qualified in second place and had scored the quickest goal of the tournament when Vaclav Masek put the ball past keeper Carbajal after just 15 seconds in their 3-1 defeat by Mexico.

The six Group Four matches were all played in Rancagua, on the small ground that belonged to the Braden Copper Company. The England team were more prepared than they had been for previous tournaments, having even had the foresight to scout the ground and find a suitable base an hour outside Rancagua. Captain Johnny Haynes was the sole survivor of the team from the previous World Cup, although by now 1958's overlooked squad member Bobby Charlton was a fixture on the left wing. In Jimmy Greaves the side could boast one of the great marksmen of his generation, while with Bobby

CAMPEONATO MUNDIAL DE FUTBOL CHILE 1962

Moore, who had broken into the first team in place of the injured Bobby Robson en route to the World Cup finals, the seeds were being sown for England's great years ahead.

"In Chile we did quite well," recalls Bobby Charlton. "We lost the first game to Hungary, then we beat Argentina, who were a strong outfit. We thought, 'Well if we can beat these, why can't we beat anybody'. But we drew with Bulgaria, which was the worst game I ever played in. I hated it. The two teams didn't want to bother – they were glad of a point and a point would've meant we went on to the next stage."

Hungary weren't the force they once were, and only keeper Gyula Grosics remained from the Magical Magyars of the early Fifties, but their team was blessed by one of the outstanding talents of the tournament, Ferencváros centre-forward Florian Albert. After harrying Johnny Haynes out of the game, Hungary went 1-0 up after a long-range shot from Lajos Tichy. Ron Flowers equalised from the penalty spot, but a superb solo goal from Albert gave Hungary a 2-1 victory.

Argentina beat Bulgaria 1-0 with an unadventurous defensive performance that inspired the necessary tactical rethink by England to deliver a 3-1 win when the two sides met. Hungary knocked four past Bulgaria in just 12 minutes, winning 6-1 with a hat-trick from Albert, before playing out a goalless draw with Argentina. Hungary and England progressed to the quarter finals, but the group had not caught the imagination of local fans, attracting an average crowd of just 7,000, with the worst attended match being England's dull 0-0 draw against Bulgaria.

Hosts Chile pulled off a surprise in the quarter-finals, knocking out the Soviet Union 2-1, while Yugoslavia beat West Germany by a single goal in Santiago. It was the third time in as many World Cups that the two sides had met at this stage. "I'm getting sick even thinking of having to play Germany again," Yugoslavia's coach Ljubomir Lovric said before the game. But when Peter Radakovic's shot hit the back

Pelé's replacement Amarildo is embraced after scoring in Brazil's victory over Spain.

of the net, the West Germans were finally made to suffer for their defensive tendencies and *catenaccio* tactics. The depressing performance of the national team even had the side effect of helping the German FA finally overhaul the country's regional football structure and replace it with a national professional league. The *Bundesliga* finally kicked off in 1963, 34 years after the formation of *Serie A* and the Spanish *Liga*, and 75 years after England's Football League.

Czechoslovakia had built a team around the successful Dukla Prague club side, with a strategy strongly built on defence. A cautious counter-attacking team, they managed to take the lead in the 12th minute of their quarter-final with Hungary through a 20-yard strike from Adolf Scherer and progressed through to the semi-finals, thanks in no small part to Wilhelm Schrioff, the goalkeeper of the tournament. He was in magnificent form, particularly in their quarter-final and semi-final clashes with Hungary and Yugoslavia, a series of magnificent saves keeping his opponents at bay in both games.

Brazil breezed through the quarter-finals, outclassing England who had finished runners-up in Group D. Garrincha shone in the match. "The dribbles that he made were just unbelievable," says Luiz Mendes. "Destabilising, extraordinary, stunning." The smallest player on the field, he opened the scoring with a header before later setting up Vavá and finding the net again in a 3-1 win.

"At 1-1, midway through the second half, we were on top and I thought we were definitely going to win," recalls England defender Jimmy Armfield. "But Garrincha beat us with a free-kick and that was one

Swiss defender Heinz Schneiter attempts to block the shot of German forward Uwe Seeler. Both players scored in the game.

of the biggest downers I've ever had. They had a good team, but at that time I thought we were as good."

"At Viña del Mar we lost to one man," says Bobby Charlton. "Little Garrincha scored with a header. He beat a lot of our big strapping centre-halfs. He out jumped them and headed the first goal and then he bent a free-kick round the wall, which you didn't really do in those days – but Brazilians seemed to be able to do it."

For the time being though, the England team were on their way home. Despite the disappointment of an early exit from the cup, this wasn't a squad totally focussed on winning at the expense of all else. Some were even pleased to be on their way home after such a long trip. "A lot of players in that team were really quite homesick," says Charlton. "There was a lot of laughing and joking afterwards, a couple of them saying they were glad that we'd lost because they'd see their families. I won't mention their names for fear of embarrassing them. We lost at the end of the day, but we played really well and 3-1 flattered them. But it was enough to make us think, 'If they're going to come and play in our place and we can play as well as this and get as close as this, why shouldn't we have a chance'. Of course Alf Ramsey soon took over as manager and said that after the performance in 1962 that he thought England would win the World Cup. I felt exactly the same myself."

As for Brazil, they were still on course for their second consecutive World Cup final and Garrincha was determined to make it happen, even though football wasn't the only thing on his mind. He had started a relationship with Elza Soares, one of the most famous samba singers in Brazil at the time. Although still married at this point, it was the romance that was to define his life. Much to his pleasure, Elza's fame had earned her an invitation to the 1962 World Cup and she looked on as Garrincha stole the show. "The 1962 World Cup was a tribute to me," says Elza Soares. "He said, 'Thank you so much for coming here, you make me so happy, I'll play better now because of it'. I was very honoured."

"She was a stimulus," says Nilton Santos, one of Garrincha's closest friends. "That championship in Chile, he was considered the best player, not just of Brazil but of the whole tournament, and she was his stimulus. She would call him on the telephone and he would just go for it. He thought mostly with his

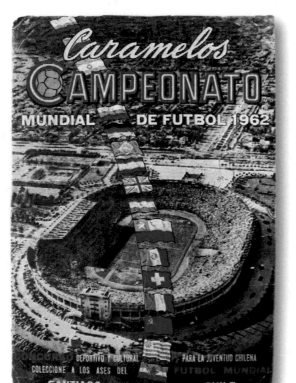

you-know-what! Imagine the two of them – God, they would have set each other alight."

The semi-final pitched Brazil against hosts Chile in an open game that was streaked with spite. Garrincha gave the holders a 2-0 lead through a volley and a header. "He was truly sensational," says Luiz Mendes. "All the Brazilian players knew exactly what to do when things looked like they were getting tough – pass the ball to Garrincha."

A Toro free-kick halved the deficit before the break. A Garrincha free-kick was then headed home by Vavá just after the interval, but Sánchez converted a penalty to keep Chile in touch. With 13 minutes remaining Zagalo dribbled through the Chilean defence and set up Vavá for another header. Shortly afterwards Chile's Landa was sent-off, and minutes later Garrincha followed, finally retaliating to one of the many kicks he had suffered during the game. Nevertheless, favourites Brazil progressed to the final.

"Garrincha never fouled people," says Nilton Santos. "He was always a victim."

Luiz Mendes: "He was spat at. He told me the Chilean player spat in his face and he couldn't restrain his anger, so he gave him a little tap on the bum. The linesman saw it and the ref sent him off. By that time it was never automatic that you would be suspended for the following match if you got sent off – there would be a judgement. So Paolo Carvalho of the Brazilian football confederation took it in his hands to make sure that the only witness to what happened went away. He was a Uruguayan and they sent him off to Montevideo and he never went to give evidence and Garrincha was absolved."

"Somehow the referee's report of the game just never surfaced," says trainer Paolo Amaral, "or it was made to be that it was never written in the match report that the player with the Number 7 shirt, Manuel dos Santos [Garrincha], was sent off. This report never surfaced. So Mané played the final, but how this was done I really don't know. It wasn't even commentated on – the only thing we knew is that on the following day the news came that he would be allowed to play the final, just that."

FIFA allowed Garrincha to play despite imposing one-match bans on all of the other five players

Opposite: The 1962 World Cup final. (above) Brazilian captain Mauro holds aloft the Jules Rimet trophy. (centre right) An emotional Mario Zagalo is helped from the field after the final. (below) Joyful scenes on the pitch after the final whistle. (overleaf) Vavá celebrates after scoring in the final.

Brazil 3 Czechoslovakia 1

0:1 JOSEF MASOPUST (CZH) 15', 1:1 AMARILDO (BRA) 17', 2:1 ZITO (BRA) 69', 3:1 VAVÁ (BRA) '78'

dismissed during the tournament. Brazil named an unchanged side and found themselves lining up against Czechoslovakia, who had reached the final by beating Yugoslavia 3-1 in front of a crowd of 5,890 in Viña del Mar.

The experienced Brazil side – nine were aged 30 years old or over – included eight members of the team that had lifted the trophy in Sweden in 1958, but still they went 1-0 down to Masopust's opening

Garrincha holds the Jules Rimet Trophy.

goal. Nilton Santos found himself picking the ball out of his own net after just 15 minutes. "I took the ball and said, 'Come on, let's start again'."

Amarildo, 'the white Pelé', scored from an acute angle near the by-line to equalise within two minutes and the match remained a closely-fought contest until the 69th minute when Amarildo's high pass was headed home by Zito. The match was decided when Czech goalkeeper Schrojf, who had a poor game after his heroics in the previous two rounds, allowed a Djalma Santos high ball to fall through his hands for Vavá to stab home. Brazil won the game 3-1. It was the best match of the tournament.

Luiz Mendes still remembers his words at the final whistle. "I had a cameraman with me and I was looking at the scoreboard and then it appeared, the words 'Brazil double champions': 'It's there, it's there, it's written on the scoreboard, behold double world champions'."

For Nilton Santos, his second World Cup final victory seemed to come as no surprise. "I never lost a big game," he recalls. "It must be really bad getting to the final and then losing because being runner-up doesn't mean anything at all, especially not for us Brazilians who are used to coming top. Either you're champion or you're nothing. Every single one of the 26 championship finals that I ever played, the following day I was always celebrating having won them. It must be really horrible to get to the top and then just not quite make it."

Garrincha had made good on his claim that he would win the World Cup for Elza Soares. The whole country could have been watching but Garrincha was aware of only one person in the crowd. "Everyone went into the locker room and she went too – even though they were naked," says Luiz Mendes. "They left that locker room totally sorted and agreed to get married."

For Brazil, the unthinkable had happened. Twelve years after the gut-wrenching disappointment of defeat in 1950, they were double world champions. It was a great time to be Brazilian, on and off the pitch. The economy was booming and social reforms were beginning to percolate through Brazilian society. It felt as if the country was finally on the move. A new generation would grow up to be inspired by the glory days of Brazil and the legends of Brazilian football. "Pelé and Garrincha really made the difference in 1958 and 1962," recalls Socrates, eight years old at the time and a Brazilian star of the future. "The country was transformed because they won those two World Cups. And they only won because they had those two players."

GROUP 1

May 30: Carlos Dittborn Stadium, Arica
Uruguay **2 - 1** Colombia

May 31: Carlos Dittborn Stadium, Arica
Soviet Union **2 - 0** Yugoslavia

June 2: Carlos Dittborn Stadium, Arica
Yugoslavia **3 - 1** Uruguay

June 3: Carlos Dittborn Stadium, Arica
Soviet Union **4 - 4** Colombia

June 6: Carlos Dittborn Stadium, Arica
Soviet Union **2 - 1** Uruguay

June 7: Carlos Dittborn Stadium, Arica
Yugoslavia **5 - 0** Colombia

	P	W	D	L	F	A	Pts
Soviet Union	3	2	1	0	8	5	5
Yugoslavia	3	2	0	1	8	3	4
Uruguay	3	1	0	2	4	6	2
Colombia	3	0	1	2	5	11	1

GROUP 2

May 30: Estadio Nacional, Santiago
Chile **3 - 1** Switzerland

May 31: Estadio Nacional, Santiago
West Germany **0 - 0** Italy

June 2: Estadio Nacional, Santiago
Chile **2 - 0** Italy

June 3: Estadio Nacional, Santiago
West Germany **2 - 1** Switzerland

June 6: Estadio Nacional, Santiago
West Germany **2 - 0** Chile

June 7: Estadio Nacional, Santiago
Italy **3 - 0** Switzerland

	P	W	D	L	F	A	Pts
West Germany	3	2	1	0	4	1	5
Chile	3	2	0	1	5	3	4
Italy	3	1	1	1	3	2	3
Switzerland	3	0	0	3	2	8	0

GROUP 3

May 30: Estadio Sausalito, Viña del Mar
Brazil **2 - 0** Mexico

May 31: Estadio Sausalito, Viña del Mar
Czechoslovakia **1 - 0** Spain

June 2: Estadio Sausalito, Viña del Mar
Brazil **0 - 0** Czechoslovakia

June 3: Estadio Sausalito, Viña del Mar
Spain **1 - 0** Mexico

June 6: Estadio Sausalito, Viña del Mar
Brazil **2 - 1** Spain

June 7: Estadio Sausalito, Viña del Mar
Mexico **3 - 1** Czechoslovakia

	P	W	D	L	F	A	Pts
Brazil	3	2	1	0	4	1	5
Czechoslovakia	3	1	1	1	2	3	3
Mexico	3	1	0	2	3	4	2
Spain	3	1	0	2	2	3	2

GROUP 4

May 30: Braden Stadium, Rancagua
Argentina **1 - 0** Bulgaria

May 31, Braden Stadium, Rancagua
Hungary **2 - 1** England

June 2: Braden Stadium, Rancagua
England **3 - 1** Argentina

June 3: Braden Stadium, Rancagua
Hungary **6 - 1** Bulgaria

June 6: Braden Stadium, Rancagua
Argentina **0 - 0** Hungary

June 7: Braden Stadium, Rancagua
England **0 - 0** Bulgaria

	P	W	D	L	F	A	Pts
Hungary	3	2	1	0	8	2	5
England	3	1	1	1	4	3	3
Argentina	3	1	1	1	2	3	3
Bulgaria	3	0	1	2	1	7	1

THE FINAL

BRAZIL	**(1) 3**
CZECHOSLOVAKIA	**(1) 1**

DATE Thursday June 17, 1962
ATTENDANCE 68,679
VENUE National Stadium, Santiago

Gilmar
Santos, D — Mauro — Zózimo — Santos, N
Zito — Didi — Zagalo
Garrincha — Vavá — Amarildo

Jelinek — Kadraba — Scherer — Pospichal
Masopust — Kvasnak
Novak — Popluhar — Pluskal — Tichy
Schrojf

BRAZIL
COACH: AYMORE MOREIRA

GILMAR
SANTOS, D
MAURO
ZOZIMO
SANTOS, N
ZITO ⚽
Goal: 69 mins
DIDI
GARRINCHA
VAVÁ ⚽
Goal: 77 mins
AMARILDO ⚽
Goal: 17 mins
ZAGALO

CZECHOSLOVAKIA
COACH: RUDOLF VYTLACIL

SCHROJF
TICHY
PLUSKAL
POPLUHAR
NOVAK
KVASNAK
MASOPUST ⚽
Goal: 16 mins
SCHERER
POSPICHAL
KADRABA
JELINEK

REFEREE: Latychev (USSR)

QUARTER-FINALS

June 10: Estadio Nacional, Santiago
Yugoslavia **1 - 0** West Germany

June 10: Estadio Sausalito, Viña del Mar
Brazil **3 - 1** England

June 10: Carlos Dittborn Stadium, Arica
Chile **2 - 1** Soviet Union

June 10: Braden Stadium, Rancagua
Czechoslovakia **1 - 0** Hungary

SEMI-FINALS

June 13: Estadio Nacional, Santiago
Brazil **4 - 2** Chile

June 13: Estadio Sausalito, Viña del Mar
Czechoslovakia **3 - 1** Yugoslavia

THIRD-PLACE PLAY-OFF

June 16: Estadio Nacional, Santiago
Chile **1 - 0** Yugoslavia

The Brazil team line-up before the final.

TOP GOALSCORERS 4 goals: Garrincha* (Brazil), Valentin Ivanov (Soviet Union), Leonel Sánchez (Chile), Florian Albert (Hungary), Drazan Jerkovic (Yugoslavia), Vavá (Brazil)
* Garrincha awarded Top Scorer prize, drawn by lot

FASTEST GOAL 15 seconds: Vaclav Masek (Czechoslovakia v Mexico)

TOTAL GOALS 89 AVERAGE GOALS 2.78 per game

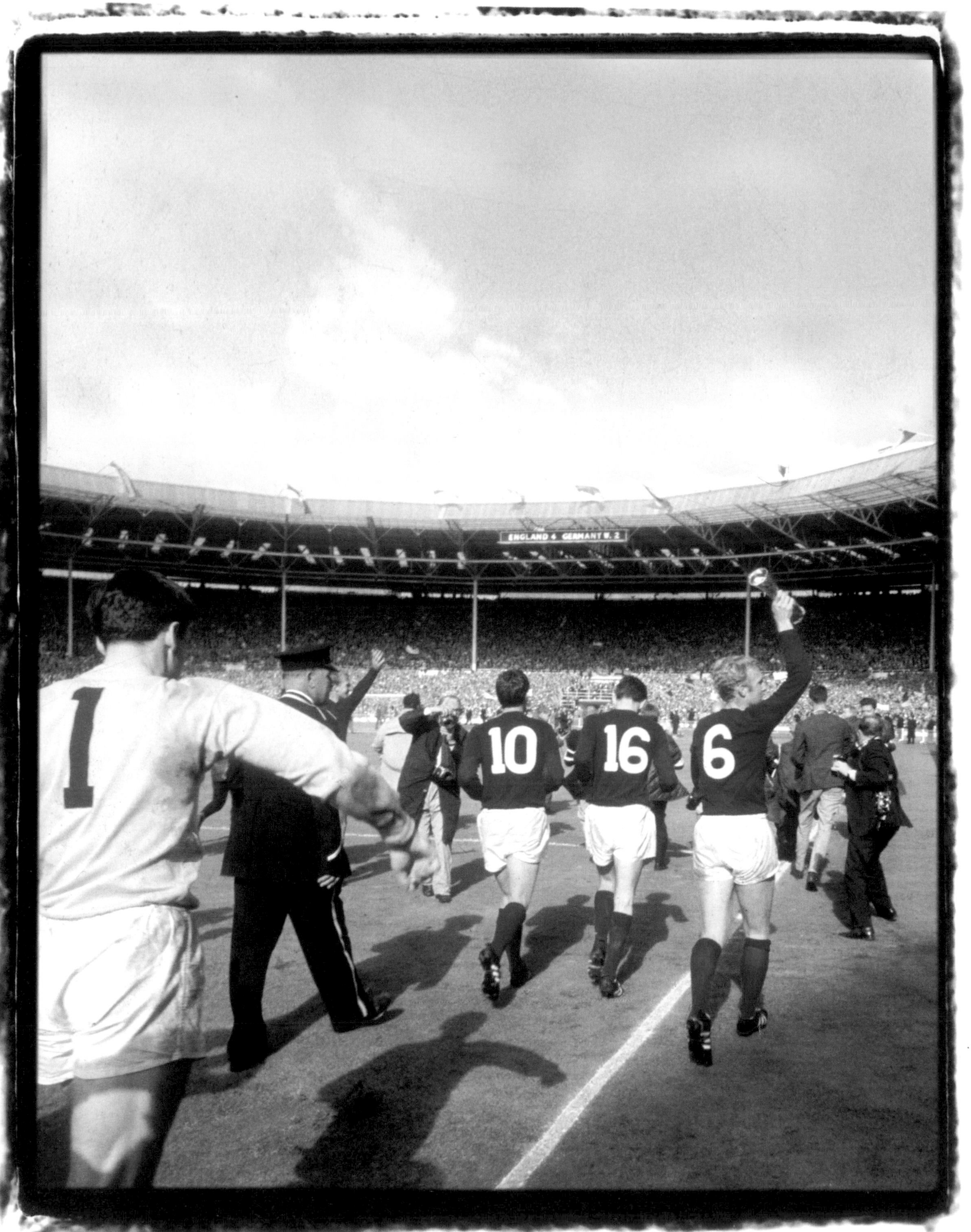
ENGLAND 4 GERMANY W. 2
1
10
16
6

WINGLESS WONDERS

England's 1966 World Cup triumph had been a long time coming. The inventors of the game had struggled to adapt to international competition, but under Alf Ramsey they finally came up with the formula for success.

In 1966 the World Cup came to England, the home of football. While it was the Brazilians who arrived as the undisputed champions, this was a tournament that saw the pragmatism of the European game outpacing the flair and style of the South Americans. As a consequence, the tournament was characterised by dour, often ugly defending, punctuated by flashes of brilliance and moments of high drama. But in the epic encounter between old adversaries England and West Germany, it was also a competition capable of springing the most fantastic of surprises, right up to the final whistle of the final match.

Although playing with home advantage in 1966, to reach this point had been a long journey for England. In their early World Cup campaigns they had found it hard to register any kind of impact on the world game. Despite supporting a thriving domestic league packed with home-grown stars, who played in front of huge crowds every week, the national team appeared not to travel well. In reality they had been left behind, surpassed by technical and tactical developments abroad. No matter how hard the English closed their eyes and thought about Queen and Empire, it didn't make them the best in the world, certainly not in football terms.

This shocking revelation had been kept from the English public, largely because of their own apathy. The USA's shock defeat of England at the 1950 World Cup had barely been reported on at home, *The Daily Telegraph*, for example, devoting just three paragraphs to the match below a picture of American tennis player Gorgeous Gussy Moran, who had caused a sensation at Wimbledon by playing in lace-trimmed

England goalscorers Geoff Hurst and Martin Peters run a lap of honour alongside England captain Bobby Moore after winning the World Cup final.

June 10, 1966: The England squad outside the National Recreation Centre at Lilleshall at the start of preparations for the World Cup.

knickers. In the days before live television transmissions, the World Cup had been a moderately appealing tournament played many miles away – no cause for any real interest or concern.

The attitude of the Football Association hadn't really helped the development of the national side. There was an over-reliance on shoehorning big name stars into the trusty old WM formation at the expense of any real team cohesion or tactical advancement. The players were chosen by the FA's International Selection Committee, a panel of eight or nine men who were supremely unqualified for the job and who had little or no playing experience at any level. The team was then presented to the coach as a *fait accompli,* and it was his responsibility to make the parts fit. It was a system that allowed for no consistency. The England team could change radically from match to match, depending entirely upon which player had caught the eye of the selector that particular week.

When the national team returned from Chile in 1962, the World Cup began to look frighteningly real – the English were waking up to the realisation that the next tournament was going to turn up on their doorstep any day soon. After four post-war attempts to gain the competition, England had finally been awarded their World Cup at the FIFA Congress in Rome on August 8, 1960, beating West Germany to become hosts. Drastic action was going to have to be taken if England were to avoid humiliation. The FA might have been able to turn a blind eye to World Cup defeat on some far away ground in South America, but on the pitch of the mighty Empire Stadium, Wembley, it would be unthinkable.

Walter Winterbottom had been the only full-time coach that the England team had ever had, holding the post since 1946. He was a schoolmasterly theorist who had started out on the books of Manchester United before injury put paid to his career. He might have once been a player, but he was an academic never fully at ease with his predominantly working class team. He would spend hours bewildering his charges with long lectures on the strengths and weaknesses of the opposition, but when it came to the training ground, in the early Fifties there was a belief among the stars of the England team that if they were good enough to be picked for their country, they really needed no coaching.

"I don't think he found it as easy when he was dealing with the likes of Matthews, Mortensen, Mannion and Lawton as he did with my generation who came in the Sixties, where we'd actually been on coaching courses and started to think about the game," suggests Jimmy Armfield.

"I had a very healthy respect for his knowledge and his desire," says Bobby Charlton. "He had everything that you needed but he just somehow didn't get that response from the players that you actually need to win."

Winterbottom resigned from his position in August 1962. "I was reaching an age when I felt I couldn't continue being an active coach, when players no longer take you seriously," he would later reflect.

It was time for a change. As a country England was changing too. In 1962 society still had one foot in the Fifties and was nervously looking to create the brave new world of the Sixties. In the 'great white heat' of Harold Wilson's technological revolution, at a time when scientific advancement was reckoned to be wholly beneficial for society, football was ready for a forward thinker, a man with a plan. Alf Ramsey fitted that bill. On October 25, 1962, he accepted the position of England manager. Shortly afterwards he announced the one thing that the FA wanted to hear more than anything. "England *will* win the World Cup in 1966".

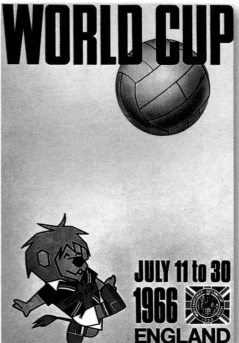

The fact that Ramsey had accepted the job on his own terms seemed to offer the first real hope that this was a new era. "I shall have complete control of the England team, the youth team and the Under-23 international side," he said on taking over. He had also insisted on seeing out the season with his club side, Ipswich Town, before formally starting his new job full-time on May 1, 1963.

As a player with Tottenham and England he had been known as 'The General', well organised and commanding. As a manager he'd taken lowly Ipswich to the Division One title. In his new job Ramsey was determined to break with the past, as England finally left the Fifties behind. He was not prepared to operate with the limited powers that the FA had afforded to his predecessor. "He chose the players, he picked the team and nobody else interfered," explains Bobby Robson. "He was such a strong character. That was the beginning of professionalism in terms of international selection and preparation."

Even revolutions take a little time to get started. Ramsey's first game was against France, but he did not start in time to take over the team selection. For the last time the International Selection Committee picked the players and England lost 5-2. Jimmy Armfield was captain and he recalls his manager's reaction to the result. "Alf came up to me in the dressing room at the end of the match and he said, 'Do we always play like that?' I said, 'No'. He said, 'That's the first bit of good news I've had all night.'"

Ramsey knew what he wanted and made it clear to his players. "This was not going to be a team of celebrities, this was going to be a unit," recalls Armfield.

"I think discipline was everything to him," says Bobby Charlton. "He was not afraid of criticising you in front of the rest of the team. If he was giving a talk and somebody had given away a goal he would totally embarrass them in front of the rest of the team, so you knew what was there if you didn't do what he wanted."

For a short while in 1964 even Ramsey's new captain, Bobby Moore, felt the quiet wrath of his manager and was stripped of the captaincy between games for a breach of discipline. For the first time the England team were truly managed. But Ramsey was wise enough not to throw out the traditional English qualities of stamina and grit. He might need them someday. He still relied on talented individuals like Bobby Moore and Bobby Charlton, but now Ramsey picked players to fit the team. Players like Nobby Stiles who could win the ball in midfield, or Jack Charlton, 29 years old when he made his England debut, who was mobile and a good header of the ball. Ramsey moulded them into a spirited unit. "We fought for each other out there, we grafted for each other, we helped each other along," says Gordon Banks. "That was what Alf was all about. He wanted a team display."

Ramsey experimented with players and tactics. Late in 1965 he converted Bobby Charlton from England's first choice left-winger into a creative midfielder, a position where his most talented player could exert more of an influence on the game. Ramsey tried out 4-2-4 in his early years in the job, but on December 8, 1965, in a match against Spain in Madrid, England won 2-0 playing an innovative, attacking 4-3-3 formation that grabbed the attention of world football. They'd experimented once before with the system, against West Germany in Nuremberg in May, but this was the first time an England team were sent out to play with no recognised wingers in the line-up. With the numbering on the back of the shirts now totally unrelated to traditional playing positions, the Spanish defenders were as confused as England had been by the visit of Hungary in 1953 and they struggled to work out who they should be marking.

In an unbeaten run Ramsey would use this formation through the next six months, experimenting with the players who could fit into it, vacillating between the idea of 4-3-3 with two strikers playing alongside a winger, and the same formation with three out-and-out strikers up front. But just six days before the World Cup, playing their last warm-up game against Poland, in a fixture that the press believed would finally showcase Ramsey's World Cup starting line-up, the formation seamlessly evolved into 4-4-2, with Hunt and Greaves playing as twin strikers. For the assembled press, worried about Ramsey's complete abandonment of alternative options, it seemed that if there was a Plan B, it didn't involve wingers.

Whichever formation England would choose to kick off the World Cup, all the pieces were now in place. Alf Ramsey and his 'wingless wonders' were ready. It was a sea change in English football. For the first time the players came second to the system, but he still managed to create a real team spirit.

"I don't think he was bothered about keeping the one team together," says Bobby Charlton. "Alf Ramsey was only bothered about one thing and that was winning the game. Some people got upset because he dropped them. Some people moved out of position but how could you argue about it when every time we went on the field we won? So we listened to him, and the players had the utmost respect for him as a manager. We went out every match frightened of nobody."

When the England football team finally flew into London Airport, returning from their ten-day tour of Scandinavia and Poland, there were just seven days to go until the tournament's opening game. "I hope this pilot knows that this landing is the only thing between England and winning the World Cup," said the irrepressible Jimmy Greaves. They had played four games in ten days and returned with a 100 per cent record. But it wasn't a widely held view at home that they would lift the Jules Rimet Trophy. In the run-up to the tournament England were rated as outsiders by many professional analysts and critics. "It's not Alf's fault," TV pundit Jimmy Hill famously said at the time, "nobody could win the World Cup with those players."

It was a telling comment. The chief criticism levelled at England coach Alf Ramsey by his own press was that he valued sweat over genius, workrate over creativity. But he had given his internationals the spirit of

Jimmy Greaves accepts the commiserations of captain Bobby Moore after being ruled out of England's quarter-final match with Argentina through injury.

a club side and they were feeling confident. "We went everywhere and we won everywhere," recalls Bobby Charlton. "It was great. I thought, 'Let's get this World Cup on while everything's going well'."

It wasn't just England who were rebuilding for the future. For West Germany it was also a new beginning. In June 1964, after 28 years in the job, Sepp Herberger had retired as coach. He had wanted World Cup-winning captain Fritz Walter to succeed him, but the *Deutscher Fussball Bund* appointed his assistant of nine years, Helmut Schön, who began fashioning a new team. An early success for Schön was the winning of his battle with the DFB to overturn the ban on players who plied their trade abroad, enabling Helmut Haller and Karl-Heinz Schnellinger to be recalled to the team for the first time in two years for the World Cup qualifier against Sweden in November 1964. The West Germans drew the match, leaving the away tie in Sweden crucial for their qualification chances, but they had not won in Sweden since 1911. To make matters worse, a career-threatening injury to Uwe Seeler meant it looked like they were going to be without their most important player. An amazing recovery by Seeler put him in contention for a recall after a successful operation to fit an artificial Achilles tendon, but he wasn't yet on his sharpest form. Even the national team physio was not confident: "If I was responsible, Seeler would not play."

It seemed, however, that Helmut Schön was prepared to take a gamble on more than Seeler. In this important match he gave an international debut to 20-year-old Franz Beckenbauer, playing in the midfield at right-half. He had previously had one try-out for the Germans in a friendly against Chelsea, which they had lost 1-0. Schön's gamble paid off. With the match 1-1 at half-time, it was Uwe Seeler who scored the winning goal from a move started by Beckenbauer, who had made the first of what would be many characteristic midfield runs. With just their away tie with Cyprus to navigate, West Germany were through to the World Cup finals having not lost a match.

At the start of the World Cup qualification process, some 70 teams entered, although only 51 actually took part. Syria withdrew, leaving Spain and the Republic of Ireland to fight each other for qualification, Spain winning in a play-off in Paris. South Africa were excluded after suspension by FIFA for violating the anti-discrimination laws that had been added to the FIFA charter at the 1960 Congress. The remaining 17 withdrawals were a protest from the African and Asian nations, aggrieved at FIFA's decision to allow only one qualifying team from these groups. North Korea were the only nation not to withdraw, and they had to play Australia over two legs to qualify. In a tight group, Scotland were edged out by Italy and, at the expense of 1962 finalists Czechoslovakia, Portugal qualified for the first time, having first tried in 1934.

In the build up to the tournament, the 1966 World Cup had a rather unusual saviour. The Jules Rimet cup was stolen while on public display at a stamp exhibition in Westminster. A nationwide hunt ensued, but it was later discovered by a dog named Pickles, wrapped in some old newspapers lying under bushes in London. England's World Cup also saw the first tournament mascot and official logo for marketing purposes. The mascot was a lion called World Cup Willie and his image appeared in the official poster.

On July 11 the tournament got underway. The draw pitted the hosts against Uruguay, Mexico and France

England's self-proclaimed cheerleader Ken Bailey before the World Cup final.

in Group One. But after all the anticipation of the build-up, the opening game was an anticlimax, with the negative Uruguayans blotting out England's sterile attack to gain a scoreless draw. In the three group games Ramsey would play a 4-3-3 formation, utilising a different winger each time. He started the tournament with largely the same team he used in the last warm-up game, but in place of Martin Peters he brought in winger John Connelly to partner Greaves and Hunt up front.

Despite all of the bold claims, the team spirit and the home advantage, the goals had dried up in their first match. "After seeing that, those who thought we were definitely going to win the World Cup were certainly having second thoughts," says Barry Davies, part of ITV's commentary team. Although a technical sell-out, Wembley had been less than full for the game, a consequence of the ticketing policy that had meant a package of tickets had to be bought in order to get one for the final. This hadn't been the game to encourage those stay-at-home ticket holders to return.

For the following game with Mexico, Martin Peters replaced Alan Ball, and winger Terry Paine came in for Connelly in attack. In a less than convincing 2-0 win, Bobby Charlton scored with a 25-yard pile-driver. "It was a good goal," he recalls. "Not so much for the way it was done but because of the importance of it. At last we'd scored a goal. That's what people expected."

"It was a goal when it left his foot and I was 100 yards away," remembers Jack Charlton. "It flew into the top corner of the net."

In the final group game with France, winger Ian Callaghan was brought in as a direct replacement for Terry Paine, who had suffered concussion in the game with Mexico. A 2-0 victory meant England had qualified for the quarter-finals, with Uruguay in second place in the group. Hunt had scored both of England's goals, while Greaves remained frustrated. But the game was most notable for a controversial foul by Nobby Stiles, who had clattered French inside-left Jacques Simon.

"A representation came from the FA to the ground and told Alf that they wanted him to drop Nobby Stiles because of this," says Brian Glanville. "The answer to that was, 'If Stiles goes, I go'. So Stiles stayed. He was absolutely a player's man at that time – and they really would go over the top for him. They knew that if they stepped out of line there would be trouble, but they also knew that he would defend them to the death and always stand up for them."

In Group Two, split between Villa Park in Birmingham and Hillsborough in Sheffield, it was felt that West Germany were no more than fancied outsiders against Argentina and Spain, with Switzerland thrown in to make up the numbers. When a journalist asked the West German team's interpreter who would win the tournament, he confidently answered, "England". It turned out to be none other than Bert Trautmann, the German-born keeper who had become a national hero in Britain after the war, having made it from POW camp inmate to FA Cup winner in just a few short years.

Pelé arrives in Liverpool with a police escort.

Always conscious of the fact that the Germans were playing in a country they had tried so hard to decimate during the blitz 26 years earlier, Helmut Schön impressed on his players the need to behave impeccably during their stay. "The main thing was that we left a good impression," keeper Hans Tilkowski would recall. "Back in 1966, the appearance and the behaviour of the team were essential."

The West Germans got off to a flying start when two goals apiece from Haller and Beckenbauer, and one from Sigfried Held, gave them a crushing 5-0 victory over Switzerland. The Swiss had played a part in their own defeat, weakening the team by suspending two key players who had broken the squad curfew. The victory helped Schön's side enlist the support of *The Sunday Mirror*, who demanded, "Show us a better team than the Germans, and you'll have the World Cup winners".

The first surprise of the tournament came when a physical Argentina came through the heavy rain at Villa Park to beat a Spanish team built around the stars of the mighty Real Madrid side. While Spain recovered to beat Switzerland at Hillsborough, West Germany played out a goalless draw with ten-man Argentina in front of 51,000 fans at Villa Park. José Albrecht was sent off following a high tackle on Wolfgang Weber, having already been cautioned after his rugby tackle on Haller. West Germany had been subjected to the kind of brutal tactics that saw the South Americans pick up a FIFA warning. It did not prevent them progressing though, Argentina clinching qualification against Switzerland in front of a hostile Hillsborough crowd. West Germany, meanwhile, qualified top after defeating Spain 2-1, with a match-winning goal from Uwe Seeler.

Group Three was undoubtedly the toughest of the four, with Brazil, Portugal and Hungary all considered serious contenders for the championship. Brazil had arrived in England unbeaten in the competition in 12 years, but with success came complacency and overconfidence. Too many ageing players were sent to England in 1966, among them 32-year-old Garrincha, who was well past his best. For many years he had been plagued by a knee injury caused by the deformity to his legs. The way his tibia met his femur meant that every time he swivelled his body, it would damage the cartilage. "I think it was a crime to take Mané there because his knee by then was totally destroyed," says his wife, singer Elza Soares "He didn't have what it took to go to that cup."

JACK CHARLTON

Just 14 months before the World Cup, the England defender couldn't have even dreamt of an England call-up, let alone a winners' medal.

"I was coming up for 30 years old when I heard I'd been called up to the England team for the first time. Leeds had just played in the semi-final of the FA Cup against Manchester United and we'd won 1-0. After the game I went into the dressing room and I was just sat there having a beer when Don Revie sat down next to me. He said, 'I've got to congratulate you. You've been selected to play for England against Scotland at Wembley'. I couldn't believe it. I said, 'Me?' I thought, 'I've got to tell our kid'. I knocked on the dressing room down the corridor and entered the Manchester United dressing room. I walked across to him and I said, 'Hey kidda, you'll never believe this but I've been selected to play for England against the Jocks at Wembley with you'. They had just lost the FA Cup semi-final and he sort of looked up at me and went, 'I'm pleased for you'. Then Dennis Law looked across and he said, 'Yes big fella, I'm delighted for you too'. And Pat Crerand looked across and he

went, 'Yes, Jack, we're all pleased for you – now piss off out of the dressing room'.

"I said to Alf once, 'Why did you pick me to play for England?' He looked at me and he said, 'Well, Jack, I had a pattern of play in my mind – but I don't necessarily always pick the best players!' That was Alf. You always had that element of fear with him though. I always felt that he didn't like me, but he very rarely held conversations. The only person I can remember him standing talking to on a regular basis was Bobby Moore. They used to stand together on the touchline. He might call one of us over and ask us something, or tell us something, but Bobby would always stand with Alf and talk to him because the two of them got on terrific together.

"I think he picked me because I was quite a mobile player. I was a good header of the ball and a very good tackler, and I scored a few goals. Once I'd got in the side against Scotland in April 1965, I played in every game right the way

through until the World Cup final. I was fully confident that I was Alf's number one choice to play alongside Bobby Moore. Before that I had never expected to be playing in a World Cup final. I didn't get into the team until a year before it actually took place, so I didn't expect it. Alf was very good in the way he picked his team. He didn't want you to do anything different to what you did with your club. That was one of his strengths: don't try things that you're not capable of. I was never the best footballer in the world but I was good at stopping people. I always felt that I needed to be effective to keep in with Alf.

"Not many people become world champions. To this day when I get introduced, they'll always say, 'Mr Jack Charlton who was in the 1966 World Cup winning team'. They always mention that, and I'm quite delighted they do."

Jack Charlton leads the England pack as Ray Wilson celebrates with the trophy.

He wasn't the only veteran in the team. Garrincha, Pelé and Gilmar might be on their third World Cup campaigns, but defender Djalmar Santos was on his fourth. Vincente Feola was once again in charge of the team, and he recalled Orlando and Bellini, the only two of his 1958 World Cup winners not to pick up a second winners medal in 1962. The side also boasted new talent, with Tostão, Jairzinho and Gérson all making their World Cup debuts in 1966.

With Garrincha and Pelé on the pitch, Brazil beat Bulgaria in their first game, both stars hitting the back of the net with swerving free-kicks. Pelé's goal made him the first player to score in three successive tournaments, while Garrincha's strike, 48 minutes later, made him the second! But it was the last time they would play together for Brazil.

Pelé rides a Bulgarian tackle at Goodison Park.

The game was marred by a series of ugly challenges, Pelé and Bulgarian defender Zhechev fighting a running battle until an injury to Pelé put him out of the next game. It was the only time Brazil would win in this tournament. They were completely unprepared for a European game that had become overtly physical. "In 1966 it was really clear that the Europeans ran so much more than the Brazilians and were physically fitter and had stronger moves," recalls centre-forward Tostão.

The Hungarians faced Portugal without their first choice goalkeeper, losing 3-1. But they fared better against a Brazil team minus the injured Pelé. In an outstanding match, the Hungarians played with skill and flair, Florian Albert's performances reminiscent of the Magical Magyars of the past. Bene gave them the lead after two minutes, Tostão equalising for Brazil against the run of play. But in the second half Hungary stepped up a gear, the brilliant Albert at the heart of their 3-1 win. It was Brazil's first World Cup defeat since Hungary in the Battle of Berne in 1954, and their first and last defeat with Garrincha in the side.

Garrincha was left out of the next game against Portugal as Brazil, in desperation to stay in the tournament, made nine changes to the team, and gave seven players their World Cup debuts. A crowd of 62,000 at Goodison Park looked on as Pelé was singled out for some particularly vicious tackles. He was carried off injured at the end of the match and threatened to retire from international football aged just 25. "I don't want to finish my life as an invalid," he said. Brazil lost the game 3-1 and were out of the cup. Portugal finished top of the group and Hungary joined them in the quarter-finals. Holders Brazil were on their way home, but they had learnt some valuable lessons that would help them in the rebuilding process.

"Because it failed in 1966 people thought that Brazilian football, the Brazilian style, would start to decline," says Tostão. "People thought that the more European style would prevail, that the collective game was more important than having good players."

"We were really bad in that competition, we were failures," says Carlos Alberto Parreira, Brazil's trainer at the following tournament. "Everyone was expecting Brazil to win the World Cup again but we were knocked out in the first round. We realised that we had the best players but they were not ready to cope with modern football, the intensity of the game, up and down for 90 minutes."

But the lessons they learnt were more than just technical. When it came to football, the memories of 1950 meant that defeat always made Brazilians even hungrier for success. "When Brazil loses a World Cup it is taken by a deep sadness, because it is as if every single one of us – the whole country – was defeated," explains Tostão. "Football transcends a sporting competition. Football is part of the national self-esteem. To lose a World Cup is a great defeat to the athletes. It's as if they were not able to attain the aspirations that the country has. But this actually helps Brazilian football. It makes the player go on to the pitch with an enormous desire to win. The player must die to achieve that."

Group Four kicked off according to form, with the Soviet Union overpowering outsiders North Korea 3-0 and the Italians beating Chile 2-0. The football fans of the host nation warmed to the North Koreans, cheering them to a draw with Chile in their next game. A curiously unbalanced Italian team were run ragged by the Soviets. Italian manager Edmondo Fabbri, having dropped creative striker Gianni Rivera, replaced him with an extra defender, signalling his intention to play for a draw. But the Soviets snatched victory in the 58th minute when Chislenko scored the only goal of the game.

Italy faced North Korea expecting to overcome their defeat to the Soviet Union and qualify in second place, but even the recall of Rivera didn't help them. The slow Italian defence proved incapable of coping with the speed and dexterity of the North Koreans, and after losing Bulgarelli to injury in the 34th minute, ten-man Italy proved no match for their opponents. Pak Doo-ik scored the winning goal and North Korea pulled off the biggest World Cup shock since the USA beat England in 1950. But it wasn't until the next day, when the Soviet Union beat Chile, that the Koreans learned that they had qualified for the knockout

North Korea celebrate after beating Italy 1-0 at Ayresome Park.

phase second to the Soviets. The Italians were out of the tournament and on their return home they would be greeted with abuse and rotten tomatoes, the loss against North Korea having been seen as a national disgrace.

England faced Argentina at Wembley in the first quarter-final. Alan Ball came in for Ian Callaghan, while Geoff Hurst replaced the injured Jimmy Greaves. Hurst had only made his debut for England in February of that year but although he had played for his country just five times, he wasn't the least capped player in the side, that honour going to Martin Peters who had made his debut two months before the tournament and had gained just three caps.

Most significantly, the line-up changes meant that England would be playing a 4-4-2 formation, or more specifically 4-1-3-2, with Hunt and Hurst playing as twin strikers, and with Nobby Stiles sitting in front of the defence as a ball winner who would feed the creative players. "I was there to protect Bobby, to win the ball. After that, if there was a white shirt, pass to it," Stiles would recall. "I was there to read the situation early. Our formation was in fact 4-1-3-2, with me playing in front of the back four and behind Ball, Charlton and Peters." It was the team that had played in the last of the pre-World Cup warm-up games against Poland, minus Greaves. This was the first time that these 11 players had been in the team together and it was the line-up that would win the World Cup for England. But first they had to get past Argentina in what journalist Hugh McIlvanney would describe as, "not so much a football match as an international incident".

"From the very beginning Argentina were committed to a policy of petty fouls. It was really stop start, stop start" recalls Brian Glanville. "Argentina were like the little boy in the storybook: when they were good they were very, very good, when they were bad they were horrid," says Jimmy Armfield, a non-playing England squad member in 1966.

England captain Bobby Moore and Argentina's Antonio Rattín lead out their sides for the World Cup quarter-final at Wembley.

England manager Alf Ramsey refuses to allow George Cohen swap his shirt with an Argentinian player after a bad tempered World Cup quarter-final.

The German referee Rudolf Kreitlein was not slow in cautioning the Argentine players, but captain Antonio Rattín had become so incensed by what he saw as yet another damning example of European bias towards Latin American football that he began a running argument with the official. "He'd already tackled Martin Peters with a thigh high tackle when the ball was on the floor," recalls Banks. "The referee warned Rattín, 'Another one of them and you're off'."

After 36 minutes the referee finally lost patience as Antonio Rattín continued to remonstrate about a foul that had been given against his team-mate. The Argentine captain was ordered from the field, sparking ten minutes of mayhem as he refused to go, bringing most of the Argentinian bench into the heated argument. For a while it seemed that the whole team would walk off in protest.

"He just would not accept a foul that the referee had given and he followed him around and kept going on about his armband, you know 'I'm the captain, I can speak to you'," recalls Bobby Charlton. "But he wouldn't go. They had to bring some of the FIFA representatives from out of the stand to get the game started again. It was good news for us that Rattín got sent off – the most influential player in the team. I couldn't believe it. He was a professional player. Who would do something so stupid?"

Ten-man Argentina held out until 13 minutes from time when a header from Hurst put England in to the semi-finals. Alf Ramsey was so incensed by the behaviour of the Argentinians that on the final whistle he took to the field, physically preventing his players from exchanging shirts with the opposition. In an ill-

Eusébio leaves the field in tears after Portugal's defeat to England in World Cup semi-final. He was regarded by many as the best player of the tournament.

advised television interview after the game he said: "We had still to produce our best and this best is not possible until we meet the right type of opposition, and that is a team who comes out to play football and not to act as animals." In Argentina, such was the furore caused by the England coach that it was as if he had called the entire nation "animals". Although Ramsey withdrew the statement under FA pressure, it would be the cause of a deeply held rivalry between the two countries that would last for many years.

The quarter-final between Uruguay and West Germany was equally unpleasant. The South Americans had looked the better side in an open first half, but the second period descended into violence. The Germans reacted to provocation, Emmerich kicking Troche, only for the Uruguayan to respond with a kick to the stomach. Troche was sent off and he slapped Seeler in the face as he left the field. Minutes later Uruguay were down to nine men and Germany cruised home with four goals in the last 20 minutes.

The Soviet Union pressed the Hungarians into making mistakes in their quarter-final at Sunderland's Roker Park, as twice goalkeeper Gelei blundered to allow the Soviets to win the tie 2-1. The popular North Koreans brought a sense of high drama to their clash with Portugal at Goodison Park, taking a 3-0 lead in just 25 minutes. But inevitably, Eusébio, the tournament's most outstanding star and its top scorer, kicked off Portugal's comeback with four goals. Augusto added a fifth to clinch the match 5-3.

West Germany took on the Soviet Union at Goodison Park in the first semi-final. It was another bruising encounter marred by poor sportsmanship and violent conduct. The Soviets ended the match with nine men, having lost 2-1. England's match with Portugal at Wembley was altogether different. Portugal struggled to breach England's resolute defence and Bobby Charlton was outstanding going forward, scoring in each half to put England two ahead. A penalty pulled one back for Portugal but it was too late and England were through to the World Cup final. "When the final whistle went in that game, we knew we had got there," says Gordon Banks. "You felt a tear in your eye and a tingling feeling knowing that England were actually going to play in a World Cup final. When we got into the dressing room, the rest of the squad were waiting for us and they'd got all the champagne and the beers ready. It was a great feeling that day."

On July 30, 1966, the crowds flocked to Wembley to see England take on West Germany. On the eve of the final the two managers had been faced with tough decisions that could affect the course of the match. Ramsey had to decide whether to recall a now fit Jimmy Greaves, or stick with a winning team and formation. He chose continuity. England's greatest striker was forced to endure the game from the stands. It was a devastating blow for Greaves, the England player who had always been most certain that England would win the World Cup.

Helmut Schön, meanwhile, was pondering a tactical dilemma – how to best use Franz Beckenbauer. Many believe the decision that he took cost his team the world title. "Before the match Helmut Schön and his assistant decided that I should mark Bobby Charlton," recalls Beckenbauer. "They knew that if I did it would reduce my own strength for attacking, but they were insistent. 'It's very important,' Schön said, 'because you're fast enough to stay with him, to control him'. At the time he was the best player in the world and he also had lungs like a horse. I never remember being as exhausted as I was playing that afternoon."

Uwe Seeler shakes hands with Bobby Moore before the start of the World Cup final.

When the match kicked off England made the worst possible start, Haller scoring for the Germans in the 13th minute from a weak clearance by Ray Wilson. Six minutes later Geoff Hurst headed in a quickly taken Bobby Moore free-kick to make it 1-1. Both sides continued to press forward in the second half, until with only 12 minutes left, Peters latched on to a poor German defensive clearance to give the hosts the lead. England looked likely winners as full-time approached, but in the final minute the referee gave a controversial free-kick to West Germany, from which Weber equalised. "As soon as we'd kicked off he blew for full time," recalls Bobby Charlton. "I'd been concentrating so much I never looked to see how much time we had left."

With 30 minutes of extra-time ahead of them, some of the exhausted West German team dropped to the pitch. "We were starting to drop on the floor too," says Gordon Banks. "Alf came round, a very shrewd man, saying, 'Get up, get up'. They were looking up at us thinking, 'Wow, they must be super-fit, they're not sitting down' – but believe me, we were tired before extra-time started."

Alf Ramsey, the General, chose the perfect words to rally his troops, as Jack Charlton recalls: "He said, 'You've won it once, now you're going to have to win it again'."

England went on the attack immediately, with Alan Ball a dynamo in midfield running tirelessly for the team. They had already gone close twice when, in the tenth minute of extra-time, Hurst thumped a pass from Alan Ball against the underside of the bar, the ball bouncing down to the goal line. England celebrated,

Opposite: The 1966 World Cup final. (above) Geoff Hurst scores England's controversial third goal. (below) Bobby Moore kisses the trophy, watched by George Cohen, Geoff Hurst and Martin Peters. (Overleaf) Bobby Charlton raises the trophy, surrounded by team-mates Gordon Banks, Ray Wilson Alan Ball, Bobby Moore and George Cohen.

England 4 West Germany 2

0:1 HELMUT HALLER (GER) 12', 1:1 GEOFF HURST (ENG) 18', 2:1 MARTIN PETERS (ENG) 78', 2:2 WOLFGANG WEBER (FRG) 89', 3:2 GEOFF HURST (ENG) 101', 4:2 GEOFF HURST (ENG) 120'.

1 — G. BANKS 2 — G. COHEN 3 — R. WILSON 4 — N. STILES 5 — J. CHARLTON 6 — R. MOORE

7 — A. BALL 8 — J. GREAVES

9 — R. CHARLTON 10 — G. HURST

11 — J. CONNELLY R. SPRINGETT

13 — P. BONETTI 14 — J. ARMFIELD

15 — G. BYRNE 16 — M. PETERS

WORLD CHAMPIONSHIP
JULES RIMET CUP
Final
ENGLAND v WEST GERMANY
SATURDAY · JULY 30 · 1966
EMPIRE STADIUM
WEMBLEY PRICE 2/6

WORLD CHAMPIONSHIP 1966
Jules Rimet Cup
FINAL TIE

17 — R. FLOWERS 18 — N. HUNTER 19 — T. PAINE 20 — I. CALLAGHAN 21 — R. HUNT 22 — G. EASTHAM

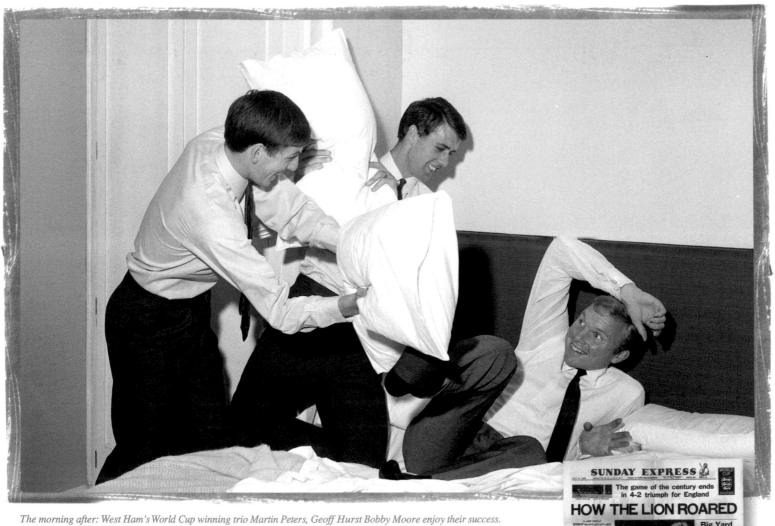

The morning after: West Ham's World Cup winning trio Martin Peters, Geoff Hurst Bobby Moore enjoy their success.

SUNDAY EXPRESS

The game of the century ends in 4-2 triumph for England

HOW THE LION ROARED

Big Yard swoop: 12 held

Callaghan may force Cabinet shuffle

Reader Harris told to repay £1,360

UNIVERSITY MEN TO BE FREED.

the West Germans protested. "I'm looking at it and it looked a goal to me," says Bobby Charlton. "Then suddenly I panicked because the referee went running over to the linesman and I thought 'he's not give it'." After consulting linesman Tofik Bakhramov, the referee gave the goal and it was 3-2 to England.

The controversy about whether the ball had crossed the line would rage for many years, but for England defender Jack Charlton there was no debate: "If the linesman says it was a goal and the referee says it was a goal, then it's a goal. They're in charge."

In the last minute the debate became academic, as Geoff Hurst became the first and only player to score a hat-trick in World Cup final history, sealing a famous win. The move started when Bobby Moore collected the ball near his own corner flag. "We're all shouting, 'Get rid of it Bobby, get rid of it'," says Gordon Banks. "He saw Geoff running and he humped it long and it sailed to Geoff. He's clean through and wallop, straight into the top corner, what a goal. I knew then that was it, we'd won the World Cup."

With Geoff Hurst bearing down on the German keeper, Kenneth Wolstenholme's BBC television commentary passed into football history as the ball hit the back of the net. "Some people are on the pitch, they think it's all over… *it is now!*"

Ramsey's approach had paid off. He'd brought change where it was needed, and kept those elements of the past that could still serve England well. A country used to living in the past was now bang up to date.

GROUP 1

July 11: Wembley Stadium, London
England **0 - 0** Uruguay

July 13: Wembley Stadium, London
France **1 - 1** Mexico

July 15: White City, London
Uruguay **2 - 1** France

July 16: Wembley Stadium, London
England **2 - 0** Mexico

July 19: Wembley Stadium, London
Uruguay **0 - 0** Mexico

July 20: Wembley Stadium, London
England **2 - 0** France

	P	W	D	L	F	A	Pts
England	3	2	1	0	4	0	5
Uruguay	3	1	2	0	2	1	4
Mexico	3	0	2	1	1	3	2
France	3	0	1	2	2	5	1

GROUP 2

July 12: Hillsborough, Sheffield
West Germany **5 - 0** Switzerland

July 13: Villa Park, Birmingham
Argentina **2 - 1** Spain

July 15: Hillsborough, Sheffield
Spain **2 - 1** Switzerland

July 16: Villa Park, Birmingham
Argentina **0 - 0** West Germany

July 19: Hillsborough, Sheffield
Argentina **2 - 0** Switzerland

July 20: Villa Park, Birmingham
West Germany **2 - 1** Spain

	P	W	D	L	F	A	Pts
West Germany	3	2	1	0	7	1	5
Argentina	3	2	1	0	4	1	5
Spain	3	1	0	2	4	5	2
Switzerland	3	0	0	3	1	9	0

GROUP 3

July 12: Goodison Park, Liverpool
Brazil **2 - 0** Bulgaria

July 13: Old Trafford, Manchester
Portugal **3 - 1** Hungary

July 15: Goodison Park, Liverpool
Hungary **3 - 1** Brazil

July 16: Old Trafford, Manchester
Portugal **3 - 0** Bulgaria

July 19: Goodison Park, Liverpool
Portugal **3 - 1** Brazil

July 20: Old Trafford, Manchester
Hungary **3 - 1** Bulgaria

	P	W	D	L	F	A	Pts
Portugal	3	3	0	0	9	2	6
Hungary	3	2	0	1	7	5	4
Brazil	3	1	0	2	4	6	2
Bulgaria	3	0	0	3	1	8	0

GROUP 4

July 12: Ayresome Park, Middlesbrough
Soviet Union **3 - 0** North Korea

July 13: Roker Park, Sunderland
Italy **2 - 0** Chile

July 15: Ayresome Park, Middlesbrough
Chile **1 - 1** North Korea

July 16: Roker Park, Sunderland
Soviet Union **1 - 0** Italy

July 19: Ayresome Park, Middlesbrough
North Korea **1 - 0** Italy

July 20: Roker Park, Sunderland
Soviet Union **2 - 1** Chile

	P	W	D	L	F	A	Pts
Soviet Union	3	3	0	0	6	1	6
North Korea	3	1	1	1	2	4	3
Italy	3	1	0	2	2	2	2
Chile	3	0	1	2	2	5	1

THE FINAL

ENGLAND (1) **4**

WEST GERMANY (1) **2**

(AET: 2-2 AT 90 MINS)

DATE Saturday July 30, 1966
ATTENDANCE 93,802
VENUE Wembley Stadium

ENGLAND
COACH: ALF RAMSEY

BANKS

COHEN

CHARLTON, J

MOORE

WILSON

STILES

CHARLTON, R

PETERS ⚽
Goal: 78 mins. Booked.

BALL

HUNT

HURST ⚽⚽⚽
Goal: 18 mins, 101 mins, 120 mins

WEST GERMANY
COACH: HELMUT SCHÖN

TILKOWSKI

HÖTTGES

SCHULZ

WEBER ⚽
Goal: 90 mins

SCHNELLINGER

HALLER ⚽
Goal: 12 mins

BECKENBAUER

OVERATH

SEELER

HELD

EMMERICH

REFEREE: Dienst (Switzerland)

QUARTER-FINALS

July 23: Wembley Stadium, London
England **1 - 0** Argentina

July 23: Hillsborough, Sheffield
West Germany **4 - 0** Uruguay

July 23: Goodison Park, Liverpool
Portugal **5 - 3** North Korea

July 23: Roker Park, Sunderland
Soviet Union **2 - 1** Hungary

SEMI-FINALS

July 25: Goodison Park, Liverpool
West Germany **2 - 1** Soviet Union

July 26: Wembley Stadium, London
England **2 - 1** Portugal

THIRD-PLACE PLAY-OFF

July 28: Wembley Stadium, London
Portugal **2 - 1** Soviet Union

Moment of indecision: Geoff Hurst waits for the linesman to call England's third goal.

 TOP GOALSCORERS 9 goals: Eusébio (Portugal) **5 goals:** Helmut Haller (West Germany) **4 goals:** Geoff Hurst (England), Franz Beckenbauer (West Germany), Ferenc Bene (Hungary), Valeri Porkujan (Soviet Union)

FASTEST GOAL 1 minute: Pak Seung-zin (North Korea v Portugal)

TOTAL GOALS: 89 **AVERAGE GOALS** 2.78 per game

THE BEAUTIFUL TEAM

Despite the altitude and the heat, Mexico 70 became the most successful tournament ever, the beautiful team of Pelé, Rivelino and Jairzinho winning Brazil's third World Cup.

A gainst all the odds, despite the heat and altitude, the scandals and the scheduling, Mexico 70 turned out to be the most exciting tournament in World Cup history. Confounding all the predictions, it proved a showcase for some of the most sublime international football ever seen, for the first time transmitted in colour around the world. Television added a new dimension to the competition, bringing the noise and the mayhem of the mighty *Stadio Azteca* to every corner of the globe – live as it happened! It also gave billions of fans worldwide the ability to pass instant opinions on decisive moments: Mexico 70 gave us the greatest game ever, the greatest save, the greatest tackle, the greatest player, and above all, in the magical Brazil side, the greatest team. Watching them on the attack was an awe-inspiring experience. This was the World Cup where football really did become 'the beautiful game'.

The decision to host the World Cup in Mexico was taken at the FIFA Congress held at the Tokyo Olympics on October 8, 1964. Mexico was already due to stage the 1968 Olympics and it seemed strange that the country should be chosen ahead of Argentina, who had been trying to host the tournament since 1938. Against a backdrop of heavy lobbying and political machinations, Mexico won the ballot by 56 votes to 32.

Mexico wasn't viewed as the ideal World Cup host. Temperatures at most venues reached well over 90 degrees, threatening to stifle any chance of free-flowing football, while the country's energy-sapping high altitude caused breathing difficulties, particularly for the European teams. To make matters worse, in an

Jairzinho is carried by fans after Brazil's World Cup final victory over Italy. He had become the first player in World Cup history to score in every match.

The Brazilians in training at the beginning of their World Cup preparations, March 1970. Pelé is third from the left.

agreement made to placate European television interests, all Sunday matches, including the final, would kick off in the intense midday sun, conditions deemed hazardous for a light stroll and madness for a high-energy football competition.

For Brazil, their triumphant performance was a giant turn around in their fortunes. The 1966 World Cup had been disastrous for them, their ageing side unable to match the endurance or aggression of the Europeans. In Río angry crowds had gathered to protest at the ineffectual displays, burning effigies in protest and waving banners denouncing coach Vincente Feola and João Havelange, president of the Brazilian Sports Confederation. Even their biggest star was becoming disillusioned with international football. "There is only one way to describe Brazil's 1966 World Cup effort," said Pelé. "And that is to declare that from beginning to end it was a total and unmitigated disaster."

Several coaches would take their turn in charge of the national team after the World Cup, but in 1969 Brazil made the strangest of appointments, giving the job to the outspoken journalist and radio commentator, João Saldanha. It was a decision viewed by the wider world as yet another sign that Brazil was a football power in terminal decline. Saldanha had played for Botafogo for a short time before going into journalism, but in 1957, despite his complete lack of managerial experience, he was the surprise selection as coach of Botafogo. An eccentric and volatile character prone to brandishing a revolver in disputes with football opponents, his spell at the club was relatively successful but very brief. The future of Brazil's national team now appeared to be in his hands.

Off the pitch the country was also experiencing a period of change and uncertainty. In 1964 Brazil's populist president João Goulart had been ousted in a non-violent *coup d'état* which saw a change in the country's constitution, allowing for a neutered Congress to elect a succession of presidential dictators from amongst the ranks of the military. Moves towards social equality had threatened the vested interests of those with power and money. The military had seized control of the government, with the ultimate goal of returning power to civilian politicians only when the left-wing threat was suppressed.

For the ordinary Brazilian, social progress seemed as far away as ever. Their passion for football, and its ability to unite the nation, was still a potent force but the military blatantly manipulated it for its own advantage. And there was no better manipulator than General Emílio Garrastazú Médici, who became President of Brazil on October 30, 1969.

Médici's great strength was that he knew how to manipulate media messages and influence the country through the use of that powerful weapon, television. He was also an ardent football fan and he understood the significant role that football played in shaping Brazil. "Football was one of the flags or shop windows that the dictatorship used," explains journalist João Maximo.

Daily life for many Brazilians had become harder under Médici, the most severe dictator the country had experienced. He established a strong military government and suppressed any opposition to his rule. Even the designer of Brazil's iconic yellow strip, Aldyr Schlee, was made to suffer for his left-wing views. "Brazil was living in the leaden years, as they are called," explains Schlee. "We had terrible experiences. In that period I was a university professor. I was the subject of 13 investigations by the military. I was arrested. I was expelled from the university. It was difficult for me to find work, just to survive."

His was a common experience, but football was treated very differently by the military dictatorship. When Pelé became the first professional to score 1,000 goals in 1969, the occasion was celebrated with an ostentatious and well-publicised gift from the President – a gold football. An armchair coach, Médici was even a familiar face at the Maracanã, where he would go to watch his beloved Flamengo, exerting his influence to encourage the club to sign his favourite player, Dario.

Brazil's new football coach João Saldanha was never going to be a favourite of the right-wing military. A communist sympathiser and a former journalist, Saldanha was ideologically opposed to a government responsible for the suppression of the free press. For a while, though, his results were enough to keep him in his job. On his appointment he had demanded complete control as he attempted to build a side totally focused on scoring goals, and under his stewardship Brazil had cruised through the World Cup qualifiers, Tostão and Pelé forging a prolific partnership up front.

General Médici came to power soon after qualification had been achieved, and he invited the successful Brazil side for lunch at the Presidential Palace. Saldanha refused to alter the team's training schedule to allow the players to attend, and in March 1970 he succeeded in compounding the insult. When asked by a journalist why he had not considered the President's favourite player Dario for selection, he replied: "I don't choose the President's ministry and he can't chose my frontline". If that wasn't bad enough, he announced that he was considering dropping Pelé. Saldanha was sacked and the establishment took the necessary steps to ensure that Pelé was back in the team. They knew the value of football all too well and the wave of optimism that a victory would generate. Médici claimed that he would not interfere directly with the team, but the new coaching staff included several military figures, including Captain Claudio Coutinho, a retired military physical training expert who had even spent time at NASA, assessing what Brazilian footballers could learn from the fitness regime of the Apollo astronauts. One and a half million dollars and three months was spent on preparing the team for the heat and altitude of Mexico under their new manager, the double World Cup winning winger Mario Zagalo.

As the Brazil team arrived in Mexico the stakes were as high as in 1950, but the players had left behind a very different country, the national pride inspired by their victories was now serving a new kind of purpose. The players tried to put this out of their minds. "We went to honour Brazil," says Rivelino. "You're wearing the yellow, the Brazil shirts, you want to do the best for your country. We weren't there to think about the problems of the country or the dictatorship or to be used by the government."

"After every victory the people celebrated in the street and that was a kind of escape," remembers captain Carlos Alberto. "That political moment in Brazil was bad for our people. We co-operated with our country to give at least a happiness for our people."

While Brazil had qualified for the finals with ease, four of the eight quarter-finalists from 1966 had failed to make it to Mexico. Argentina were knocked out by Peru, a surprise package managed by Brazilian World Cup winner Didi. Portugal's ageing stars finished bottom of a group topped by Romania, while reigning Olympic champions Hungary, tipped to be strong contenders, were knocked out after a 4-1 play-off defeat by Czechoslovakia. North Korea refused to play against Israel and were forced by FIFA to withdraw, the only one of the 71 entrants to do so this time. Italy's campaign went down to their last game, where they beat East Germany 3-0 to qualify, while West Germany set a qualification record, putting 12 goals past Cyprus in Essen, despite having only beaten them 1-0 in the away leg six months earlier. Belgium, having been accepted automatically for the first two tournaments, qualified for the finals for the first time, as did Israel.

It was also the first World Cup for El Salvador, but it didn't come without a price for the Central Americans. Their play-off game with Honduras sparked a war between two countries already mistrustful of each other for over a century. After their defeat Honduras expelled thousands of Salvadorian migrant workers. El Salvador replied by sending tanks across the border and both countries mobilised their tiny air forces. The 'Football War' lasted six days, in which time at least 2,000 were killed. It ended with a cease-fire. A peace treaty would not be signed for another ten years.

The format of the World Cup remained largely unaltered, although the tossing of a coin was introduced to settle a tie if teams were equal after extra-time in the knockout stages of the tournament. Substitutes were allowed for the first time, two per team in each game, FIFA ruling that squad members did not have to wear the Number 13 shirt if they were superstitious. The first 'official' World Cup ball was introduced too. With 32 black and white panels, the Adidas-created 'Telstar' was far more visible on TV and became the symbol of the tournament. The Telstar ball would be used again in 1974, and from that point onwards Adidas would develop a new ball for each tournament.

The 1970 World Cup also saw the first use of red and yellow cards. Following the furore caused by Argentina's Antonio Rattín at the 1966 World Cup, Ken Aston of FIFA's Referees' Committee decided that some kind of visual clarification was needed in case a player either did not understand, or chose not to understand, that he had been sent off. Not only had Aston refereed the infamous Battle of Santiago between Italy and Chile at the 1962 World Cup, he had been called to the Wembley touchline in 1966 to resolve matters after Rattín's refusal to leave the pitch. His idea for red and yellow cards was much debated by FIFA before its adoption in 1970. "That became the standard worldwide," says Antonio Rattín, the unwitting inspiration for the cards. "Had there been a yellow card in the 1966 World Cup, I wouldn't have been sent off. They would have shown me the yellow card and I would have kept my mouth shut and that would have been that and I wouldn't have had to ask for the interpreter. There needed to be some sort of distinction so that everyone knew what was going on, not just the crowds in the stadium, but also the billions of football fans watching around the world."

Hosts Mexico kicked off the tournament with a lifeless 0-0 draw against the Soviet Union at the Azteca, a glorious stadium completed four years earlier at a cost of £7 million. Their second game against the part-timers of El Salvador proved more eventful. Just before half-time, with the match goalless, El Salvador were awarded a free-kick after a foul. But to their surprise, Mexican Aarón Padilla quickly took the kick, setting up Javier Valdivia for a goal. The El Salvador players protested, but Egyptian referee Ali Kandil allowed the goal to stand. Demoralised, El Salavador went on to lose 4-0. Mexico sneaked past Belgium thanks to a disputed penalty and qualified from Group One along with the Soviet Union, the two teams dropping only a point each.

The ultra-cautious Italians qualified as leaders of Group Two without conceding a goal, scoring just once. Scarred by their early exit from the 1966 competition at the hands of North Korea, the Italians relied on a mastery of *catenaccio* to keep opponents at bay, packing men behind the ball and placing most of the goalscoring ambitions with their immensely talented striker Luigi Riva. Their football was proving so dull that after their game with Uruguay, both sets of fans booed their own players off the pitch. "It must have been bad to watch," admitted Riva. Uruguay joined Italy in the quarter-finals after Sweden had beaten the South Americans by just one goal rather than the two they required. Israel finished at the bottom of the table.

Group Three had been dubbed the 'Group of Death', pitching England against Brazil, Czechoslovakia and Romania. Alf Ramsey had been thinking of this moment since his side had lifted the trophy four years earlier. "Everyone seems concerned about what I'm going to do," Ramsey had said in the Wembley dressing room in 1966. "But there is another World Cup in Mexico in four years. It's good to have won at home. It will be good to win there."

The England team that travelled to Mexico in 1970 was fundamentally the same as the one that had won in 1966, albeit having gone through Ramsey's updating process. Attacking full-backs Keith Newton and Terry Cooper had come in for Cohen and Wilson, Brian Labone was gradually taking over from Jack Charlton,

WORLD CUP STORIES

CARLOS ALBERTO
Brazil's captain scored the winning goal in the World Cup final.

"We didn't have a good start in Brazil with the training for the World Cup, but when Mario Zagalo took over we started to understand the way to play in Mexico. In my opinion Zagalo was the cleverest coach I ever saw because it was easy to understand him, and the results were a hundred per cent better. We helped him with the experience we had. He was the kind of coach who gives the freedom to the players to talk about the best way to play different games.

"We went to Mexico one month before the competition and we were very confident with the results of the physical preparation. We felt very good. Pelé was saying that we were going to win, and if Pelé is saying that, then we are going to win the World Cup. We were very focused because many of the players knew this was the last chance to play in a World Cup. I was lucky because I scored a goal in the final. It was my first and only goal in the World Cup.

"It is difficult to describe what I felt after the game. The goal was the best moment in my career, but as captain I also went to receive a trophy that was coming to Brazil forever. I took the Jules Rimet Trophy on behalf of the one hundred million people in Brazil. We knew everybody was watching the World Cup on TV for the first time. I don't know words to describe what I felt at that moment, the moment you become champion of the world.

"After we received the trophy I was the first player to ever kiss it before it was passed to the other players. I don't know why, it was my first reaction. I didn't plan to do that. Maybe it was because the trophy is so beautiful. It's not a big trophy but it is so important."

WORLD CUP STORIES

JAIRZINHO

With seven goals in the tournament the Brazil forward became the only player in World Cup history to score in every game.

"When I first started to play in the 1970 World Cup I never had the idea of being the top scorer, and I didn't think about the possibility of winning the Golden Boot. I really played for that team. All of the players, like myself, Pelé, Tostão and Rivelino, were extremely offensive and it wasn't planned that any one of us should be the main striker for the Brazilian team. We all had the freedom to go up front and score, and all the goals that I scored just happened to come naturally.

"I think it was the only time in the history of Brazilian football that we had five players in the international side who were all strikers in their own club sides. Gérson and Rivelino were strikers playing as offensive midfielders, Tostão was a centre-forward who served all sides, Pelé was an offensive striker, and I was also an offensive right-sided striker. I started off playing as a reserve for Garrincha on the right wing, and in the finals of 1966 I even played on the left wing, but I also played as a central striker. All of us played at number 10 in our own teams.

"Gerd Müller scored a lot of goals with his head, because in European football there are a lot of plays that are done in the air, therefore it is easier for a European player to score goals. Brazilian players are more used to playing the ball on the pitch and this is what Brazilian football is all about; a lot of technique, a lot of skill. I was able to score in every round and I got a prize for that. Gerd Müller might have won the Golden Boot, but my name is more remembered from that 1970 World Cup than the name of Gerd Müller. He was one of the best players of all time, but if you go back to 1970, the name Jairzinho has a much stronger remembrance than Gerd Müller."

Jairzinho celebrates after scoring his side's third goal in the World Cup final at the Azteca Stadium.

Nobby Stiles made way for Alan Mullery, and the hard-working Francis Lee had replaced Roger Hunt. But Banks, Ball, Charlton, Moore, Hurst and Peters remained in the starting line-up, with Jack Charlton and Nobby Stiles still reliable squad members. The new team was quicker than the '66 vintage, adept at moving the ball forward at great speed to their sharp shooting frontline. "I think we have an excellent chance and we have a stronger party than in 1966," said Ramsey as his squad departed for Mexico. "Providing we can acclimatise properly I think it will take a great team to beat us." This was the first time that England had ever travelled to a World Cup with the backing of the whole nation. Their journey, however, had not been without complication.

England arrived in Mexico without their captain, Bobby Moore, who was being held by police in Colombia after being accused of shoplifting. Before beating Colombia 4-0 in a World Cup warm up match, Moore and Bobby Charlton had been questioned over the theft of an emerald bracelet from the Fuego Verde gift shop at the team's headquarters at the Tequendama Hotel in Bogotá. Initially the accusation was dismissed as a set-up and the players released, but several days later, after the belated appearance of a mysterious 'witness', Bobby Moore was arrested and charged with the theft. The England squad had to fly on to Mexico without him, Alf Ramsey announcing the shocking news to the players after their plane had taken off.

England had arrived as favourites, but Mexico provided a very different sort of challenge to that of the lush green of Wembley. "You now didn't just have to conquer the opposition," says Gordon Banks, "you had to conquer the altitude, the heat, and these were enormous things."

Alf Ramsey's brusque manner with the media had already alienated the Mexican press a year earlier on what was supposed to be England's goodwill visit to the country. Now they were waiting for him. After the Bobby Moore story, the World Cup holders were even dubbed a "team of thieves and drunks" in the Mexican press, nervous flier Jeff Astle having arrived in the country worse for wear after trying to calm his nerves on a particularly rough flight. There would be other stories for the press to chase too.

"Alf decided that the food was too dangerous there," recalls Bobby Charlton, "so we took our own chef and some of our own food – sausages and things like that. The Mexican media went crazy. They were insulted that their food wasn't good enough for the English. From the beginning we got off on the wrong foot and we were unpopular throughout the country. Nobody wanted us to win."

There had been a real fear that Bobby Moore would not be released in time for the World Cup, with even British Prime Minister Harold Wilson becoming involved in diplomatic negotiations before the England captain was finally bailed and allowed to join the team. In the meantime, Moore's former England colleague Jimmy Greaves had stopped off to visit him whilst in the middle of the first ever World Cup Rally Championship, a tortuous 16,000-mile drive that had started from Wembley Stadium. Bobby Moore's case would not formally be dropped until 1972, although he didn't receive official notification from Colombian authorities until December 1975. Moore was able to rejoin the team just five days before their first game against Romania at the Jalisco Stadium in Guadalajara. England were playing a 4-4-2, with 'Frannie' Lee partnering Hurst in attack. Despite the catcalls and boos from the Mexican crowd that greeted the team as they walked on to the pitch, they left with a 1-0 victory thanks to a 65th minute Geoff Hurst goal.

Brazil had been singled out for some particularly rough treatment at the two previous World Cups, but in 1970 FIFA had put some strict guidelines in place to stop such foul play. This allowed Brazil to play the brand of stylish, attacking football that they had once been famous for. All the better then that Mario Zagalo managed to solve Brazil's greatest conundrum – how to fit Pelé, Tostão, Gérson, Rivelino and Jairzinho into the same team. It had taken a small palace revolution to arrive at this solution. In the weeks leading up to the squad's departure from Brazil, a disillusioned Pelé, Gérson and Carlos Alberto presented Zagalo with their preferred formation. He was prepared to try out the scheme and saw that the team's shape and fluency had returned for the first time since the departure of Saldanha. "We helped Zagalo with the experience we had," recalls Carlos Alberto. "We had the freedom to exchange opinions with him. It was Zagalo's job but he gave us the freedom to talk." With Tostão playing at inside-left slightly behind Pelé and Jairzinho on the right, Rivelino was accommodated nominally on the left-wing, but in reality playing as a covering midfielder given free rein to attack on both flanks. Gérson controlled the play in midfield, with Clodoaldo guarding his rear. With a little help from his former team-mates, Zagalo had created one of the most potent forward lines in football history. In Brazil's first game, Czechoslovakia were on the receiving end of a 4-1 hiding, Jairzinho scoring twice, while Pelé and Rivelino got one apiece.

The outstanding match of the group stage was between twice-champions Brazil and the holders England, although the anti-England fervour being whipped up by the Mexican media had meant that Alf Ramsey's team had been kept awake the night before the game by the continuous noise of Mexican fans drumming, sounding car horns and chanting for Brazil.

In a wonderful end-to-end contest between two teams at the top of their powers, England and Brazil battled it out in a game many people believed should have been the World Cup final. It was a confrontation made famous by an incredible save by Gordon Banks from a goal-bound Pelé header, for an amazing tackle by Bobby Moore, and for one of the best-worked team goals ever seen. "Bobby Moore always said it was his best game for England," says Gordon Banks, "but I always said that as well, that it was *my* best game for England too."

"There were many players that made the difference in that England team because in terms of quality, they were magnificent," recalls Jairzinho. "It was a very special match and there are so many moments from that game that are still remembered, like the goal that I scored, and the save that Gordon Banks made. I remember that save well. I went to the line close to the corner and crossed the ball to Pelé, who was able to strike it with his head, but Banks was able to make a very difficult save – a brilliant save. That play, and other plays during that game, made it a historical match. It was one of the best teams that England has ever put together. Ask any Brazilian – they show games from the 1970 World Cup at least once a month and all Brazilian people have a lot of respect for that 1970 England team. That game is like a lesson. A lot of coaches throughout Brazil use that game as a reference when coaching young players."

A well-worked Jairzinho goal in the 59th minute was enough to beat England. "You want to save every shot," reflects Gordon Banks, "but I think once he had a clear shot at goal really all I could do was advance on him and try and block him, spread myself across him as best I could. But he lifted it over me."

"We should have beaten them in that match," says Bobby Charlton. "In the last five or ten minutes we had two absolute sitters. Francis Lee headed the ball and it hit the goalkeeper on the line, somebody else had a little go and it was cleared off the line. Then Jeff Astle had a sitter of a header. He was good in the air but he headed the ball straight to the goalkeeper. I honestly believe the only team that they were frightened of was us. I don't think they liked playing against us. I think it was a challenge for them to beat the European style. But once they got in front they were a nightmare to play against – they would keep the ball away from you."

This was the match that Brazil most wanted to win. "Brazil only really became the favourites after they'd played England," says Tostão, "because until then England were the real favourites."

However magical the football, those watching at home in Brazil couldn't ignore the oppression of their daily lives. The inner conflict was almost unbearable. "I was staying in the apartment of a friend and we'd

(above) England keeper Gordon Banks makes a remarkable save from a header by Pelé. (below) Gerd Müller celebrates West Germany's winning goal in the quarter-final with England. Looking on is keeper Peter Bonetti, a last minute replacement for Gordon Banks, who was felled by illness.

"You didn't just have to conquer the opposition, you had to conquer the altitude and the heat!" Gordon Banks

BOBBY CHARLTON

The England legend travelled to four World Cups, but in his last appearance he would be controversially substituted by Alf Ramsey.

"Mexico wasn't a happy place for us. It's a Latin country and they didn't want the Europeans to come and win the World Cup in Mexico. We found it quite difficult, with cars sounding their horns, driving round the hotel all night. They thought it was a way to stop us winning, but we had good players and we were not frightened of anybody. Mexico City was a strange sort of place to play. There was the heat but it was the altitude as well and you'd have to gasp for breath. It was very uncomfortable. The first couple of matches took a bit of getting used to.

"While we were in Mexico the Brazilians invited Bobby Moore and myself to go to their training camp, just to say hello. They were really keen to find out from us what sort of things we were doing at the time. The maximum wage had just been abolished in England and I think they wanted us to tell them what sort of wages we were on. They never got good money and as there was really a living to be made in England, they were very curious about it. That was the first time that I actually met Pelé. He was such a talented player with great control and his vision; he read the game and he read positions. He had an arrogance, but not in a bad way; he was a great player, so why should he not strut a little bit. But he was a magical player.

"After we played each other, England and Brazil both went forward to the next stage and we played Germany. We over ran them for the majority of the match and had a two-goal lead, but suddenly, through bad luck more than anything else, the ball just seemed to fall right for them and it was 2-2. Then it was extra-time – we lost another goal and we were out!

"It was the last time I played for England. Alf was very logical. He didn't want to pick players that weren't going to be playing at the next World Cup. I was 34 and I would have been 38. He thought it would be unthinkable that I would still be playing at that sort of level, so on the plane going home he thanked me for all that I had done and said sorry for taking me off against Germany."

Bobby Charlton leaves the pitch after his final record-breaking 106th game for England. Manager Alf Ramsey looks on.

all get together to watch the games," says Aldyr Schlee. "All of us were people who fought against the dictatorship. We decided that we were not going to support Brazil, because this would mean that we were supporting the military dictatorship that would definitely use a victory. So we were watching the game against England when Tostão took the ball, passed it to Jairzinho, who scored against Banks. And my friend took out a revolver and went to the window and was firing away saying, 'Hell! How good to be a Brazilian. What cost there is to be a Brazilian'."

In Group Four were Bulgaria, Morocco, Peru and a West Germany team who had arrived among the favourites to lift the trophy. The experience of the previous World Cup had been positive for the West Germans, who despite losing the final, returned home to a heroes' welcome. Like England they arrived in Mexico with the backbone of their 1966 team still in place, but they were rocked early in their first game when a spirited Moroccan side went into the interval leading by a single goal. When the referee started the second half, it was noticed that the game had kicked off with Moroccan keeper Allal Ben Kassu not yet on the pitch. The game continued for a minute before he rejoined the play, his goal safe until the Germans equalised in the 56th minute through Uwe Seeler, playing in his fourth World Cup. Gerd Müller scored the winner 12 minutes from time.

The West Germans gained maximum points from their games, with Gerd Müller in prolific form. He scored in every group game, including hat-tricks against both Peru and Bulgaria. In an inspired tactical decision, Helmut Schön had decided to play the young Bayern Munich striker at centre-forward in place of the hugely experienced Seeler, who he moved back into an attacking midfield role. To ensure the swap would cause no resentment, Schön had the two players room together.

Outsiders Peru had been schooled in Brazilian style and tactics by coach Didi. Despite trailing Bulgaria 2-0, in the second half the Peruvians turned the tie around, winning 3-2 thanks to a brilliant match-winning goal from Teófilo Cubillas in the 73rd minute. "Right afterwards we found out that a massive earthquake had struck Peru two days before, killing people by their thousands and destroying an entire village," Cubillas would recall. "Nobody wanted us to know prior to the match. But when we realised what had happened, the significance of the victory was trebled: it wasn't only a victory, but also a way of giving joy to people who were suffering." Cubillas scored twice more in the 3-0 victory over Morocco and once in the 3-1 defeat by West Germany, ensuring that Peru would qualify behind the Germans, with Bulgaria and Morocco bottom of the group with a point apiece.

In León the first quarter-final offered a rematch of the 1966 final, although the West Germans thought they might have the beating of the old enemy this time. Two years after their Wembley defeat, the Germans had finally settled an old score with a 1-0 win in Hanover. "It was the first time in history we had beaten the English," says Franz Beckenbauer. "That was when we realised that we could really beat them and lost some of the respect we had."

The West German players still carried something of an inferiority complex into the tie. Some of the players had actually asked Helmut Schön whether they should aim to come second in their group rather than top, so they could face Brazil rather than England in the quarter-final. Schön would have none of it, and once again insisted Beckenbauer mark Bobby Charlton, but this time with the instructions to press forward too, dragging Charlton out of position.

England would go into the game without their safety net, Gordon Banks struck down by illness on the eve of the game. Peter Bonetti had to play in his place. "The first player to go down with a bad tummy in the whole of the time that we were in Central America and it was on the first sudden death match we had to play," recalls Bobby Charlton. "I think we missed Gordon Banks that particular day. He was easily the best goalkeeper in the world at the time. He gave you that feeling of security. You know, at least if the worst comes to the worst, they'd have to get past him."

With a record British TV audience of 30 million watching back home, goals from Alan Mullery and Martin Peters gave England a 2-0 lead and put them in control by early in the second half. After the second goal Alan Ball claims he ran around the pitch shouting, "Goodnight, God bless, see you in Munich". Bobby Charlton was also feeling confident. "We over ran Germany for the majority of the match," he says. But this would be the last of Charlton's record-breaking 106 games for England. Twenty minutes from full-time Ramsey began preparing to substitute the outstanding Charlton, rather than Terry Cooper, who was noticeably flagging at left-back. With Colin Bell warming up on the touchline, Beckenbauer hit a hopeful shot that scuffed the ground and slipped underneath the unfortunate Peter Bonetti. Despite the goal Ramsey went ahead with the substitution and Bell was on the pitch for the restart. "Alf brought our kid off because of the temperatures and the heat we were playing in," says Jack Charlton, a non-playing squad member on that day. "Bobby had played in every match and Alf brought him off when he thought the game was won. Then Uwe Seeler scored the stupidest little goal. He hadn't a clue where it was going, nobody did."

With Beckenbauer free from Charlton's shadow, and the team having made attacking substitutions, West

West German midfielder Franz Beckenbauer fights for the ball with Moroccan Benkhrif Boujemaa in Leon.

Germany were right back in the game. Ramsey's approach that had worked so well in England, faced its toughest test yet. Far from the comfort of Wembley, English football was being examined as never before. The game was 2-2 after 90 minutes and once again England faced extra-time against Germany, but this time Ramsey's troops seemed to have no energy left for the fight. A Geoff Hurst goal was disallowed in the first period, before a close-range volley from Gerd Müller finally eliminated the holders.

"Playing against the Germans, you knew that if you fell below a certain level they would beat you because they were big and strong and athletic," says Bobby Charlton. "It wasn't really my going off that altered the structure of the game. I think once we'd got through the initial enthusiasm and we'd scored two goals and gone into the lead, we switched off a little bit and we used to rely on Gordon Banks – and this time he wasn't there."

In the second quarter-final in Toluca, hosts Mexico had the better of the first half against the Italians, but after the interval coach Ferruccio Valcareggi brought on European Player of the Year Gianni Rivera, who had been kept out of the starting line-up throughout the tournament in favour of Sandrino Mazzola. It was Rivera who turned the game for Italy, setting up two goals and scoring a third, Mexico losing 4-1 to an untypically free-scoring Italy

In Guadalajara, Brazil continued their irrepressible form, getting the better of Peru in a six-goal thriller, Jairzinho maintaining his record of having scored in every round. At the Azteca Uruguay narrowly defeated the Soviet Union with an extra-time goal by substitute Esparrago.

The semi-final between Italy and West Germany saw two European giants contest a thrilling game. Italy took the lead through Roberto Boninsenga, and in typical fashion withdrew to protect their lead. "We rocked the Germans with an early goal and our keeper Enrico Albertosi was the one who largely frustrated them with brilliant saves," recalls Rivera, on as a substitute for Mazzola. "Then despite me and all my team-mates employing delaying tactics, Schnellinger equalised in the last minute of injury time."

Famously, Franz Beckenbauer remained on the field for the second half with a dislocated shoulder, his arm in a sling strapped to his body. Müller edged West Germany into the lead in extra-time, while Tarcisio Burgnich and Riva put Italy back in control at 3-2. Müller – the eventual Golden Boot winner – clawed it back to 3-3 before Rivera finally clinched one of the World Cup's most epic struggles for Italy. "I was furious and I would not let victory be snatched away," recalls Rivera. "I smashed in a curled pass from Boninsenga. It was 4-3 to Italy and I had scored the winner. As soon as that goal went in an incredible feeling of peace took me away." The West Germans returned home to be viewed as 'unlucky losers', welcomed back by some 60,000 cheering fans. In Germany and Italy, despite the lifeless first 90 minutes, and the counter claims in Brazil and England, many still view this as the best match ever played.

The other semi-final pitted together the old South American foes, Uruguay against Brazil in Guadalajara. Whatever the bookies made of Brazil's chances, their semi-final opponents Uruguay were a serious threat. As a consequence of the result in 1950, they were the only side in the world that could truly unnerve Brazil before a ball was kicked. "The Brazilian press talked to us about the 'Ghost of 1950'," says Rivelino. "I said, 'I was four in 1950. How could you try and put that into my head? I wasn't even there."

"That was no good for us psychologically," says Carlos Alberto. "Between 1950 and 1970, the games between Brazil and Uruguay were terrible for us. We lost many of them because we would go to the games and they start to say, 'Hey, they beat you in 1950' and this would make the team go down."

The Uruguayans took an early lead through Cubilla, and immediately pulled men behind the ball. "The beginning of the game was terrible, terrible, terrible," says Carlos Alberto. "We didn't play and Uruguay took the advantage and they scored the first goal. Their coach was very clever because he saw that the key to our team was Jairzinho, and he put one guy to mark Jairzinho and then the team couldn't play."

Italian strikers Luigi Riva and Gianni Rivera walk on to the pitch before their World Cup match against Israel.

Mario Zagalo's side were on equal terms late in the first half when right-half Clodoaldo powered in the equaliser. In the face of some aggressive tackling from Uruguay, the Brazilians took hold of the game and goals from Jairzinho and Rivelino sealed a 3-1 victory. The yellow shirts of Brazil were deservedly through to the final. Late in the game, Pelé almost scored the goal of the tournament, outrageously dummying Uruguayan keeper Mazurkiewicz before pulling his shot just wide.

For Brazil the old enemy had been vanquished as they confronted the demons of 1950. "That phantom of Brazil against Uruguay was there until 1970 for sure," says Carlos Alberto. "But we had a very good team. Thanks to that we finished it."

The final was staged at the Azteca in Mexico City on June 21, 1970, in front of a crowd of 107,000. The global TV audience was 800 million. As Carlos Alberto led his team out it wasn't just this game that mattered.

(Overleaf) Brazil captain Carlos Alberto celebrates scoring his team's fourth goal in the World Cup final.

At stake was the permanent home of the cup itself. The trophy that Jules Rimet had created in 1930 was to be kept by the first team to win it three times. Both Italy and Brazil had won twice, so today's victor would get to keep the trophy forever. For Brazil, a country that defined its history in terms of World Cups, this could be their greatest success by far.

Despite Italy's well-organised *catenaccio* defence marshalled by veteran Giacinto Facchetti, with their deep well of attacking flair Brazil started the final as undoubted favourites. With their frail defence and goalkeeping deficiencies, Brazil were there to be attacked if the Italians chose to do so. Riva was scoring goals again and Boninsegna was on top of his game, but with Valcareggi still constructing a team that favoured Mazzola over Rivera, Italy were limiting their attacking options.

Pelé opened the scoring after 18 minutes, athletically getting his head on the end of Rivelino's cross. Against the run of play, Boninsegna pounced on a careless mistake by Clodoaldo to level the score, but Italy were unable to push on and convert their psychological advantage. They were also unable to match the Brazilians in terms of territory and possession, the skill of the men in yellow shirts leaving the *azzurri* chasing shadows.

"They were good in all areas and really deserved the World Cup," remembers Italy's reserve keeper Dino Zoff. "I don't know if it was the shock of getting that far or simply the fact that the Brazil team was so good that even when we scored, we then went under. They had a squad that was technically good, faster and stronger. We, on the other hand, possibly missed out on strength in the end."

In the 66th minute Gerson's left-footed cross-shot found the back of Albertosi's net, and it was followed by a goal from Jairzinho, making him the only player to have ever scored in every round of the World Cup. "I remember crying," recalls Tostão. "Even before the game had finished I was crying with happiness. And then there was the fourth goal…"

The *coup de grace* was delivered three minutes from time with one of the greatest and most loved goals in football history. The move began in the 86th minute with a striker, Tostão, collecting the ball in his own half. By the time the ball was in the net, eight of Brazil's ten outfield players had been involved in the move. At the conclusion Jairzinho found Pelé, who laid the ball off to his right and into the stride of Brazilian captain Carlos Alberto, who thundered it low into the corner of the goal, making it 4-1 to Brazil.

"I was lucky because I scored a goal," says Carlos Alberto. "And it is a goal that is remembered now, all these years later. Everywhere I go people remember. Even here in Brazil, young people, they didn't see me play football but they know me".

At the final whistle, fans swarmed on the pitch, swallowing up the winning team and hoisting them high upon their shoulders. Brazil had won comprehensively, but it wasn't the score that mattered – it was the way that they had won. Winning established the greatness of Brazilian football once and for all. Winning gave the whole country an escape from the horrors of dictatorship. And winning meant Brazil could keep the trophy that had come to mean so much to her football, her people, and her national identity.

Over the decades Brazil had invested so much in the World Cup that winning it outright was the end of a dream, a sensation so sweet that when captain Carlos Alberto stepped up to receive it, he kissed the tiny trophy. In Brazil victory was a release for millions suffering under an oppressive regime, a solitary ray of hope. Brazil's history had become inextricably linked to the fortunes of the national team. They would go on to win the World Cup again, and again, but it was Mexico 70 and the beautiful team that kept the trophy that bound the name of Brazil to the World Cup forever.

Opposite: The 1970 World Cup final. (top) Carlos Alberto holds aloft the Jules Rimet trophy. (inset) Pelé celebrates with Tostão, Carlos Alberto and Jairzinho. (centre) Pelé embraces Brazilian goalkeeper Ado. (bottom) Brazilian defenders Brito and Gerson tackle Italy's Alessandro Mazzola. (overleaf) The victorious Brazilian team parade the Jules Rimet trophy to jubilant fans on their return home to capital Brasilia.

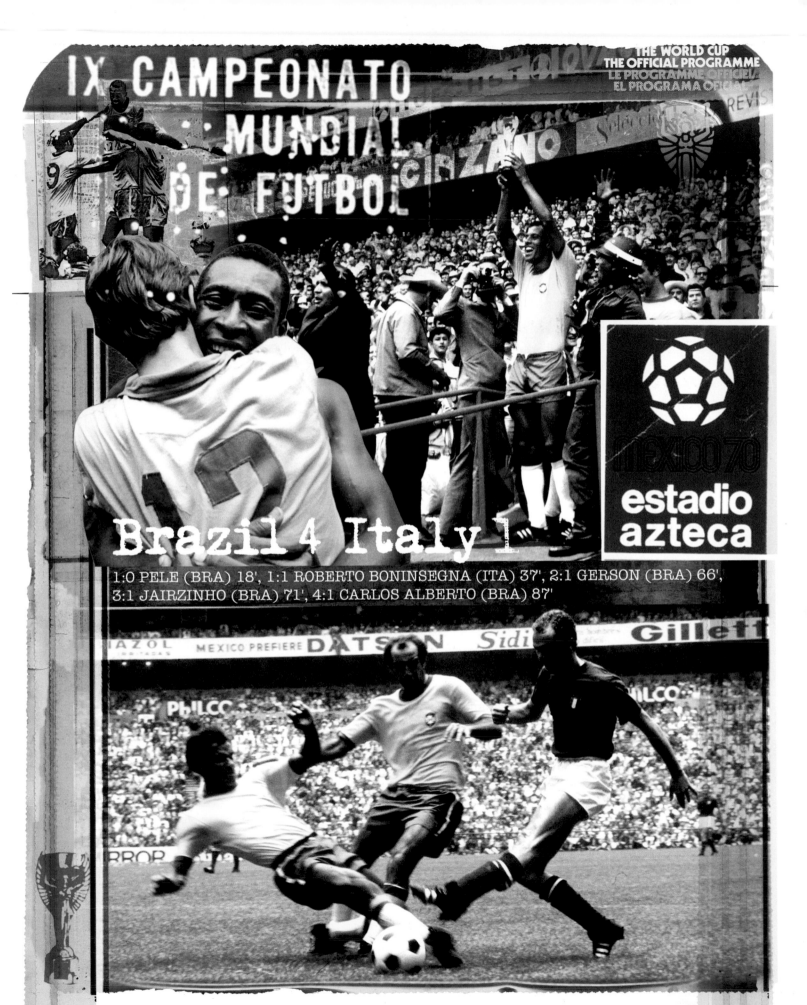

IX CAMPEONATO
MUNDIAL
DE FUTBOL

MEXICO 70
estadio azteca

Brazil 4 Italy 1

1:0 PELE (BRA) 18', 1:1 ROBERTO BONINSEGNA (ITA) 37', 2:1 GERSON (BRA) 66',
3:1 JAIRZINHO (BRA) 71', 4:1 CARLOS ALBERTO (BRA) 87'

GROUP 1

May 31: Azteca Stadium, Mexico City
Mexico **0 - 0** Soviet Union

June 3: Azteca Stadium, Mexico City
Belgium **3 - 0** El Salvador

June 6: Azteca Stadium, Mexico City
Soviet Union **4 - 1** Belgium

June 7: Azteca Stadium, Mexico City
Mexico **4 - 0** El Salvador

June 10: Azteca Stadium, Mexico City
Soviet Union **2 - 0** El Salvador

June 11: Azteca Stadium, Mexico City
Mexico **1 - 0** Belgium

	P	W	D	L	F	A	Pts
Soviet Union	3	2	1	0	6	1	5
Mexico	3	2	1	0	5	0	5
Belgium	3	1	0	2	4	5	2
El Salvador	3	0	0	3	0	9	0

GROUP 2

June 2: Cuauhtemoc Stadium, Puebla
Uruguay **2 - 0** Israel

June 3: Luis Dosal Stadium, Toluca
Italy **1 - 0** Sweden

June 6: Cuauhtemoc Stadium, Puebla
Uruguay **0 - 0** Italy

June 7: Luis Dosal Stadium, Toluca
Sweden **1 - 1** Israel

June 10: Cuauhtemoc Stadium, Puebla
Sweden **1 - 0** Uruguay

June 11: Luis Dosal Stadium, Toluca
Italy **0 - 0** Israel

	P	W	D	L	F	A	Pts
Italy	3	1	2	0	1	0	4
Uruguay	3	1	1	1	2	1	3
Sweden	3	1	1	1	2	2	3
Israel	3	0	2	1	1	3	2

GROUP 3

June 2: Jalisco Stadium, Guadalajara
England **1 - 0** Romania

June 3: Jalisco Stadium, Guadalajara
Brazil **4 - 1** Czechoslovakia

June 6: Jalisco Stadium, Guadalajara
Romania **2 - 1** Czechoslovakia

June 7: Jalisco Stadium, Guadalajara
Brazil **1 - 0** England

June 10: Jalisco Stadium, Guadalajara
Brazil **3 - 2** Romania

June 11: Jalisco Stadium, Guadalajara
England **1 - 0** Czechoslovakia

	P	W	D	L	F	A	Pts
Brazil	3	3	0	0	8	3	6
England	3	2	0	1	2	1	4
Romania	3	1	0	2	4	5	2
Czechoslovakia	3	0	0	3	2	7	0

GROUP 4

June 2: Guanajuato Stadium, León
Peru **3 - 2** Bulgaria

June 3: Guanajuato Stadium, León
West Germany **2 - 1** Morocco

June 6: Guanajuato Stadium, León
Peru **3 - 0** Morocco

June 7: Guanajuato Stadium, León
West Germany **5 - 2** Bulgaria

June 10: Guanajuato Stadium, León
West Germany **3 - 1** Peru

June 11: Guanajuato Stadium, León
Morocco **1 - 1** Bulgaria

	P	W	D	L	F	A	Pts
West Germany	3	3	0	0	10	4	6
Peru	3	2	0	1	7	5	4
Bulgaria	3	0	1	2	5	9	1
Morocco	3	0	1	2	2	6	1

THE FINAL

BRAZIL	(1) **4**
ITALY	(1) **1**

DATE Sunday June 21, 1970
ATTENDANCE 107,412
VENUE Azteca Stadium, Mexico City

Felix
Carlos Alberto — Brito — Piazza — Everaldo
Clodoaldo — Gerson
Jairzinho — Tostão — Pelé — Rivelino

Riva — Boninsegna — Domenghini
De Sisti — Mazzola — Bertini
Facchetti — Rosato — Cera — Burgnich
Albertosi

BRAZIL
COACH: MARIO ZAGALO

FÉLIX

CARLOS ALBERTO ⚽
Goal: 87 mins

BRITO

PIAZZA

EVERALDO

JAIRZINHO ⚽
Goal: 71 mins

CLODOALDO

GERSON ⚽
Goal: 66 mins

TOSTÃO

PELÉ ⚽
Goal: 18 mins

RIVELINO 🟨
Booked

ITALY
COACH: FERRUCCIO VALCAREGGI

ALBERTOSI

BURGNICH 🟨
Booked

CERA

BERTINI
Subbed: 75 mins (Juliano)

FACCHETTI

ROSATO

DOMENGHINI

DE SISTI

MAZZOLA

BONINSEGNA ⚽
Goal: 38 mins. Subbed: 84 mins (Rivera)

RIVA

sub: JULIANO

sub: RIVERA

REFEREE: Glöckner (East Germany)

QUARTER-FINALS

June 14: Guanajuato Stadium, León
West Germany **3 - 2** England
(aet)

June 14: Jalisco Stadium, Guadalajara
Brazil **4 - 2** Peru

June 14: Luis Dosal Stadium, Toluca
Italy **4 - 1** Mexico

June 14: Azteca Stadium, Mexico City
Uruguay **1 - 0** Soviet Union
(aet)

SEMI-FINALS

June 17: Azteca Stadium, Mexico City
Italy **4 - 3** West Germany
(aet)

June 17: Jalisco Stadium, Guadalajara
Brazil **3 - 1** Uruguay

THIRD-PLACE PLAY-OFF

June 20: Azteca Stadium, Mexico City
West Germany **1 - 0** Uruguay

Pelé celebrates with the Jules Rimet Trophy.

TOP GOALSCORERS 10 goals: Gerd Müller (West Germany) **7 goals:** Jairzinho (Brazil) **5 goals:** Teófilo Cubillas (Peru)

FASTEST GOAL 3 minutes: Ladislav Petras (Czechoslovakia v Romania)

TOTAL GOALS: 95 AVERAGE GOALS 2.97 per game

TOTAL FOOTBALL

Twenty years after winning the World Cup for the first time, West Germany staged their own tournament. But although they were among the favourites to win, they still had to beat the beautiful football of the Dutch.

The West German football team had come a long way in 20 years. Excluded from international football after World War II, they had struggled for re-acceptance and recognition. With determination and meticulous planning, in 1954 they had brought about a miracle that restored national pride to a broken people, achieving the greatest upset in World Cup history. But by 1974 they were no longer the underdogs. The reigning European champions who had simply dazzled with their style and finesse when winning the Henri Delaunay Trophy in Brussels in 1972, they had emerged as a football powerhouse and were competing for the World Cup at home. Their 1974 team might not have been quite as strong as two years earlier, but playing on home soil they were expected to win this World Cup.

After the intense heat of Mexico, teams had to deal with a completely new set of playing conditions in West Germany as rain blighted many of the key fixtures in the tenth World Cup. Ironically, the Germans had employed a computer to calculate the best dates to play the fixtures. FIFA went into the tournament with a new president, João Havelange becoming the first non-European to hold the post when he succeeded the 13-year rule of Sir Stanley Rous. The competition also had a new, solid gold trophy. Bigger and more dramatic, it was sculpted by Silvio Gazzaniga and called, quite simply, the FIFA World Cup. At the opening ceremony Pelé and Uwe Seeler showed off both trophies side by side, the Jules Rimet Trophy remaining in the hands of the Brazilians until it was stolen in 1983 and never recovered.

Franz Beckenbauer becomes the first captain to lift the new FIFA World Cup trophy after West Germany's win over Holland in the final.

The format of the competition changed significantly in 1974, with a second group stage replacing the knockout phase. The top two teams in each group progressed to the second round, where they were split into two further groups of four. This stage ensured that half the entrants would play at least six games, and it replaced the drama of the quarter-finals and the semi-finals, the winners of each group qualifying for the final. Another rule change that came into effect in 1974 was the replacement of goal average by goal difference to separate teams level on points.

One of the over-riding factors in the organisation of the 1974 World Cup was security. The Munich Olympics of two years earlier had been blighted by the massacre of 11 Israeli athletes by Palestinian terrorists, while West Germany itself was also suffering from its own internal urban guerrillas, the Red Army Faction – also known as the Baader-Meinhof Group – waging a damaging terror campaign in the country from the early Seventies. With the Cold War at its height, there were other security issues of concern for the hosts, brought about by the qualification of East Germany for the first time since the two countries were separated after the war. Drawn together in the same group, the competition ensured a first and only meeting for the two teams. Just weeks before the tournament, West German Chancellor, Willy Brandt, had been forced to resign after it was revealed that one of his personal assistants was an East German spy. With Cold War relations at their iciest, and the constant fear of terrorist attack, security was at an all-time high, giving the impression of a war zone rather than a World Cup.

The tight security extended to the West German training camp, in rural Malente in the north of the country. "It was a difficult time for Germany," says keeper Sepp Maier. "The Baader-Meinhof Group were at the peak of their activities. We were very heavily protected because of this, with many policemen with us in the training camp. We were a bit incarcerated, and couldn't move around as freely as footballers like. It was quite a change in circumstances."

"It was secured like a fortress," recalls West German left-back Paul Breitner. "The nature and extent of it all was actually nightmarish for us." Locked away from wives and families, their camp was a basic sports school rather than a hotel or training resort. "In those days luxury wasn't the rule at all," recalls Sepp Maier. "There wasn't a

Fußball-Weltmeisterschaft 1974
FIFA World Cup 1974
Coupe du Monde de la FIFA 1974
Copa Mundial de la FIFA 1974

telephone in every room, but there was a phone in the corridor. Sometimes you had to wait, as there were lists of who could use the telephone and when. It was a bit unusual for us. We slept three to a room there."

With little to occupy their time other than training, and under constant security supervision, the boredom at Malente caused the atmosphere to deteriorate. Captain Franz Beckenbauer had to contend with a fractious and demanding squad who had money at the top of their agenda. "The players demanded a certain fee if they won the World Cup," explains journalist Markus Brauckmann. "This was unheard of as football was considered to be sacred of money issues. It was considered an honour to play for Germany. The 1954 players were saints, they played for nothing, or for very little, so the 1974 players were expected to do the same."

Just five days before the start of the tournament, a series of heated negotiations broke out between the West German squad and the *Deutscher Fussball Bund*. The players had learned that the Italians and the Dutch had been promised bonuses in excess of DM100,000 (approximately £16,500), but the German football federation, when pushed hard, finally revealed that the figure they had under consideration was just DM30,000

(£4,900). The squad dispatched their captain, and a negotiating team of Wolfgang Overath and Horst-Dieter Höttges, to try to resolve the situation. "We formed a committee, but Overath and Beckenbauer were not really part of it," says Maier. "So we gave them the task of taking the bull by the horns and finding out what prize money we would get. There was a real haggling session. Helmut Schön said we were greedy and that people would spit on us in the street if they found out. Helmut Schön wanted to have nothing more to do with us."

When East met West: Franz Beckenbauer shakes hands with his East German counterpart Bernd Bransch.

The arguments extended through the night, and by the early hours of the morning both Paul Breitner and coach Helmut Schön had their suitcases packed. Schön had even threatened at one point to send all 22 players home and contest the World Cup with a second string squad, FIFA having been notified that there might be a last minute change. After much discussion, the *Deutscher Fussball Bund* made a final offer of DM70,000 (£11,500) per man. The squad, who had voted democratically on every offer, was split evenly, with 11 players still holding out for the DM75,000 (£12,400) they had demanded. This time Beckenbauer took the initiative and instructed the squad to accept the offer on the table. It seemed that the hosts were going to have a team for the tournament after all.

Money was a dominant theme of the 1974 World Cup, as players fought for larger rewards in the face of newspaper headlines branding them "greedy". The Scottish squad arrived in the midst of a dispute with kit manufacturer Adidas, pushing manager Willie Ormond to the edge of quitting. After describing a financial offer as "derisory", players opted to train with the company's famous logo blacked out with boot polish. The Dutch squad had been involved in some similarly hard-nosed bonus negotiations as the West German team, invoking the wrath of coach Rinus Michels before accepting a lucrative incentive scheme. Dutch captain Johan Cruyff, meanwhile, refused to wear the national team's new strip with its three Adidas stripes on the sleeve, insisting that it would be a clash of endorsements as he was signed with Puma. The Dutch football federation relented and Cruyff was allowed to play the tournament in a tailor-made kit featuring just two stripes.

Other countries weren't able to take their appearance in the World Cup finals for granted. With 89 teams starting the long and winding road that would ultimately lead 14 nations to join the hosts and the holders in West Germany, it could be a gruelling journey. The Central and North American group would see 33 matches played before Haiti finally qualified for the finals. It took even longer to arrive at the sole qualifier from the African group, with 45 matches contested before Zaire booked their place in the finals.

For some there were more important things at stake than the World Cup, and the Soviet Union, choosing principles over qualification, were eliminated without playing the final game of their campaign. Despite qualifying top of European Group Nine ahead of the Republic of Ireland and France, they had to face Chile, the winners of South American Group Three, in a play-off. After a goalless draw at home, Russia protested about being asked to play the return fixture at the *Estadio Nacional* in Santiago, taking a stand because the stadium was being used to house the political prisoners of General Augusto Pinochet's recent *coup d'etat*, during which some 3,000 Chileans were killed, or just simply 'disappeared'. FIFA decided the match should go ahead and the Chileans took to the field to complete the fixture, despite the fact that four days earlier the head of the Soviet football federation, Valentin Granatkin, had announced that, "Soviet sportsmen cannot play on a ground stained with the blood of Chilean patriots". Chile had Brazilian club side Santos on hand ready for a friendly and played that instead.

Hungary's decline in world status was confirmed after failure to qualify, despite finishing level on points with Austria and Sweden. With an identical goal difference, a play-off finally separated Sweden and Austria, the Scandinavians winning 2-1. Portugal were another football nation who had seen better years, finishing second in their group to Bulgaria, while Yugoslavia qualified at the expense of Spain in a play-off.

The England team were also among the casualties of the qualification system, starting a process of decline that would see them go 12 years between tournaments. From the minute that Alf Ramsey's squad returned from the 1970 World Cup, the press had been sharpening their knives. But Ramsey saw no reason to change his methods. "He found what he would consider to be the paraphernalia of managing the England football team very difficult to deal with," recalls TV commentator Barry Davies. "He didn't like it, he wasn't very good at it, and he felt all the time that people were trying to trip him up."

A new generation of England players had set out to qualify for the 1974 World Cup in a group with just three teams. Failure to beat the Welsh at home meant England had to defeat Poland at Wembley to qualify. From the start, keeper Peter Shilton had little to do. The pressure was all on his Polish counterpart. "To get to my first World Cup was a burning ambition and all we had to do was beat them on the night. I just stood there and I could not believe what was going on at the other end," says Peter Shilton. "The ball just would not go in the net. I never saw the defence – they were on the halfway line most of the time because we were doing most of the attacking."

But England faced a charmed goalkeeper, Jan Tomaszewski, who had been famously described before the game as a 'clown' by ITV pundit Brian Clough. "He was a very good goalkeeper but he kept goal in his style, which was very un-English," says Barry Davies. "Punching the ball away was not how the English kept goal."

The 1-1 draw was not enough for Alf Ramsey's team. "People were just in shock and in disbelief," says Barry Davies. "This didn't happen." The last time there had been a World Cup without England it was because England, the home of football, had remained aloof, refusing to take part. Now, even though they were desperate to be in it, they were not good enough to take part. In the spring of 1974 Sir Alf Ramsey was sacked from his job and English football entered its wilderness years.

The 1974 World Cup kicked off on Friday June 14 at the Olympic Stadium in Berlin, and West Germany started slowly. The behind-the-scenes bonus negotiations might have been resolved, but the side struggled to impress their own home crowd after a mediocre victory over Chile, courtesy of a single long-range goal from Paul Breitner. At the Volkspark Stadium in Hamburg they beat Australia 3-0, but it wasn't a performance that made them popular, the cheers turning to jeers towards the end of the game, with Beckenbauer spitting at the crowd after being abused for giving the ball away. The crowd had turned against Germany's negative approach and there was an atmosphere of mutual disdain. But all that could be turned around if they could only beat East Germany. It was what the country expected, and what their Dresden-born coach Helmut Schön wanted more than anything. The stage was set for the match everyone had been waiting for, the head-to-head between two Germanys and two ideologies.

"Football in the German Democratic Republic [East Germany] was at that time not so popular with the officials, because it did not yield medals at the Olympics," recalls East German midfielder Jürgen Sparwasser. "Once they wanted to forbid it, but then the people went on the barricades and the State couldn't do anything about it. To begin with people were very happy to have qualified. Then, of course, came the draw and there was a hullabaloo, because many people also supported West Germany. They said, 'Well, at last it comes to this duel, you'll have to prove how strong you are'. Many expected that we were going to leave the stadium having lost 5-0."

Sepp Maier remembers how the loyalties were split between the two German nations. "When we had to drive from Malente to Berlin we passed through the GDR," he recalls. "People on the streets were waving flags – not GDR flags but German flags. They gave us the thumbs up, although the GDR was in fact an opponent in our group."

"Where I lived in the East you could view Western television so we experienced the tension of the run up that was happening in the West," says Sparwasser. "The first games didn't seem so important, but that game was in the news every day."

West Germany had qualified for the next round already while, after beating Australia and drawing with Chile, the East Germans needed just a point to be certain of progressing, but this didn't detract from the significance of the game or from the pressure on Helmut Schön's team. The West German coach had been forced to leave the East in May 1950 to stay true to his football principles and winning the match would vindicate his defection. But the match didn't go according to Schön's script, his team unable to break through the East German wall of resistance. Frustration was spreading on and off the pitch. Then in the 77th minute, frustration turned into disaster for the West Germans, Sparwasser collecting a long ball from Hamman, rounding a

East Germany's Jürgen Sparwasser scores the winning goal past West German defenders Horst Höttges, Berti Vogts and keeper Sepp Maier.

defender and lifting the ball over Maier. The only Germans making a noise were 2,000 fans from the GDR who had been specially vetted by the Party and deemed politically correct enough to attend. "There was deadly silence," recalls Sparwasser. "The stadium was quiet. Our 2,000 fans made a noise for 10,000, but it was accompanied by booing and whistling. We had hit the enemy where it hurts him most – which was football. It certainly stung the West badly."

For Helmut Schön the defeat was particularly devastating. "After supper the players sat together until three or four in the morning, drinking and smoking," says Maier. "Schön came in and said, 'Cigars and all this smoking won't help'. Then he went to bed and we were left alone again."

Paul Breitner: "After the panic of initially just wanting to go home we realised we didn't want that, we didn't want to look ridiculous. Earlier we'd been negotiating like megalomaniacs about what we would get when we were world champions, and now it looked like we would be going home in the second round. That could not be allowed."

Schön took the defeat so badly that the next morning he was still locked in his room alone, refusing to eat with the players. In the afternoon a packed press conference had be cancelled. With Schön unable to speak, the West German football federation had to accept that their coach was facing up to something approaching a nervous breakdown. "Helmut Schön was an extremely sensitive person," explains Breitner. "He even went as far as saying to himself, 'I'm going home now, I don't want to expose myself to this any longer'."

His right hand on the pitch, Franz Beckenbauer, was the man who came to the rescue. From that point Beckenbauer attended press conferences alongside Schön, speaking eloquently for the coach about the games and tactics, and

Johan Cruyff dribbles past Argentinian goalkeeper Daniel Carnevali on his way to scoring.

deflecting all the media attention. Beckenbauer's thoughts on a restructuring of the line-up, including dropping Uli Hoeness who he had heavily critisised, were implemented as the West German captain transformed the attitude and the look of his team. "From then Helmut Schön did not make the calls by himself," says Markus Brauckmann. "It was Franz Beckenbauer who made the calls, maybe not visible to the outside back then but definitely known to the team." The West Germans were gathering strength at just the right time, and by finishing behind East Germany in their group, it meant that they had avoided Holland, Argentina and Brazil in the second group phase.

While the West Germans had been struggling to kick-start their World Cup, a new team were putting some colour into the tournament. Led by the charismatic Johan Cruyff and followed by an army of *Oranje* fans, Holland set the opening round alight. The Dutch had no real pedigree on the world stage, having made just fleeting appearances at the 1934 and 1938 World Cup finals, playing once at each. Even their current team had struggled slightly during the qualifying stages, but the appointment of Barcelona manager Rinus Michels as coach just three months before the tournament was the catalyst for the side of 1974. A former Ajax coach, his team was built around the stars of the all-conquering Ajax club side. They cut a swathe through the group stages, their unique and spellbinding brand of 'Total Football', in which players switched positions and roles with astonishing versatility, won the heart of the competition – and to a certain extent, of a generation.

For Michels, playing beautiful football was a serious business and he demanded a high level of professionalism from his team on the pitch. When they were off it, however, the Dutch appeared to approach life in a more relaxed manner than the bickering West Germans (although, in reality, they had pushed Michels just as close to the edge with their bonus demands as the Germans had with Helmut Schön). With their beautiful long hair, laid-back attitude and hippy love beads, the stars of the Dutch team were the pin-ups of the 1974 World Cup. In contrast to the Germans, locked away like monks at their Malente training base, here was a team who liked a good time. "We were very easy living and we had parties," recalls Arie Haan. "Because we did not know anything about a world tournament, how you have to behave, we were just normal. We played our game and after the game you were free."

Holland began the tournament with a comfortable 2-0 win over the very first world champions, Uruguay, both goals coming from Ajax star Johnny Rep. Uruguay were no longer anything like a serious football power and, on arriving in West Germany, both their players and coaching staff had become embroiled in a serious dispute about money, refusing to give any press or television interviews without payment. Finishing bottom of their group, Uruguay soon proved to be of no real interest to anyone. Holland qualified with a goalless draw against Sweden and an impressive 4-1 rout of Bulgaria, enough for them to top the group and qualify for the last eight along with the Swedes.

While the tournament's new champions of free-flowing football were cruising through their opening group, the once mighty Brazil were proving that they were clearly not the force that they had once been, playing a more cynical, defensive game to compensate for the fact that their team no longer boasted the same level of individual skills. Rivelino, Jairzinho and Piazza were the only remaining stars from their great team of 1970. They scraped through the first stage thanks to goalless draws with Yugoslavia and Scotland, and a 3-0 win over a hapless Zaire side who had conceded nine against Yugoslavia. The group finished with Yugoslavia, Brazil and Scotland sharing the same amount of points at the top of the table, but it was hard luck on the Scottish who were knocked out of the competition on goal difference, despite having not lost a game. Their captain Billy Bremner had been on world-class form, but ultimately Scotland paid the price for not scoring more than two goals against Zaire.

Poland and Argentina progressed from Group Four at the expense of the Italians, who had arrived at the competition with goalkeeper Dino Zoff in outstanding form, having not conceded a goal in almost 1,100 minutes of international football. After being outplayed in their 1-1 draw with Argentina, the Italians went into their final game needing a point to stay in the competition, but after dropping their two ineffective stars, Luigi Riva and Gianni Rivera, they were defeated 2-1 by an outstanding Polish side.

The eight teams who had qualified for the second round were again split into two groups of four teams, Argentina, Brazil, East Germany and Holland in Group A; Poland, Sweden, West Germany and Yugoslavia in Group B. With no semi-finals, the teams who finished top of their groups would go straight through to the World Cup final.

Brazil had started the second stage with something approaching their old swagger, beating East Germany 1-0, thanks to a second-half strike from Rivelino. He scored again, along with Jairzinho, as they beat Argentina 2-1. But despite improving form, the Brazilians found it impossible to live with a Dutch side approaching the peak of their powers, the South Americans resorting to a series of brutal tackles in their attempt to keep in the game. Two second-half goals, Cruyff's strike in the 65th minute following Neeskens' gorgeous lob in the 50th, saw Holland run out 2-0 winners, the self-destructing Brazilians finishing with ten men after the dismissal of Luis Pereira for a high tackle on Neeskens. Brazil had tarnished their golden reputation, while Holland had scored 14 goals and conceded only once on the way to the final. Many now assumed they were well on their way to a first and hugely deserved world championship. "It was fantastic," recalls Dutch defender Ruud Krol. "But of course you realised that by beating the world champions, it did not mean that you become world champions."

In Group B, slowly but surely, the West Germans had finally started to play as a team. Spurred on by an inspirational Franz Beckenbauer, they started the second group stage impressively, beating Yugoslavia 2-0 with goals from Paul Breitner and Gerd Müller. A 4-2 victory over Sweden in torrential rain in Düsseldorf set up a crucial decider with Poland, a match the West Germans only needed to draw. Poland were yet to be defeated at the World Cup, and in Grzegorz Lato they had the tournament's most prolific striker. He had scored a vital second-half winner in the 2-1 victory over Yugoslavia that brought Poland face-to-face with West Germany for a place in the final.

It proved an exciting clash. When the game eventually got underway, both sides attempted to play attractive football despite the conditions. The kick-off had initially been delayed due to a waterlogged pitch, with the Frankfurt

Torrential rain hits the crowd and TV crews during Holland's game with Argentina in Gelsenkirchen.

fire brigade brought in to pump water from the quagmire. "The first 20 minutes were more like a game of chance," recalls Sepp Maier. "You couldn't play a straight ball because it kept getting stuck. If it hadn't been a World Cup match, an important one, you could have written it off as a big laugh."

Poland's best chances came in the first half, Robert Gadocha and the effervescent Lato forcing Maier into a couple of excellent saves. "As a footballer my aim was to once deliver a perfect game," says Paul Breitner. "That means 90 minutes without making the smallest mistake, to have played perfectly. I have never achieved it, but Sepp Maier achieved it in this game. You can't play better as a goalkeeper than Sepp played on that day." In the second half it was the turn of Maier's opposite number to shine, Tomaszewski saving a penalty from Uli Hoeness. West Germany snatched the winner 14 minutes from time, when Hoeness's shot deflected into the path of Müller, who clinically buried the ball into the back of the net.

Picking up consolation medals after a 1-0 win over Brazil in the third place play-off victory was scant consolation for the Poles, who had surely been the tournament's biggest surprise. The final, however, was now to be contested between hosts West Germany, who hadn't won the tournament since 1954, and Holland, who hadn't even managed to qualify since 1938: efficiency, organisation and hard work against versatility, vision and precocious talent.

On the surface the two teams couldn't have been more different, but in reality both were exponents of their own kind of Total Football. West Germany had set the European Nations Cup alight with their dazzling performances in 1972, described by *The Times* as "elegance and inventiveness", while the backbone of the Dutch team had done the same with Ajax, three times European Cup winners. This new and exciting style of football had turned the defensive sweeper of *catenaccio* into an attacking defender capable of shaking up the game with surging forward runs. It was the role that Franz Beckenbauer had created when reinventing his role, first at Bayern Munich and then with the national team.

The Dutch Total Football of Rinus Michels placed the emphasis on footballers who could play in any position on the field and were intelligent enough to know exactly when to switch roles, Arie Haan playing the Beckenbauer role. "The idea of Total Football was that that everybody can play in every position, that everybody plays in the team and could go where he wants," explains Ruud Krol. "It takes a lot of discipline. You must have the freedom to go forward, knowing that the position behind will be filled. You need quality players. At that time we had one super player and maybe five or six world-class players, and the rest were of top European level."

The Dutch may have been disciplined on the pitch, but off it their approach to the tournament was famously cavalier. On the eve of the final, their casual attitude came back to haunt them. Under the headline 'Cruyff, Champagne and Naked Girls', German tabloid *Bild Zeitung* published a story claiming that the night before the Holland-Brazil game there had been a 'naked party' in the swimming pool of their hotel, involving four unnamed Holland players and two German girls. The newspaper claimed to have pictures but none were ever published.

"Johan said, 'There's a big problem'," recalls Arie Haan. "I read the paper and we were a little surprised, a little bit confused. This was the first time we were confronted with this kind of journalism."

"I don't think it affected us," says Ruud Krol. "Of course we read it, but we were focussed on the final. They would try to do anything to win for the home country. Everywhere is the same."

"We changed a little bit that night," says Arie Haan. "Before we did not think, but afterwards we were starting to know what it was like to be famous, to be the best. Everybody was looking at you and everybody was following you. That started with the articles. Then came the pressure and the stress – the women were on the phone."

Whether the story was true or not, and it has never been proved either way, it has been said that Johan Cruyff's wife kept him on the telephone all night. "Players wives were coming on the phone and asking, 'What's going on, I thought you were playing football, not swimming in hotel pools with naked German girls'," says journalist Auke Kok. "The worst was Danny Cruyff as she just kept calling and calling."

Where before everything had been peace and harmony, now, with the final just hours away, instability threatened the Dutch camp. The West Germans, meanwhile, were brimming with self-confidence and self-belief and there was only one thing that could now come between them and the World Cup – a better team. For all their problems caused by the 'swimming pool scandal', the Dutch were certain that they were a better team. "They were confident because they had played a marvellous tournament with beautiful victories in a spectacular and impressive playing style," Rinus Michels would recall. "There was a lot of confidence that they could repeat it against Germany."

As a nation, the Dutch still had very strong feelings about the Germans, an enmity that dated back to the occupation of Holland during World War II. The memories were still fresh for many people, not least Wim van Hanegem, who would give the best Dutch performance in the final. "Every time I played against German players I had a problem because of the war," he has said. "Eighty per cent of my family died in the war; my daddy, my sister, my two brothers. And every game against players from Germany makes me angry. The Germans were good players but arrogant."

To the Germans, Dutch confidence appeared more like arrogant overconfidence. "About one hour before the game the Dutch were behaving as if they were at the Oktoberfest," says Paul Breitner. "They were singing, they were bawling out, they were already celebrating as if they were world champions. That, of course, made it easier for us to deal with the Dutch."

"I still recall them playing 'Tulips From Amsterdam'," says Maier. "And then I thought, 'We'll pluck those tulips today alright!'"

The West Germans finally had unanimous support from their fans and had managed to turn their World Cup form around, but now they were up against the tournament's most inspirational player, Johan Cruyff. The 1974 World Cup final kicked off in front of a crowd of 77,833 in the Olympic Stadium in Munich on July 7, but not without a slight hitch. "Every referee dreams of having a World Cup final," says referee Jack Taylor. "The thing I remember most is that with all the German efficiency, we were just about to kick off and I noticed that there were no corner flags. We had to wait, with millions of people watching around the world, while some little man runs all the way round the ground to put the corner flags in position."

The game would prove just as eventful. The Dutch kicked off, moving the ball around from player to player, just out of reach of the Germans. The home crowd whistled in anger as they saw the inability of their players to touch the ball. Cruyff picked up the ball in the centre circle, ambled towards goal, accelerated past his marker Berti Vogts and into the box, only to be felled inches inside the 18-yard line by a tackle from Uli Hoeness. Referee Jack Taylor pointed to the spot. After a move of 17 passes, Holland were awarded the first ever penalty in a World Cup final. "The Germans hadn't even touched the ball and all of a sudden we've got a penalty in under a minute," recalls Taylor. "It was very simple – an orange jersey going through the box and a white jersey fetched him down. It was a penalty, a blatant penalty."

Franz Beckenbauer celebrates with coach Helmut Schön after winning the World Cup final.

In an attempt to intimidate the referee and to imply he was biased, Beckenbauer waved his arm at Taylor and said, "You are an Englishman, of course". Johan Neeskens hammered the ball home from the spot and when Sepp Maier picked it out of the net, he became the first German to have touched the ball in the game. In the initial aftermath of the goal, the Germans went into shock. But rather than take advantage by piling on the pressure, the Dutch team, certain of their own victory after just two minutes, inexplicably decided that they wanted to humiliate the Germans on the pitch. "For a moment we were paralysed," says Breitner. "They didn't realised how far down we were, how demoralised we were."

"We had kept an eye on the Dutch on TV and they really were the best team at the tournament," says Sepp Maier. "They played superbly and beat all the big teams. Then they thought, 'Good, here come the Germans, we'll send them packing'. That's how they started in Munich. They were arrogant. They went into the lead and thought they'd easily get three or four. The relationship between Holland and Germany was difficult, and still is today, but was far worse at that time. The two countries could barely stand each other. They wanted to show us up a bit, but they didn't succeed."

"We *were* a little bit arrogant on the pitch," says Ruud Krol. "We had so much confidence in ourselves, that we could win. Because we had so many Ajax players in the team at that time, we had a little bit of that mentality, to be a little bit arrogant."

The Dutch continued to dominate with their taunting game of possession football. "We were surprised that the Germans didn't attack," says Arie Haan. "We were 1-0 up and we were happy to keep the ball, no problem." But they couldn't have foreseen what would happen next. In the 25th minute a surging run from Bernd Hölzenbein was brought to an abrupt end as he threw himself over a tackle with the ball running out of his reach. Taylor blew for a penalty, although to many in the crowd it appeared to be a *schwalbe*, or swallow, the German term for what the English would call a dive. It was something that Hölzenbein had quite a reputation for. "He ran against the player's leg and immediately went down," Franz Beckenbauer has recalled. "That was his speciality. Shortly before, he had stopped Bayern from reaching the German Cup final by doing that." Sepp Maier agrees. "I have to say it was no penalty. Those who knew Hölzenbein knew very well. Hölzenbein simply flew over."

"People have suggested that Hölzenbein was prone to exaggerate, for want of a better word," says Jack Taylor.

Opposite: The 1974 World Cup final. (left) Gerd Müller holds the World Cup. (top right) Sepp Maier beats Johan Cruyff to the ball. (centre) Cruyff jumps a tackle. (centre right) Gerd Müller scores West Germany's second goal before Ruud Krol can tackle him. (bottom) Beckenbauer holds the trophy next to a relaxed Helmut Schön. (Overleaf) Dutch midfielder Johan Neeskens scores the first ever penalty in a World Cup final.

WORLD CUP '74 FINAL

West Germany 2 Holland 1

0:1 JOHAN NEESKENS (HOL) 2' (pen), 1:1 PAUL BREITNER (GER) 25' (pen), 2:1 GERD MÜLLER (GER) 43

"He was notorious for doing that. But the law says 'tripping or attempting to trip'. It was just a penalty as I saw it. I was happy with the decisions then; I can't say I've been happy with decisions all my life, but whatever I've done has been with total honesty and total integrity."

Paul Breitner converted the spot-kick, and the Germans went on to snatch a decisive lead two minutes before half-time. In a flash Gerd Müller turned on a loose ball in the box, feinted to shoot through keeper Jongbloed and the incoming Krol at the near post, before snapping the ball across the goal towards the unguarded far side of the net. In Holland TV commentator Herman Kuiphof uttered the line that would always encapsulate the moment for many of his viewers. *"Zijn we er toch nog ingetuind"*, he exclaimed, "They've tricked us again".

So cagey for so long, West Germany were back in the game. It was now the Germans who looked like the disciples of Total Football, as they took the Dutch on at their own game. Crucially, the terrier-like Berti Vogts was getting

the better of an insipid-looking Cruyff. The frustration was starting to tell on the inspirational Dutch captain, who had been yellow-carded for berating the referee while walking off the pitch at half-time. The West Germans were now in the driving seat in every way. "It was 2-1 when we came off at half-time," remembers Maier. "Schön said, 'Just another 45 minutes and we've won the World Cup'. But things aren't that simple."

The Dutch were down, but with their richness of talent they were far from out. "We tried to make pressure, pressure, pressure," says Krol, "but the ball didn't want to go in." They were determined to equalise and continued their relentless attack on Sepp Maier's goal. "To me five minutes seemed like three hours," says Maier. "When I had time I kept looking at the stadium clock wondering how long we still had to go. When the Dutch came at me again, as they did all the time in the last half hour of the second half, I didn't even have time to look at the clock any more."

Finally the sound the whole of West Germany had been praying for: Jack Taylor blew for full-time. "It's a joy which is indescribable," says Maier. Paul Breitner agrees. "It's indescribable, because you don't know at the time what it means. I was 22 and it was a reward for me for nine years of the most intensive training. As a child I never dreamed of becoming world champion – it was never imaginable, never reachable, never achievable. But at that moment I was incredibly satisfied with myself."

In his third World Cup Franz Beckenbauer had finally led West Germany to the top spot, 20 years and three days after the Miracle of Berne. Wolfgang Overath picked up a winners' medal to go with his medals for coming second and third, the only player in World Cup history to have won all three. But although the Germans were delighted, the victory wasn't without its tarnish. Later that evening, as the players arrived at Munich's Hilton Hotel for the post match banquet, they discovered that their wives were not welcome, and that Susi Hoeness, who was already at the table, was being asked to leave on the instructions of Hans Deckert, head of the German delegation. A row ensued and Uli Hoeness found himself reprimanded. "It's not for you to demand things that you're not entitled to," instructed Deckert. Hoeness and his wife promptly left the building to celebrate in a Munich bar, followed by Franz Beckenbauer and many of the players. That night a dismayed Gerd Müller, the highest-scoring player in World Cup history, announced that he was quitting international football at 28 years of age.

For the Dutch the defeat was catastrophic, particularly for Wim van Hanegem. Johan Cruyff, then only 27, announced he would not compete in the next World Cup, unprepared to leave his wife and family again for such a long period. Four years later, despite huge efforts to change his mind, Holland went to Argentina without him. Beckenbauer would go on to win the World Cup again, this time as manager, when he led a newly unified Germany to a third World Cup victory in 1990. But in 1974 the Germans had proved yet again that through resilience, determination and sheer hard work, they were unbeatable.

The West German team do a lap of honour.

THE FINAL

WEST GERMANY	(2) 2
HOLLAND	(1) 1

DATE SUNDAY July 7, 1974
ATTENDANCE 77,822
VENUE Olympic Stadium, Munich

WEST GERMANY
COACH: HELMUT SCHÖN

MAIER
VOGTS
Booked: 3 mins
SCHWARZENBECK
BECKENBAUER
BREITNER
Goal: 25 mins (pen)
BONHOF
HOENESS
OVERATH
GRABOWSKI
MÜLLER
Goal: 43 mins
HÖLZENBEIN

HOLLAND
COACH: RINUS MICHELS

JONGBLOED
SUURBIER
RIJSBERGEN
Subbed: 69 mins (De Jong)
HAAN
KROL
JANSEN
NEESKENS
Goal: 2 mins (pen). Booked: 39 mins
VAN HANEGEM
Booked: 22 mins
REP
CRUYFF
Booked: 45 mins
RENSENBRINK
Subbed: 46 mins (R Van De Kerkhof)

sub: R VAN DE KERKHOF
sub: DE JONG

REFEREE: Taylor (England)

GROUP 1

June 14: Olympic Stadium, Berlin
West Germany **1 - 0** Chile

June 14: Volkspark Stadium, Hamburg
East Germany **2 - 0** Australia

June 18: Volkspark Stadium, Hamburg
West Germany **3 - 0** Australia

June 18: Olympic Stadium, Berlin
East Germany **1 - 1** Chile

June 22: Olympic Stadium, Berlin
Australia **0 - 0** Chile

June 22: Volkspark Stadium, Hamburg
East Germany **1 - 0** West Germany

	P	W	D	L	F	A	Pts
East Germany	3	2	1	0	4	1	5
West Germany	3	2	0	1	4	1	4
Chile	3	0	2	1	1	2	2
Australia	3	0	1	2	0	5	1

GROUP 2

June 13: Wald Stadium, Frankfurt
Brazil **0 - 0** Yugoslavia

June 14: Westfalen Stadium, Dortmund
Scotland **2 - 0** Zaïre

June 18: Wald Stadium, Frankfurt
Brazil **0 - 0** Scotland

June 18: Park Stadium, Gelsenkirchen
Yugoslavia **9 - 0** Zaïre

June 22: Wald Stadium, Frankfurt
Yugoslavia **1 - 1** Scotland

June 22: Park Stadium, Gelsenkirchen
Brazil **3 - 0** Zaïre

	P	W	D	L	F	A	Pts
Yugoslavia	3	1	2	0	10	1	4
Brazil	3	1	2	0	3	0	4
Scotland	3	1	2	0	3	1	4
Zaïre	3	0	0	3	0	14	0

GROUP 3

June 15: Niedersachsen Stadium, Hanover
Holland **2 - 0** Uruguay

June 15: Rhein Stadium, Düsseldorf
Bulgaria **0 - 0** Sweden

June 19: Westfalen Stadium, Dortmund
Holland **0 - 0** Sweden

June 19: Niedersachsen Stadium, Hanover
Bulgaria **1 - 1** Uruguay

June 23: Westfalen Stadium, Dortmund
Holland **4 - 1** Bulgaria

June 23: Rhein Stadium, Düsseldorf
Sweden **3 - 0** Uruguay

	P	W	D	L	F	A	Pts
Holland	3	2	1	0	6	1	5
Sweden	3	1	2	0	3	0	4
Bulgaria	3	0	2	1	2	5	2
Uruguay	3	0	1	2	1	6	1

GROUP 4

June 15: Olympic Stadium, Munich
Italy **3 - 1** Haiti

June 15: Neckar Stadium, Stuttgart
Poland **3 - 2** Argentina

June 19: Neckar Stadium, Stuttgart
Argentina **1 - 1** Italy

June 19: Olympic Stadium, Munich
Poland **7 - 0** Haiti

June 23: Olympic Stadium, Munich
Argentina **4 - 1** Haiti

June 23: Neckar Stadium, Stuttgart
Poland **2 - 1** Italy

	P	W	D	L	F	A	Pts
Poland	3	3	0	0	12	3	6
Argentina	3	1	1	1	7	5	3
Italy	3	1	1	1	5	4	3
Haiti	3	0	0	3	2	14	0

SECOND ROUND GROUP A

June 26: Niedersachsen Stadium, Hanover
Brazil **1 - 0** East Germany

June 26: Park Stadium, Gelsenkirchen
Holland **4 - 0** Argentina

June 30: Park Stadium, Gelsenkirchen
Holland **2 - 0** East Germany

June 30: Niedersachsen Stadium, Hanover
Brazil **2 - 1** Argentina

July 3: Park Stadium, Gelsenkirchen
East Germany **1 - 1** Argentina

July 3: Westfalen Stadium, Dortmund
Holland **2 - 0** Brazil

	P	W	D	L	F	A	Pts
Holland	3	3	0	0	8	0	6
Brazil	3	2	0	1	3	3	4
East Germany	3	0	1	2	1	4	1
Argentina	3	0	1	2	2	7	1

SECOND ROUND GROUP B

June 26: Neckar Stadium, Stuttgart
Poland **1 - 0** Sweden

June 26: Rhein Stadium, Düsseldorf
West Germany **2 - 0** Yugoslavia

June 30: Wald Stadium, Frankfurt
Poland **2 - 1** Yugoslavia

June 30: Rhein Stadium, Düsseldorf
West Germany **4 - 2** Sweden

July 3: Rhein Stadium, Düsseldorf
Sweden **2 - 1** Yugoslavia

July 3: Wald Stadium, Frankfurt
West Germany **1 - 0** Poland

	P	W	D	L	F	A	Pts
West Germany	3	3	0	0	7	2	6
Poland	3	2	0	1	3	2	4
Sweden	3	1	0	2	4	6	2
Yugoslavia	3	0	0	3	2	6	0

THIRD-PLACE PLAY-OFF

July 6: Olympic Stadium, Munich
Poland **1 - 0** Brazil

Paul Breitner scores a penalty in the final.

TOP GOALSCORERS 7 goals: Gregorz Lato (Poland); **5 goals:** Johan Neeskens (Holland), Anrdrzej Szarmach (Poland); **4 goals:** Gerd Müller (Germany), Ralf Edström (Sweden), Johnny Rep (Holland)

FASTEST GOAL 80 seconds: Johan Neeskens (Holland v West Germany)

TOTAL GOALS: 97 **AVERAGE GOALS** 2.55 per game

MONUMENTAL VICTORY

The decision to stage the 1978 World Cup in Argentina was controversial. With the country in the grip of a ruthless military dictatorship, the Argentine players wanted to give the nation something to cheer about.

When the 1978 World Cup finals kicked off at the Monumental Stadium in Buenos Aires, Argentina was a far different country from the one that had been awarded the tournament at the 35th FIFA congress in London on July 6, 1966. Having been a finalist in the very first competition in 1930, this passionate football nation was made to wait another 48 years until it could stage its own World Cup. That they made it through to the final was an even more extraordinary achievement, throwing up a multitude of conspiracy theories. But when Daniel Passarella lifted the trophy, amid an explosion of tickertape and a backdrop of flag-waving fervour, it was one of the most romantic and tragic moments in football history. Just to have staged the event was an incredible achievement for Argentina given the political turmoil that had prompted several participants to talk of a boycott. To then win the trophy sent the nation ecstatic.

Buenos Aires might have celebrated, but away from the euphoria of the World Cup, Argentina was not a happy country. The military had seized power two years earlier, ousting ineffective President Isabella Perón and pursuing a policy of state terrorism against those who opposed, or were suspected of opposing, the dictatorship. In what became known as the 'Dirty War', a military junta headed by General Jorge Videla was responsible for the illegal arrest, torture, killing or forced disappearance of thousands of Argentinians. With the population living under such an oppressive regime, Videla could see the advantages to be gained from supporting the World Cup, both in terms of the feel-good factor it could bring to the country, and in the improvement of his regime's standing abroad.

Mario Kempes celebrates scoring against Holland in the World Cup final.

To make sure that the right message was sent out about Argentina, top American Public Relations firm Burson-Marsteller was hired, its report on the challenge ahead titled *What Is True For Products Is Also True For Countries*. "The World Cup will be just the occasion to show the Argentine's real way of life," said General Merlo. But to ensure that visiting tourists would see only the acceptable face of Argentina, the shantytowns on the edge of the major cities – the *villas miserias* – were bulldozed and their inhabitants banished to areas of the country not staging World Cup games. In Rosario a wall was built alongside the main road into the city to hide

the slums that lay behind it. Decorated with the colourful facades of beautiful houses, it became known as the 'Misery Wall'. The government attempted to sweep any politically unsound citizens out of the sight of foreign tourists and journalists – in the run up to the tournament 200 people a day were made to 'disappear' during Operation *El Barrido*.

Huge sums of money were invested in the country's infrastructure to help promote the national image during the World Cup, most notably in the development of new road and rail networks, and in the $60 million construction of a television centre, Argentina Televisora Color, capable of broadcasting a colour signal to the country for the first time. The regime also embarked on a major programme of stadia construction. The legendary Monumental Stadium was significantly redeveloped, as were the Velez Sarsfield Stadium and Rosario's Gigante de Arroyito, while new stadia were built in Mar del Plata, Mendoza and Córdoba. As costs spiralled out of control, the junta's slogan for the tournament, '25 Million Argentinians Will Play In The World Cup', was soon popularised in the country as '25 Million Argentinians Will *Pay* For The World Cup'.

The original estimated cost of staging the tournament had been no more than $100 million, but the Perónists had been off the pace with their planning. The military junta speeded up the preparations, placing the tournament in the hands of an autonomous organising body, Ente Autuartico Mundial, known as EAM'78. This succeeded in quickening the process but didn't rein in the costs. Mistakes were being made too. The Monumental Stadium might have been rebuilt, but a decision to sprinkle the pitch with seawater killed off the grass, and the hastily laid replacement turf suffered from the most uneven bounce. Although the true cost of staging the competition would never be made public, four months before the tournament the Finance Secretary of the military government, Juan Alemann, admitted that the final bill would probably exceed $700 million.

This would be the biggest and most costly World Cup yet. By the time the deadline for entries closed on August 31, 1975, 106 nations had applied to take part, although after withdrawals only 96 actually played in the qualifiers. Iran and Tunisia made it to their first finals, yet some old faces again failed to qualify, including former champions England and Uruguay. The English finished their group level on points with Italy, but were nudged out of the finals on goal difference. Manager Don Revie had quit his post midway through the campaign to sign a £340,000, four-year contract to coach the United Arab Emirates. The FA imposed a ten-year ban from English football on Revie for bringing the game into disrepute, enraged that he would have the temerity to resign before they could sack him.

Austria reached their first finals in 20 years, while Poland's good run continued as they qualified unbeaten, just dropping a point at home to second-placed Portugal. Holland and neighbours Belgium shared a group with Northern Ireland and Iceland, but it was the Dutch who proved the most dominant, qualifying five points clear of their nearest rivals. From the complicated South American groups, Brazil and Peru qualified directly, while Bolivia had to play-off with Hungary, who had been the winners of European Group Nine at the expense of the Soviet Union. Hungary

Argentina fans prepare for the start of the World Cup final.

won both legs, booking their place in the finals. Tunisia claimed the sole African spot in the finals in a qualification group that involved 45 games.

The World Cup had a new ball, the Adidas designed Tango, but the competition followed the same format as 1974, with two group stages and no knockout phase. The top two teams in four groups would progress into a second group stage, with the winners going into the final.

Given the nature of the military junta's regime, questions had been raised about how appropriate it would be to hold the tournament in Argentina, and several European countries, most notably Holland, had threatened to pull out in protest. "It was very difficult because a lot of important people in Holland were against us going," recalls Arie Haan. Although Amnesty International's awareness campaign had persuaded European stars like Paolo Rossi and Sepp Maier to sign petitions protesting against the torture of political prisoners, the threatened boycott never materialised and all 16 teams arrived in Argentina. At the opening match between holders West Germany and Poland, kicking off at the Monumental Stadium, Buenos Aires, on June 1, President Videla gave a moving speech at the opening ceremony, but his message of harmony and friendship was in strong contrast to the human rights violations practised almost as a matter of course by his regime. He had promised a "World Cup of Peace", but for the junta the tournament was an opportunity to unite Argentina behind their vision of national salvation. For the players, though, as long as Argentina was living in an atmosphere of fear and repression, they saw the World Cup as achieving a different goal.

LEOPOLDO LUQUE

For the Argentina striker, the World Cup really was a matter of life and death.

"The game against France was one of my best ever matches for the national side. I scored a great goal that helped us progress to the second round. Ardíles gave me the ball and I was very selfish and didn't give it back to him. Since I had the ball in a very good position I decided to shoot, and I think the goalkeeper was surprised – actually, everyone in the stadium and around Argentina was surprised, because I managed to score from very far out.

"I was injured in that game with only a few minutes left. I was trying to follow a move and I fell and dislocated my elbow, which was rather serious because I did not play in the following two matches. It was also sad, very sad, because my brother learned about my injury and drove to Buenos Aires to see if I was okay, and somewhere near San Isidro, he and his friend crashed and he died.

"Somehow one has the premonition that some things will happen. I am not telling you it was a premonition, no, but still I said, 'Hey, let me go back on the pitch for a little while so my folks in Santa Fe will see I am fine'. And the doctor let me go back on, because although I was injured there was only ten minutes left. So I went back on to the pitch with a bandage, but it was only for the sake of my family, for their peace of mind. But my brother was concerned and wanted to see me. He crashed and died near the bridge in San Isidro on the Panamericana Highway.

"Two days later my father came to give me the news. When I saw them I thought they had come to see me because of my injury. It was the saddest news I've had in my life. My father told me, 'Well, just as last time we came to give you a surprise for your birthday, now we have bad news'. He told me about my brother and I went back to Santa Fe with them, injured as I was, feeling the physical pain and the pain in my soul. Daniel Passarella kept phoning me to say, 'We need you', but I know he only said it to take my mind off the tragedy.

"I came back to play in the World Cup because my parents asked me to. I thought to myself, 'Well, I've done my bit, now I want to be with my parents', but they drove me and told me, 'You must go on playing, you will reach the final and you will have to play'. So I made up my mind and did my best, despite the pain, and I made it to the final.

"It was very sad, I was 28 and my brother was 25. I am the eldest and he came next, and I have four younger sisters too. It was sad. Losing a brother is very hard, but losing a son, that must be horrible, and I saw my parents in a very bad shape, devastated, and that is why I wanted to stay with them. But they always supported me as a football player, they drove me to Rosario and I carried on.

"After we had won the final, after I had received my medal, I left the party early because I wanted to get home. I saw people at every street corner with flags. Everybody was outside celebrating – but I was happier than them, because in spite of my sadness and my eagerness to be with my parents, with my heart divided due to my brother's death and my victory, I had been one of those that gave happiness to these people."

Leopoldo Luque jumps to avoid the tackle of Dutch defender Ernie Brandts in the World Cup final.

"We wanted to give the people some joy," says defender Alberto Tarantini. "We wanted people to forget a little about what we were all living through during the month of the World Cup. Sure, the pressure was on us but that team had the personality to handle it."

What the junta wanted from the World Cup was clear to Argentina's coach, the 40-year-old chain-smoker César Luis Menotti, but he encouraged a belief amongst his players that they were playing for the fans, not for General Jorge Videla and the country that he represented. During 30 days of football an extraordinary rapport developed between squad and supporters. "They would run alongside the bus," recalls centre-forward, Leopoldo Luque. "There were people who waved at us holding an image of the Sacred Heart or some other holy image. So we felt a commitment, warmth and a desire which those people had awakened in us."

There was an increasing sense that, after the disappointments of the past, Argentina's time had now come. Because Menotti believed that this was the people's game he told his team to play in an entertaining and attacking style. In the Monumental Stadium, Menotti's team put his philosophy into practice, playing football with passion. But it hadn't been an easy journey for him. On taking the job, he had been forced to confront Argentina's historic club before country approach to the game. After being denied the players of the dominant Boca Juniors and River Plate in 1975, Menotti selected a side from the less fashionable regional clubs, many of whom would remain the backbone of his team all the way to the 1982 World Cup: full-back Galván, midfielders Ardíles, Gallego and Kempes, and striker Luque. Even 17-year-old Diego Maradona had been close to inclusion in the 1978 squad, axed at the last minute when the 25-man preliminary squad had to be cut down to the final 22. "That was the most bitter moment of my career," he has said. "I cried, and I still cry when I remember it."

Menotti had wanted to bring the squad together for several months of team-building before the tournament, but in the face of an exodus of Argentine talent to Europe after the 1974 World Cup, to allow enough preparation time he had also vowed to select just three of his country's overseas stars. Ultimately, though, he only picked one, Valencia's Mario Kempes. "Menotti's great virtue was to give players a lot of freedom," says Kempes. "He gave them a lot of confidence. Of course, the player had to handle the three or four tasks he assigned each player for the team but, beyond these, players had full freedom to do what they would usually do for their own club. He was not restrictive; he would give you as much freedom as possible so you would feel comfortable on the pitch."

"Menotti was a breath of fresh air for Argentinian football," says Osvaldo Ardíles. "His methods were completely different to what had come before but, in fact, were the essence of Argentinian football. He represented a return to traditional Argentine ways of playing. He put special emphasis on the idea that we had to return to first principles – a relationship with the ball, treating it well and with skill."

In the slight, graceful Ardíles, Argentines saw the virtues of a specifically Argentinian way of playing, what they called in Spanish *La Nuestra* – Our Way. This was a style of football shaped by the same forces that created modern Argentina. Introduced at the end of the 19th Century by the English, football was at first viewed as the sport of the economic elite, but the football of *La Nuestra* was created by the poor immigrants from Italy and Spain who passed through the port of La Boca in Buenos Aires. They took this English invention and made it their own. "The English talked a lot about fair play but when they saw the kind of spirit Argentinians brought to their football they distanced themselves from the game," says journalist Ezequiel Fernandez Moores. "Other immigrants, the Italians and the Spanish, saw football very differently. They adapted more easily."

Like the tango, Argentine football came from the country's underclass, and like the music, the people's game was full of graceful movement, vibrant energy and passion. In this immigrant nation of many languages, creeds and cultures, the national team became a unique source of pride and identity. When Argentina played in the 1978 World Cup, matches had the exact same patriotic function – one nation under the flag. Everything that General Videla wanted.

The hosts were drawn in the toughest group, alongside Italy, France and Hungary, but after dominating an exciting clash against the Hungarians, their fans had every reason to expect the team to progress. In this atmosphere even those who the military junta had demonised as enemies of the state were behind the team. Less than half a mile from the Monumental Stadium – at the Argentine Navy Mechanical School – was a detention and torture centre. Here prisoners could hear the roar from the stadium as the games were played. "There were over 300 of these centres all over Argentina but this was the main one," explains Ezequiel Fernandez Moores. "Over 5,000 people passed through there. Later I found out that the prisoners heard the goals from the stadium, and they told me that even chained up, with their heads covered in hoods, they cheered the goals. And they could hear almost at the same time the screams of their tortured cellmates."

A solitary defeat to Italy in their last match of the first round meant that Menotti's Argentina squad would have

Dominique Rocheteau models the green and white shirts France borrowed from a local club side to play their match with Hungary.

to leave Buenos Aires for the next stage of the tournament, playing their second round games in Rosario. The Italians had proved the dominant force in the group, their coach Enzo Bearzot attempting to ditch the team's traditionally defensive tactics in favour of something approaching Total Football. A 2-1 victory over the French helped Argentina finish second in the table, but France had every reason to feel aggrieved, two harsh refereeing decisions – the award of a penalty against them and the denying of one in their favour – influencing the outcome of the match.

It hadn't been a happy tournament for Michel Platini and the French team, the players training with the Adidas stripes erased from their boots as a result of a financial dispute with the company. For coach Michel Hidalgo it was yet another shock, he and his wife having already survived an attempted kidnapping at home shortly before departing for Argentina. But there were still more bizarre hurdles for the French to clear before they could return home. Arriving at the *Estadio Mar del Plata* for their final game with Hungary with just their white-shirted change strip, the French discovered that FIFA had already asked the Hungarians to change to all white. Without an alternate kit, the French would be forced to forfeit the match, so the kick-off was delayed as police were dispatched to commandeer the playing strip of local second division side Kimberley. For the one and only time in their history, the French wore vertical green and white striped shirts along with their own blue shorts. They won the match 3-1 but were out of the competition.

Scotland arrived in Argentina with perhaps their greatest ever team, boasting players of the calibre of Archie Gemmill, Lou Macari, Graeme Souness, Kenny Dalglish and Joe Jordan, but their shambolic campaign, under the increasingly erratic decision-making of Ally MacLeod who had decided to leave a fit Andy Gray at home, degenerated into farce and acrimony. A 3-1 defeat to Peru in their first game was a jolt. The Scots had grotesquely underestimated their opponents, and for all of their star talent, they had proved unable to cope with the midfield threat of Teófilo Cubillas, who scored twice for Peru in the last 20 minutes of the game. After the final whistle, their winger Willie Johnston failed a drugs test, having taken two Fencamfamin pills. Protesting his innocence he

Kenny Dalglish exchanges shirts with Teófilo Cubillas, after Peru's 3-1 victory over Scotland in Córdoba.

was sent home in disgrace. A 1-1 draw with Iran ensured that his team-mates would be on their way home too. Only then, when it was too late, did the Scots show what they were capable of by beating the Dutch 3-2, Archie Gemmill scoring one of the tournament's finest goals in the process.

Qualifying top of the group, Peru had proven they weren't the expected push over, while doubts persisted whether second-placed Holland, without Cruyff, could mount a serious challenge. "I think it's a pity that Johan did not play more World Cups," says Dutch defender Arie Haan. "For me he was still the best player in the world, not Maradona, not Beckenbauer, but they are more famous because they played more times in the World Cup."

Cruyff wasn't the only Dutchman who had refused to go to the tournament. They were also without Wim van Hanegem, their best player in the 1974 final, who had pulled out of the squad the night before they were due to fly to Argentina. His absence was attributed to a dispute with Holland's Austrian manager Ernst Happel over the likelihood of his place in the starting line-up, but in reality it was caused by another money dispute in the Dutch team. Irked that some senior players preferred to keep individual sponsorship and advertising revenues for themselves, rather than pay everything into a central players' pool to be divided out among the whole squad, van Hanegem quit the team in disgust and sat out the tournament on a beach in Spain, tuning in for just one game: the final.

West Germany were also without their greatest player, Franz Beckenbauer having been overlooked by the *Deutscher Fussball Bund* from the point when, in April 1977, he announced he would be joining the New York Cosmos. Still under the control of Helmut Schön, who had been persuaded to stay on for one more World Cup after the victory of 1974, the West German team, combining the experience of Sepp Maier and Berti Vogts with young talent like Karl-Heinz Rummenigge and Hansi Müller, qualified in unimpressive style as runners-up to Poland in perhaps the weakest group of the tournament. They even struggled to a scoreless draw with Tunisia, although their six goals against Mexico proved they could work well in front of goal when so inclined.

The German campaign wasn't without controversy off the field. Hermann Neuberger, president of the DFB and vice-president of FIFA, had invited Hans Ulrich Rudel, an unrepentant former Nazi fighter pilot and war hero exiled in South America, to the squad's training camp in Ascochinga, while not allowing Günter Netzer, who was working for a newspaper. The scandal it caused in the German papers was second only to that inspired by the team's lacklustre performances.

Brazil, under 39-year-old coach Claudio Coutinho, had gone from the poetic to the pragmatic in just eight years. Coutinho was the army captain who had been brought in to assist the team with modern fitness techniques for the World Cup in Mexico. His 1978 Brazil team were not of the same vintage, focusing on fitness and European-inspired defensive tactics. Under Coutinho, Brazil were far from convincing, Rivelino the only man standing from the beautiful team of 1970. They managed only two goals in their first round group, but they had their share of bad luck in the match against Sweden, the outstanding Zico scoring what would have been the winner direct from a corner, had referee Clive Thomas not blown for full-time a split second before the ball hit the net. Along with Austria, Brazil squeezed through ahead of Spain and Sweden.

Despite their indifferent showings, all of the favourites had spluttered into a second round that fizzed with exciting fixtures. Group A featured European superpowers West Germany, Holland and Italy, plus a useful Austrian side, fronted by the prolific Hans Krankl. Group B included the Poles and Peru, plus arguably the fiercest rivals in world football – Argentina and Brazil. Playing their second round ties in the smaller, more compact stadium of the provincial city of Rosario, the hosts now found themselves closer to the fans than in River Plate's giant Monumental Stadium. For striker Mario Kempes, this was a sentimental return to the ground where he had first played as a professional. "Returning to Rosario was lovely," he recalls. "I had played on that very pitch. This was a return to the ground where I had scored so many beautiful goals. Playing there, things changed completely for me. I believe Rosario gave me a push, so I could start showing why Menotti had brought me in. The River Stadium is very nice, very big, but it has that synthetic track around the pitch, so the crowd is a bit further away, while in Rosario the whole crowd is right there, next to the fence. You feel more pressure, maybe more so for the opposition than for us, and maybe this helped us a bit to get through."

Kempes, the player the fans liked to call *El Matador*, was fast becoming the heartbeat of the team. A new hero for the nation, he scored the two goals that finished off Poland. Brazil had beaten Peru 3-0 in their first game, and when they eventually faced Argentina, the weight of history and the fear of defeat were too much to bear for both sides and the match fizzled into an ill-tempered 0-0 draw. Providing both teams could win their last matches, the finalist would be decided on goal difference. When Brazil overcame Poland 3-1 in Mendoza, the balance of power appeared to have swung their way. But despite the fact that in the other group the final games kicked off simultaneously, in Group B schedules had been drawn up to favour the hosts, Argentina kicking-off their last game against Peru in Rosario 45 minutes after the Brazil-Poland encounter had finished. Cesar Menotti's side had the massive advantage of knowing they had to win by four clear goals to reach the final, although Argentina had not beaten Peru by that margin since their very first meeting in 1927.

The Estadio Monumental Antonio V Liberti in Buenos Aires, otherwise known as River Plate stadium.

The decisive game against Peru would leave many lingering question marks over the achievements of Menotti and his team. General Videla was in the stands to give his support, and just before the match he had made the curious decision to visit the dressing room of his team's opponents. "The Peruvian player Oblitas told me that Videla spoke about Latin American brotherhood," says Ezequiel Fernandez Moores, "about this great opportunity Latin America had to show itself to the world, about Latin American unity. According to what Oblitas told me these were words from a dictator which intimidated a group of young players."

Peru, who had looked so accomplished early in the tournament, at first appeared up for the challenge, hitting the post near the beginning of the game. Then, in one of the most talked about matches in World Cup history, they rolled over and the goals began to flow for Argentina and their five-man strikeforce. "I was doing the commentary on what I saw as a normal match," says Victor Hugo Morales. "It was fear, stage fright from the Peruvians. The fact that Argentina were playing at home and were three or four goals ahead didn't seem absurd. When you can win by three or four goals, to extend that to six or seven doesn't take much."

There were immediate suspicions that the game had been fixed, and these seemed to be confirmed with later allegations that bribes had been paid and deals done between Argentine and Peruvian Generals. In 1986 *The Sunday Times* published an article by Maria Laura Avignolo. Based on the word of anonymous Argentine football and civil service sources, it alleged that Argentina had shipped 35,000 tons of free grain to Peru, and possibly arms too, while the Argentine central bank unfroze $50 million in credits. The journalist was put on trial in Argentina, accused of 'moral turpitude', but was eventually acquitted.

There were other elements to the conspiracy theory. Peru played the match in red, rather than their famed white shirt with its diagonal red stripe; eccentric goalkeeper, Ramon Quiroga, known as 'El Loco', was in fact born in

MARIO KEMPES

Argentina's Mario Kempes scored twice in the World Cup final and won the Golden Boot.

"I believe Argentina won the World Cup because at the time all of the players were playing in Argentina, except me. I was playing in Europe for Valencia. They worked together for three months before the World Cup started – being 'focused' for three months is usually too much, but when I got there I found a fantastic group. There was no infighting, no shouting, nobody was any more dominant than the others, but rather we were all the same. There were no special stars and there were no differences among us.

"The selection of Ardíles and Galván was questioned more than anybody else in the team; people did not like them, and that was strange, because Ardíles had already shown, first at Instituto de Cordoba and later at Huracán, that he was a very good player. But of course everybody thought that with Ardíles being so small, and with all those giants from Europe, he would not be able to play the way he played for Huracán. Nevertheless, he did what he did and people had to shut up. He walked over all of them. He ended up being one of the stalwarts of the team, indefatigable both in defence and attack. He would get to the opponents' goal, he would defend very well and he knew how to handle the ball.

"Argentina has always had very good players in all departments; the thing is that with this style of football, it is usually the forwards that shine, but in 1978 Menotti worked very well with the whole team. There were not just 11 players, but 22 of us in the squad and we all worked together. When the time came to defend, we would all defend; and when time came to attack, we would attack in numbers. We combined both tasks very well.

"For the first match, Menotti used me as a left-winger and I seldom played that way. I was used to starting further back, to be in contact with the ball, so this first match was quite tough for me. For the second match, he placed me a bit further back, so I had a better perspective of the goal and I had more contact with the ball, and that's when I started developing my best football.

"For the first match I had a beard and a moustache, but for the second and third match only a moustache. Menotti told me, 'Well, now we've played the first three matches you can shave and maybe you will start scoring'. When I started shaving I also started scoring.

"When we came on the pitch for the World Cup final there was confetti everywhere and you could hardly see anything. You could hear the shouting and the cheering, but once the match starts you forget everything around you. Only when you score do you feel what's around you again, but that's 45 seconds or so, no more, just time to celebrate and then kick off once more from the centre circle. But to play in a World Cup final and feel that emotion in your own country, with all those people cheering… we could not fail them, and indeed we did not.

"When we were presented with the World Cup trophy I didn't get to touch it, because it was a moment when many of the boys were so full of expectancy that when I got there they had taken it away already. But being unable to touch it is minor. Having done what we had done we had to feel happy, joyful, we had finally given the World Cup to Argentina and put the country in the place it deserved. We had always had very good national sides with very good players, but we had never won the World Cup. And that was the great moment, the great opportunity and we managed to take advantage of it."

Mario Kempes celebrates scoring his second goal in the final while Ruud Krol looks on.

Rosario in Argentina, to Argentine parents, before emigrating to Peru; while reserve keeper Manzo reportedly admitted to the fix while drunk, retracting his words the next day. "Everything that was later talked about was very difficult for me to come to terms with, because I had to own up to my own naivety," says Victor Hugo Morales. "At the time I hadn't considered this at all."

"We thought it was very strange at the time," says Rivelino. "Losing, that's part of football, but the way they lost was very strange. Brazil and Argentina should have played their games at the same time. They got Brazil to play Poland, and Argentina played later. Three years later the Peruvian goalkeeper said, 'Yes, it was all a fix'. That's not great."

The Argentine players remain vehement about their own innocence, and whilst acknowledging the junta's capacity for criminality, they remain sceptical about the allegations. "I believe not and I hope not," says Ardíles. "If it were true it would diminish our winning of the World Cup. Looked at another way, if these people were capable of such atrocities, they wouldn't have had any qualms about fixing a match. Personally I don't think they did it. Not because they had the moral principles not to do it, but I don't see how they could have done it."

As fans celebrated General Videla now came into the Argentine dressing room to offer his thanks. Here was an opportunity for revenge for defender Alberto Tarantini. Despite the euphoria of reaching a World Cup final, Tarantini remembered the victims of Videla's Dirty War – a part of his life that allowed no forgiveness or forgetting. "I had three friends who disappeared at the time of the military and I went to ask about them," remembers Tarantini. "They didn't pay me the slightest bit of notice, didn't even give me the time of day. So I said to Daniel Passarella, 'I'll bet you a thousand dollars that if Videla comes I'll rub soap all over my balls, and when he comes up to me I'll shake his hand'. So he said, 'You're on'. Videla came to meet us as I was soaping my balls and he had to shake hands with me, with all the photographers and journalists there, and then he pulled a face! It was all very funny but I had to go abroad to play afterwards. I am very proud of what I did and I don't regret it. I did not agree at all with what they were doing."

When the dust settled, Argentina – 48 years after they had lost the first World Cup to Uruguay – had booked themselves a ticket to the final of their own fiesta. In the other group, Holland exploded into life with a 5-1 destruction of Austria to take an early stranglehold on the group, while Italy and West Germany drew 0-0. Holland strengthened their hand when, in a repeat of the 1974 final, goals from Haan and René van der Kerkhof earned them a useful 2-2 draw with West Germany. With Italy beating Austria 1-0, the Dutch knew that unless the West Germans could manage to win by a landslide against Austria, a draw against Italy would be sufficient. The West German team, a shadow of their 1974 side, were put out of their misery when they lost 3-2 to the already-eliminated Austrians. Holland did all that was required and more by beating Italy 2-1.

In the third-place play-off, Brazil overcame Enzo Bearzot's Italy 2-1 to maintain the only unbeaten record of the tournament. But in some ways the victory only upset them even more because for the first time in the competition they shed their inhibitions and played in the great Brazilian tradition. As for the Italians, 1978 would prove a valuable educational experience. "We played good football and we won lots of matches," says Italian defender, Claudio Gentile. "But I would say that we were quite young and inexperienced and we missed getting to the final as a result of that inexperience, and some bad luck. We didn't repeat the same mistakes in 1982."

The day of the final people poured on to the streets of Buenos Aires in a state of frenzied expectation. Argentina was now one game away from winning its first World Cup final. "It was just amazing," recalls Tarantini. "You stepped out on to the pitch and you could feel it moving, the people screaming – it's so hard to explain. I thought I could feel their breath on the back of my neck."

"Holland had been showing what a great side they were," says Kempes, "but we were in our own country and had the support of our people. It was a very difficult match, that's for sure, but there was a special atmosphere prevailing, not just at the stadium but throughout the country, and I believe there was nobody left in the streets of Argentina, everybody was hooked to their TV sets."

Before the game, Argentina had already played gamesmanship over the choice of referee, refusing to accept FIFA's selection of the Israeli, Abraham Klein. They claimed that because of Holland's close political ties with Israel, Klein would be unsuitable. It could be no coincidence, too, that he had been the referee for Argentina's first round game with Italy, the only match they had lost on the way to the final. FIFA caved in and appointed the Italian, Sergio Gonella, to officiate.

Argentina continued the psychological warfare on match day, attempting to unnerve the Dutch by keeping them on the pitch for five minutes before their arrival to a sea of sky blue and white flags. Daniel Passarella then objected

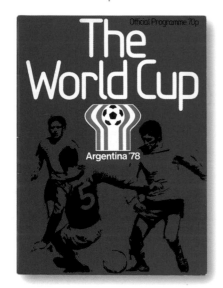

to the lightweight cast on René van der Kerkhof's arm, which he had worn in the five previous matches. The game was delayed while the referee insisted that yet another bandage was applied over the top. "I played a major role in this incident," reveals Ossie Ardíles. "When we exchanged pennants I shook hands with Van der Kerkhof and I thought, 'He's got a cast'. I told Passarella, and Passarella told Menotti, and suddenly it turned messy and the game was further delayed. I wish I had not said anything because the whole thing was blown out of proportion. But I personally thought that he could not play with that thing on, that it really was dangerous. That's how I saw it."

When play began, high skill mingled with barely restrained contempt. The Argentines were up against what many considered the best team of the Seventies. It took courage and agility for Ubaldo Fillol to keep them at bay, Johnny Rep squandering a great chance for Holland. "He was around the penalty spot," says Fillol. "He was alone, received the ball, stopped and whacked it like a missile. It looked certain it would go in. But my reflexes are one of the best things about me and they saved me, because I jumped, extended my hand backwards and I felt the ball hitting my hand and going out of play. I made two very important saves in the first half."

In the first half hour the Dutch had the better of the play, then up stepped *El Matador*, Kempes putting Argentina ahead on 37 minutes. "In my whole football career I had never scored a goal like that one," he says. "Ardíles passed it to me and I dribbled past one guy and I'm running level, then I slid on the ground and when the goalie came out I shot and it rolled under him. That was the first goal." Argentina kept hold of their slim lead through much of the match, the Dutch growing feverish with frustration until substitute Dick Nanninga made up the difference. All week he had to been predicting to journalists that he would come on and score with ten minutes left, and in the 81st minute he headed the ball into the net from a René van de Kerkhof cross. Then, with just a minute to go, Rensenbrink struck the foot of the post. "I was in the middle of the pitch so I could see the move," recalls Luque. "I felt the silence when it hit the post. Everybody's hearts stopped."

With the match level after 90 minutes, the two sides faced extra-time. According to Fillol, Menotti tried to convince his players that Holland's moment had passed. "He said, 'Lads, that ball didn't go in, we are the new champions, but we have to put in more effort in these last 30 minutes. They're dead. They don't want it any more.'"

As both sides began to tire there was one last flourish from Kempes, who beat three defenders and keeper Jan Jongbloed to slot the ball home, securing the World Cup for Argentina and the Golden Boot for himself. "It was

Opposite: The 1978 World Cup final. (top & overleaf) Argentina captain Daniel Passarella holds the World Cup trophy as he is carried on the shoulders of fans. (bottom) Mario Kempes celebrates his second goal in front of Daniel Bertoni and Dutch defenders Wim Suurbier and a crouching Ruud Krol.

Argentina 3 Holland 1

1:0 MARIO KEMPES (ARG) 38', 1:1 DICK NANNINGA (HOL) 82', 2:1 MARIO KEMPES (ARG) 105,
3:1 DANIEL BERTONI (ARG) 115'

a goal full of emotion, a goal that had suspense," he says, "because the move was beautiful and the finish almost gave you a heart attack because the two Dutch guys were on the ground and I'm turning round to see if the ball had gone in. At the moment of celebration I didn't know who to hug."

An assist from Kempes allowed Bertoni to make it 3-1 to Argentina in the 25th minute of extra-time. The final whistle prompted dazed moments of ecstasy and one moment of Holy Communion between players and fans. "My legs gave way and I fell on my knees," says Fillol. "I fell on my knees, I crossed my arms – and I saw the image of God in front of me."

Tarantini: "I knelt down and crossed myself, went towards the centre of the pitch. I didn't know what I did then. Somehow I went back and I saw Fillol kneeling down, also praying."

"Tarantini comes over, he kneels down in front of me, hugs me," says Fillol. "Along comes a boy, with no arms, and he throws himself on top of us both." This photograph – what is known as the 'Hug of the Soul' – would become in Argentina the defining image of this exhilarating but turbulent tournament.

For the Dutch, defeat again was particularly hard to take. "We were a little bit unlucky to play two finals against the host country," sighs Ruud Krol. "It's never easy and it has never happened again, but it happened to us." In a politically motivated gesture the Dutch passed on greeting the Argentine military leadership during the presentations. It wasn't the grand snub that they had planned – the team had earlier decided to refuse to accept the trophy if they had won. "We always said if we became winners, we would not take the cup from Videla," says Arie Haan. "We didn't even go for our medals." After the match the team refused to attend the closing dinner. They would spend the evening locked away in their hotel for the second consecutive time. The team that had illuminated football in the Seventies, that probably did more to create the modern game than any other, were destined to end the decade without a major honour.

For Argentine centre-forward Leopoldo Luque and keeper Ubaldo Fillol, the joy of winning the World Cup was not in any way enhanced by the experience of being presented to General Videla. "I did not shake hands with Videla when he handed us the medal and the cup," says Fillol. "We knew something had been going on in the country because news reached us through foreign media."

"As a present for winning the World Cup, Videla gave me a cigar holder," says Luque. "Of course I accepted it, but I said, 'Thank you, but I am a football player, I don't smoke'. They did not have the slightest notion, not the slightest idea!"

In the evening the focus of Argentine celebrations moved from the Monumental Stadium to the streets of Buenos Aires. At a time when public demonstrations were banned, celebrating footballing glory allowed a night of liberation for the crowds. "I know of people who because of the World Cup went on to the streets for the first time since the military coup," says Ezequiel Fernandez Moores. "Big gatherings had been banned. A lot of people who went out to party managed to meet people they hadn't seen since the coup, political activists, for example, who had gone underground."

The day after the victory celebrations, General Videla went on to the balcony of the Presidential Palace – the Pink House – to receive the acclaim of the people. But he hadn't achieved all of his aims. Little had been known around the world about the crimes of his regime, but the World Cup helped to shine a bright light on all of the subjects that Videla had wanted swept under the carpet. "Because the tournament was there, everybody learned what was happening in Argentina," explains Arie Haan. "They had wanted to use it to show the positive side, but there was also a negative side for Argentina and the press were now writing about it, so it was not bad that we went there after all."

The tournament itself had not been a classic, but while Argentina 78 lacked a genuine superstar or a great team, the extreme emotions it generated – not to mention the whiff of scandal – ensured its place in football folklore.

GROUP 1

June 2: Monumental Stadium, Buenos Aires
Argentina **2 - 1** Hungary

June 2: Estadio Mar del Plata, Mar del Plata
Italy **2 - 1** France

June 6: Monumental Stadium, Buenos Aires
Argentina **2 - 1** France

June 6: Estadio Mar del Plata, Mar del Plata
Italy **3 - 1** Hungary

June 10: Monumental Stadium, Buenos Aires
Italy **1 - 0** Argentina

June 10: Estadio Mar del Plata, Mar del Plata
France **3 - 1** Hungary

	P	W	D	L	F	A	Pts
Italy	3	3	0	0	6	2	6
Argentina	3	2	0	1	4	3	4
France	3	1	0	2	5	5	2
Hungary	3	0	0	3	3	8	0

GROUP 2

June 1: Monumental Stadium, Buenos Aires
West Germany **0 - 0** Poland

June 2: New Rosario Stadium, Rosario
Tunisia **3 - 1** Mexico

June 6: New Rosario Stadium, Rosario
Poland **1 - 0** Tunisia

June 6: Estadio Córdoba, Córdoba
West Germany **6 - 0** Mexico

June 10: New Rosario Stadium, Rosario
Poland **3 - 1** Mexico

June 10: Estadio Córdoba, Córdoba
West Germany **0 - 0** Tunisia

	P	W	D	L	F	A	Pts
Poland	3	2	1	0	4	1	5
West Germany	3	1	2	0	6	0	4
Tunisia	3	1	1	1	3	2	3
Mexico	3	0	0	3	2	12	0

GROUP 3

June 3: Estadio José Amalfitani, Buenos Aires
Austria **2 - 1** Spain

June 3: Estadio Mar del Plata, Mar del Plata
Sweden **1 - 1** Brazil

June 7: Estadio José Amalfitani, Buenos Aires
Austria **1 - 0** Sweden

June 7: Estadio Mar del Plata, Mar del Plata
Brazil **0 - 0** Spain

June 11: Estadio José Amalfitani, Buenos Aires
Spain **1 - 0** Sweden

June 11: Estadio Mar del Plata, Mar del Plata
Brazil **1 - 0** Austria

	P	W	D	L	F	A	Pts
Austria	3	2	0	1	3	2	4
Brazil	3	1	2	0	2	1	4
Spain	3	1	1	1	2	2	3
Sweden	3	0	1	2	1	3	1

GROUP 4

June 3: Estadio Córdoba, Córdoba
Peru **3 - 1** Scotland

June 3: Estadio Mendoza, Mendoza
Holland **3 - 0** Iran

June 7: Estadio Córdoba, Córdoba
Scotland **1 - 1** Iran

June 7: Estadio Mendoza, Mendoza
Holland **0 - 0** Peru

June 11: Estadio Córdoba, Córdoba
Peru **4 - 1** Iran

June 11: Estadio Mendoza, Mendoza
Scotland **3 - 2** Holland

	P	W	D	L	F	A	Pts
Peru	3	2	1	0	7	2	5
Holland	3	1	1	1	5	3	3
Scotland	3	1	1	1	5	6	3
Iran	3	0	1	2	2	8	1

THE FINAL

ARGENTINA	(1) **3**
HOLLAND	(1) **1**

(AET; 1-1 at 90 mins)

DATE SUNDAY June 25, 1978
ATTENDANCE 77,260
VENUE River Plate Stadium, Buenos Aires

Fillol

Olguin Galvan Passarella Tarantini

Ardiles Gallego Ortiz Bertoni

Luque Kempes

Rensenbrink Rep

v d Kerkhof, R v d Kerkhof, W Haan Neeskens

Jansen Brandts Krol Poortvliet

Jongbloed

ARGENTINA
COACH: CESAR LUIS MENOTTI

FILLOL
OLGUIN
GALVAN
PASSARELLA
TARANTINI
ARDÍLES ▯
Booked: 40 mins. Subbed: 66 mins (Larossa)
GALLEGO
ORTIZ
Subbed: 75 mins (Houseman)
BERTONI ⊕
Goal: 115 mins
LUQUE
KEMPES ⊕⊕
Goal: 38, 105 mins
sub: LAROSSA ▯
Booked: 94 mins
sub: HOUSEMAN

HOLLAND
COACH: RINUS MICHELS

JONGBLOED
POORTVLIET ▯
Booked: 96 mins
KROL ▯
Booked: 15 mins
BRANDTS
JANSEN
Subbed: 73 mins (Suurbier)
NEESKENS
HAAN
VAN DE KERKHOF, W
VAN DE KERKHOF, R
REP
Subbed: 59 mins (Nanninga)
RENSENBRINK
sub: NANNINGA ⊕
Goal: 82 mins
sub: SUURBIER ▯
Booked: 94

REFEREE: Gonella (Italy)

SECOND ROUND GROUP A

June 14: Monumental Stadium, Buenos Aires
Italy **0 - 0** West Germany

June 14: Estadio Córdoba, Córdoba
Holland **5 - 1** Austria

June 18: Monumental Stadium, Buenos Aires
Italy **1 - 0** Austria

June 18: Estadio Córdoba, Córdoba
Holland **2 - 2** West Germany

June 21: Monumental Stadium, Buenos Aires
Holland **2 - 1** Italy

June 21: Estadio Córdoba, Córdoba
Austria **3 - 2** West Germany

	P	W	D	L	F	A	Pts
Holland	3	2	1	0	9	4	5
Italy	3	1	1	1	2	2	3
West Germany	3	0	2	1	4	5	2
Austria	3	1	0	2	4	8	2

SECOND ROUND GROUP B

June 14: New Rosario Stadium, Rosario
Argentina **2 - 0** Poland

June 14: Estadio Mendoza, Mendoza
Brazil **3 - 0** Peru

June 18: New Rosario Stadium, Rosario
Argentina **0 - 0** Brazil

June 18: Estadio Mendoza, Mendoza
Poland **1 - 0** Peru

June 21: Estadio Mendoza, Mendoza
Brazil **3 - 1** Poland

June 21: New Rosario Stadium, Rosario
Argentina **6 - 0** Peru

	P	W	D	L	F	A	Pts
Argentina	3	2	1	0	8	0	5
Brazil	3	2	1	0	6	1	5
Poland	3	1	0	2	2	5	2
Peru	3	0	0	3	0	10	0

THIRD PLACE PLAY-OFF

June 24: Monumental Stadium, Buenos Aires
Brazil **2 - 1** Italy

Playing for time: Argentina on their way to victory in the World Cup final.

TOP GOALSCORERS 6 goals: Mario Kempes (Argentina) **5 goals:** Teófilo Cubillas (Peru), Rob Rensenbrink (Holland) **4 goals:** Hans Krankl (Austria), Leopoldo Luque (Argentina)

FASTEST GOAL 31 seconds: Bernard Lacombe (France v Italy)

TOTAL GOALS: 102 **AVERAGE GOALS** 2.68 per game:

CAMPIONI DEL MONDO

The stars shone brightly in 1982, but it wasn't Platini or Maradona who grabbed the headlines. That honour went to Paolo Rossi, who transformed his tarnished reputation when he made Italy champions of the world.

It had been decided that Spain should host the 1982 World Cup as early as 1964, confirmed two years later at the FIFA Congress in London. Some £40 million was spent on redeveloping stadia to World Cup standard, and a further £60 million on the organisational costs, but still there were many doubts about Spain's ability to host such a major sporting event, and those fears were heightened as the draw turned into farce. Taking place in Madrid on January 16, 1982, the balls representing Peru and Chile were accidentally left in the draw from the start, when it was FIFA policy to keep them out initially in order to ensure the teams were kept apart from their more illustrious neighbours, Brazil and Argentina. Scotland, meanwhile, were mistakenly put in Argentina's group in place of Belgium, before being moved into their correct pool with Brazil. The confusion led to a halt in proceedings, then to compound the situation, the cage containing the balls jammed and one ball split in half. It all made for compelling television, but the charade was met with worldwide condemnation.

With the tournament's expansion to 24 teams, there was a real fear that sides like Kuwait, Honduras and El Salvador would amount to little more than cannon fodder for the major footballing nations, but the magic of the World Cup always throws up the most unexpected of surprises, and 1982 proved no exception. Increasing the size of the tournament had been an ambition of former FIFA president Sir Stanley Rous and had been taken up as a campaign promise by João Havelange when he succeeded Rous in 1974, gaining extra votes in return for his promise to increase representation from the African and Asian federations. The expansion of the tournament meant

Marco Tardelli kisses the World Cup trophy after Italy's triumph at the Bernabéu Stadium in Madrid.

Kevin Keegan is besieged by reporters as he arrives in Bilbao. Injury would keep Keegan out of the World Cup until England's last game.

another new format. The 24 teams were divided into six groups of four, the two top teams qualifying for a second phase of four groups, the winners of which would pass into a semi-final knock-out stage. This was the only World Cup to use this format. Adidas introduced yet another new ball in 1982, the Tango España. With rubber inlaid over the seams, it was the first ball with water-resistant qualities, but wear and tear to the rubber often meant the ball needed to be replaced during matches. It was the last genuine leather ball used at the World Cup.

A total of 109 teams entered the 12th World Cup, 105 actually taking part after the withdrawal of Ghana, Iran, Libya and Uganda. The European groups had grown in size, with six of the seven containing five teams, but to compensate, the top two nations in each would now qualify. West Germany finished their campaign with a 100 per cent record, scoring seven goals against Finland and eight against Albania. They qualified top of the table, along with Austria. England, meanwhile, very nearly missed out on qualification from an easy group. After losing their away games to Romania, Switzerland and Norway, they needed a single Paul Mariner goal against table-topping Hungary at Wembley to finish second. Italy also failed to top their group, progressing behind Yugoslavia. The Republic of Ireland missed out on making it to their first World Cup on goal difference, Belgium and France qualifying, with Holland finishing a disappointing fourth out of five.

Brazil qualified without dropping a point under manager Telê Santana. Former coach, Claudio Coutinho, who had taken Brazil to the two previous World Cups, had drowned the previous November, aged just 42. Peru made it to the finals at the expense of Uruguay, while Chile finished top of their group ahead of reigning South American champions Paraguay. In the Central and North American group, Honduras and El Salvador qualified ahead of Mexico, while Algeria and Cameroon made up the African representation. In the Asia/Oceania group, Kuwait finished top and were led to the finals by future World Cup winning coach Carlos Alberto Parreira. New Zealand remarkably beat Saudi Arabia by five goals in their last game to force a play-off, and just six days before the World Cup draw, they beat China 2-1 in Singapore to qualify.

Paolo Rossi also made a late bid for the World Cup, only becoming available for selection a matter of weeks before the tournament. He would emerge as the big surprise star of the 1982 World Cup. Although he had impressed four years earlier in Argentina, his stock had been significantly devalued following his alleged involvement in an Italian match-fixing scandal that had become known as *Totonero*.

Corruption had long been a problem for Italian football. The mid Sixties had seen a huge investment in the game, and along with money came the desire to win at all costs. "It was quite horrific really as the corruption was absolutely infamous," explains journalist Brian Glanville. "It was difficult to find any player from any level in *Serie A* who wouldn't go along with it. It was a question of who *hadn't* been bribed." Betting on individual games was illegal in Italy and the only way to gamble on football was through *Totocalcio*, the Italian football pools. This restriction gave rise to a huge black economy of illegal gambling. "It was only a few years after the introduction of the pools that the first rumours of scandal emerged," says author Simon Martin. "Thereafter it was a consistent feature of Italian football, with a number of players and squads being punished quite heavily for fixing matches."

COPA DEL MUNDO DE FUTBOL ESPAÑA 82

The most significant of these scandals hit the news in 1980, when many well known Italian players were accused of rigging results. But the biggest name of all was that of Italian football's golden boy, Paulo Rossi, who was accused of taking a bribe while playing on loan for Perugia against Avellino on December 30, 1979. The match had ended 2-2, with Rossi scoring both of Perugia's goals, but after an inquiry the following year, Rossi and several team-mates were accused and convicted of 'fixing' the result. Rossi claimed that his reply to a question asked by an opposition player – "2-2? If you want!" – was entirely innocent.

The scandal was brought to light after the men behind the fix became aggrieved with the amount of money they were regularly losing when players failed to deliver the promised result. They first tried to blackmail the Italian football federation with threats of going public, and absurdly blew the whistle while trying to have criminal charges pressed against the players for defrauding them. Even the president of AC Milan became implicated and by the time the scandal had run its course, some 50 years of bans had been apportioned and 25 points deducted from various clubs, relegating Milan and Lazio to *Serie B*. "The fact that top stars let themselves be caught into this network of illegal betting with all sorts of underworld syndicates was a major shock," says journalist Giancarlo Galvalotti. "For someone like Paulo Rossi to be implicated was really a shock within the shock."

In spite of his denials, and the weak evidence against him compared to many of the other cases, Rossi was suspended for three years, later reduced on appeal to two years. He would always maintain his innocence, claiming that he had been used as a high profile warning to others. His suspension ended on April 29, 1982, allowing him to play just three games for Juventus – who had bought him while banned – before the end of the season. Italian coach Enzo Bearzot caused a sensation when he called Rossi up to the Italian squad for the World Cup, despite his complete lack of match fitness.

The 1982 World Cup kicked off on June 13 in front of a crowd of 95,000 at Barcelona's Nou Camp, with a match between Belgium and the defending champions. The Argentinian team was still under the command of coach César Luis Menotti, who would pay the price for the loyalty he showed his world champions. Passarella aside, they were not playing with the same conviction they had displayed four years earlier. Back in Argentina little had changed, the feel-good factor created by their 1978 World Cup had quickly evaporated and for the military junta it was business as usual, the torture still continuing in the *Escuela Mechanica de la Armada*. Drugged victims were taken in unmarked cars out of a back entrance, transferred to planes and helicopters, and then dropped into the waters of the River Plate. It is thought up to 30,000 disappeared in these years of military rule, but weekly protests by the 'Mothers of the Disappeared' in front of the Presidential Palace also continued, as awareness of the junta's crimes increased. There was now a confidence to take on the military. "In March 1982 it was the first time the people fiercely protested against the dictatorship," says journalist Ezequiel Fernandez Moores.

With their popularity ebbing away, the junta – now fronted by General Galtieri – decided on a little patriotic diversion, one that they hoped would have the same unifying effect as the regime's other great national triumph, the 1978 World Cup. In April 1982, as troops landed on the Falklands, the national team was at home in Argentina, training for the forthcoming World Cup. Like the majority of the country, the squad were no different in believing that *Las Islas Malvinas* belonged to Argentina. "Without doubt we supported the fact that Argentina should recover the islands," says Osvaldo Ardíles. "In Argentina we are born believing those islands are ours, that they have been stolen from us and therefore to recover the islands is a matter of national pride."

In early May the squad travelled to Spain, leaving Argentina in a state of patriotic frenzy. The population was subjected to an unprecedented propaganda campaign promising imminent victory in the war, and winning another World Cup could only bring further glory to the nation. As the tournament began, Argentina were looking a good bet to retain the World Cup. "It was tremendously exciting," says Ardíles. "We were convinced we were going to win. Basically it was the same squad from 1978, but every one was more experienced. We were better players without doubt. Individually we had grown."

Alongside the heroes of 1978, there was a new star, Diego Armando Maradona. "Diego had this really rare ability," says Socrates of Brazil. "Few players have had this ability, we call it a sixth sense, someone who can make the ball do whatever he wants." Like many Latin American footballers, Maradona learnt his skills during games played on wastelands, in Argentina what is called the *potrero*. "In the old days, it was the norm to get together with a bunch of mates, put four bricks down and play ball," recalls Mario Kempes. "Any space was good enough."

Maradona made his first appearance for Argentina against Hungary in 1977, at the age of only 16. Controversially omitted from the squad for the following year's World Cup, he led Argentina to victory in the World Youth Cup in 1979. From the start of his professional career it was clear that Maradona was a footballer apart, a phenomenon. "He's a monster," says commentator Juan Sasturain. "A monster is someone without equal, someone who doesn't belong to any class, he's in a class of his own. When something is monstrous, it can be something beautiful or something terrible."

Before the 1982 World Cup Maradona had been playing his club football at *La Bombonara,* home of Boca Juniors in the docklands of Buenos Aires, where football had arrived by boat a century earlier. Maradona, a descendent of immigrants, made it clear he was a man of the people – he scored fabulous goals and was idolised for it. By the beginning of the World Cup – the climax of the Falklands War – Argentina looked to Maradona to become the saviour of national pride, because by then it was becoming apparent that the military had lied, that the war to liberate the *Malvinas* was being lost, not won.

"Perhaps our trip to Spain could have been cancelled," suggests Mario Kempes, "but it was all planned by the military to relieve some of the pressure they were under. Whether we played or not, there was nothing we could have done. We only learned how things really were later on, not while things were happening."

OSVALDO ARDÍLES

For the Argentinian midfielder, 1982 was not just the year of the World Cup, it was the time of the Falklands War.

"Just before the World Cup, Argentina regained the Falkland Islands. I was playing in England at the time and had an FA Cup semi-final to play with Tottenham. We won and reached the final, but it had already been agreed between Argentine coach César Luis Menotti and Tottenham manager Keith Burkinshaw that after that game, regardless of the outcome, I would leave for Argentina. I think Argentina took the Islands on April 2, I played the semi-final on April 3, and arrived back home on April 4. But it was not, as many people thought, that I left because the whole thing was starting. When England sent the Navy, I was already in Argentina with the team, getting ready to play at the World Cup in Spain.

"As the national side, we had a very important role to play. We raised funds and we gave our unqualified support to the junta. Today I would see it differently, but at the time I fully supported it all. The Falklands are Argentine and our support was absolutely unequivocal. Almost from the day we are born, it is *'Las Malvinas son Argentinas'*. If you ask me now, everything that causes war is absurd. The two countries did it simply because Galtieri in Argentina and Thatcher in England wanted to stay in power, it's as simple as that, and because of that hunger for power so many people died.

"Menotti did not ask us to support the war, each one of us was free to do as he pleased, but it was absolutely unanimous, with all the players and the technical staff. It was not a difficult decision to take. Not that we supported the war, but we definitely supported the fact that Argentina had recovered the Islands.

"When fighting began, there were people dying on both sides – my country and the country I lived in, which I loved so much. They were at war one against the other and I felt both the Argentinian losses and the English losses. Both were horrible. The whole thing was terrible, perhaps the bleakest period in my life.

"It was a bit strange to play football at this time, but it was our patriotic duty to go to the World Cup in Spain, and if possible, to win it. That was our role in the war; that is how we saw it. Later on, many people used the whole situation as a pretext to justify why we did not play well, but it was just an excuse. We were football players and there was no way we could help our country other than by doing well in the World Cup, winning it if possible. That was our patriotic duty.

"We were in Spain when Argentina surrendered and the war ended. It was a shock in the sense that when we left Argentina we were winning the war and when we arrived in Spain we were already losing it, according to the Spanish and English newspapers. We realised that things were not quite how we had been told, that things were going really badly in the Falklands. This was a political realisation and a psychological one too.

"For me the Falklands War was an episode that destroyed my world as it was at the time. Everything was going incredibly well, I was playing the best football I had ever played and I was very happy in England. I was in the Argentina side to play at the World Cup, everything was going really smoothly – and that perfect world came to an end with the war. After the World Cup I went to play in France and I have never played so badly in my entire life. My head was simply destroyed, beginning with the Falklands War, and it took me years to recover."

Osvaldo Ardíles battles with Italy's Gabriele Oriali and Francesco Graziani.

"The hardest thing was that when we left here we were winning the war. That's what we were told by the military junta, that's what they made people believe," recalls defender, Alberto Tarantini. "We faced reality when we got to Spain and saw what was happening. I think that was a really hard blow for the team, to see boys who were dying of cold, with terrible problems… in that shitty war."

"I was living in Spain already and when I arrived back in Argentina I found a totally disconcerting journalistic reality," remembers Jorge Valdano, whose World Cup would come to a premature end after injury in the second game. "What the Argentine media were saying about the war had nothing to do with the information I had read in Spanish papers and when I wanted to talk about it, I received rather aggressive reactions, some of them a bit violent, even within the squad. I was accused with a very fashionable epithet at the time: anti-Argentinian.

"Somehow we were the sporting ambassadors of a country at war, and we were given some instructions in case the media asked us about the conflict, but those instructions were given to us without much conviction, so nobody followed them. Personally I was not for the war and the media were eagerly trying to find out what we, sportsmen, thought about the war. I remember answering with complete freedom."

By the time of Argentina's first match against Belgium, the country had temporarily lost its enormous appetite for football. A goal from Belgium's Erwin Vandenbergh made certain that this would be the first opening game in 20 years that didn't end in a draw. It was also the first time since 1950 that the defending champions had lost their opening game. The new superstar of world football, Diego Maradona, recently signed by Barcelona for £4 million and making his first appearance at the ground of his new club, was subdued by efficient Belgian defending. The day after this shock defeat, British armed forces accepted the final Argentine surrender in Port Stanley.

"I don't believe any of the players managed to forget the Falklands issue and just focus on football," says Tarantini. "You don't think about the things that are going on, but the issue is always present. It would not be fair to say that the war did affect our performance, but we did not manage to eradicate that damn war from our minds, that is true." At a time when it was hard to concentrate on football, Argentina finished second in the group to Belgium, at least having convincingly beaten a Hungary side that had put ten goals past El Salvador.

Cameroon's Roger Milla steps past Italy's Claudio Gentile.

Despite their poor showings in the two previous tournaments, Brazil were among the favourites to lift the cup. The flair and breathtaking skill – so absent four years earlier – had returned, while in Zico, Socrates, Falção and Junior, they had a prowess that few could match, attacking to the sound of the terrace samba beat. The 4-1 victory against Scotland – in which David Narey had the audacity to score first – and a 4-0 win over New Zealand indicated their intention. They qualified comfortably for the second phase without dropping a point, the Soviet Union snatching second place from Scotland on goal difference.

Their rivals did not have it so easy. The Italians made a less than auspicious start. As the World Cup got underway the Italian press were scathing in their criticism of the players and their sizeable win bonuses. Paolo Rossi's two-year break from international football seemed to have sapped his confidence. He failed to score against Poland, he was substituted after a dreadful first half with Peru, and in Italy's third group game he again fired blanks against a Cameroon side that boasted future luminaries of African football, keeper Thomas N'Kono and the charismatic star of *Italia 90*, Roger Milla. Much later accusations of match fixing were to surface, not helped by Cameroon's strange tactic of defending a 1-1 draw when they needed another goal to progress. Italy had drawn all three of their group games, scoring just twice, and although Graziani's header against Cameroon secured them safe passage to the next round, it wasn't even on goal difference, but by dint of having scored one more goal than the Africans. Back home the Italian press were waging a war of words against the team. "Every news conference after a match became a trial," recalls the team's spokesman, Dino Zoff. "Instead of talking about football, we had to defend ourselves."

Defending their performance on the field was one thing but it seemed that the press would use any tactic to smear the players. "There had been a lot of criticism about the national team before the World Cup," says commentator, Fabio Caressa, "but a couple of journalists started talking about 'relationships' within the team."

"There was a rumour going round that Cabrini and Rossi were having an affair," says John Foot, author of *Calcio: A History Of Italian Football*. "They shared the same room and this just came about as they were leaning out of their hotel window with their tops off. Someone made some joke about it. They joked back and it got into the press. Then it became true. People will still tell you that there was something going on."

"Homosexuality in that period was a real tough subject in Italy," says Fabio Caressa. "So when that gossip came out, the team decided not to speak with anybody any more."

"We'd seen in the papers stories which simply weren't true," says Roma winger Bruno Conti. "The most horrible was that Rossi was 'with' Cabrini and that players were seen in bars or shooting up drugs. This didn't go with what we were trying to do or represent, so we got together and created a news blackout." As a result of this media boycott, this *silenzio stampa*, the Italian team found themselves united against the rest of the world. "Bearzot was behaving exactly like Vittorio Pozzo

Claudio Gentile preventing Brazil's Zico to the ball at the Nou Camp in Barcelona.

had, keeping the group together," says FIFA historian Pierre Lanfranchi. "They invented one phrase, *silenzio stampa,* and they didn't speak to the press during the whole tournament to keep the group together."

West Germany had arrived in Spain under the stewardship of Jupp Derwall, who had been Helmut Schön's assistant since 1970. In under a year in the job, Derwall had taken the team to triumph at the European Championship and had maintained an unbeaten record through the first two years of his tenure. For the first time, however, German football fans were going to learn that there were more important things than winning. After losing their opening game to Algeria, Derwall's team contributed to one of the most distasteful moments in World Cup history. Having scored against neighbours Austria through a header from Hrubesch after just ten minutes, the remainder of the game descended into a travesty of time wasting, as the two countries played out a result that would take them both through to the second phase at the expense of Algeria. Both teams would leave the pitch of Gijón's El Molinón Stadium with abuse ringing in their ears. Watching from the stands, French coach Michel Hidalgo suggested that the teams be given the Nobel Peace Prize, while the crowd waved white handkerchiefs at the players to suggest that a truce had been agreed.

A Spanish newspaper called the match, *El Anschluss,* while at home West Germany's largest tabloid newspaper reflected the views of the country with its headline, 'Shame On You'. "What's happening here is disgraceful and has nothing to do with football," was how the German television commentary had called it during the match. "We wanted to progress, not play football," said Derwall, lamely trying to defend the performance. Lothar Matthäus, echoing the views of his coach, said, "We have gone through, that's all that counts." In the ultimate show of disregard for their public, from the safety of their luxury rooms the West German players hurled water-filled balloons at fans who had gathered outside the team's hotel in the hope of an explanation for the shameful performance.

It wasn't to prove a successful tournament for the hosts, who failed to shine under the leadership of their Uruguayan coach, José Santamaría. He had constructed a team around the stars of Spanish champions Real Sociedad, but whereas Sociedad employed a highly successful defensive game, Santamaría tried to have his team to play like Real Madrid. After a shock draw with the 500-1 outsiders Honduras, and a narrow victory over Yugoslavia, Spain were left sweating on their chance of progress as a Gerry Armstrong goal for Northern Ireland stunned the home support in Valencia. Keeper Pat Jennings was in outstanding form to keep the Spanish at bay, but the 1-0 defeat proved enough to ensure that both teams qualified for the second stage, with Billy Bingham's Northern Ireland side topping the group. The Irish also created history when their winger, Norman Whiteside, became the youngest player to appear in the finals, aged 17 years and 41 days.

Europe's other leading lights, France and England, were left to battle out in Group Four. Aggrieved at England's seeding despite their fairly disastrous qualification record, the French would get off to a poor start, losing 3-1 to the English and conceding – to Bryan Robson in just 27 seconds – what was believed at the time to be the fastest goal in World Cup history. Despite this setback, the 1982 World Cup would prove to be the catalyst for the future successes of French football and their most successful tournament since Albert Batteux's great attacking team of 1958. For a quarter of a century after the 1958 World Cup, winning matches was to become a rarity for the French team. With the return to power of President Charles de Gaulle in France in 1958, a period of conservatism was born, both off and on the field. Albert Batteux, a disciple of entertaining football, was replaced in 1962 by Georges Boulogne, who instigated a more pragmatic approach to playing.

Bryan Robson scores in 27 seconds – just 12 seconds slower than Václav Masek's World Cup finals record, set in 1962.

"It was a grim affair," says cultural historian Andrew Hussey. "It was all about teamwork, defence, moving the ball, passing the ball and not daring to do any of the top end champagne football stuff. As a manager Boulogne reflected the political culture of the time. The Gaullist values of home, safety and caution – the safety of mediocrity."

Between the late Fifties and the early Eighties, France failed to qualify for the World Cup on three separate occasions. When they did qualify they were eliminated in the first round. But in 1981 a new era began in France. "With the election of Francois Mitterrand there was a complete change of the moral climate," says politician Jack Lang, French Cultural Minister at the time of the World Cup. "A breeze of liberty was brought to the people, the feeling that many things could be possible."

It was a sentiment shared by France coach, Michel Hidalgo, who had been rebuilding the national team since his appointment in 1976. His approach was a return to the creative vision of Albert Batteaux, for whom he had played at Stade de Reims. "I had a preference for creative players," says Hidalgo. "The team I got played very quick football, they were quick-thinking and fast-moving. It was the type of football that I'd come to love through my experience with Albert Batteux."

Hidalgo was fortunate to have a player in his team who would become a symbol of the new wave in French football: Michel Platini. "We understood each other," says Platini. "We spoke the same language, we both knew the football we needed to play: the passionate football, the street football, the pass football, the 'knowing how to play' football."

"Platini was the kind of player you don't find very often," says Jérôme Bureau, editor of *L'Equipe*. "He was not an athletic football player. As he once said, 'You can find three million French people who run faster than me, who jump higher than me', but you couldn't find a single man playing football better than him."

The 1982 team were fully prepared for the World Cup in Spain, but as usual there was no great interest from the French public at home, who believed their team to be only capable of defeat. For a nation of football underachievers, it seemed no surprise when France conceded a goal to England in just 27 seconds. But despite this defeat, Platini's team were far from finished. "The English people were laughing when they played against France," says Platini. "But after that they weren't laughing so much."

England progressed to the second phase with maximum points, although they looked less than impressive in beating Czechoslovakia and Kuwait. The French followed them through, helped by a 4-1 victory over Kuwait, a game remembered for its famous disallowed 'goal'. Alain Giresse hammered home from close range but Kuwait's defence claimed they had stopped on hearing a whistle, possibly from the crowd. The referee let the goal stand, at which point Prince Fahid, president of the Kuwaiti FA, appeared on the pitch to protest, while it seemed his players were being encouraged to walk off. Unbelievably, in the midst of this confusion, Russian referee Miroslav Stupar reversed his decision and disallowed the goal, Michel Hidalgo having to be restrained by the police. The French scored once more before the end of the match, and subsequently the Kuwait FA were fined £8,000 for Prince Fahid's interference in the game.

With the second phase split into four groups of three, and with only the top side guaranteed a semi-final place, victory was imperative in the tough Group C, containing Brazil, Argentina and Italy. Argentina were still to find their best form and in their first match of the round they came up against the Italians. Maradona was not only tightly-marked, he was kicked out of the game by defender Claudio Gentile. "I studied him for two days, watching videos, and realised there was a strategy I could use against him," says Gentile. "That was to make sure he was so well-marked that he couldn't get the ball from his team-mates. Once he has possession of the ball, that's when he becomes a problem."

"It went on for the whole match, because Diego was a player you just couldn't neglect," says Mario Kempes. "Gentile was one of those typical Italian hunting dogs who would follow you for 90 minutes. He was on top of you, following you wherever you went... if you went to the toilet he'd follow you there."

"Gentile was a great defender," says John Foot. "His nickname was Gaddafi as he was born in Libya. And he had this moustache, a very scary character and he cancelled out Maradona – he denied him the right to play, fairly and unfairly. That is seen by Italians as a defining moment of that World Cup."

The tactic employed angered the Argentinians, who complained that Gentile's spoiling tactics were unsporting. "I played with my shirt torn, permanently discussing with the referee, permanently arguing," says Ardíles. "We totally lost our concentration from what we were supposed to be doing on the pitch, which was to play football."

WORLD CUP STORIES

MICHEL HIDALGO
The France coach recalls his side conceding a goal in 27 seconds.

"I don't remember us having that many hopes and dreams when we qualified for the 1982 World Cup. We did, however, prepare as if we were going to have a great World Cup. We took some experienced players and we did have some expectations, but we really didn't know how far we would be able to get.

"Our first game of that World Cup was against England and it was a real disappointment. We'd done some altitude training before the start of the championship and it had been relatively cold up there, but our first game against England was played in the searing heat. The players I had selected were all big players and none of them could stand the heat that well.

"England scored against us within a few seconds; I think it's one of the fastest goals ever scored in a World Cup. We never recovered from that and I recall that at half-time, it had got so hot that the players all got undressed. They stripped naked and lay down flat on the tiles in the showers. I know that the English players passed around blocks of ice and rubbed them all over their bodies for the whole of the half-time break.

"They fully deserved their victory but the critics still had a field day, asking us why we'd gone to prepare in the mountains, when the World Cup was being played in Spain. Luckily for us, the heatwave only lasted a day."

"The Argentinians don't have anything to complain about," retorts Gentile. "It's obvious that when you're losing you look for excuses. Tarantini, Passarella and Gallego were no angels themselves." In the tradition of *catenaccio*, Gentile had managed to keep Maradona out of the game and the rest of the team grew in confidence, helping them achieve a morale-boosting 2-1 victory.

In the next game, Argentina and Brazil squared up to each other for the second consecutive tournament, the bitterest of rivals battling for a place in the World Cup semi-finals. "It's pure rivalry," says Socrates. "They're right by us, but we're two very different cultures, very different peoples. Their origins are purely European, but Brazilians are much more of a mix with the Africans. I think this rivalry is going to be eternal. There is a brutal difference in sporting behaviour between the two countries. Argentinians are much more aggressive. When an Argentinian gets on the pitch, you know he doesn't think about the consequences, he just needs to get victory. Brazilians are much more like the good little boys, you know, they're not really violent against anyone. It's the difference in culture between the countries. We play football for fun, for entertainment's sake, for the spectacle, for the beauty, whereas Argentinians play to win."

After the debacle of the Falklands War there was yet another national humiliation for the Argentines, as Brazil gleefully exposed the failings of Menotti's team, beating their neighbours 3-1. Unable to play the central role he craved, Maradona became frustrated. In the last five minutes of the match he exploded and was sent off for a high kick at Batista. The champions were out of the World Cup. "After the match we went back to the hotel to have dinner," remembers Argentine keeper, Ubaldo Fillol. "It was late and I cried a lot. At the dinner table I just burst into tears. I could not hold back the anguish inside me. Sitting at the dinner table with my team-mates, I burst into tears like a child. The brutal relief and the tremendous pain that I felt, everything came out after that game. It was a really painful thing."

The deciding group game between Brazil and Italy was billed as the clash of the tournament. But Brazil only needed a draw against Italy to go through to the semi-final. They were considered the strongest team in the tournament and to beat them would take a heroic effort. "Brazil were an incredible team, especially in midfield, but their defence left a bit to be desired," says Giuseppe Bergomi. "We were on excellent form and took advantage of this." In a seesaw match, it was the superlative finishing of Paolo Rossi that made all the difference to the outcome and ensured Italy's 3-2 victory. His hat-trick, completed 15 minutes from time, not only disposed of the game's most attractive team, but created a new World Cup hero and revitalised a football mad nation. "For Rossi to score three goals like that against Brazil got him past his barren spell and away from the notoriety," says Bergomi.

England's progress, meanwhile, was faltering due to the bluntness of their attack, and with the creativity of Kevin Keegan and Trevor Brooking still missing through injury, a sterile goalless draw with West Germany meant they would need to beat Spain by two goals. Another goalless draw prevailed, despite a desperate last throw of the dice by manager Ron Greenwood. He plunged both Keegan and Brooking into their first action of the tournament with just 27 minutes remaining, but a clearly unfit Keegan fluffed a simple header that could have provided the impetus so desperately needed. France and Poland completed the semi-final line-up.

The Italians had the easiest route to the final against Poland, who sorely missed their best striker Boniek, who was suspended for two cautions received earlier in the tournament. Rossi further enhanced his credentials, scoring the two goals that would take Italy to the World Cup final. "The whole country took to the streets, just yelling and swimming in the fountains," says Fabio Caressa. "It was a great moment for our country. We discovered how to be Italians again."

In the other semi-final, West Germany and France played out one of the most gripping games in World Cup

Diego Maradona jumps over the tackle of Hungarian Sándor Sallai in Alicante.

GIUSEPPE BERGOMI

Just 18 years old, the Italy defender never imagined he would get to play in the World Cup final.

"I was 18 and a half when I was called up to the Italian squad for the 1982 World Cup and I will always be grateful to Enzo Bearzot for giving me that chance. You have to remember, it wasn't like now where everyone gets to sit on the bench. In those days the first 11 went through with the rest following on behind, and if I was lucky I'd perhaps get on the bench.

"I got my chance in the game against Brazil. I came on the pitch in the 34th minute in the place of Collovati, who had hurt himself. I was on to mark Serginho. They were an incredible team, especially in midfield where they had Falção and Socrates, and up front they had Zico and Serginho. I was a little bit frightened as Bearzot had said to me, 'Look, you go on and let's see how you do'. With that kind of innocence you don't think of anything else, you just throw yourself into it. It was an incredible victory.

"Getting through to the second round had been exhilarating, as it had meant that we were in a group with Argentina, who were world champions, and Brazil, neither of whom thought much of us. Once we'd overcome these obstacles, we knew we had a chance of winning, but we just concentrated on the semi-final match with Poland.

"Beating Poland in Barcelona, in that beautiful stadium, was an incredible experience. The sensation of getting to the World Cup final was amazing, especially for me. I was only 18 and I wasn't even sure if I was going to get a game, as Antognoni was due to play. In the end he couldn't, so it was me. They were incredible feelings.

"There was a feeling of great strength, of invincibility, of being the superior team. Playing in the final puts you through maximum emotions, but putting on that blue strip gives me such a sensation that I would honestly love all players to feel that emotion, to put this strip on just once.

"My job was to mark Rummenigge. The man was a symbol for Germany, even if he wasn't up to it physically. He'd played in the semi-final and had just turned up and scored the goal that retrieved the situation, so it was a huge responsibility. I was 18 but the team helped me. That was the best thing about it – being 18 I had nothing to worry about and I could go on and play and know at that moment I could achieve something great.

"Once we'd unleashed the goals there really wasn't anything they could do. The last ball of the World Cup was tapped by me – and then the Brazilian referee blew his whistle and held the ball high above his head. I will always have that memory in my mind. Watching Dino Zoff lifting the cup at 40 years old was unbelievable. There was him, then Gentile, then me. I was third in line and I just wanted to touch the cup. To lift it up to the skies was the most emotional moment.

"The reaction was just so incredible, especially when we returned home in the private plane and landed at Ciampino Airport. I lived in a small village, but it was so full of people you couldn't move, so I had to cross lots of tiny courtyards and through tiny streets and climb over walls so I could get into my house. There was an enormous crowd of people, all very enthusiastic, all wanting to celebrate.

"It had been an amazing World Cup tournament. Italy had a team that really worked. They were all in their late twenties, they had all played in the previous World Cup, so four years later they all came together at just the right time to meet the objective of winning the World Cup. I came in for the last three games and took part in this, and even though I played in a further four World Cups and was captain in 1990, this was the best team, this was the strongest."

Giuseppe Bergomi celebrates at the end of the World Cup final.

history. "We had all the grandeur of a team with high hopes," says Michel Hidalgo. "We were hoping to be the first ever French team in a World Cup final."

After an early goal by the Germans, the scores were levelled by a penalty from Platini, who kissed the ball before slamming it home. The turning point of the game would come in quite controversial circumstances, highlighting again the ruthless tactics of Jupp Derwall's team, most notably the German keeper, Harald 'Toni' Schumacher.

"He was very aggressive from the start," recalls Giresse. "I think Schumacher reflected the mood of the German team. He knew France were playing well and thought a bit of aggression would do the trick."

In the second half, French midfielder Genghini was substituted, but his replacement Patrick Battiston was to spend a mere ten minutes on the pitch. "Platini released Battiston, who went for it on his own," says Giresse. "The German defence was out of position and Schumacher had to come out. He was clearly beaten. He couldn't get the ball so he went for the player instead. Everyone saw it, both the players and the fans, but the referee didn't seem to notice a thing."

Schumacher had clattered the French substitute, leaping and turning his upper body as he charged, protecting himself from the impact but catching Battiston in the face with his hip bone and knocking him unconscious. The distraught French players ran to the aid of their fallen team-mate, but Schumacher seemed unconcerned. "We thought that Patrick had a serious problem," says Platini. "A really serious problem and we thought that the referee should do something but he didn't."

Although Battiston was knocked unconscious, lost two teeth, had his vertebrae broken and was put out of the game for months, no penalty was awarded and no foul given. Schumacher escaped without even a booking. Michel Hidalgo could not believe what had happened. "We had been the victims of a grave injustice. The match reignited the old Franco-German antagonism that wasn't there before the start of the match."

Michel Platini and Didier Six tend to Patrick Battiston after he had been knocked unconscious by West German keeper Harald Schumacher.

Schumacher was unrepentant and taunted the French fans, but *Les Bleus* fought back. After the game had gone into extra-time, Marius Tresor put the French ahead, and six minutes later Alain Girrese made it 3-1.

"Even though I was only ten years old I remember Alain Giresse's goal," says Zinédine Zidane, the star of France's 1998 World Cup campaign. "That's a really clear image for everyone, not only for French people. I think that image went all the way round the world, because he had a real anger and a desire when he scored the goal. That's the image that comes out of that World Cup."

"When you see the way I celebrated," says Giresse, "you could see that all of us believed we were in the final." But the champagne would have to wait for another day, as France allowed their opponents back into the game, the Germans typically refusing to quit. Derwall gambled by introducing his half-fit captain, Karl-Heinz Rummenigge, who beat the French defence to bring the score to 3-2 after just six minutes on the pitch. "The competition got very heated," says Michel Hidalgo. "The sun in Seville burns everything it touches and the competition matched the heat that they're used to in Andalusía. At the same time, we felt the cold of Germany's calculating game."

In the 108th minute Fischer levelled the score with an overhead kick. "We are responsible for what happened next," says Giresse. "We should have been a little more calculating and put some thought in to staying ahead, but that wasn't really our style." With the scores tied at the end of extra-time, the match would be decided by a penalty shoot-out, the first in World Cup history. "It was a very long distance to travel," says Giresse, who squared up to the first spot-kick. "It was only 30 or 40 meters but it felt like kilometres to me. My nerves were on edge and I was emotionally shattered. I tried not to look at the goalie but that was really hard. I really didn't want to look at him considering what he'd done to us during the game."

With the teams all square after five penalties each, the game went to sudden death. Defender Maxime Bossis stepped up for the most important shot of his life, but Schumacher made the save, leaving Horst Hrubesch to take the spot-kick that put Germany into their fourth World Cup final. "Before the match, I had a team of men who, once they'd put the French shirt on, looked bigger than their real size," says Michel Hidalgo. "After the game, they looked like a team of primary school kids. They were all crying like children in the dressing rooms. We had to force them to undress and get into the showers, they were inconsolable."

The formidable security force assembled for the final of the World Cup at the Santiago Bernabéu Stadium, Madrid.

The game won West Germany few admirers, but it would have its consequences for them. "We wanted to fly from Seville to Madrid that very night," remembers Paul Breitner. "But we had extra-time and a penalty shoot-out, and as a result of that – and because of a strike by airport personnel in Seville – we didn't fly until four o'clock in the morning, without us getting anything to eat or drink. The Italians had already played their semi-final on Wednesday but we didn't get back to our hotel in Madrid until 6.30am on Friday morning, with the final on Sunday. We had already lost one night's sleep and, because of the missing fitness, we had just one chance on the Sunday – if we could score the first goal, and then defend. But we knew that we would never have the strength to catch up once we were down in the score."

The *azzurri* had reached the World Cup final against all expectations and on July 11, 1982, they walked out on to the pitch of the Bernebéu Stadium in Madrid to face West Germany. They would be playing in front of a crowd of 90,000, including the Spanish Royal family and the popular Italian president, Sandro Pertini. "When we walked on to that pitch, seeing all those people in the Bernabéu, all those Italian flags," says Marco Tardelli, "it's something that stays with you for the rest of your life, you never forget it."

As the teams lined-up before the kick off it was a tense moment, particularly for 18-year-old Giuseppe Bergomi, who was a last minute replacement for the injured Antognoni. "When I lined up for the final I thought of my father," he say. "I lost my father when I was 16. He never got to see me play at this kind of level. So playing in the final and thinking of my dad was highly emotional."

Italy were the favourites to win their third World Cup but with midfielder Antognoni ruled out of the match, their anxieties were heightened further when Graziani left the field with an injured shoulder inside ten minutes. The game was a fairly even contest for the first 25 minutes, until Briegel brought down Conti in the box. Left-back Antonio Cabrini stepped up to take the penalty, but when his shot went wide of the post it became the first ever penalty miss in a World Cup final. "This was a defining moment in the first half," says Bergomi. "We could have been 1-0 ahead if not for this mistake."

Opposite: The 1982 World Cup final. (top) Paolo Rossi turns away to celebrate scoring the first goal of the final. (centre) Dino Zoff lifts the trophy. (bottom left) Italy celebrate at the final whistle. (bottom right) Claudio Gentile raises the World Cup with his team-mates. (overleaf) Paolo Rossi with the trophy during the lap of honour.

Italy 3 West Germany 1

1:0 PAOLO ROSSI (ITA) 57', 2:0 MARCO TARDELLI (ITA) 69', 3:0 ALESSANDRO ALTOBELLI (ITA) 81',
3:1 PAUL BREITNER (FRG) 83'

COPA MUNDIAL · FIFA · ESPAÑA 82

Although the game was still goalless at half-time, for Cabrini the missed penalty was hard to forget. It was time for captain Dino Zoff to pull his team together. "At half-time I spoke to him, tried to joke with him, that it didn't matter, that we'd turn the game around and get a goal."

In the second half the team re-focused in an attempt to break the stalemate. In the 57th minute Tardelli wasted no time in taking a free-kick to Gentile on the right, who crossed to the three blue-shirted players in the box. Paolo Rossi connected with the ball to push home his sixth goal of the tournament. In the main tribune, Italian president Pertini was unable to contain his joy. The goal also sparked the game into life. "They needed to attack," says Bergomi. "That gave us the space to keep playing a fast game with players like Conti, Altobelli and Rossi."

Paolo Rossi presents Italian president Sandro Pertini with a team shirt on the day of the final.

After 68 minutes Tardelli made it 2-0, sweeping home a long range shot from just outside the area. Tardelli went into ecstasy, running as if he would never stop. "Where was I going? I don't know, I really don't know – you just go mad in that moment in time. It was the pinnacle of joy. My kids give me joy but there's nothing like that one moment. In sport or in life, nothing compares to that moment." Tardelli's reaction to scoring has become iconic in Italian culture and is known as 'Tardelli's scream'.

Nine minutes before the end of the game, Conti burst down the right wing, crossing for Altobelli to seal the victory, setting in motion celebrations that not even Paul Breitner's consolation goal could dampen. When Mexican referee Arnaldo Coelho blew the final whistle, theatrically hoisting the ball high above his head, Italy had regained the World Cup for the first time since 1938. Commentator Nando Martellini brought the victory to his viewers in the most simple of ways. "*Campioni del mondo, Campioni del mondo, Campioni del mondo,*" he announced, as if telling himself it was true. The next day the headline of *La Gazzetta dello Sport* offered the same message, selling a record one and a half million copies.

In the most amazing career turnaround, Paulo Rossi was awarded the Golden Boot as the tournament's top goalscorer. The Germans were left to pay the price for their epic semi-final victory, while for Italy the triumph was a defining moment in the nation's history. "It's something I'll never forget," says Bergomi. "Great emotions and then to go up and receive the cup, passing Pertini and King Juan Carlos of Spain, that was a really beautiful experience."

"We'd reached the top with this incredible satisfaction and happiness," says Zoff. "For me personally, being captain and 40 years old, it wasn't a small thing. The happiness was extraordinary. We came back on the plane with the president, who'd been with us throughout. He was amazing, friendly and open, and we had a great relationship with him."

This wasn't just another politician exploiting the popularity of football. Pertini was a socialist who had been a resistance fighter in the war against Fascism. He had personally given the order in April 1945 that Benito Mussolini should be executed if caught. Winning the World Cup seemed to release the Italian people from 40 years of frustration and gloom. The economy was on the up and Italian football was going from strength to strength. *Serie A* became the most powerful domestic league in the world, Italian club sides a force to be reckoned with in European competition. Victory at the 1982 World Cup became a symbol of rebirth for Italy.

GROUP 1

June 14: Balaídos Stadium, Vigo
Italy **0 - 0** Poland

June 15: Riazor Stadium, La Coruña
Peru **0 - 0** Cameroon

June 18: Balaídos Stadium, Vigo
Italy **1 - 1** Peru

June 19: Riazor Stadium, La Coruña
Poland **0 - 0** Cameroon

June 22: Riazor Stadium, La Coruña
Poland **5 - 1** Peru

June 23: Balaídos Stadium, Vigo
Italy **1 - 1** Cameroon

	P	W	D	L	F	A	Pts
Poland	3	1	2	0	5	1	4
Italy	3	0	3	0	2	2	3
Cameroon	3	0	3	0	1	1	3
Peru	3	0	2	1	2	6	2

GROUP 2

June 16: El Molinón Stadium, Gijón
Algeria **2 - 1** West Germany

June 17: Carlos Tartiere Stadium, Oviedo
Austria **1 - 0** Chile

June 20: El Molinón Stadium, Gijón
West Germany **4 - 1** Chile

June 21: Carlos Tartiere Stadium, Oviedo
Austria **2 - 0** Algeria

June 24: Carlos Tartiere Stadium, Oviedo
Algeria **3 - 2** Chile

June 25: El Molinón Stadium, Gijón
West Germany **1 - 0** Austria

	P	W	D	L	F	A	Pts
West Germany	3	2	0	1	6	3	4
Austria	3	2	0	1	3	1	4
Algeria	3	2	0	1	5	5	4
Chile	3	0	0	3	3	8	0

GROUP 3

June 13: Nou Camp Stadium, Barcelona
Belgium **1 - 0** Argentina

June 16: Nuevo Estadio, Elche
Hungary **10 - 1** El Salvador

June 18: José Rico Perez Stadium, Alicante
Argentina **4 - 1** Hungary

June 19: Nuevo Estadio, Elche
Belgium **1 - 0** El Salvador

June 22: Nuevo Estadio, Elche
Belgium **1 - 1** Hungary

June 23: José Rico Perez Stadium, Alicante
Argentina **2 - 0** El Salvador

	P	W	D	L	F	A	Pts
Belgium	3	2	1	0	3	1	5
Argentina	3	2	0	1	6	2	4
Hungary	3	1	1	1	12	6	3
El Salvador	3	0	0	3	1	13	0

GROUP 4

June 16: San Mamés Stadium, Bilbao
England **3 - 1** France

June 17: Nuevo Estadio José Zorrilla, Valladolid
Czechoslovakia **1 - 1** Kuwait

June 20: San Mamés Stadium, Bilbao
England **2 - 0** Czechoslovakia

June 21: Nuevo Estadio José Zorrilla, Valladolid
France **4 - 1** Kuwait

June 24: Nuevo Estadio José Zorrilla, Valladolid
France **1 - 1** Czechoslovakia

June 25: San Mamés Stadium, Bilbao
England **1 - 0** Kuwait

	P	W	D	L	F	A	Pts
England	3	3	0	0	6	1	6
France	3	1	1	1	6	5	3
Czechoslovakia	3	0	2	1	2	4	2
Kuwait	3	0	1	2	2	6	1

GROUP 5

June 16: Luis Casanova Stadium, Valencia
Spain **1 - 1** Honduras

June 17: La Romereda Stadium, Zaragoza
Northern Ireland **0 - 0** Yugoslavia

June 20: Luis Casanova Stadium, Valencia
Spain **2 - 1** Yugoslavia

June 21: La Romereda Stadium, Zaragoza
Northern Ireland **1 - 1** Honduras

June 24: La Romereda Stadium, Zaragoza
Yugoslavia **1 - 0** Honduras

June 25: Luis Casanova Stadium, Valencia
Northern Ireland **1 - 0** Spain

	P	W	D	L	F	A	Pts
Northern Ireland	3	1	2	0	2	1	4
Spain	3	1	1	1	3	3	3
Yugoslavia	3	1	1	1	2	2	3
Honduras	3	0	2	1	2	3	2

GROUP 6

June 14: Sánchez Pizjuán Stadium, Seville
Brazil **2 - 1** Soviet Union

June 15: La Rosaleda Stadium, Málaga
Scotland **5 - 2** New Zealand

June 18: Benito Villamarín Stadium, Seville
Brazil **4 - 1** Scotland

June 19: La Rosaleda Stadium, Málaga
Soviet Union **3 - 0** New Zealand

June 22: La Rosaleda Stadium, Málaga
Scotland **2 - 2** Soviet Union

June 23: Benito Villamarín Stadium, Seville
Brazil **4 - 0** New Zealand

	P	W	D	L	F	A	Pts
Brazil	3	3	0	0	10	2	6
Soviet Union	3	1	1	1	6	4	3
Scotland	3	1	1	1	8	8	3
New Zealand	3	0	0	3	2	12	0

SECOND ROUND GROUP A

June 28: Nou Camp Stadium, Barcelona
Poland **3 - 0** Belgium

July 1: Nou Camp Stadium, Barcelona
Soviet Union **1 - 0** Belgium

July 4: Nou Camp Stadium, Barcelona
Soviet Union **0 - 0** Poland

	P	W	D	L	F	A	Pts
Poland	2	1	1	0	3	0	3
Soviet Union	2	1	1	0	1	0	3
Belgium	2	0	0	2	0	4	0

SECOND ROUND GROUP B

June 29: Santiago Bernabéu Stadium, Madrid
West Germany **0 - 0** England

July 2: Santiago Bernabéu Stadium, Madrid
West Germany **2 - 1** Spain

July 5: Santiago Bernabéu Stadium, Madrid
England **0 - 0** Spain

	P	W	D	L	F	A	Pts
West Germany	2	1	1	0	2	1	3
England	2	0	2	0	0	0	2
Spain	2	0	1	1	1	2	1

SECOND ROUND GROUP C

June 29: Sarriá Stadium, Barcelona
Italy **2 - 1** Argentina

July 2: Sarriá Stadium, Barcelona
Brazil **3 - 1** Argentina

July 5: Sarriá Stadium, Barcelona
Italy **3 - 2** Brazil

	P	W	D	L	F	A	Pts
Italy	2	2	0	0	5	3	4
Brazil	2	1	0	1	5	4	2
Argentina	2	0	0	2	2	5	0

SECOND ROUND GROUP D

June 28: Vicente Calderón Stadium, Madrid
France **1 - 0** Austria

July 1: Vicente Calderón Stadium, Madrid
Northern Ireland **2 - 2** Austria

July 4: Vicente Calderón Stadium, Madrid
France **4 - 1** Northern Ireland

	P	W	D	L	F	A	Pts
France	2	2	0	0	5	1	4
Austria	2	0	1	1	2	3	1
Nothern Ireland	2	0	1	1	3	6	1

SEMI-FINALS

July 8: Nou Camp Stadium, Barcelona
Italy **2 - 0** Poland

July 8: Sánchez Pizjuán Stadium, Seville
West Germany **3 - 3** France
(aet)
West Germany won 5-4 on penalties

THIRD PLACE PLAY-OFF

July 10: José Rico Perez Stadium, Alicante
Poland **3 - 2** France

THE FINAL

ITALY (0) 3
WEST GERMANY (0) 1

DATE Sunday July 11, 1982
ATTENDANCE 77,260
VENUE Santiago Bernabéu, Madrid

Lineup:
Zoff
Cabrini — Scirea — Gentile — Collovati
Oriali — Bergomi — Tardelli
Conti — Rossi — Graziani
Fischer — Rummenigge
Littbarski
Dremmler — Briegel — Breitner
Förster, B — Förster, K-H — Stielike — Kaltz
Schumacher

ITALY

COACH: ENZO BEARZOT

ZOFF
GENTILE
SCIREA
COLLOVATI
BERGOMI
CABRINI
Missed pen: 25 mins
ORIALI
Booked: 73 mins
TARDELLI
Goal: 69 mins
CONTI
Booked: 31 mins
GRAZIANI
Subbed: 8 mins (Altobelli)
ROSSI
Goal: 57 mins
sub: ALTOBELLI
Goal: 81 mins. Subbed: 88 mins (Causio)
sub: CAUSIO

WEST GERMANY

COACH: JUPP DERWALL

SCHUMACHER
KALTZ
STIELIKE
Booked: 73 mins
FÖRSTER, K-H
FÖRSTER, B
LITTBARSKI
Booked: 88 mins
DREMMLER
Booked: 61 mins. Subbed 63 mins (Hrubesch)
BREITNER
Goal: 83 mins
BRIEGEL
FISCHER
RUMMENIGGE
Subbed: 70 mins (Muller H)
sub: HRUBESCH
sub: MULLER H

REFEREE: Coelho (Mexico)

TOP GOALSCORERS 6 goals: Paolo Rossi (Italy) **5 goals:** Karl-Heinz Rummenigge (West Germany) **4 goals:** Zbigniew Boniek (Poland), Zico (Brazil)

FASTEST GOAL 27 seconds: Bryan Robson (England v France)

TOTAL GOALS: 146 AVERAGE GOALS 2.8 per game:

THE HAND OF GOD

With several works of magic and one irrepressible flash of mischief, Diego Maradona stamped his identity all over the 1986 World Cup finals. With a little help from the 'Hand of God', Argentina were champions again.

W hen the 1986 World Cup kicked off, Mexico became the first country to host the tournament on two occasions. But 16 years after the fondly remembered Mexico 70, this time they came to the competition as stand-in hosts. In 1974 the tournament had originally been awarded to Colombia, but a new venue was required in late 1982 after Colombian authorities declared that they could no longer underwrite the costs of staging the event. FIFA weren't short of alternative candidates, with Brazil, Canada and the USA prepared to take on the challenge. But when the FIFA committee met in Stockholm on May 20, 1983, Mexico was selected without even the formal consideration of a USA bid, despite the heavyweight presence of diplomat and longtime football fan Henry Kissinger among the American delegation.

With their own financial crisis and unemployment at record levels, the decision to give the tournament to Mexico looked precarious when compared to the stability provided by the rival USA bid. When it was revealed that the tournament would be staged by Mexican TV network Televisa, whose president was a close friend of FIFA president João Havelange, the decision drew outrage from the Americans. Further doubt was cast over Mexico's ability to safely stage the event after a severe earthquake hit Mexico on September 19, 1985. Killing an estimated 20,000 and leaving a further 150,000 homeless, it caused $4 billion worth of damage in just three minutes, and with the World Cup only eight months away, it was something of a surprise that the Mexicans were allowed to press on with their organisation regardless.

Diego Maradona raises the World Cup trophy after Argentina beat West Germany in the final.

Argentina coach Carlos Bilardo and Diego Maradona stand together before their match with South Korea.

Against all the odds, Mexico staged another successful tournament, illuminated by the incandescent brilliance of Diego Armando Maradona, who would both thrill with his ball skills and enrage with the sheer temerity of his self-proclaimed 'Hand of God'. The world's greatest player was desperate to exorcise the ghosts of Spain 82, when a lunge at Italian defender Batista had ended his participation in the tournament's second round, red-carded just minutes before the referee's final whistle would end the campaign of his team-mates. But in 1986 he was representing a different Argentina. At home the disastrous Falklands War of four years earlier had accelerated the collapse of the military dictatorship, and in September 1983 there had been a peaceful return to democracy for the country, the military junta put on trial in 1985 for crimes against humanity, allowing Argentina the luxury of at last being able to look to the future.

In this new era of democracy, Argentina's national team had qualified for the World Cup in Mexico with a new manager, Dr Carlos Bilardo. As a player he had plied his trade as a left-half for the tough-tackling Estudiantes team of the late Sixties, but his career had taken him in the direction of serious medical research. When he took over as Argentina's coach he proved unpopular with fans, his tactics even causing outrage at the highest levels of government as he constructed a team that played to the strengths of his players and excluded the weaknesses, most noticeably the lack of wingers. "We had a very strong and united group, but some of our players had zero approval from fans, journalists and from football leaders," says defender, José Luis 'Tata' Brown. "Bilardo was the only one who had trusted us. We went to play the World Cup and had to leave a month early, because rumours had it that the Secretary for Sport would have Bilardo fired. So Bilardo arranged everything in just two days and we went to Norway, from Norway to Israel, and on to Switzerland. Would you believe we got to Mexico a month before the World Cup was scheduled to start and already we had been abroad, wandering around Europe for some 20 days?"

Former coach Menotti had set high standards for Argentine football, but Bilardo had his own ideas about how the game should be played, even if it deviated from traditional Argentine expectations. "For Menotti football is joy, for Bilardo football is part of the civic mission of an army which fights for every inch of the battlefield and every second of the game," explains Maradona's strike partner Jorge Valdano, the 'Philosopher of Football'. "For Menotti football is part of the popular culture of a country; for Bilardo it is a sort of holy war. For Menotti the ball is the very centre of the problem and possession is a major element of a game where one finds beauty and aesthetic pleasure; Bilardo, instead, is much more concerned with men and spaces. Both have a true passion for football and that perhaps is their only point in common."

"Bilardo had different ideas and a different point of view," says midfielder, Jorge Burruchaga. "He saw football in a way we were not used to in Argentina – tactical, the way you were supposed to live, the way you were expected to think. As a coach, first of all he thinks about the 'nil', making sure no goals are scored against you. He would make us work back from midfield, we were supposed to be very strict, strategic in our approach, the roles well defined. But from midfield forward we had plenty of freedom to move as we pleased. That is precisely what he asked us to do."

Playing with a revolutionary 3-5-2 formation, with a sweeper in front of two central markers, five across the midfield and with two strikers, many of Bilardo's tactical changes were forced by necessity. Even the withdrawal through injury of the long-serving Daniel Passarella, soon after arriving in Mexico, allowed for the promotion to *libero* of 28-year-old José Luis Brown, who was even without a club at the outset of the tournament. Brown had returned home from playing his football in Colombia to concentrate on preparations for the World Cup, but no-one signed him in Argentina, leaving him to train for the finals alone. His sacrifices would be well rewarded.

In a controversial move, signalling another break with the past, the coach made Maradona captain, giving him responsibility for not just his own supreme talents, but for the team as well. This inspired decision brought out the best in the player and allowed Bilardo the luxury of building a team around his captain. "He made Diego understand that that World Cup had to be *his* World Cup," says José Luis Brown. Bilardo wanted to harness the magic of this special player in every way that he could, knowing the psychological advantage that Maradona could give them over their opponents. "You know how both teams line up together to go out on to the pitch," says Brown. "There was this superstition we had – we liked the opponents to get there first. And when we arrived you could see our opponents eyeing Diego up as if they were wondering, 'How will I be able to stop this guy'."

Maradona's team-mates could also see that this was a genius at the very top of his game. "There was only one disadvantage, sometimes he turned you into a spectator," says Valdano. "When he passed the ball to you, he surprised you – he woke you up, because he did such spectacular things, so fascinating that you would be hypnotised."

"He was capable of standing with his back to you and it was like he had eyes in the back of his head," says Burruchaga. "For him it was possible to do what none of us could ever do in a million years."

When the draw for the finals took place in Mexico City on December 15, 1985, the competition looked like it was shaping up to be a powerful showcase for all that was great in football, a record 110 teams having started out on the long road to qualification 19 months earlier. In four of the seven European groups the top two teams were to qualify and one each from the remaining groups, with another chance via a play-off place for the unlucky runners-up. A strong Poland side qualified automatically on goals scored, having finished level on points and goal difference with Belgium. After a play-off victory against Holland, the Belgians also booked a ticket to Mexico. West Germany dropped four points in qualifying from Group Two, followed by Portugal, whose 1-0 away win in Stuttgart had assured them of second spot and their first finals since Eusébio's magical team of 1966. England and Northern Ireland qualified together from Group Three, the English knocking 13 goals past Turkey over two matches. Goals from Michel Platini brought France victory against Yugoslavia, ensuring that the reigning European champions would edge into the finals along with Bulgaria, while Spain qualified from

(top) A Mexican wave: waiting for the opening ceremony.
(bottom) England captain Bryan Robson is helped off the pitch after injury ends his World Cup.

Group Seven despite losing to both Wales and second-placed Scotland. In the face of the death of their manager, Jock Stein, during their last group game away in Cardiff, the Scots qualified for the World Cup after beating Australia in a two-legged play-off, Frank McAvennie scoring on his international debut in the home leg.

Argentina, Uruguay and Brazil all qualified from the South American groups, while for the first time since 1958 Paraguay would be at the World Cup, making it through the region's convoluted play-off system after beating Chile. With hosts Mexico already assured of their place in the finals, the Central and North American region threw up Canada as its representative, while Morocco and Algeria emerged from the African group, and Iraq and South Korea qualified from Asia.

Once again, the format of the competition was changed: the 24 qualifying teams were divided into six groups of four, but the second round featured a knockout competition, made up of the six group winners, the six runners-up, and the four best third-placed teams. After the controversial game between West Germany and Austria at the previous tournament, FIFA decided that the final two matches in all groups should kick off simultaneously, a system that has been used for all subsequent World Cup finals.

With a crowd of 95,000 in the Azteca Stadium, the 1986 World Cup kicked off with Italy facing Bulgaria, appropriately enough using Adidas's new synthetic ball, the Azteca. The Italians had been struggling to score goals in their approach to the tournament and Paolo Rossi was dropped from the starting line-up for the first game, while the Bulgarian team had been decimated the previous year after a notorious brawl at their cup final between CSKA and PFC Levski Sofia had resulted in numerous lengthy suspensions, including a lifetime ban for 19-year-old star Hristo Stoitchkov (eventually commuted to a one-year suspension). The champions were limited to a 1-1 draw, thanks largely to the goalkeeping of Borislav Mikhailov, whose ban had been overturned to enable him to play in Mexico.

Along with the holders, Argentina were the other team most likely to progress from Group A, although with a record transfer fee of £6.9 million hanging over his head, Maradona was as much of a marked man as he had been in 1982. The succession of fouls inflicted by South Korea gave an indication of the fear he instilled. Yet he destroyed his opponents, setting up goals for Valdano and Ruggeri in a 3-1 victory. A truer test came against champions Italy. No team knew the diminutive star better, yet he shone in a game of chess-like intrigue. In the 34th minute he eluded

On the way to a hat-trick: Gary Lineker shoots past Polish defender Stefan Majewski.

Ayyyy!

Napoli team-mate, Bagni, his low centre of gravity enabling him to score from an acute angle. The goal cancelled out Altobelli's sixth minute penalty, but both teams progressed to the knock-out phase, Italy beating South Korea 3-2 in Puebla to ensure there were no repeats of the nightmares they had suffered 20 years earlier after defeat to the northern half of Korea.

The hosts went into the competition under the direction of a Yugoslav, Bora Milutinoviç. It was his debut at the World Cup, but he would go on to become the first coach to lead five different nations at the finals. Mexico enjoyed the passionate support of the 110,000 fans that had filled the Azteca Stadium for their opening 2-1 win against Belgium. On the pitch they were supported by the undeniable talents of Real Madrid striker Hugo Sánchez, while off it they had the 'Mexican Wave', a phenomenon that was seen via the magic of television and copied by football fans the world over. Quirarte opened the scoring for Mexico, the second goal coming from Hugo Sánchez, whose feats would rival those of Maradona in the eyes of the home fans. He was equally impressive in the draw with Paraguay, although his brilliance was somewhat tarnished when a last minute penalty was saved by keeper Fernández. Both teams progressed to the second round, along with Belgium as one of the best third-placed teams.

With the high altitude, European nations were given little chance of success in Mexico. On paper France were deemed a threat, Platini, Battiston, Bossis, Tigana and Giresse all capable of performing at the highest level. But with Platini strangely out of sorts, a 1-0 victory against Canada was less than convincing, while a 1-1 draw with an impressive Soviet Union side left the European champions sweating on their progress. "In 1986 France were coming to win the World Cup," Platini said 20 years later, but their eventual qualification had more to do with the ineptitude of the Canadians and Hungary, rather than their own creativity.

England arrived at the World Cup under the stewardship of Bobby Robson, who had been appointed to the role in 1983. The FA had been looking for the new Alf Ramsey, and in Robson they thought they had found him. Like Ramsey he had played for England, and like his predecessor he had success managing Ipswich Town. As a club manager he had embraced players from abroad, and with England he would welcome those with continental experience. Nevertheless, England still made heavy work of qualification from their group, as a 1-0 defeat by Portugal was followed by a sorry draw with Morocco, Ray Wilkins sent off for throwing the ball down in disagreement with a refereeing decision. More disastrously, England's most influential player, Bryan Robson, dislocated his shoulder once again. There had been talk of the midfielder playing on with his arm strapped up, but when the majority of the team opposed this idea, Bobby Robson's love affair with his captain was over for this tournament at least. Results had made victory against Poland crucial, but a rejuvenated midfield of Trevor Steven, Peter Reid, Steve Hodge and Glenn Hoddle made England look like a different team, Gary Lineker combining well up front with Peter Beardsley, who had been omitted from England's starting line-up for the first two games. Lineker scored the hat-trick that would keep Bobby Robson's side in the tournament.

In the early stages of the competition, Denmark appeared the European side best equipped to succeed. With Michael Laudrup in outstanding form, their 1-0 win against Scotland was merely a warm-up for the Danes' inspired 6-1 demolition of Uruguay. They pulled off another shock with their 2-0 victory over West Germany, although both teams had rested several key players. Scotland, under the stewardship of Alex Ferguson, were without some of their brightest stars, centre-back Alan Hansen controversially omitted from the squad, while

Franz Beckenbauer rises to the occasion at the beginning of his World Cup campaign.

their most capped player, Kenny Dalglish, pulled out through injury. They played some bright and inventive football, but the results went against them and they finished bottom of this tournament's 'group of death'.

West Germany progressed to the second round behind Denmark but after the debacle of Spain 82, this was a team in transition. Jupp Derwall and the *Deutscher Fussball Bund* had parted company just a few days after West Germany had been eliminated from the group stages of the 1984 European Championships at the hands of Spain. After the defeat, French newspaper *Libération* wrote, "German football, this brute of an animal, deserved to be drowned in its own urine". It was time for a change. More than anyone else, the DFB wanted Franz Beckenbauer to take over the national team, but the Kaiser had made it plain since his retirement that coaching really was not for him. Next on the DFB's list was Helmut Benthaus, coach of reigning *Bundesliga* champions Stuttgart. But before any approach could be made, *Bild* ran with the headline: 'Franz: I'm Ready'. There was no substance to the story, a fabrication concocted by the newspaper and Beckenbauer's agent, keen to see if public pressure would make his client warm to the idea of coaching the national team. The story led Beckenbauer to accept the job on a temporary basis, until Benthaus could find a way out of his contract with Stuttgart. But once in the job, the Kaiser made it his own.

With no formal coaching experience, he shouldn't have even been allowed to train the team if the DFB's strict guidelines and precedents were adhered to. Lacking the relevant coaching qualifications, he was categorised as 'team supervisor' instead of 'national coach'. But he didn't need a piece of paper to tell him how dire was the state of German football. "I considered what I had seen in the *Bundesliga* and I realised that there wasn't much apart from the proverbial German virtues: fighting spirit and solid defending," he would later say. These were qualities that would stand his team in good stead for the remainder of the tournament.

As soon as the knock-out phase of the competition was underway, it was apparent that Brazil were once again

JOSÉ LUIS BROWN

The Argentine sweeper didn't expect to play at the 1986 World Cup, let alone score in the final.

"From the day we left for the World Cup until the day we returned, we were away from home for 72 days. I told my ex-wife, 'Phone me only if something serious happens to the kids, otherwise I am not there for anybody'. I was there to play football and that was that. I left fully focused and, as our coach Carlos Bilardo had said, I took with me just one suit and a sheet. He has said, 'If we win the World Cup, we come back wearing the suit; if we don't, we will put on a white sheet and travel to Arabia instead, because here they will kill us all'.

"When I lined up before the World Cup final I got all emotional, because it was what I had dreamed about all my life. I went to play for Estudiantes when I was 14 years old. Later, when I started playing for a club side, I would have been happy to just make the B team there – and when I was 15 I was already playing for the B team. Then I wanted to play for their first team, then I wanted to make the national side, and once in the Argentinian side, I wanted to win the World Cup. I achieved all I ever wanted in football, even scoring in the World Cup final.

"So many things went through my head, such as the time when I hitch-hiked to get to training in Estudiantes; I thought about my family, my brothers, my children and most of all, what I had to do. But the thing is, that is a time in your football career when the most important moment of all is about to happen. It is very difficult to explain what you feel before the final of the World Cup.

"I could not believe it when the game started and I scored! It was much too big a reward for my efforts, it was as if it were too big a prize for everything I had done, because it was very hard for me to get there. I went to a World Cup without a team and I trained all alone. I trained with the Argentinian side every Monday and then all the other players would return to their clubs, while I trained alone with *el profesor* of the Argentinian team.

I belonged to Nacional de Medellin of Colombia, but if I returned there I could not train with the Argentine squad, so I decided to stay and train all alone. Three or four days a week I would train alone with *el profesor*. It really had been hard for me. I was not paid, not a penny. My one and only objective was to be among the 22 names on the list of players going to Mexico 86, that was all I wanted. And everything went my way. I was on the list as Daniel Passarella's substitute, but

José Luis Brown leaps into England's Terry Butcher in the World Cup quarter-final.

Passarella became ill. We were room-mates, Passarella and I, and it was my turn to play. I was aiming higher all the time and I ended up playing in the final, scoring and becoming world champion.

"I will be honest, scoring in the World Cup is something that goes through my mind every day of my life. Apart from the birth of my children, it is the best thing that ever happened to me. For a football player there is nothing more beautiful than scoring in a World Cup final. It is very hard to explain what it means – it was as if the gates of heaven had opened up for me. But in fact it was a move we had practised with Burruchaga – he knew where he had to hit the ball and we all

knew where we were expected to be. When I saw the ball up in the air and Schumacher coming out, I thought, 'Where is he going?' I jumped up, headed the ball and I didn't even look because I knew I had scored. One of my strengths was my aerial game. It is like giving Diego Maradona or Gary Lineker the ball in the penalty box, with the goal wide open – it will be a goal. I landed on top of Diego and then, of course, I started running and celebrating.

"I felt my chest would explode. I said to myself, time and again, 'What have I done?' and I went down on my knees and wished the game would come to an end because I wanted all the glory for me. I wished the game would finish right away and we were world champions. But there was plenty of time left, it was only 21 minutes into the first half.

"At the end of the match I hugged all the lads and went for the lap of honour. When we got to the first corner I remembered *el profesor*, Ricardo Echevarria, who had helped me so much, the man who trained me alone, who supported me all the time. I turned around and saw him standing in the middle of the pitch and I ran back and hugged him and we went for the lap of honour together, both of us crying. He was a father to us all because he built the team, he was the man who always had a word of encouragement for everybody, a very special and very knowledgeable man, well chosen by our coach Carlos Bilardo.

"I don't have the words to quite express the sort of happiness a player feels when he scores a goal in the World Cup final. Only very few of us have done so. I have travelled the world and everywhere I go, the introduction is always my image scoring the goal that changed my life. It is something that made me feel very proud, as I managed to do something very important for my country."

France captain Michel Platini celebrates a goal during the World Cup quarter-final against Brazil at the Jalisco Stadium in Guadalajara.

playing a flamboyant game reminiscent of the glory days. Having cruised through their group against Spain, Algeria and Northern Ireland, they crushed Poland 4-0 in the second round, Edinho firing home a Careca backheel for a third goal that had the crowd in Guadalajara mesmerised. With just a few minutes remaining and the match lost, the Poles brought on substitute Wladislav Zmuda to equal Uwe Seeler's World Cup appearance record of 21 games.

The Danes had looked effective in their group, but an emphatic 5-1 defeat at the hands of Spain ended their World Cup, Emilio Butragueño scoring four goals. He became the first player to do so in the World Cup finals since Eusébio 20 years earlier. The Italians, meanwhile, succumbed to a much-improved French side. Bearzot had disrupted the flow of his team, sacrificing the creative Di Gennaro in order to man-mark Platini with Giuseppe Baresi, whom Bearzot insisted always played well against the Frenchman in *Serie A*. But Platini again demonstrated his world class, setting up a comfortable 2-0 win with a casual chip over Galli in the 14th minute. The champions were out of the World Cup and it would be the end of Enzo Bearzot's tenure as national team coach.

The French, playing as potential champions, would have to overcome Brazil in the quarter-finals if they had realistic world title ambitions, and with so much riding on the outcome, a game of cat and mouse ensued. With substitute Zico missing a crucial late penalty just four minutes after coming on the pitch as a sub for Muller, the match finished with one goal apiece and was decided by a penalty shoot-out. France emerged victorious 4-3, despite a miss by Platini. Shoot-outs decided three of the four quarter-final ties, Belgium overcoming Spain and West Germany edging past Mexico, thanks to two penalty saves from Schumacher, the villain of the 1982 World Cup. The process of elimination led to calls for sudden death football, yet if this was knee-jerk anger from the losers, their pain was nothing compared to that felt by the English following their exit against Argentina.

England had progressed through to the second round with a 3-0 win over Paraguay, Gary Lineker scoring two goals either side of a strike from Peter Beardsley. After a couple of strong early chances from Canete, the Paraguayans had little to offer other than roughhousing. Peter Shilton was in outstanding form, but Maradona's Argentina would prove a far sterner test for him.

When the two sides met in the Azteca, it was their third World Cup encounter, England having won both previous games. But this time history had conspired to add tension to the pre-match build-up. It was the first time the teams had met since the Falklands War, and while the participants wanted to play this down, it gave the press plenty to write about. "I knew that they were going to bring up the Falklands War," says Bobby Robson. "But that had nothing to do with Argentina versus England on a football pitch. They would have loved to have equated one battle with another battle, but that wasn't for me."

"Nobody talked about politics and nobody talked about the Falkland Islands," says Carlos Bilardo. "I had spoken a lot to many of our young men who were in the Falklands, which was an episode to forget, but many of those young men had good things to say about the English soldiers. They would tell you how they had taken good care of them. But we never, not once, mixed those discussions with football."

"Everybody in that squad knew of someone who had been sent to fight for the country and each one of us had our own feelings," says José Luis Brown. "But because it was the World Cup, we never thought of it as a revenge for events in the Falklands, because I believe that if leaders at the time were not smart enough to solve it by talking, we could not solve it with a game of football."

In the build up to the game, Robson had pondered the best way to eliminate the threat of Maradona. He knew full well that this one player made the difference between Argentina being a *good* team and a *great* team, but after discussing the possibilities with his players, he decided that he did not want to interrupt England's rhythm by assigning just one man to mark the Argentine Number 10. "The nearest man goes to Maradona, kills him, and if he doesn't, the next one does, simple as that," were his instructions for the game.

When the football match kicked off there were few chances on goal in a cagey first half, but in the 51st minute Steve Hodge played a slightly reckless lobbed backpass to Peter Shilton, only for Diego Maradona to jump for the ball, intercepting it by any means necessary. Radio commentator Victor Hugo Morales was a witness to the infamous 'Hand of God'. "I could see Diego punching the ball," he says. "The way Diego runs away says it all and should have given the referee a clue. The way he glances to see if he can cheer, and when he sees the ref and linesman have not noticed anything, only then does he let himself go. But it's like the behaviour of someone who knows he's done wrong."

On the touchline Bobby Robson wasn't immediately in a state of panic. From where he was standing, the handball had been so obvious that he was certain that the goal would be overruled. "Where I was at pitch level, it was clear as a bell that Maradona couldn't reach it with his head and beat Shilton to the punch with his left hand," he says. But the inexperienced Tunisian referee, Ali Ben Naceur, gave the goal, ignoring the protests of Terry Fenwick and Glenn Hoddle who chased him back to the centre-circle, angrily indicating a handball.

Maradona would remain unrepentant about the goal, only admitting to the crime nearly 20 years later and coyly referring to it at the time as being, "A little of the hand of God, and a little of the head of Maradona". "If I'd have gone up and it had hit my hand and gone in, would I have turned to the referee and said something?" ponders Gary Lineker. "I don't know, but whether I would have tried it in the first place is a completely different matter. I'm not sure it's in my psyche to do that, but I've seen it happen lots of times."

For all Argentines – on and off the pitch – pickpocketing the English in this way was a deeply satisfying experience, even affecting the television commentary of Victor Hugo Morales. "I ended up saying something not very professional," he recalls. "I was on high with emotions the war might have set off and I said, 'What can I say against the English, we even use the hand'."

"Of course I celebrated it," says Jorge Valdano. "There isn't a single Argentinian willing to go and say to the referee, 'Look it wasn't a goal'. We have been brought up to celebrate cheekiness and cunning. For us this was just another way of playing. For the Argentinian it is *viveza*. I want you to understand that I am not telling you

this with any sort of personal pride. Perhaps many of the social and economic problems we've had in Argentina would have been solved if we could understand that what *we* call *viveza* is in other countries regarded as crime. *Viveza* is deeply rooted in the average Argentinian, and when you get away with it, you celebrate: you are 'smartest' compared to others."

For Bobby Robson, no amount of rationalising the goal in the context of Argentine cultural mores would make it any more acceptable. "They wouldn't think about the sporting aspect of the game," says Bobby Robson. "If it gives them a chance of winning and it's illegal, who cares. Maradona didn't care. He'd actually gone to the crowd for adulation and raised his fists as a superstar, but he was a cheat."

The 'Hand of God' only served to inspire Maradona's second goal, a fantastic solo effort six minutes later that put the quarter-final beyond doubt. Throughout the game Maradona had been trying to unlock the English defence using the trick he had learned as a boy, the Argentine art of dribbling, known as the *Gambetta*. One particular *Gambetta* created a path directly to Peter Shilton and the English goal. "I saw Maradona breaking

Peter Shilton attempts to punch the ball clear, but he can't beat the 'Hand of God'.

away half way up the pitch," says Victor Hugo Morales. "I'm thinking that once Maradona begins his run there will be a goal. I think that Maradona is going to end up giving us something amazing so I start to say a few words – 'genius, genius, genius' – until the goal is scored, as if I'm trying to be a part of something great that was about to unfold."

"When he finishes the goal and goes to the corner flag I was the first one to reach him," says Jorge Burruchaga. "I was happy, shouting, joyous, and then I said to him, 'It's impossible what you've just done, you son of a bitch'."

At the other end of the pitch his opposite number, Gary Lineker, watched in amazement. "The second goal was, and still remains, the best goal ever scored. You have to take into account the significance of the football match and the conditions, as it was unbelievably hot and we were playing on a pitch that moved with you every time you put your foot down to go the other way. It was pretty unplayable. To do what he did was just extraordinary. I have to say I just stood there on the halfway line and thought, 'Wow'. That could have meant we were out of the World Cup, but it was just breathtaking."

"The second goal was a great bit of skill by Maradona," agrees Peter Shilton, "but it's very difficult to explain how you feel when you know you've been cheated with the first goal of such an important game. Maradona *was* a great player, but it disguised the fact that we helped him on that second goal by our lack of concentration, due to it happening so quickly after the 'Hand of God' goal."

According to Jorge Valdano, the goal was inspired by Maradona's performance at Wembley in 1980. "In the shower after the match he told me that when he reached the goalkeeper he thought he would shoot to the far post, but then he recalled a similar move in England, some years before, when he finished that way and his brother had told him that he should have *Gambeteado* the goalkeeper as well. So, as a flash, he also went past the goalkeeper. This is very interesting because those flashes go through the mind of a genius during a move and it helps understand the process of a genius in action."

A late flurry yielded Gary Lineker's sixth goal of the tournament, earning him the Golden Boot. But Maradona's performance, in equal measures genius and pickpocket, left the English with a lingering sense of dissatisfaction that would build on the historic enmity between the two nations that dated back to Antonio Rattín's histrionics at Wembley 20 years earlier. For Rattín himself, covering the tournament for Argentine

England and Argentina walk out for the World Cup quarter-final at the Azteca Stadium in Mexico City.

television, the victory meant more to him than mere revenge. "I'm not the sort of person who is after revenge," he says. "I was happy Argentina won because it was on its way to winning the World Cup, but not because I wanted to defeat England."

In 30 seconds of football, Maradona's perfect balance of strength and beauty transformed this glorious piece of dribbling, this *Gambetta,* into a metaphor for Argentine life. "It's another kind of tango," says Valdano. "It's the pleasure of adding those extra flourishes, those twists and turns. There are two elements in the *Gambetta.* The first is skill to show that I, with my foot, have the skill to do anything – this gives a person dignity. The second is deceit. You have to fool the defender into believing exactly the opposite of what you are actually going to do. This taste for deceit is also very Argentinian. When you combine these two traits, then you have the most celebrated football move in Argentina, the *Gambetta.*"

Three days later, against Belgium in the semi-final, Maradona did it all again with a virtuoso performance that included two breathtaking second-half strikes. "They were key goals and I believe they put an end to that game," says Carlos Bilardo. "Diego was going from strength to strength after playing against England. He was ready to be crowned best player."

Maradona's goals against Belgium had set Argentina up for a final clash with West Germany, who had once again eased past France in the semi-final, 34-year-old Platini saying goodbye to the World Cup by throwing his shirt to the fans as he walked despondently off the field of the Jalisco Stadium in Guadalajara. For the French it was not just the end of an era, but the beginning of the meticulous long term planning for a new one. Although boasting some of the world's great players, this French line-up had twice fallen at the final hurdle, their cavalier flair crushed by the resilience and efficiency of the Germans. "We had a certain way of playing football, but that way led us to play well and to win matches," says Platini. "The two matches that we lost were World Cup semi-finals. Otherwise this generation, with its two World Cup semi-finals and one European Championships win, was a good generation. Teams that play good football are always remembered. We will remember the 1982 Brazilian team that played good football more than the 1994 team that won the World Cup, and I think that we were a team that people remember too."

"Reaching any summit is never easy but it's even harder to stay at the top," sums up Michel Hidalgo. "The 1986 World Cup really was the end of an era, the end of a generation of players who had ten years experience in international football. Refreshing a team can be done if you have average players, but people like Platini are irreplaceable. You can't train a player to be as good as he was. His type of player is like a beautiful flower that you pick in a field – but finding a bouquet of flowers is extremely difficult. After 1986, the process of building up a new team had to be started all over again for France."

Although the West Germans had performed way above their abilities to reach the final, beating Mexico with ten men in the quarter-final, it hadn't been a smooth campaign for Beckenbauer, who had sent home keeper Uli Stein for calling him a clown. He failed to command the respect of some other players and he frequently lost his temper with the press. On the night before the final he even offered his resignation to the DFB. Later, when the dust had settled on the tournament, Beckenbauer would laugh at the thought of this World Cup, asking a journalist, "Can you believe we reached the final of a World Cup with these players?" He was a man learning his job and the diplomacy that went with it – while this tournament would belong to Maradona, Beckenbauer's day would come.

Just before kick-off in the Azteca Stadium on June 29, 1986, Maradona gave an unexpected team talk. "Diego always had this extraordinary intuition to say the right thing at exactly the right time," recalls Jorge Valdano. "I remember before the final Diego shouting, 'I'm scared Tota, come to me, help me, help me, give me some love',

Opposite: The 1986 World Cup final. (top) Ricardo Giusti is carried by fans. (inset) Pedro Pasculli celebrates with coach Carlos Bilardo. (bottom left) Maradona avoids the attention of Felix Magath. (bottom right) Maradona lifts the trophy.

Argentina 3 West Germany 2

1:0 JOSÉ LUIS BROWN (ARG) 23', 2:0 JORGE VALDANO (ARG) 55', 2:1 KARL-HEINZ RUMMENIGGE (GER) 74',
2:2 RUDI VÖLLER (GER) 80', 3:2 JORGE BURRUCHAGA (ARG) 83'

calling to his mother. But it was his way of saying to us, 'We're nervous, we're worried, we're afraid. Even I'm scared. It's normal'."

"We needed the final effort against a team we knew well," says Bilardo. "We had beaten them in a friendly game in Düsseldorf in 1984, precisely the day when Beckenbauer became their coach but I thought it was going to be a tough game." Bilardo had calculated that the West Germans would try to mark Maradona out of the game, but the *albicelestes* – quite literally, the white and sky blues – proved they were no one-man team, their superior skill and creativity allowing them to take control of the match. Beckenbauer had assigned Lothar Matthäus the job of shadowing the Argentine captain, but it was his cynical foul on Maradona that led defender José Luis Brown to score his first and only goal for Argentina in the 23rd minute. The elegant Jorge Valdano made it 2-0 after the break. "I followed the ball, praying, 'Go in, please go in' – all I had to do is look at the goalie and decide when to finish," he remembers. "It was a good goal."

"The goal Valdano scored was one of the sweetest," says Bilardo. "It was really good because it started back in our box on the right and he advanced and kept moving forward and ended up scoring from the left, so that was super. From my point of view it was a tactical beauty, plus it gave us incredible peace of mind because it is very hard to even up a final when you are two goals down."

The Germans, who had so successfully stifled their opposition en route to the final, struggled for an answer as the South Americans were already dreaming of another ticker-tape celebration. But with the end of the match in sight, Rummenigge and Völler scored headed goals just a few minutes apart. The Germans had levelled the match with less than ten minutes remaining. "We felt helpless, just helpless," says Brown. "We had thought we were world champions before the match was over, and that's the worst thing you can feel." But Maradona, so subdued through much of the match, once more provided the impetus to stir Argentina to glory, hitting an inch-perfect pass to Burruchaga, who beat the offside trap to power the ball past Schumacher in the final moments of the match.

A pitch invasion at the final whistle, just as with Mexico 70, turned the celebration scenes into chaos. According to José Luis Brown, in the dressing room Maradona led the celebrations with a terrace song voicing revenge against the critics who had doubted his team. "It goes like this: *'Argentina's going to be champions, Argentina's going to be champions – we dedicate this to you all, even the fucking whore who gave birth to you'*. It was the whole dressing room – imagine. It was a really emotional moment."

For Bilardo, who had been vilified at home before the tournament, it was final vindication. A banner behind one of the goals in the Azteca had read, 'Sorry, Bilardo. Thank you', while in due course his 3-5-2 formation would be taken up around the world. But even at the point of his greatest triumph he was unable to enjoy the party. "We were in the showers, singing, jumping and so on," says Brown, "and he came to tell us, 'Just remember we've got a World Cup to defend in 1990'. He took care of every little detail, I think his life is all about being obsessive in every aspect – only a half hour before we had won the World Cup and he was already thinking about the next one. Even Carlos would say that he was sorry he had missed the beautiful moments in life."

As the team returned from Mexico to Buenos Aires there was a feeling that this victory tasted somehow sweeter than 1978. "It was great because it was a victory during a time of democracy," says Victor Hugo Morales. "It was a victory that wasn't achieved at home with the military looking on, trying to turn the whole thing to their advantage."

Unlike 1978, the balcony of the presidential palace – the Pink House – was given over to just the footballers. Receiving the adoration of the people was captain Diego Maradona, not the Argentine President Raul Alfonsin. "For me Alfonsin's gesture is unforgettable," says Jorge Valdano. "He was saying to us, 'There are the people, this is the balcony, thank you very much for coming', and he disappeared from the scene."

This small but symbolic gesture had confirmed to Argentines that after a decade of terror and war, their country had emerged from the darkness as true champions.

GROUP A

May 31: Azteca Stadium, Mexico City
Bulgaria **1 - 1** Italy

June 2: Estadio Olimpico '68, Mexico City
Argentina **3 - 1** South Korea

June 5: Cuauhtemoc Stadium, Puebla
Italy **1 - 1** Argentina

June 5: Estadio Olimpico '68, Mexico City
Bulgaria **1 - 1** South Korea

June 10: Estadio Olimpico '68, Mexico City
Argentina **2 - 0** Bulgaria

June 10: Cuauhtemoc Stadium, Puebla
Italy **3 - 2** South Korea

	P	W	D	L	F	A	Pts
Argentina	3	2	1	0	6	2	5
Italy	3	1	2	0	5	4	4
Bulgaria	3	0	2	1	2	4	2
South Korea	3	0	1	2	4	7	1

GROUP B

June 3: Azteca Stadium, Mexico City
Mexico **2 - 1** Belgium

June 4: Bombonera Stadium, Toluca
Paraguay **1 - 0** Iraq

June 7: Azteca Stadium, Mexico City
Mexico **1 - 1** Paraguay

June 8: Bombonera Stadium, Toluca
Belgium **2 - 1** Iraq

June 11: Bombonera Stadium, Toluca
Paraguay **2 - 2** Belgium

June 11: Azteca Stadium, Mexico City
Mexico **1 - 0** Iraq

	P	W	D	L	F	A	Pts
Mexico	3	2	1	0	4	2	5
Paraguay	3	1	2	0	4	3	4
Belgium	3	1	1	1	5	5	3
Iraq	3	0	0	3	1	4	0

GROUP C

June 2: Irapuato Stadium, Irapuato
Soviet Union **6 - 0** Hungary

June 1: Nou Camp Stadium, León
France **1 - 0** Canada

June 5: Nou Camp Stadium, León
Soviet Union **1 - 1** France

June 6: Irapuato Stadium, Irapuato
Hungary **2 - 0** Canada

June 9: Nou Camp Stadium, León
France **3 - 0** Hungary

June 9: Irapuato Stadium, Irapuato
Soviet Union **2 - 0** Canada

	P	W	D	L	F	A	Pts
Soviet Union	3	2	1	0	9	1	5
France	3	2	1	0	5	1	5
Hungary	3	1	0	2	2	9	2
Canada	3	0	0	3	0	5	0

GROUP D

June 1: Jalisco Stadium, Guadalajara
Brazil **1 - 0** Spain

June 3: Trez de Marzo Stadium, Guadalajara
Northern Ireland **1 - 1** Algeria

June 7: Trez de Marzo Stadium, Guadalajara
Spain **2 - 1** Northern Ireland

June 6: Jalisco Stadium, Guadalajara
Brazil **1 - 0** Algeria

June 12: Tecnológico Stadium, Monterrey
Spain **3 - 0** Algeria

June 12: Jalisco Stadium, Guadalajara
Brazil **3 - 0** Northern Ireland

	P	W	D	L	F	A	Pts
Brazil	3	3	0	0	5	0	6
Spain	3	2	0	1	5	2	4
Northern Ireland	3	0	1	2	2	6	1
Algeria	3	0	1	2	1	5	1

THE FINAL

ARGENTINA	**(1) 3**
WEST GERMANY	**(0) 2**

DATE Sunday June 29, 1986
ATTENDANCE 116,026
VENUE Azteca Stadium, Mexico City

Pumpido

Ruggeri — Brown — Cuciuffo

Giusti — Batista — Burruchaga — Enrique — Olarticoechea

Valdano — Maradona

Allofs — Rummenigge

Briegel — Eder — Magath — Matthäus — Berthold

Forster, K-H — Jakobs — Brehme

Schumacher

ARGENTINA
COACH: CARLOS BILARDO

PUMPIDO 🟨
Booked: 85 mins

BROWN ⚽
Goal: 23 mins

CUCIUFFO

RUGGERI

OLARTICOECHEA 🟨
Booked: 77 mins

GIUSTI

BATISTA

BURRUCHAGA ⚽
Goal: 88 mins. Subbed: 89 mins (Trobbiani)

ENRIQUE 🟨
Booked: 81 mins

MARADONA 🟨
Booked: 17 mins

VALDANO ⚽
Goal: 56 mins

sub: **TROBBIANI**

WEST GERMANY
COACH: FRANZ BECKENBAUER

SCHUMACHER

JAKOBS

BERTHOLD

FÖRSTER, K-H

BRIEGEL 🟨
Booked: 62 mins

MATTHÄUS 🟨
Booked: 21 mins

BREHME

MAGATH
Subbed: 63 mins (Hoeness D)

EDER

RUMMENIGGE ⚽
Goal: 74 mins

ALLOFS
Subbed: 46 mins (Völler)

sub: **HOENESS D**

sub: **VÖLLER** ⚽
Goal: 82 mins

REFEREE: Arppi Filho (Brazil)

GROUP E

June 4: La Corregidora Stadium, Querétaro
West Germany **1 - 1** Uruguay

June 4: Neza 86 Stadium, Nezahualcoyotl, Toluca
Denmark **1 - 0** Scotland

June 8: Neza 86 Stadium, Nezahualcoyotl, Toluca
Denmark **6 - 1** Uruguay

June 8: La Corregidora Stadium, Querétaro
West Germany **2 - 1** Scotland

June 13: Neza 86 Stadium, Nezahualcoyotl, Toluca
Scotland **0 - 0** Uruguay

June 13: La Corregidora Stadium, Querétaro
Denmark **2 - 0** West Germany

	P	W	D	L	F	A	Pts
Denmark	3	3	0	0	9	1	6
West Germany	3	1	1	1	3	4	3
Uruguay	3	0	2	1	2	7	2
Scotland	3	0	1	2	1	3	1

GROUP F

June 2: Universitario Stadium, Monterrey
Morocco **0 - 0** Poland

June 3: Tecnológico Stadium, Monterrey
Portugal **1 - 0** England

June 6: Tecnológico Stadium, Monterrey
England **0 - 0** Morocco

June 7: Universitario Stadium, Monterrey
Poland **1 - 0** Portugal

June 11: Universitario Stadium, Monterrey
England **3 - 0** Poland

June 11: Jalisco Stadium, Guadalajara
Morocco **3 - 1** Portugal

	P	W	D	L	F	A	Pts
Morocco	3	1	2	0	3	1	4
England	3	1	1	1	3	1	3
Poland	3	1	1	1	1	3	3
Portugal	3	1	0	2	2	4	2

SECOND ROUND

June 15: Azteca Stadium, Mexico City
Mexico **2 - 0** Bulgaria

June 15: Nou Camp Stadium, León
Belgium **4 - 3** Soviet Union
(aet)

June 16: Jalisco Stadium, Guadalajara
Brazil **4 - 0** Poland

June 16: Cuauhtemoc Stadium, Puebla
Argentina **1 - 0** Uruguay

June 17: Estadio Olimpico '68, Mexico City
France **2 - 0** Italy

June 17: Universitario Stadium, Monterrey
West Germany **1 - 0** Morocco

June 18: Azteca Stadium, Mexico City
England **3 - 0** Paraguay

June 18: La Corregidora Stadium, Querétaro
Spain **5 - 1** Denmark

QUARTER-FINALS

June 21: Jalisco Stadium, Guadalajara
France **1 - 1** Brazil
(aet)
France won 4-3 on penalties

June 21: Universitario Stadium, Monterrey
West Germany **0 - 0** Mexico
(aet)
West Germany won 4-1 on penalties

June 22: Azteca Stadium, Mexico City
Argentina **2 - 1** England

June 22: Cuauhtemoc Stadium, Puebla
Spain **1 - 1** Belgium
(aet)
Belgium won 5-4 on penalties

SEMI-FINALS

June 25: Azteca Stadium, Mexico City
Argentina **2 - 0** Belgium

June 25: Jalisco Stadium, Guadalajara
West Germany **2 - 0** France

THIRD-PLACE PLAY-OFF

June 28: Cuauhtemoc Stadium, Puebla
France **4 - 2** Belgium

TOP GOALSCORERS 6 goals: Gary Lineker (England) **5 goals:** Emilio Butragueño (Spain), Careca (Brazil), Diego Maradona (Argentina)

FASTEST GOAL 63 seconds: Emilio Butragueño (Spain v Northern Ireland)

TOTAL GOALS: 132 **AVERAGE GOALS** 2.54 per game

THE GOOD, THE BAD & THE UGLY

While two football heavyweights cynically slugged it out for the world title, the true drama of Italia 90 lay in the penalty shoot-out anguish of the defeated semi-finalists, England and Italy.

taly had still been world champions when they were awarded the 14th World Cup on May 19, 1984, beating off the challenge of the Soviet Union. England and Greece had also been involved in the bidding process, but it was somehow appropriate that 56 years after they had first staged and won the competition, the Italians should get the chance to play hosts once again, at a time when their club football was stronger than it had ever been, *Serie A* regarded as the best league in the world.

Italia 90 was the tournament where FIFA stepped up its campaign to have the World Cup recognised as a global marketing phenomenon, and by the end of the competition a TV audience of 26 billion had watched the 52 matches, double the record for 1986. To get a piece of the action wasn't cheap either, sponsors paying £10 million each to associate themselves with the tournament. There could be no better country to put on such a major showcase for the sport than Italy, one of the truly great nations of football history. No expense was spared as the Italians embarked on a major overhaul of ten of their existing football stadia, building two more from scratch in Bari and Turin. Although breathtaking, the space age Stadio Sant Nicola in Bari, designed by Renzo Piano, one of the architects of the Pompidou Centre, was far too big with its 60,000 capacity for the club that would support it after the tournament. In Turin costs went through the roof as the Stadio Delle Alpi was in construction, and both Torino and Juventus were forced to share a ground that neither club wanted: inconveniently situated, too large, and with an unpopular running track around the pitch that made watching football a distant spectacle for many fans.

Jurgen Klinsmann celebrates West Germany's victory in the World Cup final in Rome.

England's Bobby Robson and Thijs Librechts of Holland look at their group during the World Cup draw in Rome on December 9, 1989. By the time the tournament came around, Leo Beenhakker had taken over as Dutch coach.

At the San Siro in Milan, a third tier was added at enormous cost, but the pitch never recovered its former glory after the construction work had finished. In Rome a new tube line was built just for the World Cup, but the line closed immediately after the tournament and has never since reopened. The Italian state spent public money freely on the preparations, and in the early Nineties one of the biggest judicial investigations in Italian history would expose the corrupt system of politically organised kickbacks that helped to make large sums of this money vanish in the build up to the tournament.

The World Cup did leave Italy with a selection of sporting facilities befitting a league as strong and as rich as *Serie A*, but sadly the quality of play at Italia 90 failed to live up to the vast hype and the carefully negotiated corporate endorsements, the competition being characterised by negativity, foul play and penalties.

When the draw took place in Zurich on December 12, 1987, 111 teams had entered the competition, including the hosts and the champions. Before the qualifying campaign had started, Bahrain, India, Lesotho, Nepal, Rwanda, South Yemen and Togo had all withdrawn, Libya pulling out after playing three matches, leaving 101 countries to battle for the 22 available places, the hosts and the holders having qualified as usual by right. Mexico were unable to compete, having been suspended from international competition for fielding overage players in a youth tournament. Although Chile had failed to qualify, they would be banned from entering the subsequent World Cup as a result of their gamesmanship during the 1990 qualifiers. Needing to win by two goals, their keeper Roberto Rojas attempted to fake serious injury after a firework landed on the pitch near him during Chile's last qualifier against Brazil in Río. The Chilean team left the field claiming they were neither mentally nor physically able to continue. The game had to be abandoned after 65 minutes, with Brazil 1-0 in front. FIFA awarded the tie to the Brazilians and imposed a series of penalties against Chilean players, medical staff and federation officials, including a lifetime ban for Rojas. Along with Brazil, Uruguay and Colombia qualified from the three South American groups, the latter beating Israel, the best that the Oceania group had to offer, in a play-off.

Some strong teams were absent from the finals, most notably France, semi-finalists in the two previous competitions. Coached now by their star of those campaigns, Michel Platini, the team finished third in their group behind Yugoslavia and Scotland. England qualified without conceding a single goal, but still managed to finish second in their group to Sweden, having to qualify as one of the two best runners-up from the four-team groups. Denmark missed out on a place in the finals after finishing behind Romania, but at least they would have the consolation of going on to win the subsequent European Championship instead. Holland finished at the top of Group Four, West Germany qualifying behind them through the same back door as England. Both teams were undefeated in the campaign. Spain and the Republic of Ireland qualified from Group Six. Under the stewardship of English World Cup winner Jack Charlton, it was the first time that the Irish had reached the finals. Belgium and Czechoslovakia qualified ahead of Portugal, and the Soviet Union and Austria progressed at the expense of Turkey.

Egypt and Cameroon were the representatives of Africa, while the USA received a huge boost in credibility ahead of their hosting of the 1994 World Cup by qualifying along with Costa Rica from the Central and North American group, thanks largely to the enforced absence of Mexico. Costa Rica would be led to the finals by Bora Milutinoviç, the country's fifth coach since the qualifying campaign had begun. From the Asia groupings, South Korea finished top and qualified along with the United Arab Emirates, who only made it after the Chinese had conceded two goals in the last four minutes of their final qualifying game with Qatar.

The format remained the same as at the previous World Cup, with 24 teams competing in six groups of four, the top two teams and the four best third-placed sides progressing through to a knock-out second round. Adidas had designed yet another new ball for the tournament, the snappily named Etrvsco Unico.

Kicking off at the San Siro in Milan on June 8, the first game of Italia 90 pitted Argentina against the underdogs of Cameroon, who bullied their way through the match to pull off the biggest World Cup upset since North Korea had beaten Italy in 1966. Finishing the match with just nine players on the pitch after the dismissal of Andre Kana-Biyik and Benjamin Massing, Cameroon mugged the reigning champions with a goal from François Omam-Biyik. To add insult to injury, Maradona was jeered throughout the match by a partisan Milanese crowd. From the point that he signed for Napoli in 1984, Maradona had become embroiled in a fierce regional loathing that went far beyond traditional football rivalries. A figure of hate in the north already, during the build up to the World Cup he had claimed that the tournament was 'fixed' in favour of the Italians.

When Maradona had arrived in Naples six years earlier, he immediately brought with him a new era of hope and glory for his team and for the region, challenging the traditional dominance of the major clubs of the north: AC Milan, Inter and Juventus. In its 60-year history, Napoli had never won a major trophy, but Maradona led them to the *Serie A* title twice in four years and helped them to lift the *Coppa Italia*, the *Supercoppa Italiana* and the UEFA Cup. At the time of the World Cup, Napoli were reigning champions and Maradona had come to symbolise everything that the more affluent north Italians hated about the poor south. Northern politicians already vilified Maradona as the personification of southern untrustworthiness. For the Neapolitans, however,

Maradona was a football Messiah and he gave them the chance to enjoy a rare feeling of superiority. "For a long time Naples has been a difficult city, with a lot of poverty and a lot of social problems," says Fabio Caressa. "For them Maradona was the chance to be first in this country." There was a hope in some quarters that the unifying effects of a successful World Cup campaign for Italy would heal the regional divides, but as the tournament progressed Maradona would have something very important to say about that.

Argentina stuttered into the second round through the back door after finishing their group in third place behind Cameroon and Romania. While the champions struggled, the hosts started the campaign as hot favourites. They didn't have Paolo Rossi this time, or Enzo Bearzot for that matter, but people were still hoping that under the direction of coach Azeglio Vicini, their Italia 90 team would repeat the success of 1982. The country's club sides had managed a complete sweep of all European trophies a month earlier, bringing the European Cup (AC Milan), the UEFA Cup (Juventus) and the Cup Winners' Cup (Sampdoria) back to Italy, and nothing less was expected of the national team.

Franco Baresi in action during Italy's match against Austria at the Olympic Stadium in Rome.

All the ingredients were there. Italy boasted an exciting young team with the potential to perform at the highest level. Backed by the support of a passionate home crowd, everything was achievable. Up front they had the fearsome Gianluca Vialli, a deadly striker who had taken Sampdoria to their first European trophy that year, his two goals winning the European Cup Winners' Cup just weeks before the tournament. There was also Roberto Baggio, the most skilful Italian forward of his generation, and Andrea Carnevale, the coach's favoured strike partner for Vialli. In midfield, the Italians could proudly boast of the creative talents of Roma playmaker Giancarlo Giannini, while during the tournament eccentric goalkeeper Walter Zenga would break the record for the length of time between conceding World Cup goals. He would be aided by an impenetrable defence, superbly marshalled by Franco Baresi and built in Milan, Paolo Maldini and Baresi from the red half of the city, Ricardo Ferri and Giuseppe Bergomi from the blue. "We trusted a lot in that team, more than in 1982," says Fabio Caressa. "After Bearzot, Vicini started a new way of understanding and thinking, mixing an attacking way of playing with great experience and young guys."

"I was captain in that World Cup," says Giuseppe Bergomi. "We were playing at home, we had the public behind us and a tremendous amount of positive feelings. There were great expectations." But in the *azzurri's* first game against Austria, despite the support of 72,000 in Rome's magnificent Olympic Stadium, expectations failed to translate into goals. Neither side had scored, and for Italy, Vialli and Carnevale appeared bereft of ideas. With only 15 minutes remaining, the match looked certain to end in a goalless draw. But then Vicini decided to introduce the relatively unknown Juventus forward, Salvatore 'Totò' Schillaci. "He was a surprise," says Fabio Caressa. "We didn't know him very well at all."

A late blossoming 26-year-old with just one *Serie A* campaign to his name, he had been plying his trade in the lower leagues for most of his career, a 23-goal season's tally for Messina in *Serie B* bringing him to the attention of Juventus, who signed him the year before the World Cup. Unexpectedly receiving an international call-up for an away friendly with Switzerland two months before the tournament began, as far as most Italian fans were concerned, Schillaci had slipped into the squad almost as an afterthought. He was from a poor, mafia-ridden neighbourhood of Sicily and, although a prolific striker with a lethal right foot, he was often considered the outsider. With just one international appearance under his belt, it was thought that he would serve little purpose other than keeping the bench warm.

As he prepared to go on to face Austria, his Juve team-mate, Stefano Tacconi, urged him to, "Go on and score a header like John Charles", that other great Juve forward of years gone by. "I came on in the 75th minute," says Schillaci. "I was so tense and so scared. It was a huge responsibility. I was worried what would happen, all these people in the stadium around me shouting." Within four minutes of coming on, Schillaci rose to meet an incredible cross from Vialli on the by-line, and headed the ball into the back of the net. As soon as he scored, any resentment of where he was from was forgotten. People started comparing him to Paolo Rossi, the star of 1982, and he became a national hero overnight. "I became the symbol, the beloved of Italian football," recalls Schillaci himself. "Everybody spoke about me, wrote about me and turned me into a hero for the fans."

Rudi Völler of West Germany comes within spitting distance of Holland's Frank Rijkaard at the San Siro.

Schillaci was left out of the starting line-up for the following game against the USA, but came on again to replace Carnevale, whose abusive gesture at being substituted hardly endeared him to his coach. Lacking in confidence throughout the tournament, Vialli missed a penalty and the Italians scraped a 1-0 win through a Giannini goal. With both sides assured of a place in the second round, Schillaci started the game against Czechoslovakia, partnering £7.7 million striker Roberto Baggio up front. Both players scored and Baggio's strike was particularly memorable, a superb individual goal that saw him cruise through the Czech defence.

With the exception of the Costa Ricans, who reached the last 16 in their very first World Cup finals after beating Scotland and Sweden, the first round turned out much as expected. Of the main contenders, both Brazil and Holland went out tamely in the second round. Utilising a sweeper and once again reverting to a more European style of play under Sebastiao Lazaroni, Brazil lacked the harmony of their great sides of the past. They had easily topped a weak group featuring Sweden, Scotland and Costa Rica, but in the second round they lacked the firepower to finish off Argentina when they had a chance, despite dominating much of the match. Afterwards Brazil's Branco accused the Argentine bench of handing him a bottle of drugged Gatorade.

European champions Holland could draw on the stellar talents of Ruud Gullit, Frank Rijkaard and Marco van Basten, but under the direction of coach Leo Beenhakker they were the biggest disappointments of 1990. The team seemed troubled and Beenhakker failed to motivate his stars to any performances of note, their second round defeat to West Germany being best remembered for Frank Rijkaard's rather too literal spat with Rudi Völler. "You just don't know what you would do if something like that happened to you," recalls West German striker, Jurgen Klinsmann. "I was happy with the way Rudi Völler reacted. He got mad but he didn't get out of control. Afterwards, obviously, Frank Rijkaard apologised and said he was just over-motivated – he didn't have himself under control." West Germany were at their best in the first round, scoring 12 goals in three matches, but they would only score one per game in the knockout phase en route to the final.

For a while Cameroon looked like they might make history by winning the tournament. After beating Argentina in the opening game, the 'Indomitable Lions' became the first African nation to reach the last eight when they beat Colombia after extra-time. Mixing vibrant skills with a powerful physical presence, the unquenchable spirit of the Cameroon team was embodied by Roger Milla, a goal-scoring talisman who danced around the corner

TOTÒ SCHILLACI

The surprise star of Italia 90, the Italy striker came from nowhere to win the Golden Boot.

"All children dream of being a footballer. I was one of those children, but I would never have dreamt that one day I would play for the national side. After playing for Messina for seven years, starting off in *Serie C*, signing for Juventus was amazing. As a child I had been a fan of Juventus and when I was first able to put on their strip it was incredible. For me, they were the most loved, most important team and it was a dream come true.

"I had a great championship campaign in the year after signing for them and I scored 21 goals, 15 in the championship and six in Europe, winning the UEFA Cup and the Italian Cup. I was a promising player and, coming from Messina, both the media and the fans pushed me forward and encouraged me. I was one of the few players to go on to the national squad without trialling.

"My greatest satisfaction was being selected as one of the 22 for the Italian World Cup squad. I was just one of the 22 and I had no responsibilities, but even if I didn't play, I would have been just as happy to be sitting on the bench. Even that was still amazing to me. It was during practice matches that I was able to show my skill and qualities and our coach, Vicini, considered letting me play. My first match at the World Cup was also my first competitive game for the national team.

"As soon as I was put on the pitch my main concern was to do well, but I didn't even think about scoring because it all happened so quickly. It was a matter of seconds, I was to go out there and score goals. For an attacker, the whole purpose is to score, especially in the World Cup. It is just amazing to win there. It signifies that you get the recognition everywhere and

people will praise you for what you have done. Thanks to the World Cup, even when I go abroad people know who I am. For any footballer, playing for your country should be your first priority because it can change your life in the way that it changed mine.

"I think we all played as well as we could. We all came away with something. Personally, I had the satisfaction of having been the competition's highest scorer, but I would have happily given that up in order to have won the World Cup.

"I would wish all footballers the sort of luck I had. I've been lucky enough to have done so much in one year – from *Serie B* to *Serie A* to the national squad and the highest scorer in the World Cup in just one year was a dream come true."

An overnight success: Totò Schillaci celebrates scoring the winning goal during Italy's quarter-final with the Republic of Ireland.

flag after each of his four strikes as a substitute. Milla was 38 years old and playing for JS Saint-Pierroise, a local team from Reunion Island, when he had been persuaded to come out of retirement to play in the tournament. He became the oldest goalscorer in World Cup history when he struck against Romania. He would extend this record further at the 1994 World Cup, but as far as 1990 was concerned, it would be Cameroon's recklessness in the tackle would eventually prove to be their undoing when they came up against England in the quarter-finals.

The England squad had travelled to the World Cup more in hope than expectation. Bobby Robson's seven years as England manager had taken in World Cup exit via the 'Hand of God' in 1986 and the disastrous European Championship campaign of 1988, which led to his vilification by the English tabloid press. He was criticised for his team selection and tactics, while his personal life was scrutinised to the point that before the squad left for the World Cup, the FA had already been forced to announce that they would not be renewing Robson's contract. Regardless of whether Bobby Robson won the World Cup or came home after the first round, the FA had had already made known that his successor would be Aston Villa's Graham Taylor.

Roger Milla of Cameroon celebrates scoring during the match with Colombia in Naples.

At Italia 90 Bobby Robson was in charge of an England team of undoubted talent, if it could only buy itself the time to grow with confidence as the tournament progressed. In Gary Lineker the side had a proven goalscorer, there was genuine world-class creativity in a midfield featuring Chris Waddle and Paul Gascoigne, and as the last line of defence was the vastly experienced keeper Peter Shilton, who had not conceded a goal in 540 minutes of play during qualification. England had made hard work of their group, progressing via lamentable draws with the Republic of Ireland and Holland, and a 1-0 victory over Egypt. Unusually for an England team, Robson contradicted his traditional stance on sweepers, utilising Mark Wright in the role against the Dutch. Once again England lost their best player and captain through injury early on, Bryan Robson pulling out of the squad and returning home after the second game. But in his absence, the England midfield was blessed by the inventiveness of Paul Gascoigne, who was flourishing on the international stage.

In the second round England stumbled past Belgium 1-0, but it was David Platt's memorable volley 30 seconds before the end of extra-time that helped the team grow in confidence. Having come on as a 71st minute substitute for Steve McMahon, Platt swivelled in the box to connect with Paul Gascoigne's neatly flighted free-kick and scored one of the most memorable World Cup goals ever. It made him an overnight star. "I got off the plane at Naples after I'd scored against Belgium and the camera crews just rushed up to me and started jabbering on in Italian," he recalls. "Gary Lineker could see me almost panic because I didn't know what was going on. He said, 'Just be polite'. That's the kind of advice you need, because Gary had been there before in 1986 and he'd had it all."

Platt would become one of the most significant players in England's World Cup campaign and his goal triggered an unprecedented wave of optimism at home. Suddenly, thanks to one last minute volley, it appeared that with this team anything was possible. But they still had to get past Cameroon in the quarter-final, and by the 1990 World Cup there really were no easy games in international football. "They were the biggest team I'd ever seen in my life and they were a good team," remembers Bobby Robson.

In the starting line-up for the first time, David Platt nodded home a Stuart Pearce cross in the 26th minute to give England the lead, but after Gascoigne fouled Roger Milla in the area, Emmanuel Kunde scored a 61st minute equaliser from the penalty spot. Four minutes later Cameroon took the lead, midfielder Ekeke striding through the defence to place the ball past the advancing Shilton. The English were struggling to cope with the power of the Cameroon attack, but although 2-1 down, this team had enough grit and determination to stage a comeback. With seven minutes of normal time remaining, Gary Lineker was hauled down as he darted into the box. "My immediate reaction was 'penalty'," recalls Lineker. "I saw the ref point to the spot and I thought, 'Yes, we're back in it'."

"Stuart Pearce was our penalty taker before the tournament started and Gary Lineker actually came to me and asked whether I would mind if he took the penalties," explains Bobby Robson. "I quite liked that, the fact that he wanted to. I remember asking why, and he said, 'Well, I could win the Golden Boot and it just might boost my earnings'. I quite liked that."

"I always practiced penalties, loads of them every day, even during the World Cup," says Lineker. "But I only practice one penalty, so come a match I wouldn't change my mind. I thought, 'Well, just hit the penalty you've practiced and hit it sweet'." Lineker converted the penalty, firing smartly into the right hand side of the goal, but 15 minutes into extra-time he found himself in the same position again, having been brought down by the keeper, Thomas N'Kono. "The thing I didn't plan for was having a second penalty," recalls the England striker. "I thought, 'Now what do I do?' Having practiced just the one all the time, I couldn't hit the same one again, so I thought

Italy's Paulo Maldini and Ray Houghton of the
Republic of Ireland during their match in Rome.

I'd just hit it down the middle. Thankfully he dived out of the way."

Overnight, the emotion of two dramatic wins had helped to create a new England, a team capable of beating anyone. "The sense of hysteria was uncontrollable," says Bobby Robson. "We'd got to the semi-final. It was quite amazing. You're in a battle and you're winning battles, so the solidarity within the team just went up."

The Republic of Ireland's first World Cup campaign ended in the quarter-finals as they lost to the hosts by a single goal. Jack Charlton's team had placed Walter Zenga's goal under sustained attack, but as the tournament progressed it was hard to see how any team would be capable of penetrating the watertight Italian defence. The only goal of the game came courtesy of new national hero, Totò Schillaci. After his instant impact, Schillaci had become a permanent choice in the starting line-up and his goals helped the hosts progress smoothly through their group games in the Olympic Stadium in Rome. The support they could rely on in the huge arena was immeasurable. "The warmth of the reception in Rome gave this World Cup a special significance," says striker Aldo Serena. "It made us feel so powerful. When we entered the Olympic stadium it was already full of people waving flags and it felt like we had already won. We felt like we had so much strength."

Italy had enjoyed the support of the Rome crowd for all of their games, but after their 2-0 quarter-final victory over Uruguay, thanks to goals from Schillaci and Serena, they found that things were going to be a little different for their semi-final clash with Argentina. They would have to travel south to Naples, where they would be playing in the San Paolo Stadium, home ground of Italian champions Napoli, whose star player just happened to be the Argentine captain. "Maradona is God in Naples," says Fabio Caressa. "He is a God and you can probably trust him more than the real God, because you can see him and see what he can do on the pitch."

Argentina had beaten Yugoslavia in their quarter-final through a penalty shoot-out that had featured five missed spot-kicks, one by Maradona. With a semi-final showdown with the hosts ahead of him, the Argentine captain saw a chance to get his revenge on the Italians who had booed him at the opening game, exploiting the North-South divide by appealing directly to the people of Naples to back him rather than their own country. "For 364 days a year you are treated like dirt," he said, "and then they ask you to support them."

"Maradona had been sneaky, sly and clever during the week, making very provocative statements to annoy the Italian fans and stir up the Napoli fans," says Serena. The die-hard Napoli fans replied to him with a slightly ambiguous banner, 'We love you Maradona, but Italy is also our country'. "It's still an open wound," says Giuseppe Bergomi. "When we had played in Rome the crowd roared when you walked on to the pitch and it gave you an energy and a positive feeling. Maradona had turned the people of Naples against us and when we entered the stadium the public were divided. Some of them applauded, others whistled and called for Maradona and this definitely helped them."

It was clear from the kick off that the Italians were feeling nervous. "We weren't a balanced team, not as concentrated or solid as at other times," says Serena. "The team didn't have its usual legs, it felt like a different team." Despite this, 17 minutes into the game there was a chance for Totò Schillaci to be the hero once more, pouncing on Goycochea's partial save from Vialli to score his fifth goal of the tournament. "After making it 1-0 I felt very secure as I believed in the team around me," says Schillaci. "We had a great defence with Baresi, Bergomi and Maldini; scoring against us was going to be difficult and I was certain to score."

Diego Maradona comes under pressure from Italian defender Giuseppe Bergomi in the semi-final.

The goal should have been a relief but the Italians continued to play an anxious game relying on defensive tactics to combat the Argentines, who had a special reason for wanting victory. "The Italians were rude to us, they did not respect us as a team, not as world champions," says Jorge Burruchaga. "They felt they were in the final already. That deeply wounded our pride. It was the best game Argentina played and it was a game we should have won before the penalty shoot-out."

The Argentines came back into the game thanks to a headed goal from Caniggia. "Unfortunately we made one mistake, when Zenga came out to get the ball," says Schillaci. "When a keeper makes a mistake it's usually fatal." It was the first goal that Zenga had conceded in 517 minutes of World Cup football, beating by 18 minutes Peter Shilton's record spanning the two previous tournaments. Nevertheless, he would be vilified for his mistake. In an attempt to play a more attacking game Baggio and Serena were brought on. "When I came on I realised that the team were having difficulties and were disjointed," says Serena. "We just couldn't get into their area."

The Italians struggled on for the rest of the match with the tensions between the two sides escalating. In extra-time things got even more heated and Giusti was red carded for an off the ball incident. But even then Italy couldn't take advantage. After the referee had allowed a record nine minutes of added time, at the final whistle it was still a frustrating stalemate. There was only one way the game could now be decided. For Italy this was the first time in a World Cup that they would have to face the penalty shoot-out. But it wasn't clear who would take their penalties. "I had a muscular injury to my leg and was tired so I thought I'd leave it to someone in better condition than me, someone better at taking penalties," says Schillaci. "I'm not a great penalty taker. I've got lucky with some and I've missed some. When you're taking a penalty shot you think of lots of things, failure and achievement, and at such an important event there is fear of getting it all wrong. It's a huge responsibility

Argentina keeper Sergio Goycochea celebrates after saving from Italian Roberto Donadoni during the penalty shoot-out in the semi-final.

to take on. I would have liked to have had a shot, but I couldn't even kick properly. I'm not backward, even if I'd missed the penalty, I'd already scored five goals, so it wasn't going to be my fault."

"I was sat quietly and Vicini did the first trawl for players to take the first five penalties, but he was finding it difficult," says Serena. "Not everyone wanted to take one. After a couple of seconds he came back and said, 'There is no one else', so I said I'd take it. I was going to be the fifth one, the final penalty."

Both sides scored their first three penalties as the nerves within an already tense stadium reached an unbearable level; Baresi, Baggio and de Agostini for Italy, Serrizuela, Burruchaga and Olarticoechea for Argentina. Roberto Donadoni, Italy's fourth penalty taker, hit it hard to the right but saw his kick saved by one of the true stars of the tournament, Sergio Goycochea, who had only taken over as first choice keeper after Nery Pumpido had broken his leg in the second game. Maradona was next. After toying with the fans emotions before the match, he now proved the one to break the country's heart. "This was the Maradona we all knew," says Bergomi. "We knew he wouldn't miss. We thought one of his team-mates might, but not him."

Italy's final penalty taker had to score for the hosts to have any chance of staying in the World Cup. Their last thread of hope, their ultimate fate, lay at the feet of Aldo Serena. "I lost lucidity and I couldn't hear sounds around me," he recalls. "As I walked towards the goal I realised that I was no longer feeling balanced. I'd become very tense so I tried to calm myself by taking deep breaths, but as I continued towards the goal it seemed to be shrinking. It's the cross I still carry. For a footballer to miss a penalty is down to how he feels at the time and the tension within him. I had the technical ability to score that penalty but it was the tension and the pressure which got to me."

Diego Maradona celebrates Claudio Caniggia's goal during the World Cup semi-final between Argentina and Italy.

Serena's spot-kick was saved by Goycochea, leaving Italy in shock and out of their own World Cup. "We had luck on our side because we had won the quarter-final game against Yugoslavia on a penalty shoot-out and Italy had never been in that situation," says Jorge Burruchaga. "Perhaps we were a bit more confident, but I remember very well when Goycochea saved the final penalty kick, the joy we felt was very much the same as in 1986, because it was Italy. Zenga was a real troublemaker, clowning around, thinking he could catch the penalty kicks with his clowning. That game was our final, the one we wanted to win."

"I wanted to remember as little of that moment, of their joy and our sadness, so I left as fast as possible," says Bergomi. "It was hard to take in," says Schillaci. "It was as if a large building had toppled on me. I spent two hours in the changing room, crying and smoking."

The Italians had not been able to repeat the miracle of 1982 when winning the World Cup had united the country, creating a collective euphoria not seen since the end of the war. In failing to reach those heights Italia 90 had exposed old divisions and insecurities. It also marked the beginning of an era of self-doubt, as the *azzurri* would continue to be haunted by the nightmare of penalty shoot-outs in future World Cups.

England's opponents for the semi-final in Turin's Delle Alpi stadium were old rivals West Germany yet again. Their manager was still Franz Beckenbauer, who had played a part in the two epic World Cup encounters with England in 1966 and 1970. The Kaiser had grown into the job in the four years between tournaments. Now he was the model of respectability compared to the bad tempered coach of 1986, who had demonstrated such little faith in his players.

West Germany had been the team of the tournament, but England were still highly confident of victory. "We went into that match believing we could do it," says Robson. "Everybody, from Shilton to Waddle, from one to eleven." England took control of the game immediately and dominated much of the first half. "I felt we were on top, I felt defensively we were handling them pretty well and we were always lively going forward," says Lineker. But in the 14th minute of the second period, a cruel piece of luck saw a Brehme free-kick deflected by the onrushing Paul Parker. "It was a good wall and we had a good kamikaze guy to press the ball," says Bobby Robson. "Parker would attack the ball and try to block the shot, but the ball spun off him and right over Shilton. There was about an 18 inch gap between the bar and Shilton's hand and that's where the ball went."

"Anything over the wall I'd got covered," says Peter Shilton. "A direct shot I'd got covered, but the ball was knocked square so the wall doesn't exist. I came off my line to narrow the angle, and I was left in no man's land. If it had gone six inches higher it would have hit the crossbar and gone over and if it had gone six inches lower I'd have pushed it over."

It was rough justice, but England were far from beaten. They kept pushing forward and, with just ten minutes remaining, they finally got their just reward when Lineker scored an equaliser. "It fell on my left foot and I thought I better just whack it and thankfully it went through the guy's legs and right into the corner. It was quite a moment."

The game was locked at 1-1 after 90 minutes. In 1966 English football's greatest glory had come in extra-time against West Germany. In 1970, it had precipitated their fall from grace. So much rested on the next 30 minutes. For the third time, these two sides played extra-time, both hitting the woodwork in an end-to-end battle. In one of the defining moments of the tournament, Paul Gascoigne was booked for a reckless challenge on Berthold, meaning that if England made the final, their most inspirational star would be suspended. Gazza's tears at the end of the match would provide a picture that would move the world, but for the time being he played on, firing the team with his skill and originality. Ultimately there was only one way to separate the two teams. The game went to penalties. "I wasn't worried about penalties," says Bobby Robson. "We'd practiced penalties, we'd talked about penalties, we had good guys who were going to keep their nerve, there wasn't any doubt about that. Any volunteers? Hands up straight away. Lineker, Beardsley, Platt, Pearce, Waddle. Couldn't beat it."

"I never envisaged anything but victory in the penalty shoot-out," says Lineker. "It seemed to me that it was the ultimate test of your bottle." Robson scheduled his best penalty takers, Gary Lineker and Stuart Pearce, for what he regarded as the two most important spot-kicks: the first and the fourth. Lineker, Beardsley and Platt converted the first three penalties for England, while Brehme, Matthäus and Riedle completed their task for West Germany. Stuart Pearce blasted the fourth towards the goal, but it hit Bodo Illgner's legs. "After Lineker I suspect that Pearce would have been the second in the list of favourites to be certain of scoring," says Barry Davies. "Not that night."

Thon put West Germany in front and Chris Waddle blazed England's final penalty over the crossbar. "We were lucky because you need luck in a penalty shoot-out," says Jurgen Klinsmann, "but also maybe we were just able to control our nerves a little bit better." The England team were disconsolate. "We'd lost a match we shouldn't have lost," says Bobby Robson. "The pull for the country was such that we wanted to win it for everyone back home. To have won the World Cup outside of England as well would have been great for us. We had the team to do it."

"It fell on my left foot and I thought I better just whack it. It was quite a moment." England's
Gary Lineker celebrates scoring the equaliser against West Germany in the semi-final.

They may have lost the match, but they had captured the imagination of the English people and on their arrival home they would receive an unprecedented heroes' welcome from the 150,000 fans that lined the 20 mile route from Luton airport. "We'd done a tremendous job. It was the best achievement of any England side abroad and I think we really did the country proud," says Peter Shilton. Bobby Robson unsurprisingly agrees: "That game restored the English people's faith in our national game." It was the match that kick-started the phenomenon of the travelling England fan, the idea that a game of football could be such a piece of high drama that you had to be there whatever it took. More than 30 million people had watched the match on television in England, the biggest TV audience in the country's history for a sporting event. Such was the impact of the match on the English psyche, at least one stage play came out of the experience; the comedy drama 'An Evening With Gary Lineker' managing to encourage people who had never set foot in a theatre before to relive the emotional rollercoaster of that Turin night.

In the third place play-off Italy beat a watered down England side 2-1, Totò Schillaci scoring from the penalty spot to clinch the Golden Boot. "Baggio asked me to take it. He said, 'You take it and you can be top scorer'. I accepted this offer from Baggio and with this penalty I became the highest scorer." But Italy's new national hero would play just eight more times for his country, scoring one more goal. He never repeated his form of that magical summer and four years later he signed for Japanese J-League side Jubilo Iwata, with whom he ended his career in 1997. "Schillaci's success at the World Cup was a surprise to all of us," says Giuseppe Bergomi. "We thought it was going to be the World Cup for Vialli or Carnevale, they were the main names, but in the end it was Totò Schillaci. He had such a great personality. He was loved by everyone for his enthusiasm and the twinkle in his eye, and for his very distinctive way of playing. He gave so much to Italian football and he deserved his reputation."

Although West Germany had been a little fortunate to survive the semi-final, by the time they lined up against Argentina for the final at Rome's Olympic Stadium on July 8, they had proved themselves to be the tournament's most outstanding team. With Matthäus and Klinsmann both at the peak of their powers, they had grown in stature as the competition progressed. However, for all their strengths, West Germany did nothing to help Italia 90 finish on a high. Only 115 goals were scored at the tournament, at a ratio of 2.21 per game, yet there were a record 16 dismissals and 164 bookings. From a football perspective it had been a poor tournament and it was gifted the final it truly deserved: stale, cynical football punctuated by fouls, histrionic diving and petulance.

Argentina weren't the inspirational team that had lifted the trophy four years earlier, but they were prepared to fight for this World Cup. "There was something that the 1990 team had," says Burruchaga, "and that was courage. We had courage as big as our country. We went there to defend something and we fought for it with tooth and nail. We said we were going to sweat blood. We had to play the best national sides in the world, crippled by all the fitness problems we had. Perhaps our performances weren't as good as in 1986, but if we are talking about effectiveness, well, we reached the World Cup final."

The confrontation between West Germany, playing their third consecutive final, and holders Argentina ranks as the worst final in the tournament's history, the game characterised by negativity and bad sportsmanship. "Argentina had made it to the final through a lot of luck," says Rudi Völler. "They then played for a draw from the kick off, to get a penalty shoot-out, which had been their forte through the tournament. As a team they were nowhere near as strong as they had been in 1986. That's why we felt we would manage to beat them."

As the sides lined up before the match, the Italian crowd booed Maradona throughout the Argentine national

Opposite: The 1990 World Cup final. (top) Andreas Brehme scores West Germany's only goal from the penalty spot. (centre) Maradona dramatically hits the deck. (bottom right) Lothar Mattäus celebrates with the trophy.

Coppa del Mondo FIFA 1990

West Germany 1 Argentina 0

1:0 ANDREAS BREHME (GER) 85', penalty

Gara
Match

FINAL

ITALIA'90

Citta City	Data Date	Ora Hour
ROMA	8-7-1990	20.00

STADIO OLIMPICO

anthem. He could clearly be seen to mouth, *"Hijos de puta"* – sons of bitches – on the television screen. "The Italian team had been eliminated and the *tifosi* now kept their fingers crossed for us, everyone could feel that," says Völler. "Rome's Olympic Stadium was my ground. I played there for Roma for five years."

The Argentina team arrived at the final with a record of a foul every four minutes and were missing four players through suspension. It wasn't a statistic that impressed their former coach, César Luis Menotti. "I'm ashamed as an Argentinian, because what I see of my country at this World Cup has nothing to do with our true character," he said at the time. In the final, however, both teams were guilty of deeply cynical play.

West Germany held the upper hand for much of the match but the contest degenerated as time wore on. Pedro Monzon became the first player to be sent off in a World Cup final for a wild lunge at Klinsmann, and it was no surprise when the match was settled by a spot-kick after Völler's *schwalbe* in the penalty

Franz Beckenbauer and the West German team arrive home with the World Cup trophy.

box. "It was certainly not a clear penalty and Rudi said as much straight afterwards too," recalls Klinsmann. "The clear penalty was just before that actually, from the Argentina goalkeeper on Klaus Augenthaler. I think the referee was saying, 'I missed the call right before', so he called it in that moment."

"Many people say it wasn't a foul," says Völler. "But I always say this: it was the accumulation of the many fouls during the match that did it. At this point the ref simply said, 'Enough is enough!'" Lothar Matthäus was the team's designated penalty taker but, after having to change the boot on his favoured right foot at half-time, he didn't feel comfortable enough to take the kick. Brehme stepped up instead, firing the ball into the back of the net. With just five minutes remaining, the only sensation experienced by the fans was relief that another 30 minutes would not have to be endured. The Argentines lost their heads in the aftermath of the penalty, and two minutes later Dezotti also received his marching orders as the referee was subjected to abuse, pushed and jostled. "It was an aggressive game," says Klinsmann. "There were two sent off and it was just unfortunate that they didn't open the game up. They were just sitting back and were just trying to kill the rhythm of the game rather than playing their own game. Unfortunately it was decided by a penalty, but we were clearly the better team. Argentina never had a chance in that game – they were simply sitting back and hoping for maybe one magical counter-attack through Maradona."

After the final whistle, as his team celebrated, Franz Beckenbauer strolled slowly across the pitch, his winners' medal around his neck. It would be his last game as West German manager and he was going out on a high, having joined Mario Zagalo in that elite who had lifted the World Cup as both a player and a coach. At the post-match press conference he was back to his usual controversial self: "I'm sorry for the other countries, but now that we will be able to incorporate all the great players from the East, the German team will be unbeatable for a long time to come." While his prediction did not come true, it would be the last time a West German team would be seen in the final – from here on in, it would simply be Germany once again.

The final of the 1990 World Cup had been poor and Maradona had never looked in the same form as the charismatic magician who had performed wonders in Mexico in 1986. In the Olympic Stadium he had mischievously conducted his side's theatrics and it seems fitting that the enduring image of that Rome evening is not Lothar Matthäus holding aloft the World Cup, but the Argentine captain's tear-stained face.

GROUP A

June 9: Stadio Olimpico, Rome
Italy **1 - 0** Austria

June 10: Stadio Comunale, Florence
Czechoslovakia **5 - 1** USA

June 14: Stadio Olimpico, Rome
Italy **1 - 0** USA

June 15: Stadio Comunale, Florence
Czechoslovakia **1 - 0** Austria

June 19: Stadio Olimpico, Rome
Italy **2 - 0** Czechoslovakia

June 19: Stadio Comunale, Florence
Austria **2 - 1** USA

	P	W	D	L	F	A	Pts
Italy	3	3	0	0	4	0	6
Czechoslovakia	3	2	0	1	6	3	4
Austria	3	1	0	2	2	3	2
USA	3	0	0	3	2	8	0

GROUP B

June 8: San Siro, Milan
Cameroon **1 - 0** Argentina

June 9: Stadio Sant Nicola, Bari
Romania **2 - 0** Soviet Union

June 13: Stadio San Paolo, Naples
Argentina **2 - 0** Soviet Union

June 14: Stadio Sant Nicola, Bari
Cameroon **2 - 1** Romania

June 18: Stadio San Paolo, Naples
Argentina **1 - 1** Romania

June 18: Stadio Sant Nicola, Bari
Soviet Union **4 - 0** Cameroon

	P	W	D	L	F	A	Pts
Cameroon	3	2	0	1	3	5	4
Romania	3	1	1	1	4	3	3
Argentina	3	1	1	1	3	2	3
Soviet Union	3	1	0	2	4	4	2

GROUP C

June 10: Stadio Delle Alpi, Turin
Brazil **2 - 1** Sweden

June 11: Stadio Luigi Ferraris, Genoa
Costa Rica **1 - 0** Scotland

June 16: Stadio Delle Alpi, Turin
Brazil **1 - 0** Costa Rica

June 16: Stadio Luigi Ferraris, Genoa
Scotland **2 - 1** Sweden

June 20: Stadio Delle Alpi, Turin
Brazil **1 - 0** Scotland

June 20: Stadio Luigi Ferraris, Genoa
Costa Rica **2 - 1** Sweden

	P	W	D	L	F	A	Pts
Brazil	3	3	0	0	4	1	6
Costa Rica	3	2	0	1	3	2	4
Scotland	3	1	0	2	2	3	2
Sweden	3	0	0	3	3	6	0

GROUP D

June 9: Stadio Renato Dall'Ara, Bologna
Colombia **2 - 0** UAE

June 10: San Siro, Milan
West Germany **4 - 1** Yugoslavia

June 14: Stadio Renato Dall'Ara, Bologna
Yugoslavia **1 - 0** Colombia

June 15: San Siro, Milan
West Germany **5 - 1** UAE

June 19: San Siro, Milan
West Germany **1 - 1** Colombia

June 19: Stadio Renato Dall'Ara, Bologna
Yugoslavia **4 - 1** UAE

	P	W	D	L	F	A	Pts
West Germany	3	2	1	0	10	3	5
Yugoslavia	3	2	0	1	6	5	4
Colombia	3	1	1	1	3	2	3
UAE	3	0	0	3	2	11	0

THE FINAL

WEST GERMANY	(0) **1**
ARGENTINA	(0) **0**

DATE Sunday July 8, 1990
ATTENDANCE 73,603
VENUE Olympic Stadium, Rome

Illgner
Berthold — Kohler — Buchwald — Brehme
Augenthaler
Hässler — Matthäus — Littbarski
Völler — Klinsmann

Dezotti — Maradona
Lorenzo — Troglio — Burruchaga — Basualdo — Sensini
Serrizuela — Simón — Ruggeri
Goycoechea

WEST GERMANY
COACH: FRANZ BECKENBAUER

ILLGNER
AUGENTHALER
BERTHOLD
Subbed: 75 mins (Reuter)
KOHLER
BUCHWALD
BREHME ⊕
Goal: 85 mins (pen)
HÄSSLER
MATTHÄUS
LITTBARSKI
KLINSMANN
VÖLLER 🟨
Booked: 52 mins

sub: REUTER

ARGENTINA
COACH: CARLOS BILARDO

GOYCOECHEA
SIMÓN
SERRIZUELA
RUGGERI
Subbed: 46 mins (Monzon)
TROGLIO 🟨
Booked: 84 mins
SENSINI
BURRUCHAGA
Subbed: 54 mins (Calderon)
BASUALDO
LORENZO
DEZOTTI 🟥
Sent-off: 65 mins
MARADONA 🟨
Booked: 87 mins

sub: MONZON 🟥
Sent-off: 87 mins

sub: CALDERON

REFEREE: Codesal (Mexico)

GROUP E

June 12: Stadio Marc Antonio Bentegodi, Verona
Belgium **2 - 0** South Korea

June 13: Stadio Friuli, Udine
Uruguay **0 - 0** Spain

June 17, Stadio Marc Antonio Bentegodi, Verona
Belgium **3 - 1** Uruguay

June 17: Stadio Friuli, Udine
Spain **3 - 1** South Korea

June 21: Stadio Marc Antonio Bentegodi, Verona
Spain **2 - 1** Belgium

June 21: Stadio Friuli, Udine
Uruguay **1 - 0** South Korea

	P	W	D	L	F	A	Pts
Spain	3	2	1	0	5	2	5
Belgium	3	2	0	1	6	3	4
Uruguay	3	1	1	1	2	3	3
South Korea	3	0	0	3	1	6	0

GROUP F

June 11: Stadio Sant 'Elia, Cagliari
England **1 - 1** Rep. Of Ireland

June 12: Stadio Della Favorita, Palermo
Holland **1 - 1** Egypt

June 16: Stadio Sant 'Elia, Cagliari
England **0 - 0** Holland

June 17: stadio Della Favorita, Palermo
Egypt **0 - 0** Rep. Of Ireland

June 21: Stadio Sant 'Elia, Cagliari
England **1 - 0** Egypt

June 21: Stadio Della Favorita, Palermo
Holland **1 - 1** Rep. Of Ireland

	P	W	D	L	F	A	Pts
England	3	1	2	0	2	1	4
Rep. Of Ireland	3	0	3	0	2	2	3
Holland	3	0	3	0	2	2	3
Egypt	3	0	2	1	1	2	2

SECOND ROUND

June 23: Stadio San Paolo, Naples
Cameroon **2 - 1** Colombia
(aet)

June 23: Stadio Sant Nicola, Bari
Czechoslovakia **4 - 1** Costa Rica

June 24: Stadio Delle Alpi, Turin
Argentina **1 - 0** Brazil

June 24: San Siro, Milan
West Germany **2 - 1** Holland

June 25: Stadio Luigi Ferraris, Genoa
Rep. Of Ireland **0 - 0** Romania
(aet)
Rep. Of Ireland won 5-4 on penalties

June 25: Stadio Olimpico, Rome
Italy **2 - 0** Uruguay

June 26: Stadio Marc Antonio Bentegodi, Verona
Yugoslavia **2 - 1** Spain
(aet)

June 26: Stadio Dall'Ara, Bologna
England **1 - 0** Belgium
(aet)

QUARTER-FINALS

June 30: Stadio Comunale, Florence
Argentina **0 - 0** Yugoslavia
(aet)
Argentina won 3-2 on penalties

June 30: Stadio Olimpico, Rome
Italy **1 - 0** Rep. Of Ireland

July 1: San Siro, Milan
West Germany **1 - 0** Czechoslovakia

July 1: Stadio San Paolo, Naples
England **3 - 2** Cameroon
(aet)

SEMI-FINALS

July 3: Stadio San Paolo, Naples
Argentina **1 - 1** Italy
(aet)
Argentina won 4-3 on penalties

July 4: Stadio Delle Alpi, Turin
West Germany **1 - 1** England
(aet)
West Germany won 4-3 on penalties

THIRD-PLACE PLAY-OFF

July 7: Stadio Sant Nicola, Bari
Italy **2 - 1** England

TOP GOALSCORERS 6 goals: Salvatore Schillaci (Italy) **5 goals:** Tomás Skuhravy (Czech)
4 goals: Michel (Spain), Roger Milla (Cameroon), Gary Lineker (England), Lothar Matthäus (Germany)

FASTEST GOAL 4 minutes: Safet Susic (Yugoslavia v United Arab Emirates)

TOTAL GOALS: 115 **AVERAGE GOALS** 2.21 per game

THE FINAL FRONTIER

Despite a lacklustre final showcasing insipid displays from both Brazil and Italy, the World Cup in America confounded all expectations when it broke tournament attendance records that had stood since 1950.

In light of FIFA's long held ambition to conquer football's one final frontier, there was an air of inevitability when the United States were finally awarded the 1994 tournament after the snub of 1986. With rivals Morocco and Brazil unable to match the superior infrastructure, a lack of tradition held no barriers when FIFA presented the Americans with football's greatest responsibility on, appropriately enough, American Independence Day, 1988. The power and wealth of the USA had beaten the Moroccan bid by ten votes to seven.

Not everyone in America had wanted the privilege of hosting the World Cup, some seeing the growing interest in football as a potential threat to existing American sporting interests and, in the most extreme view, to the American way of life itself. In 1986 Jack Kemp, a former American Football quarterback and Republican politician, took to the floor of United States Congress to condemn a resolution supporting the USA's campaign to host the World Cup. "I think it is important for all those young out there," he said, "who someday hope to play real football, where you throw it and kick it and run with it and put it in your hands, a distinction should be made that football is democratic capitalism, whereas soccer is a European socialist [sport]."

Outside of America, there were also concerns that the competition would fail to capture the imagination, and the cringing embarrassment caused by watching Diana Ross attempt to score from the penalty spot at the opening ceremony cemented this apprehension. Yet USA 94 would prove a great success. Three points for a victory ended those lifeless group games, while the introduction of motorised carts to evacuate 'injured' players from the pitch

Brazil captain Dunga raises the World Cup at the Rose Bowl in Pasadena, California.

The Opening ceremony of the World Cup at Soldier Field, Chicago.

saw a decrease in the feigning of injuries. Stadiums were full throughout the tournament, Americans proving that whether they like a sport or not, they are suckers for a big occasion. All the signs had been there for those who took the time to look beyond the country's traditional 'anti soccer' stance. Despite the failure of the North American Soccer League in early Eighties, the football tournament at the 1984 Los Angeles Olympics had drawn huge crowds. Contradicting all advance predictions, the average World Cup attendance of nearly 69,000 smashed the competition record that had stood since 1950. With 3,587,538 fans passing through the turnstiles, USA 94 remains the best-attended World Cup ever, even despite the expansion of the competition to 32 teams in 1998.

Only the actions of one player blighted the festival. Diego Maradona came to America looking to reach his third final and, on form, there was every chance the dream could become reality. However, after testing positive for five variants of the stimulant ephedrine, his 1994 World Cup aspirations were at an end after just two games and one goal. Arrogantly proclaiming his innocence, he stayed on at the World Cup as a television summariser.

FIFA's desire to hold the World Cup in the USA meant that the stringent stadium criteria they had imposed upon Italia 90 was discarded in favour of a selection of exotic venue choices. The Pontiac Silverdome, for instance, gave the World Cup its first indoor match, the pitch having to be grown in California and transported across country in large blocks of turf ready for relaying.

By the deadline for entries on September 15, 1991, 147 teams had entered the 15th World Cup, with 133 actually playing in the qualification tournament. Some 16 of those were taking part for the first time – among them South Africa, back in international sporting competition after a lengthy exclusion. Yugoslavia, in a state of civil war, were excluded. Several of European football's big names did not make the cut, including England and France. Under Graham Taylor, England's disastrous campaign stuttered to a halt as they finished behind Norway and Holland in their group. Travelling to Bologna in Italy to play their final qualifier against tiny San Marino, England had needed to win by eight clear goals and hope that Poland could beat Holland. After the initial shock of conceding a goal in eight seconds, the fastest in international football, they managed a 7-1 win, but it proved academic, as Poland had been unable to contain the Dutch.

Already certain of hosting the 1998 World Cup finals, France looked set to qualify comfortably for USA 94, but after a shock home defeat by Israel, they were beaten in Paris by Bulgaria in their final game, losing 2-1 thanks to an Emil Kostadinov counter-attack in the dying seconds. Sweden topped the group and Bulgaria snatched the second qualifying slot from France by just a point, having beaten them home and away. Reigning European champions Denmark also failed to qualify. They lost their final game away to group leaders Spain and were edged out of the second spot on goal difference by the Republic of Ireland. Portugal were another casualty, finishing behind Italy and Switzerland, who had qualified for the first time in 30 years under the quiet coaching genius of Englishman Roy Hodgson.

In South America the Colombians were the only team to qualify with any degree of certainty. Undefeated in their group, they managed to finish ahead of Argentina, who had to endure a play-off with Australia, a 1-0 home win booking their place at USA 94. In the other group Brazil and Bolivia only managed to confirm their qualification at the final whistle of the last matches, Brazil having lost their first ever World Cup qualifier along the way, a 2-0 defeat to Bolivia in La Paz.

Mexico qualified from the Central and North American group, while in the Asian group Japan slipped up in their last game, drawing 2-2 with Iraq to allow Saudi Arabia and South Korea to qualify above them, the latter just by goal difference. The success of Cameroon at the 1990 World Cup meant that for the first time, three African countries would be able to qualify, Cameroon being joined by Morocco and Nigeria. Zambia had come so close to reaching the finals, despite the tragedy of losing their manager and the entire squad in a plane crash while en route for their qualifier with Senegal. Their captain and most experienced player, Kalusha Bwalya, was not on the flight, intending to join the team directly from Holland where he had been playing for PSV. As a mark of respect to the 18 players who had died, Zambia completed their campaign, needing just a draw in their final game with Morocco to qualify. Unfortunately they lost 1-0 in controversial circumstances.

Presaged by an elaborate and theatrical opening ceremony, the first game of the 1994 World Cup kicked off on June 17 at Chicago's Soldier Field, with holders Germany beating surprise qualifiers Bolivia 1-0 through a quickly worked Jurgen Klinsmann goal in the 61st minute. The result was overshadowed by the red card awarded to Bolivia's Marco Etcheverry, who had come on as a late second-half substitute just four minutes earlier. A few hours later, in the same group, Spanish defender Nadal was dismissed after just 25 minutes of their game against South Korea. Having taken a 2-0 lead through Salinas and Goicoechea, the Spaniards threw away their advantage, conceding two goals in the last five minutes. With their match against Germany also ending in stalemate, both European teams progressed as Caminero scored twice to help Spain to a 3-1 victory over Bolivia, Klinsmann taking his personal tally to four in a 3-2 win for the Germans against South Korea.

After Franz Beckenbauer's triumph at the 1990 World Cup, the Germans were now coached by Berti Vogts, another playing legend from their great team of the early Seventies. But under Vogts, just as under Derwall, discipline was lax and a poor team spirit resulted. After allowing a three-goal lead against South Korea to slip to

3-2, Vogts substituted Stefan Effenberg for the more defensive Thomas Helmer. Jeered as he walked off the pitch, Effenberg flashed an abusive gesture at the German fans. This proved too much for the new DFB president Egidius Braun. "Many fans from Germany paid a lot of money to follow us to the USA," he said "There is no excuse for insulting these people." Effenberg was placed on the first plane home, with the words of Berti Vogts ringing in his ears: "For as long as I'm coaching this team, Effenberg will not play for Germany again."

Having defeated Argentina 5-0 in qualifying, the Colombian team were tipped to do well, yet a 3-1 defeat against Romania and a subsequent defeat against the hosts sealed their fate. The USA result had tragic consequences, as Pablo Escobar – blamed for the defeat after scoring an own goal – was murdered shortly after his return home. After an altercation with a group of men outside a restaurant in Medellin, he was shot 12 times, the accomplices yelling 'Goal' each time the trigger was pulled.

Brazil were under the direction of Carlos Alberto Parreira in 1994, the latest in a long line of coaches who

Jack Charlton stands to attention for the Republic of Ireland.

wanted to 'modernise' the natural flair right out of the side. Parreira had been a part of Brazil's training staff at Mexico 70 and had coached the United Arab Emirates at Italia 90. Brazil had looked unsteady in qualification, but the coach was happy with the side as they started a new World Cup campaign. "In 1994 I think our preparation was perfect and the team grew during the competition," he says. "They watched a lot of video tapes and there was a lot of tactical training. There were not many free days and no families there to join them. It was a place just for the Brazilian team, full of concentration for the competition. We had doctors, nutritionists, physiotherapists; we had 60 people with us working as staff. When the preparation is good, when the planning is okay, when everything works together, then it is very difficult to stop Brazil."

A depleted Russian side tried their best to stop the Brazilians in the first game, but with Bebeto and Romario forging a formidable partnership up front, it took just 27 minutes for the three-time World Cup winners to take the lead, Romario turning in Bebeto's inswinging corner. Raí made it 2-0 from the penalty spot in the 53rd minute. After a dispute with coach Pavel Sadyrin, the Russians had arrived in the USA without several key members of their squad, players of the calibre of Andre Kanchelskis, Sergei Kiriakov and Igor Shalimov. Without them the Russians failed to progress to the next phase, finishing behind Brazil and Sweden, with Cameroon propping up the table. The Africans had arrived in the USA with high expectations, following their powerful display in reaching the quarter-finals of the 1990 World Cup, yet they took their football association to the brink of a crisis two days before the game with Brazil, the players refusing to play without payment. It was rumoured that a suitcase packed with $450,000 arrived secretly, allowing the 'Indomitable Lions' to continue, but with Romario and Bebeto in outstanding form they lost 3-0 to Brazil and finished their campaign with a lacklustre display against Russia, losing 6-1 in San Francisco. Oleg Salenko became the first player to score five goals in a World Cup game, while that popular veteran of African football, 42-year-old Roger Milla, waved goodbye to the World Cup with one more goal, breaking his own record for the oldest goalscorer in the tournament's history.

Prior to Maradona's positive drugs test, Argentina had the look of potential champions, the Argentine captain appearing to have recaptured some of that form of old. An emphatic 4-0 defeat of Greece was followed with victory against Nigeria, signalling Batistuta's arrival with three goals. But without Maradona, a despondent Argentina lost to Bulgaria and limped into the next round at the bottom of a three-way tie with Nigeria and Bulgaria at the top of the table.

Despite stumbling during qualification for the tournament, Italy were regarded as certainties in Group E. Under the guidance of new coach, the much-criticised Arrigo Sacchi, the Italians had at last moved away from their traditional use of *catenaccio*, abandoning the *libero* in favour of a formation that veered between 4-4-2 and 4-3-3. Sacchi's unpopularity was based on his insistence on tactics over individual skill, but he was never able to develop a settled side, his constant tinkering and poor man management alienating him from key members of his team. In his 53 games as national coach he would use 77 players, never fielding the same team twice. For the 1994 World Cup he would be saved by the skill of the exquisitely talented Roberto Baggio, but under Sacchi there was never any certainty of when – or where – Baggio would play. Like Azeglio Vicini before him, Sacchi preferred to use Baggio in a striking role, rather than the player's own preferred deeper positioning.

Maradona faces the press after failing a dope test. It would prove to be the end of his World Cup.

Given the shortage of strikers at his disposal, it was a surprise that Sacchi opted to leave Gianluca Vialli behind. At the back, Franco Baresi had come out of retirement to add experience to the defence, but he was at fault for the only goal of their first game against the Republic of Ireland, his poor headed clearance chested down by Ray Houghton and driven into the net from 20 yards. It was a tremendous moment for the Irish, played at the Giants Stadium in New York in front of 75,000 predominantly Irish fans. "It was a marvellous occasion," recalls Brian Glanville. "Everyone thought that with all the Italian-Americans in New York they would absolutely pack out the stadium, but it was practically all Irish green."

"For a country the size of Ireland to beat Italy, well it doesn't happen very often, does it?" ponders Jack Charlton. "It was a very special moment and it probably surpasses all of my playing achievements in terms of emotion."

Defeat for the Italians meant that victory against Norway would be imperative, but after the sending-off of goalkeeper Gianluca Pagliuca and injury to Franco Baresi, it took Dino Baggio's 69th minute goal to rescue the game. Sacchi already had a strained relationship with Roberto Baggio and this wasn't helped when he substituted the player after just 22 minutes. Baggio was seen to mouth the words, "This is mad". A subsequent draw with Mexico meant that all the teams were tied on four points, Italy progressing as one of the best third-placed teams behind Mexico and Ireland.

The usual destructive internal disputes undermined Holland's chances once more. A spat between Dick Advocaat and Ruud Gullit, who arrogantly refused to play to the coach's instructions, led to the 32-year-old star's withdrawal from the squad. A less than convincing 2-1 win against Saudi Arabia confirmed their troubles. The Saudis became the tournament's surprise team, beating Morocco 2-1, before Saeed Owairan, 'The Desert Pelé', ran 60 yards through the Belgium rearguard, beating five players and the keeper to secure victory and qualification to the second phase.

Rudi Völler inspired a 3-2 second round win over Belgium for the Germans, while Spain's defeat of Switzerland was closer than the 3-0 scoreline suggested. Two goals from Kennet Andersson at the Cotton Bowl in Dallas enhanced his reputation as Sweden beat Saudi Arabia 3-2, while the tie of the round saw Argentina paired with

Romania. Ariel Ortega did his best to replace Maradona, yet it was opposing playmaker Gheorghe Hagi, the 'Maradona of the Carpathians', who pulled the strings in a 3-2 victory. Argentina had ultimately been let down by the absence of their favourite son, who could be found watching the match from the safety of the press box.

The heat of Orlando caused problems for Ireland, with errors by Terry Phelan and Pat Bonner helping the Dutch to a 2-0 victory. The USA's good run, meanwhile, ended at the Stanford Stadium in Palo Alta, a single Bebeto goal in the 72nd minute killing off their challenge on American Independence Day. Brazil played half the match with ten men, Leonardo sent off for cynically smashing an elbow into the face of midfielder Tab Ramos, the USA's most creative player. He was later diagnosed with a fractured skull.

Despite the undoubted talent in their ranks, the Italians were 1 0 down to Nigeria with 90 seconds left and only ten men on the field, substitute Gianfranco Zola having been controversially sent off after just 12 minutes on the pitch. In the dying seconds Roberto Baggio popped up to send the game into extra-time, running to the television cameras in celebration, screaming "God exists, God exists!" Just a couple of minutes earlier Italian TV commentator Bruno Pizzul had said, "It looks like we are slipping out of the World Cup without having left even a trace". Now Baggio was a player transformed. Filled with renewed confidence, he scored the winner from the penalty spot and would go on to shape Italian destiny for the remainder of the competition.

Letchkov of Bulgaria celebrates scoring the winning goal in the World Cup quarter-final against Germany.

The final second round clash between Bulgaria and Mexico was delayed when a goalpost collapsed, Marcelino Bernal having fallen backwards into the net after clearing a corner. The game went to penalties, Aspe, Bernal and Rodriguez missing for Mexico to send Bulgaria though to the quarter-finals.

Seven of the eight European sides had made it through to the quarter-finals, with Italy looking like a team in the ascendant. Dino and Roberto Baggio both scoring to edge a thriller 2-1 against Spain, while Brazil and Holland dished up a similarly scintillating show in Dallas. Romario's drive and Bebeto's cool finish appeared to have won the game, but Dennis Bergkamp and Aron Winter levelled the score, setting up a grandstand finish, which Brazil won thanks to Branco's free-kick. Bulgaria provided the biggest shock, beating Germany 2-1 thanks to a goal from Stoitchkov and a text-book header by Letchkov, the tournament's star midfielder. It was Germany's earliest World Cup exit since 1962. "That free-kick was definitely the best moment of my career," recalls Hristo Stoitchkov. "I was fouled just outside the box and I thought to myself, 'This is the moment'. I needed to keep my nerves cool and then I hit the ball over the wall and into the net. I was especially pleased when Yordan Letchkov got the winner, because it had been his tackle on Jurgen Klinsmann that had given away a penalty. What was important was that we stuck together for the whole 90 minutes, played like a real team and won the game."

With Romania leading Sweden 2-1 in a tense quarter-final in Palo Alta, Stefan Schwarz's red card in the 11th minute of extra-time seemed to have killed off all hope for the Scandinavians, but Kennet Andersson's goal took the game to penalties and the Swedes tasted victory when Thomas Ravelli saved from Miodrag Belodedici. In the semi-final against Brazil at the Pasadena Rose Bowl, Ravelli was in inspired form once again, but with only ten men for the last 30 minutes after the expulsion of Jonas Thern, Brazil proved too powerful. Romario's headed

Brazil 0 Italy 0

BRAZIL WIN 3-2 ON PENALTIES

goal in the 80th minute put the South Americans through to their fifth World Cup final. There they would meet Italy, two goals from the 'Divine Ponytail', Roberto Baggio, having defeated Bulgaria in the other semi-final.

The Brazilians had reached the final through their consistency of play, whereas Italy had relied entirely on the skill of Roberto Baggio. Back in Brazil, there were murmurings of discontent, a desire to see the national team jettison the negative European ways of defensive football and return to the beautiful game that seemed to have been lost forever. "The great thing about football is that it's the only sport where the worst team can win," says Brazil legend Socrates, whose brother Raí was on the bench for the 1994 final. "Just because you might be in control of a lot of the match doesn't mean that you're going to win it. It's the unique characteristic of football."

Brazil's hopes were pinned on Romario and Bebeto, that magical pairing responsible for 33 goals in 57 games together, while Sacchi pinned all of his hopes on the experience of Daniele Massaro and the skill of Roberto Baggio, who had overcome a hamstring injury received in the semi-final to play with a heavily bandaged right leg. There was also room in the side for veteran Franco Baresi, only three weeks after a knee operation. "In 1994 Milan were the top team in Europe, with Baresi, Massaro, Albertini, Maldini and Donadoni, so Italy were a very experienced side," says Carlos Alberto Parreira. "They were a wonderful team so it would be a very difficult game."

For all the fevered hype and speculation about team selection in the build up to the game, when the World Cup final kicked off at the Pasadena Rose Bowl on July 17, the match proved to be a disappointingly cagey affair. "The way that Italy plays is like a counterpoint to the way Brazil plays," explains Socrates. "Brazilian football needs freedom, Italians will try and take away all freedom. So it's the most uncomfortable type of team to play against."

Brazil walked on to the pitch hand-in-hand, as if to reaffirm that team unity would triumph over individual skill. "People don't realise how difficult that game was," says Parreira. "The Brazilians were a good team but Italy were wonderful. It was like a chess game, the one who moves the wrong piece loses the World Cup. It was very beautiful to see people who understand football on a tactical level."

The 90 minutes saw just one clear opportunity, when Pagliuca pushed Silva's effort on to a post, Bebeto and Baggio both spurning chances in extra-time. The game was decided by a penalty shoot-out, the first in a World Cup final. Baresi's opening miss set the trend for the drama to follow. Santos then missed for Brazil, but after successful spot-kicks from Albertini and Evani for Italy and Romario and Branco for Brazil, Massaro saw his effort stopped by Taffarel. Brazilian captain Dunga converted his spot-kick, leaving an exhausted Roberto Baggio needing to score. But like Baresi, the hero of Italy's campaign spooned his effort over the bar. Taffarel sank to his knees in joy, Baggio froze to the spot, his head bowed in despair and disbelief. "I have never known such a low point in my career and I don't think there will ever be another one like it," said Baggio afterwards. He had single-handedly powered Italy to the final, but he would also remain a symbol of their defeat.

With the end of the game Brazil could celebrate their fourth World Cup triumph. "The pressure we had during three years was unbelievable," says Parreira. "At the end of the match there was a feeling of relief. It was like a weight had been taken off my shoulders and it was mission accomplished. Afterwards I could rejoice, but in that moment there was relief, nothing else."

For Sacchi, reaching the final would be enough to keep him in the job for another two years, although he would ultimately resign after Italy's disastrous 1996 European Championships. "I don't think Sacchi was an outstanding manager yet he did get them to the World Cup final," says Brian Glanville. "They probably could have won it, because it wasn't a great Brazil team, but it would have been despite Sacchi rather than because of him."

For the first time in 24 years Brazil were champions again, and as they passed the World Cup trophy around the pitch, for a moment it rested in the grip of one of their youngest squad members, the 17-year-old Cruzeiro striker Ronaldo. In 1994 this young star had not managed to make it on to the pitch, but he would certainly shape the destiny of future tournaments and go on to become one of the World Cup's brightest stars.

GROUP A

June 18: Pontiac Silverdome, Detroit
USA **1 - 1** Switzerland

June 18: Rose Bowl, Pasadena
Colombia **1 - 3** Romania

June 22: Rose Bowl, Pasadena
USA **2 - 1** Colombia

June 22: Pontiac Silverdome, Detroit
Romania **1 - 4** Switzerland

June 26: Rose Bowl, Pasadena
USA **0 - 1** Romania

June 26: Stanford, Palo Alto
Switzerland **0 - 2** Colombia

	P	W	D	L	F	A	Pts
Romania	3	2	0	1	5	5	6
Switzerland	3	1	1	1	5	4	4
USA	3	1	1	1	3	3	4
Colombia	3	1	0	2	4	5	3

GROUP B

June 19: Rose Bowl, Pasadena
Cameroon **2 - 2** Sweden

June 20: Stanford, Palo Alto
Brazil **2 - 0** Russia

June 24: Stanford, Palo Alto
Brazil **3 - 0** Cameroon

June 24: Pontiac Silverdome, Detroit
Sweden **3 - 1** Russia

June 28: Stanford, Palo Alto
Russia **6 - 1** Cameroon

June 28: Pontiac Silverdome, Detroit
Brazil **1 - 1** Sweden

	P	W	D	L	F	A	Pts
Brazil	3	2	1	0	5	1	7
Sweden	3	1	2	0	6	4	5
Russia	3	1	0	2	7	6	3
Cameroon	3	0	1	2	3	11	1

GROUP C

June 17: Soldier Field, Chicago
Germany **1 - 0** Bolivia

June 17: Cotton Bowl, Dallas
Spain **2 - 2** South Korea

June 21: Soldier Field, Chicago
Germany **1 - 1** Spain

June 23: Foxboro, Boston
South Korea **0 - 0** Bolivia

June 27: Soldier Field, Chicago
Bolivia **1 - 3** Spain

June 27: Cotton Bowl, Dallas
Germany **3 - 2** South Korea

	P	W	D	L	F	A	Pts
Germany	3	2	1	0	5	3	7
Spain	3	1	2	0	6	4	5
South Korea	3	0	2	1	4	5	2
Bolivia	3	0	1	2	1	4	1

GROUP D

June 21: Foxboro, Boston
Argentina **4 - 0** Greece

June 21: Cotton Bowl, Dallas
Nigeria **3 - 0** Bulgaria

June 25: Foxboro, Boston
Argentina **2 - 1** Nigeria

June 26: Soldier Field, Chicago
Bulgaria **4 - 0** Greece

June 30: Foxboro, Boston
Greece **0 - 2** Nigeria

June 30: Cotton Bowl, Dallas
Argentina **0 - 2** Bulgaria

	P	W	D	L	F	A	Pts
Nigeria	3	2	0	1	6	2	6
Bulgaria	3	2	0	1	6	3	6
Argentina	3	2	0	1	6	3	6
Greece	3	0	0	3	0	10	0

THE FINAL

BRAZIL	**(0) 0**
ITALY	**(0) 0**

(aet: Brazil won 3-2 on penalties)

DATE Sunday July 17, 1994
ATTENDANCE 94,194
VENUE Pasadena Rose Bowl, Los Angeles

Taffarel

Jorginho — Aldair — Marcio Santos — Branco

Mazinho — Mauro Silva — Dunga — Zinho

Bebeto — Romario

Massaro — Baggio, R

Donadoni — Albertini — Baggio, D — Berti

Benarrivo — Maldini — Baresi — Mussi

Pagliuca

BRAZIL
COACH: CARLOS PARREIRA

TAFFAREL

JORGINHO
Subbed: 22 mins (Cafu)

ALDAIR

MARCIO SANTOS

BRANCO

MAZINHO
Booked: 4 mins

MAURO SILVA

DUNGA

ZINHO
Subbed: 106 mins (Viola)

BEBETO

ROMARIO
sub: Cafu Booked: 87 mins

sub: VIOLA

ITALY
COACH: ARRIGO SACCHI

PAGLIUCA

MUSSI
Subbed: 34 mins (Apolloni)

BARESI

MALDINI

BENARRIVO

BERTI

BAGGIO, D
Subbed: 95 mins (Evani)

ALBERTINI
Booked: 42 mins

DONADONI

BAGGIO, R

MASSARO
sub: Apolloni Booked: 41 mins

sub: EVANI

REFEREE: Puhl (Hungary)

GROUP E

June 18: Giants Stadium, New Jersey
Italy **0 - 1** Rep. Of Ireland

June 19: Robert F Kennedy, Washington DC
Norway **1 - 0** Mexico

June 23: Giants Stadium, New Jersey
Italy **1 - 0** Norway

June 24: Citrus Bowl, Orlando
Mexico **2 - 1** Rep. Of Ireland

June 28: Giants Stadium, New Jersey
Rep. Of Ireland **0 - 0** Norway

June 28: Robert F Kennedy, Washington DC
Italy **1 - 1** Mexico

	P	W	D	L	F	A	Pts
Mexico	3	1	1	1	3	3	4
Rep. Of Ireland	3	1	1	1	2	2	4
Italy	3	1	1	1	2	2	4
Norway	3	1	1	1	1	1	4

GROUP F

June 19: Citrus Bowl, Orlando
Belgium **1 - 0** Morocco

June 20: Robert F Kennedy, Washington DC
Holland **2 - 1** Saudi Arabia

June 25: Citrus Bowl, Orlando
Belgium **1 - 0** Holland

June 25: Giants Stadium, New Jersey
Saudi Arabia **2 - 1** Morocco

June 29: Citrus Bowl, Orlando
Morocco **1 - 2** Holland

June 29: Robert F Kennedy, Washington DC
Belgium **0 - 1** Saudi Arabia

	P	W	D	L	F	A	Pts
Holland	3	2	0	1	4	3	6
Saudi Arabia	3	2	0	1	4	3	6
Belgium	3	2	0	1	2	1	6
Morocco	3	0	0	3	2	5	0

SECOND ROUND

July 2: Soldier Field, Chicago
Germany **3 - 2** Belgium

July 2: Robert F Kennedy, Washington DC
Spain **3 - 0** Switzerland

July 3: Cotton Bowl, Dallas
Saudi Arabia **1 - 3** Sweden

July 3: Rose Bowl, Pasadena
Romania **3 - 2** Argentina

July 4: Citrus Bowl, Orlando
Holland **2 - 0** Rep. Of Ireland

July 4: Stanford, Palo Alto
Brazil **1 - 0** USA

July 5: Foxboro, Boston
Nigeria **1 - 2** Italy
(aet)

July 5: Giants Stadium, New Jersey
Mexico **1 - 1** Bulgaria
(aet)
Bulgaria won 3-1 on penalties

QUARTER-FINALS

July 9: Foxboro, Boston
Italy **2 - 1** Spain

July 9: Cotton Bowl, Dallas
Holland **2 - 3** Brazil

July 10: Giants Stadium, New Jersey
Germany **1 - 2** Bulgaria

July 10: Stanford, Palo Alto
Sweden **2 - 2** Romania
(aet)
Sweden won 5-4 on penalties

SEMI-FINALS

July 13: Rose Bowl, Pasadena
Brazil **1 - 0** Sweden

July 13: Giants Stadium, New Jersey
Italy **2 - 1** Bulgaria

THIRD-PLACE PLAY-OFF

July 16: Rose Bowl, Pasadena
Sweden **4 - 0** Bulgaria

TOP GOALSCORERS 6 goals: Oleg Salenko (Russia), Hristo Stoichkov (Bulgaria)
5 goals: Kennet Andersson (Sweden), Roberto Baggio (Italy), Jurgen Klinsmann (Germany), Romario (Brazil)

FASTEST GOAL 2 minutes: Gabriel Batistuta (Argentina v Greece)

TOTAL GOALS: 141 **AVERAGE GOALS** 2.71 per game:

VIVE LA FRANCE

For a nation who had given so much to the history of the World Cup, France had always failed to perform when it really mattered. But in 1998 Aimé Jacquet's 'rainbow warriors' finally showed the country how to win.

The 16th World Cup was staged on an infinitely bigger and grander scale than any before. USA 94 had done fantastically at the box office, but as an advert for the game of football, the sterile final at the Pasadena Rose Bowl failed to capture the imagination. In comparison, France '98 came like a breath of fresh air, providing all the passion, excitement and controversy that makes the competition such a special occasion. The unsolved mystery surrounding the World Cup final performance of the planet's best footballer, Ronaldo, only added extra drama to the proceedings, and would serve to inflame the passions of conspiracy theorists for many years after the final whistle had called time on the tournament.

For France, hosting the World Cup wasn't without significance. The brainchild of a Frenchman, the nation was yet to win the World Cup despite the riches of skilled talent that it had possessed over the years. If staging the tournament hadn't really captured the imagination of the country at the outset of the competition, by the time the final came about, the French were fully-fledged believers in the game.

The magnificent *Stade de France* was built especially for the occasion in St Denis, in the suburbs of Paris. But behind the façade of this fine new stadium, France was hiding a darker reality. As one of the most racially troubled countries in Europe, the French were divided by the question of immigration. "France had a real problem concerning immigration and the integration of immigrant communities into French society," says defender Marcel Desailly. "The media suggested that it was coloured people who were causing the country all these

France finally experience the liberating sensation that only World Cup victory can bring. Bernard Diomede, Robert Pires, Bixente Lizarazu and Zinédine Zidane lift the trophy.

problems." But it was not just the media who fuelled French discontent. The leader of the far right National Front Party, Jean Marie Le Pen, actually attacked the multi-racial make-up of Aimé Jacquet's France team to further inflame the immigration issue. "I think that was cheap talk," says striker Thierry Henry. "France has always been great at welcoming people. As soon as we were wearing the French shirt, it didn't matter where you are coming from. Everybody was proud to be French."

"I think Jean Marie Le Pen was a supreme opportunist," suggests cultural historian Andrew Hussey. "He just took the right moment to have a kick at the French team as representative of everything that was decadent and rotten about France in the Nineties." Le Pen claimed that to call Jacquet's squad of foreigners French would be a sham. "I think that the remark was out of place," says captain Didier Deschamps. "All the players who were there didn't ask themselves questions about their origins, they were proud to represent France and they made every effort so that France could win, regardless of whether they were black, mixed or white."

What Le Pen was choosing to ignore was that French football had always reflected the country's racial diversity. Many of France's greatest players had come from immigrant backgrounds, including Raymond Kopa and Michel Platini. But even their flair, talent and extravagant play had not managed to bring footballing glory to France.

The French team was now under the direction of coach Aimé Jacquet. He had been appointed to the job after France had failed to qualify for the World Cup in 1994 and was given four years to turn around the fortunes of the national team before the French played hosts to the World Cup for the second time. With the tournament staged on home soil, France could not afford another disastrous defeat like the semi-final of 1982, when they had thrown away a two-goal lead against West Germany. Jacquet had been coach of Bordeaux at the time and many of his players were in the French squad. "I was absolutely furious," recalls Jacquet. "I always said to

them, 'When we have a two goal lead, it's a different kind of football'. You have to know how to control the game, to stall, to destabilise the opponent psychologically. You think that when you're 3-1 up against the best team in the world that you're in control. That's a mistake, it's unthinkable." It was to take another 12 years of missed opportunities by the French national team before Aimé Jacquet was able to start putting into practice the lessons of Seville.

In his first two years in the job France had a remarkable record, Jacquet dropping two of the side's more cavalier talents – Eric Cantona and David Ginola – in favour of a team ethic. But after losing on penalties in the semi-final of the 1996 European Championship, Jacquet became a regular figure of ridicule in the French media, particularly in the pages of national sports paper *L'Équipe*, who were highly critical of his every decision. "Nobody believed in the French team," says Jacquet. "I lived through hell, from critics but also even from the public. There was never a quiet day, because I was getting it from all sides."

As the World Cup approached *L'Équipe* claimed that Jacquet was ill prepared to lead the national side, their criticism turning personal as he was vilified less for his technical ability and more for his social background. "They said he was somebody from the middle of France," says Emmanuel Petit, "that he didn't deserve to be the leader of the national team, that he came from the backwater, that he was not the right person. Do you have to come from high school to direct the football team?"

Jacquet had a vision for the French squad that emphasised teamwork above all else, but with a solid group of players behind him he was able to take a gamble with one of the most creative but unpredictable footballers in France, midfielder Zinédine Zidane. "For me Zidane was out of the ordinary, the exception, but he didn't have his influence yet," says Jacquet. "He hadn't yet acquired his personal dimension and he played football

Brazil's Cesar Sampaio celebrates scoring the opening goal of the World Cup finals against Scotland at the Stade de France.

to enjoy himself. He had exceptional skills, but he didn't have the team in him. When he came to the French team, he joined other talents that took him on to an international level."

"What he can do with his feet, some people can't even do with their hands," says Henry. "That's why he will always do something that will get the fans on their feet, because it's just magical. Sometimes when he plays it seems like he is dancing with the ball." The Zidane magic was evident from an early age when he could be seen playing outside his flat in hometown Marseilles. "We had real fun playing our own World Cup on the *Place de la Tartane*, in the *La Castellane* estate where I was bought up," says Zidane. "We each had our own team but at that age you don't think it's going to be a reality." Everyday reality in France for Zidane, a second-generation Algerian immigrant, gave him little scope for dreaming. His estate was a notorious no-go area that offered little other than high unemployment, limited educational opportunities and a lack of public services. It was given the title of '*Une Quartier Difficile*', a problem area, and its problems were blamed on its immigrant population. The 1998 World Cup would allow Zinédine Zidane to rise from his background and show the whole of France that anything was possible.

For the first time the competition featured 32 teams, more than ever before. That meant not only more matches, but more sides from the emerging regions of football's world game. Among those making a debut at the finals were Japan, Jamaica, South Africa and Croatia. There was also the introduction of the 'golden goal': if a game went into extra-time, the first goal scored would decide the match. By the time the deadline for World Cup entries closed on September 30, 1995, including the hosts and the holders some 174 teams had entered – 168 teams actually taking part in the qualification process, 32 of these for the first time.

With more places available to European teams than ever before, the winners of all nine groups, plus the best runner-up, would qualify for the finals automatically, while the eight remaining second-placed teams would do battle in the play-offs for the last four places. Germany, Norway, Romania and Spain all qualified undefeated at the top of their groups, but even an undefeated campaign was not enough to enable Italy to finish above England in Group Two. Their qualification contest had gone right down to the wire. A goal at Wembley from Italy's Premiership-based striker Gianfranco Zola gave England manager Glenn Hoddle his first defeat early in the qualifying campaign, with stand-in goalkeeper Ian Walker heavily blamed. For the return fixture, England had to travel to Rome's Olympic Stadium for their final group game and battled for a scoreless draw to finish top of the table. Italy were left to beat Russia in the play-offs to ensure their place in the finals.

Holland qualified top of their group, a 3-1 victory over neighbours Belgium in the penultimate game clinching their qualification. A goal from Tony Cascarino against table topping Romania earned the Republic of Ireland a place in the play-offs, only to have their aspirations ended by a 2-1 defeat to Belgium in Brussels. Hungary were also unlucky in the play-offs, losing 12-1 on aggregate to Yugoslavia over two legs.

Iran proved one of the big surprises of the qualification process, beating the Maldives 17-0, the widest margin in World Cup history at the time, Karim Bagheri scoring a record seven goals. Despite having trailed 2-0 in their play off with Australia in front of a crowd of 85,000 at the Melbourne Cricket Ground, Iran would qualify for the finals on the away goals rule after equalising through goals from Karim Bagheri and Khodadad Azizi.

In South America the qualification process was based around a single group of nine teams for the first time, with the top four qualifying automatically. Argentina won the group drawing six of their games. Paraguay, Colombia and Chile also booked their places in the finals, while Mexico, the USA and Jamaica qualified as

The Divine Ponytail picks up where he left off in 1994. Roberto Baggio at the penalty spot for Italy against Chile.

the three representatives of the North and Central American region. After qualifying undefeated, Mexico sacked their coach Bora Milutinoviç, but he made it to the finals in charge of the Nigerian team. Cameroon, Morocco, South Africa and Tunisia were the other qualifiers from the African group.

The opening game of the 1998 World Cup finals kicked off on June 10 between Brazil and Scotland, using the new Adidas Tricolore ball. The holders went ahead after just four minutes through midfielder Cesar Sampaio, who headed past keeper Jim Leighton from four yards. Sampaio was involved in the action again 34 minutes later, as his foul on Kevin Gallacher allowed Scotland to equalise from the penalty spot courtesy of their best player, the sophisticated Monaco midfielder John Collins. A deflected own goal from Tommy Boyd ultimately proved Scotland's undoing and handed victory to Brazil in the 73rd minute. They had acquitted themselves well against the holders, but following a 1-1 draw with Norway, and a 3-0 defeat against Morocco, they were once again on their way home before the start of the second round. Brazil's subsequent defeat by Norway didn't prevent them from topping the group, with the Norwegians qualifying in second place.

In Group B Italy lived up to their reputation as slow starters, trailing Chile 2-1 in their first game until an 85th minute penalty, Roberto Baggio putting his 1994 World Cup final miss behind him to level the scores. With Arrigo Sacchi a distant memory, the Italians were now under the control of the veteran coach, Cesare Maldini, father of the side's captain, Paolo Maldini. With the 66-year-old's belief in *catenaccio* and his preference for selecting the out-of-form Alessandro Del Piero in place of Roberto Baggio, the Italians once more seemed to be creating problems for themselves rather than for their opponents. Nevertheless, with victories over Austria and Cameroon, Italy eased through to the next round along with group runners-up Chile.

YOURI DJORKAEFF

For the France striker it was good old-fashioned team spirit that won the World Cup.

"In 1990 the French team wasn't at the World Cup in Italy, and at the last second we didn't qualify to go to the United States in 1994. In 1998 we were playing at home so we qualified automatically. There were no qualification matches to judge how good the team was, which meant there was a huge pressure because the French media were not really behind the team, and especially the coach. But from 1995 the team was very strong and didn't lose many matches, so we were well prepared and wanted to win. There was a unity in the squad, a solidarity. Aimé Jacquet managed to build a team spirit and the French team became like a club. It became *our* club. That was amazing.

"When you live in France, when you were born in France, when you wear the blue shirt, I think it's important to feel 100 per cent French. My parents were born in France and so was I, so I'm French. But we shouldn't forget our origins, and I think the French team's strength was that mix, the strengths we each brought to the team: a little bit of Guyana, Armenia, Algeria. That's why there was something really extraordinary.

"Jean-Marie Le Pen criticised the team, saying we didn't know the words to the national anthem. But that wasn't true because of the 22 players, nearly 20 had been in the French army, and that's where people learn *'La Marseillaise'*. We don't learn it at school; we learn it in the army. So we all knew it and we sang it before each match. We had a ritual of standing close to each other and holding on to each other's shoulders while we were singing it. We did it once and it brought us luck, so we carried on.

"I had known *'La Marseillaise'* since I was young. My father was a footballer and he played for the French team. When I was about six, I saw my father on TV and saw that *'La Marseillaise'* was played. My brother and I stood up, because you have to stand for the national anthem, that's respect. That's why wearing the blue shirt and singing *'La Marseillaise'* is important to me. It's good motivation. It's something very powerful. When you hear *'La Marseillaise'* you don't need to warm up.

"When I scored against Denmark it was amazing because it was in Lyon, my home city, the place where I grew up. All my family and friends were there and the stadium had a crazy atmosphere. It's a great memory. We played in Marseilles, Paris, Lyon and we didn't feel one had a greater atmosphere than the other. That was extraordinary, because normally when we played in Lyon we thought it was not going to be as crazy as Marseilles, or that Paris would be more difficult than Lens. But the French team were at home everywhere in 1998.

"When you're a kid you can only dream of playing in a World Cup final one day, but suddenly you find yourself there. It's the achievement of your sporting career, but we knew we were strong, we knew that the whole country would support us, and that it was the right day for us.

"I think everybody cries when they become world champion, because you are like Pelé, like Maradona, like all those mythical players you watched as a child. You used to see them with the World Cup, kissing it, holding it – and now here you are as well! There were tears of joy that day. We had managed to do something unique, to win the World Cup for France."

Youri Djorkaeff holds of Alessandro Costacurta during France's quarter-final with Italy.

France came into the tournament under pressure. The team's many critics claimed they were lacking strikers and too focused on defence, but Aimé Jacquet had full confidence in his team's preparation. "I was aware of how to do my job well," he says. "And I was sure that with the resources I had, I knew I was going to make a success of something." A 3-0 win in their first game, however, said little about how they had struggled to find a way past an uninventive South Africa, and Jacquet's confidence did not seem to be shared by his team. "We were apprehensive," says Marcel Desailly. "We started doubting the training we'd had. I think I've never doubted so much at any other time in my career."

"When we first played against South Africa in Marseilles, the pressure in the bus before we arrived at the game was so intense," says Emmanuel Petit. The match had been just as tense but largely uneventful for the French until Christophe Dugarry made the first breakthrough in the 35th minute. Spurred on by this success and a South African own goal, Monaco's Thierry Henry scored a third for France, collecting the ball 20 yards out, slipping into the area past Willem Jackson and putting the ball over keeper Hans Vonk. "In the spur of the moment I just turned and chipped the ball over the goalkeeper and the ball was in," says Henry. "I was pretty happy as my dad and brother were in the stadium. Scoring in the World Cup at home, in front of the family, was just crazy."

After the first victory had been secured the sense of relief could be felt by the whole of France. "In the end it went well for us in spite of a difficult start to the game," says Zinédine Zidane. "We got back in the changing room feeling stronger." But for Zidane, the next match would hold less happy memories. Saudi Arabia were

Zinédine Zidane sees red. Aimé Jacquet can hardly hide his anger as France's best player is sent off.

not expected to give France much of a headache and were reduced to ten men after 18 minutes, Mohammed Al-Khlaiwa red-carded for a foul on Lizarazu. With Henry scoring in the first half, and David Trezeguet increasing the lead in the 68th minute, France appeared to be coasting towards victory, but then disaster struck. Zinédine Zidane was sent off for violent misconduct after stamping on Amin Fuad-Anwar. "I felt terrible when I got sent off," says Zidane. "I took it badly because I let my team-mates down and I was going to miss games."

"When you see Zidane leaving the pitch and you see Jacquet, he didn't even look at him. He was focusing on the guys who were on the pitch," says Henry. "Zinédine's red card was terrible, because the best player was going," says Jacquet. "What were we going to do? I can tell you that we were very worried. But I did not want to show it."

Even without Zidane France were able to overwhelm Saudi Arabia, with additional goals from Henry and Lizarazu. The team celebrated safe in the knowledge that they had qualified for the second round with a game to spare. Jacquet's vision for the team appeared to be working, with or without their biggest star. "It's interesting to listen to the accents bounding around the dressing room," says Andrew Hussey. "There are accents from all over the place, different parts of France as well as different parts of the colonies, but what's interesting is when you look at the team together, how they function, how they bond. They're taking the piss out of each other, they're having fun with each other, but they're completely relaxed in this dual identity of being Algerian, being Basque, and being French."

After the game, Saudi Arabia sacked their manager Carlos Alberto Parreira with one game still to play. Parreira had coached Brazil to World Cup success in 1994, but now he had become Saudi Arabia's eighth managerial casualty in just four years. Prince Faisal Bin Fadh decided that assistant coach Mohamed Al-Khuraishi should take charge of the team for its final game against South Africa and a committee was also formed to investigate the poor showing of the players.

Nigeria were the surprise winners of Group D, their talented team boasting the exquisite midfield play of Jay-Jay Okocha, while the Spanish once again failed to live up to expectations. Under the direction of coach Javier Clemente, and despite the powerful club sides housed within *La Liga*, Spain's poor run at major tournaments continued as they narrowly lost a five-goal thriller against the Nigerians and drew 0-0 with Paraguay. Despite a valiant effort in their last match, where they beat Bulgaria 6-1, it was Paraguay who progressed in second place. The controversial Paraguayan keeper Jose Luis Chilavert continued to create headlines, as two Argentinian politicians lobbied for him to be banned for life from his club side after he had appeared on Japanese television giving advice on how Japan could beat Argentina in their opening group game.

Jay-Jay Okocha of Nigeria in action against Denmark at the Stade de France.

Holland qualified at the top of Group E. Under Guus Hiddink much was expected of the Dutch, with a team boasting Patrick Kluivert, Dennis Bergkamp, Marc Overmars and Edgar Davids. They put five goals past South Korea in their opening game, but after a goalless draw with Belgium they had to beat Mexico in the final decisive match that saw both teams go through to the second round. Germany and Yugoslavia made easy work of Group F, the ageing German team offering a last chance for further glory to Jurgen Klinsmann. The most talked about match of the group involved the two bottom placed teams, Iran packing their defence to beat the USA 2-1 in a match rich in political significance. On the final whistle the Iranians celebrated as if they had won the World Cup itself.

Romania topped Group G, Dan Petrescu's last-minute goal helping them to a 2-1 victory over England, who clinched second place with a 2-0 victory over Colombia, thanks to goals from Darren Anderton and David Beckham. Argentina pipped Croatia to the top of Group H after a Gabriel Batistuta hat-trick helped then to a 5-0 victory over the 'Reggae Boyz' of Jamaica at the Parc des Princes stadium in Paris.

In their second round match France faced up to their sternest test yet against Paraguay in a tightly fought match. "Physically it was a nightmare," says Emmanuel Petit. "They were marking man-to-man all over pitch. Even if you decided to go to the toilet, they were following you!" The French appeared nervous and clumsy, Trezeguet, Diomede and Henry all wasting good chances in front of goal. Without the incisiveness of Zidane, luck seemed to be running out for France. "We started to really suffer because we thought, 'How are we going to score?' We tried everything," says Youri Djorkaeff. "It was intense," says Emmanuel Petit. "We hit the woodwork and we missed a couple of chances."

As the game entered extra-time, Djorkaeff saw a free-kick deflected wide as Paraguay hung on. But with just six minutes left on the clock, substitute Robert Pires picked up the ball on the edge of the Paraguayan area and clipped a lofted pass to Trezeguet, who cushioned a header into the path of Laurent Blanc, who rifled a right-footed shot past the onrushing Chilavert. It was the first golden goal in World Cup history. The French had good reason to celebrate. Not only were they through to the quarter-finals, but their playmaker Zinédine Zidane would be back from his two-match suspension.

In the tie of the round, old foes England and Argentina faced up to each other in St Etienne. Gabriel Batistuta gave the South Americans an early lead through a penalty, before Alan Shearer equalised from the spot in the

EMMANUEL PETIT

The France midfielder scored the winning goal in the 1998 World Cup final, but he remembers more about the World Cups he watched as a child.

"I remember the World Cup semi-final against West Germany in 1982. I remember running in my parents' garden for the penalties. It's one of the best memories of the World Cup from when I was a kid. It was a beautiful game to watch and very intense. France were winning 3-1 at one point and I remember the specific moment when Schumacher, the German keeper, smashed the head of Patrick Battiston. The referee didn't even give a free-kick or a card, nothing at all. Battiston was taken off the pitch unconscious by the emergency services. I remember the Germans scored two more goals after that. It went to extra-time and we lost on penalties. I was so frustrated that I hated the Germans for a couple of days, but I hated the referee too.

"I think that game was typically French; when you know that you're going to win, but you can't really win until the last second of the game. I think France were probably too

confident then. There was always a little bit too much arrogance. But winning the World Cup in 1998 had a great impact on the French people and the mentality has changed. Now people know we cannot win until we've finished the job."

"Aimé Jacquet was the architect of our victory because most people think that you have to have the best players to win, but that's not true. It's not the best player that wins, but the best team. Aimé Jacquet had a vision. He brought 22 players together and made them the best team possible. Nobody was more important than the team. A player cannot make the team, but the team can make a player. For me, that's the truth.

"Jacquet was lucky too because he arrived at a good time when there were a lot of very talented players. Like a good bottle of wine you have to wait a certain amount of years to drink it and when

Jacquet arrived with the national team he was a manager with a lot of experience behind him and it was the same for many of the players. They were all playing at a high level at most of the famous European clubs. We arrived at the same point together at the same time, so it was a perfect match.

"I don't remember much about the goal I scored in the final. It's called the 'Goal Of Liberation' because there was no way back for Brazil. I've watched it probably three times and I couldn't believe it was me who scored. I watched it to try and get some memories, because I have none inside my head. I knew that I had scored a goal because I remember Patrick Vieira coming up to me when I was on my knees. But I have no memories other than that."

Match-winning goal scorer Emmanuel Petit celebrates after victory in the World Cup final.

tenth minute, 18-year-old striker Michael Owen having been felled in the area by Ayala. Six minutes later Owen controlled a long pass from David Beckham and raced towards the Argentine goal, leaving defenders in his wake, before beating keeper Carlos Roa with an unstoppable shot from 15 yards. It was one of those memorable World Cup moments on which reputations are built. England maintained their lead until just before the interval, when a clever free-kick routine saw Zanetti equalise. The second half brought drama of a different kind. Within minutes of the restart, Diego Simeone brought down Beckham and, while on the ground, the Englishman kicked out, receiving a red card for his petulance. Playing the second half and 30 minutes of extra-time with ten men, England held their own, even having an effort from Sol Campbell disallowed and a penalty appeal refused. In the deciding penalty shoot-out David Batty's spot-kick was saved by Roa and England fans were left blaming Beckham rather than Batty.

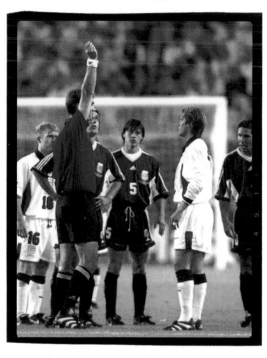

Referee Kim Nielsen shows David Beckham the red card in England's second round game with Argentina.

In the remaining second round matches, Brazil looked impressive in their 4-1 defeat of Chile, while Italy and Croatia both crept through to the quarter-finals by a single goal. Germany edged out Mexico thanks to goals from Klinsmann and their star of the 1996 European Championships, Oliver Bierhoff, while the Danes crushed the main African threat with a 4-1 victory over Nigeria at the *Stade de France*. The Dutch beat Yugoslavia 2-1 in a thrilling game, Edgar Davids deciding the tie with a last minute winner.

In the most exciting quarter-final, Denmark gave Brazil an early shock when Udinese's Martin Jorgensen scored in the second minute, but the South Americans played with confidence, winning 3-2 thanks to a winner from Rivaldo, his second goal of the game. In the quarter-final between Holland and Argentina, both teams were reduced to ten men in the last 15 minutes. Ariel Ortega was red-carded for head-butting goalkeeper Edwin van der Sar in the 88th minute, and from the free-kick the ball was played to Dennis Bergkamp who hit a fierce, rising shot across the goal and into the roof of the net.

Croatia caused the upset of the round, a late goal from Davor Suker sealing a 3-0 win over Germany. The Germans had opened the game well, but had been dealt a major blow when Christian Wörns was sent-off for a foul on Suker. Although no-one but the German team found fault with the red card, coach Berti Vogts would cause a small controversy by hinting that the referee had acted on "orders from above" because the Germans had been "too successful in the past". Appalled at the behaviour of the manager of their national team, *Bild* ran with the headline 'Stop Whining!' and campaigned for Vogts to be sacked.

Italy and France played out a dull quarter-final at the *Stade de France*. With the tie undecided after 120 minutes of play, the teams were left to contest a penalty shoot-out. After four successful penalties from the French and three from Italy, Luigi Di Biaggio had to score to keep Italy in the game – but his spot-kick cannoned off the bar. "Because I was concentrating so hard, the moment he hit the crossbar I didn't realise the match had finished," says keeper Fabien Barthez. "I was still in penalty mode, concentrating. Then I saw everyone running towards me. I thought, 'Oh, it's finished, we've won!'"

"After this game we realised that we were equal to the whole generation of Platini, when they went to the semi-finals," says Petit. "Whatever happened next could only be better." The party atmosphere on the pitch was becoming infectious, as the whole of France got behind their team. "We couldn't avoid seeing what was going on when we went through towns and estates on the team bus," says Desailly. "Africans, Algerians,

Two goals from defender Lilian Thuram ensured France victory over Croatia to reach their first ever World Cup final.

Arabs and Moroccans were all at their windows with French flags. They were mixing with French people and everyone was singing together and everybody had their faces painted in blue, white and red."

In the first semi-final Holland seemed to have the beating of Brazil until a lapse just 22 seconds into the second half, when Frank de Boer tried to catch Brazil offside, only to see Ronaldo steer the ball under Edwin van der Sar. The goal looked enough to win the game, until Patrick Kluivert rose to head home Ronald de Boer's cross in the 87th minute. Neither side managed to gain the upper hand in extra-time, and the semi-final had to be settled by penalties, the reigning champions winning 4-2 after Phillip Cocu and Ronald de Boer both missed spot-kicks for the Dutch. "It was a very hard match," said Rivaldo afterwards. "There were times when we were afraid and when Holland were also afraid. That's why the match went to penalties."

As France had never progressed beyond the semi-final in any World Cup competition, the weight of expectation became unbearable in the run up to their decisive match with Croatia. The French again started nervously, and in a surprisingly difficult first half they struggled to make any headway. During the break Jacquet's team talk left nothing to the imagination: "We're losing all our chances," he told his players, captured in the changing room by French television cameras. "It's not that complicated: either we react, or we go, because there is a final at the end, or you let it go… What are you scared of? Who are you scared of? You're going to lose guys, and its no wonder."

One minute after Jacquet's warning, the unthinkable happened. With the French defence watching the ball rather than the opposition, Davor Suker made a run into the box to score, a rare lapse of concentration from defender Lilian Thuram playing him onside. Thuram's error produced a rage that no-one could have expected, and one minute after Suker's goal he found himself spearheading the French attack. "The ball came to me,"

Dunga scores Brazil's last spot-kick in their penalty shoot-out victory over Holland in the semi-final.

says Djorkaeff. "I saw a player to the side, a blue shirt, so I hit it towards him. I never thought it would be Thuram – why would he be there?"

It was Thuram's first international goal, and it couldn't have come at a more important moment. "He turned around and took a few steps towards his team-mates, he looked out into the crowd and realised what had just happened to him," says Desailly. "He lost consciousness. It's not like he passed out, but he was unconscious with his eyes open, he just didn't know where he was. For about 40 seconds Thuram didn't know what was going on around him. We were all celebrating and we hugged him and told him how awesome he was, but he can't remember a thing. It will always be a magical moment for me."

Thuram wasn't finished yet. In the 70th minute he curled a wonderful left-footed 20-yard shot just inside the post. He had amazed not only his team-mates, but the whole of the country. It was enough to put the French into their first ever World Cup final. "For one night I think if he had said he wanted to be president of France, everyone would have voted for him," says Henry.

With victory in sight it was now time for the real president to follow the lead of the country and join in the celebrations. "I think Chirac is perceived by most French people to be a deeply cynical and opportunistic politician and it is no surprise whatsoever that he put himself around with the team," says Andrew Hussey. "He wore the Number 23 shirt and he identified himself with a proletarian sport that he quite evidently despised. It was foul beyond belief."

As the team made its way to the *Stade de France*, the magnitude of the event began to hit the players. "We are going to play the World Cup final, can you believe it?" laughs Youri Djorkaeff. "It's the final!" But as the team prepared themselves for the most historic day in French football, rumours began to circulate that Brazil's

World Player of the Year was looking likely to miss the game. The name of Ronaldo wasn't included on coach Mario Zagalo's team sheet when it was first submitted and circulated around the press box. There was no explanation and the mystery would go unanswered for many months. Team doctor Lidio Toledo would later reveal that Ronaldo had been rushed to hospital after suffering a convulsion in his sleep on the afternoon of the game. "I don't remember what happened but I went to sleep and it seems I had a fit for about 30 or 40 seconds," the striker explained much later.

Ronaldo's room-mate, Roberto Carlos, was on hand to call for help. "Ronaldo was scared about what lay ahead," he would explain. "The pressure had got to him and he couldn't stop crying. If anything it got worse, because at about four o'clock he started being sick. That's when I called the team doctor and told him to get over to our room as fast as he could." In the days immediately after the final, hotel director Paul Chevalier would paint a more graphic picture of events on the afternoon of the final, the 21-year-old striker reportedly having swallowed his tongue. "There was general alarm with yells and shouts which woke up all the players, who were in the middle of their siesta. For a time we heard people saying, 'He's dead, dead, dead'. It created a terrible atmosphere around the team which was clearly demonstrated later on the pitch."

Ronaldo's place was initially given to Edmundo, and when coach Mario Zagalo gave a team talk before leaving the hotel he reminded his players about the World Cup in Chile, when he and his Brazil team-mates of 1962 had won the World Cup without the injured Pelé. "When they left the hotel at about 6pm for the *Stade de France*, there was complete silence on the bus," said Chevalier. "We who knew them personally understood at that moment that there was no cohesion and they had lost the cup." When Ronaldo later arrived at the stadium he declared himself fit to play and he was reinstated on the team sheet. His inclusion would be the cause of heated debate and forensic enquiries for many years to come.

Word of problems in the Brazil camp had reached the French team before the final. "We were aware of what was going on with Ronaldo," says Fabien Barthez, "but we wanted to play against the real Brazilian team, with Ronaldo carrying the flag. We wanted to see how we measured up to this legendary team, Brazil for real."

On July 12, a crowd of 75,000 packed the *Stade de France* for the World Cup final, with an estimated 25 million watching on television around the country. The French dominated the match for the first 20 minutes, their efficient defence extinguishing any semblance of a Brazilian attack. In the 27th minute Zinédine Zidane showed the world exactly why Aimé Jacquet had placed so much faith in him. Rising to head home a corner supplied by Emmanuel Petit, Zidane scored the goal that the whole of France was waiting for. "Even if you do dream about it, think about it, want to do it," says Zidane, "you tell yourself it's not possible. That's why I said afterwards that in my life nothing was going to be impossible any more."

The Brazilians pushed forward, but Zidane slipped away from Dunga to head home a mirror image goal from Djorkaeff's inswinging corner just before half-time. Brazil looked short of ideas, Ronaldo's performance nothing short of insipid. As the interval was called, Aimé Jacquet rallied his team, determined that the advantage was not lost by the same kind of over-confidence that had cost France defeat in the 1982 World Cup semi-final. "The manager came back and he said, 'Would you all shut up in the dressing room, calm down, relax, legs up'," recounts Emmanuel Petit. "He said, 'Concentrate on what you have to do in the second half and then when the job is finished, then you can talk.'"

As the second half began, 45 minutes separated France from victory. But within minutes Desailly was booked. A second booking in the 68th minute saw him sent from the pitch. "I knew that behind Cafu there weren't any more defenders, which meant that if I could intercept the ball, I could go for goal on my own,"

Opposite: The 1998 World Cup final. (top left) Zinédine Zidane lifts the trophy. (top left) Emmanuel Petit scores France's 'goal of liberation'. (bottom) France celebrate on the pitch. (overleaf) The architect of victory: Aimé Jacquet with the trophy the country thought he couldn't win.

COUPE DU MONDE DE FOOTBALL · FRANCE - BRESIL · FRANCE 98

12-7-1998
93 ST DENIS

15 THURAM Lilian
18 LEBOEUF Frank
6 DJORKAEFF Youri
7 DESCHAMPS Didier
10 ZIDANE Zinédine
7 PETIT Emmanuel
19 KAREMBEU Christian

SAINT-DENIS - STADE DE FRANCE

DIMANCHE 12 JUILLET 1998 A 21H00

FINALE

FIFA
For the Good of the Game.

FRANCE 98

France 3 Brazil 0

1:0 ZINÉDINE ZIDANE (FRA) 27', 2:0 ZINÉDINE ZIDANE (FRA) 46', 3:0 EMMANUEL PETIT (FRA) 90'.

he says. "I got a bit carried away by my excitement, by the dream of scoring a goal in the World Cup final, and I got caught out by my commitment to that."

Just like their semi-final against Brazil in 1958, France were down to ten men, but Jacquet had trained the team for an eventuality like this and nothing was going to rock his defence. The Brazilians were becoming frustrated. "We were winning 2-0 and I remember two Brazilian players were shouting at each other, screaming things, bad things," says Petit. "I did not understand but I could see that they weren't talking nice to each other."

Emmanuel Petit confirmed the win in the 90th minute with France's third goal, his Arsenal team-mate Patrick Vieira feeding him the ball on the edge of the area, Petit firing a low left-footed shot past keeper Claudio Taffarel. "I was running with two defenders and I saw the goalkeeper coming towards me," says Petit. "I didn't know that I was going to score the goal, but I had the feeling that they didn't really attack me. I think they gave up straight away. I don't have a lot of memories of that goal. The only thing I remember is, 'It's me!'"

"The moment when Petit scored the third goal I said to my trainer, 'We're world champions'," says Jacquet. "He said to me, 'We have been for a long time'. I never noticed when the whistle blew. I had a mental block. I don't remember anything."

As France were hosts, it was the job of President Chirac to award the World Cup to the French team. On the way to pick up the trophy captain Didier Deschamps was congratulated by Michel Platini, who had been head of the tournament's organising committee. "It was an amazing privilege," says Deschamps, "because I was the first, I was captain. You feel like stopping time so that everything stands still. It can't get any better than that. It's the result of an enormous effort and lots of hard work and it is a massive reward."

After World Cup final victory Paris celebrates, saying 'merci' to the French team on the Arc de Triomphe.

The French performance in the World Cup final had turned a country more interested in solo sports, such as tennis and cycling, football crazy. Even the president's wife had been swept along with the enthusiasm, admitting to having a crush on goalscorer Emmanuel Petit. "After the celebration at the Champs Elysées, the president came up to me, we shook hands and he looked at me and said, 'You are the one my wife prefers'."

On the Champs Elysées in Paris more than a million people gathered in a massive outpouring of national euphoria, and similar scenes were witnessed across the country. With French flags and Algerian flags flying happily alongside each other, the victory was seen as a triumph for multicultural France, Zinédine Zidane the talisman of French victory. The city of Paris said its own thanks to Zidane, projecting the words 'Merci Zizou' on to the Arc de Triomphe. "I went to the Champs Elysées to participate," says the leading French politician and former Minister for Culture Jack Lang. "When I saw the image of Zidane on the Arc de Triomphe, it was something so strong. For the people of my generation the Arc de Triomphe was the symbol of patriotic ceremonies. For the first time I saw the face of a man coming through his parents from Algeria. I can't find the words to express how happy I was. For me it was one of the most beautiful days of my life."

With the French victory in 1998, Aimé Jacquet and his team had proved their critics wrong. They had shown the world that France was a nation with the mentality to win. But more importantly, the French multicultural team had shown the country the rewards of racial tolerance. That night Aimé Jacquet stepped down from the job of coach to the French national team – and in an act of sweet revenge, he also launched an embittered attack on *L'Équipe*, the newspaper that had tried so hard to destroy him.

GROUP A

June 10: Stade de France, Saint-Denis
Brazil **2 - 1** Scotland

June 10: La Mosson, Montpellier
Morocco **2 - 2** Norway

June 16: La Beaujoire, Nantes
Brazil **3 - 0** Morocco

June 16: Parc Lescure, Bordeaux
Scotland **1 - 1** Norway

June 23: Velodrome, Marseilles
Brazil **1 - 2** Norway

June 23: Geoffroy-Guichard St. Etienne
Scotland **0 - 3** Morocco

	P	W	D	L	F	A	Pts
Brazil	3	2	0	1	6	3	6
Norway	3	1	2	0	5	4	5
Morocco	3	1	1	1	5	5	4
Scotland	3	0	1	2	2	6	1

GROUP B

June 11: Parc Lescure, Bordeaux
Italy **2 - 2** Chile

June 11: Municipal, Toulouse
Austria **1 - 1** Cameroon

June 17: Geoffroy-Guichard, St Etienne
Chile **1 - 1** Austria

June 17: La Mosson, Montpellier
Italy **3 - 0** Cameroon

June 23: La Beaujoire, Nantes
Chile **1 - 1** Cameroon

June 23: Stade de France, Saint-Denis
Italy **2 - 1** Austria

	P	W	D	L	F	A	Pts
Italy	3	2	1	0	7	3	7
Chile	3	0	3	0	4	4	3
Austria	3	0	2	1	3	4	2
Cameroon	3	0	2	1	2	5	2

GROUP C

June 12: Felix Bollaert, Lens
Saudi Arabia **0 - 1** Denmark

June 12: Velodrome, Marseilles
France **3 - 0** South Africa

June 18: Stade de France, Saint-Denis
France **4 - 0** Saudi Arabia

June 18: Municipal, Toulouse
South Africa **1 - 1** Denmark

June 24: Gerland, Lyon
France **2 - 1** Denmark

June 24: Parc Lescure, Bordeaux
South Africa **2 - 2** Saudi Arabia

	P	W	D	L	F	A	Pts
France	3	3	0	0	9	1	9
Denmark	3	1	1	1	3	3	4
South Africa	3	0	2	1	3	6	2
Saudi Arabia	3	0	1	2	2	7	1

GROUP D

June 12: La Mosson, Montpellier
Paraguay **0 - 0** Bulgaria

June 13: La Beaujoire, Nantes
Spain **2 - 3** Nigeria

June 19: Parc des Princes, Paris
Nigeria **1 - 0** Bulgaria

June 19: Geoffroy-Guichard, St. Etienne
Spain **0 - 0** Paraguay

June 24: Municipal, Toulouse
Nigeria **1 - 3** Paraguay

June 24: Felix Bollaert, Lens
Spain **6 - 1** Bulgaria

	P	W	D	L	F	A	Pts
Nigeria	3	2	0	1	5	5	6
Paraguay	3	1	2	0	3	1	5
Spain	3	1	1	1	8	4	4
Bulgaria	3	0	1	2	1	7	1

GROUP E

June 13: Gerland, Lyon
South Korea **1 - 3** Mexico

June 13: Stade de France, Saint-Denis
Holland **0 - 0** Belgium

June 20: Parc Lescure, Bordeaux
Belgium **2 - 2** Mexico

June 20: Velodrome, Marseilles
Holland **5 - 0** South Korea

June 25: Parc des Princes, Paris
Belgium **1 - 1** South Korea

June 25: Geoffroy-Guichard, St Etienne
Holland **2 - 2** Mexico

	P	W	D	L	F	A	Pts
Holland	3	1	2	0	7	2	5
Mexico	3	1	2	0	7	5	5
Belgium	3	0	3	0	3	3	3
South Korea	3	0	1	2	2	9	1

THE FINAL

FRANCE	**(2) 3**
BRAZIL	**(0) 0**

DATE Sunday July 12, 1998
ATTENDANCE 75,000
VENUE Stade de France, Paris

Barthez

Thuram — Desailly — Leboeuf — Lizarazu

Karembeu — Deschamps — Petit

Zidane

Djorkaeff — Guivarc'h

Bebeto — Ronaldo

Rivaldo — Dunga — Cesar Sampaio — Leonardo

Roberto Carlos — Aldair — Junior Baiano — Cafu

Taffarel

FRANCE
COACH: AIMÉ JACQUET

BARTHEZ
THURAM
DESAILLY
Booked: 48 mins. Sent off (second booking) 68 mins
LEBOEUF
LIZARAZU
DESCHAMPS
Booked: 39 mins
ZIDANE
Goal: 27 mins, 45 mins
PETIT
Goal: 90 mins
KAREMBEU
Booked: 56 mins. Subbed: 56 mins (Boghossian)
DJORKAEFF
Subbed: 74 mins (Vieira)
GUIVARC'H
Subbed: 66 mins (Dugarry)
sub: BOGHOSSIAN
sub: DUGARRY
sub: VIEIRA

BRAZIL
COACH: MARIO ZAGALO

TAFFAREL
CAFU
JUNIOR BAIANO
Booked: 33 mins
ALDAIR
ROBERTO CARLOS
CESAR SAMPAIO
Subbed: 57 mins (Edmundo)
LEONARDO
Subbed: 46 mins (Denilson)
DUNGA
RIVALDO
RONALDO
BEBETO
sub: DENILSON
sub: EDMUNDO

REFEREE: S Belqola (Morocco)

GROUP F

June 15: Parc des Princes, Paris
Germany **2 - 0** USA

June 14: Geoffroy-Guichard, St Etienne
Yugoslavia **1 - 0** Iran

June 21: Felix Bollaert, Lens
Germany **2 - 2** Yugoslavia

June 21: Gerland, Lyon
USA **1 - 2** Iran

June 25: La Mosson, Montpellier
Germany **2 - 0** Iran

June 25: La Beaujoire, Nantes
USA **0 - 1** Yugoslavia

	P	W	D	L	F	A	Pts
Germany	3	2	1	0	6	2	7
Yugoslavia	3	2	1	0	4	2	7
Iran	3	1	0	2	2	4	3
USA	3	0	0	3	1	5	0

GROUP G

June 15: Velodrome, Marseilles
England **2 - 0** Tunisia

June 15: Gerland, Lyon
Romania **1 - 0** Colombia

June 22: La Mosson, Montpellier
Colombia **1 - 0** Tunisia

June 22: Municipal, Toulouse
Romania **2 - 1** England

June 26: Stade de France, Saint-Denis
Romania **1 - 1** Tunisia

26 June: Felix Bollaert, Lens
Colombia **0 - 2** England

	P	W	D	L	F	A	Pts
Romania	3	2	1	0	4	2	7
England	3	2	0	1	5	2	6
Colombia	3	1	0	2	1	3	3
Tunisia	3	0	1	2	1	4	1

GROUP H

June 14: Municipal, Lyon
Argentina **1 - 0** Japan

June 14: Felix Bollaert, Lens
Jamaica **1 - 3** Croatia

June 20: La Beaujoire, Nantes
Japan **0 - 1** Croatia

June 21: Parc des Princes, Paris
Argentina **5 - 0** Jamaica

June 26: Parc Lescure, Bordeaux
Argentina **1 - 0** Croatia

June 26: Gerland, Lyon
Japan **1 - 2** Jamaica

	P	W	D	L	F	A	Pts
Argentina	3	3	0	0	7	0	9
Croatia	3	2	0	1	4	2	6
Jamaica	3	1	0	2	3	9	3
Japan	3	0	0	3	1	4	0

SECOND ROUND

June 27: Velodrome, Marseilles
Italy **1 - 0** Norway

June 27: Parc des Princes, Paris
Brazil **4 - 1** Chile

June 28: Felix Bollaert, Lens
France **1 - 0** Paraguay
(aet)
France won with golden goal

June 28: Stade de France, Saint-Denis
Nigeria **1 - 4** Denmark

June 29: La Mosson, Montpellier
Germany **2 - 1** Mexico

June 29: Municipal, Toulouse
Holland **2 - 1** Yugoslavia

June 30: Parc Lescure, Bordeaux
Romania **0 - 1** Croatia

June 30: Geoffroy-Guichard, St Etienne
Argentina **2 - 2** England
(aet)
Argentina won 4-3 on penalties

QUARTER-FINALS

July 3: Stade de France, Saint-Denis
Italy **0 - 0** France
(aet)
France won 4-3 on penalties

July 3: La Beaujoire, Nantes
Brazil **3 - 2** Denmark

July 4: Velodrome, Marseilles
Holland **2 - 1** Argentina

July 4: Gerland, Lyon
Germany **0 - 3** Croatia

SEMI-FINALS

July 7: Velodrome, Marseilles
Brazil **1 - 1** Holland
(aet)
Brazil won 4-2 on penalties

July 8: Stade de France, Saint-Denis
France **2 - 1** Croatia

THIRD-PLACE PLAY-OFF

July 11: Parc des Princes, Paris
Holland **1 - 2** Croatia

TOP GOALSCORERS 6 goals: Davor Suker (Croatia) **5 goals:** Gabriel Batistuta (Argentina)

FASTEST GOAL 53 seconds: Celso Ayala (Paraguay v Nigeria)

TOTAL GOALS: 171 **AVERAGE GOALS** 2.67 per game:

BATTLE OF THE GIANTS

From its opening day shock, the 2002 World Cup saw successes for many unfancied nations. But ultimately the competition was decided by a duel between two football giants, meeting in the final for the first time.

When FIFA awarded the 17th World Cup to Japan and South Korea on May 31, 1996, it was by acclamation rather than a formal vote. Forever wanting to extend the frontiers of the world game, this would be the first tournament to be staged outside of Europe and the Americas. Despite a less than impressive record in international football before the 2002 World Cup, the two hosts threw themselves wholly into the challenge of staging a memorable sporting event, generating huge public excitement in a region not previously known for its great interest in the sport.

In their own distinctive ways, the fans of both countries made this tournament a special event. The South Koreans turned matches red with colour, sweeping their team along on a tidal wave of enthusiasm. The Japanese, meanwhile, cast aside their traditional conservatism and transformed themselves into easily excitable football fans, their wide-eyed enthusiasm one of the lasting memories of a successful World Cup.

It will also be remembered as the tournament where the smaller football nations fought back, and very nearly succeeded in overthrowing the existing global power base. As if to signify a shift in the balance of football dominance, from the very first game it was to be a competition full of shocks and surprise results. It was a tournament that saw plenty of countries with established reputations and big name players knocked out of the competition long before they would have expected, while it was also notable for the success of many unfancied countries, such as Senegal, Turkey and South Korea. For the very first time in World Cup history, teams from

Ronaldo and Rivaldo demonstrate how pleased they are to have finally won the World Cup.

The opening match of the 2002 World Cup threw up a major shock, when unfancied Senegal beat holders France.

Europe, North America, South America, Africa, and Asia reached the quarter-finals. Despite this, the final was to be played out between Germany and Brazil, the World Cup's two most established and successful sides.

Going into the tournament Germany and Brazil were considered to be fielding their weakest teams in living memory and both had stumbled through the qualification process. At one point it had seemed highly possible that Brazil would fail to reach the finals for the first time in their history, and the Germans only made it to Korea/Japan through the backdoor of the play-offs.

For German fans the disastrous performance at the European Championships of 2000 had been hard to stomach for a country so used to success, and their team's 5-1 World Cup qualification defeat to England at the impenetrable bastion of German football, the Olympic Stadium in Munich, was a humiliation more than they could bear. The result left Germany going into the last round of group games level on points with England but with an inferior goal difference. When the final whistle blew on Germany's 0-0 draw with Finland, the last few seconds were still being played out at Old Trafford, England 2-1 down to Greece. The German team were crowded around a tiny TV set on the touchline in Gelsenkirchen when, a minute and a half into injury time, David Beckham stepped up to take a free kick from distance. "There was no doubt that Beckham would narrowly miss, probably hitting the post or the bar," said Greece's German coach Otto Rehhagel. "That was the God-given rule: England were always denied when it counted, Germany always got the lucky breaks. And so Beckham struck. And the ball hit the back of the net." In a new experience for the Germans, their team was consigned to the play-offs.

A decisive 4-1 home victory against Ukraine saw them through to the finals and for the first time a German team was going to the World Cup as an outsider. This created a strange dynamic, bonding the players and bringing the German nation behind them in a way not experienced for many years. Even at his peak as a player Franz Beckenbauer had been unpopular with the fans, and they had little love for the squad of Jupp Derwall, but now Germany had a team of players that they actually liked, underdogs that they could root for. It mattered little that the German media had written off the team as a bunch of no-hopers, the fans geared themselves up for an enjoyable World Cup unhindered by the responsibility of expectations. The accepted wisdom was that they would qualify from their weak group without a problem and reach the quarter-final before being knocked out by Italy. While they attempted to do so, the country went football mad like never before.

With the tournament split across two countries for the first time, three teams qualified automatically: the two hosts Japan and Korea, plus the holders, France. A further 196 countries entered the preliminary qualification process, although after withdrawals, only 193 nations actually took part, with more than 17 million fans passing through the turnstiles before all 29 countries had booked their places in the finals. Once again the qualification process had its casualties, none bigger than Holland. Despite a star-studded team of world-class talent, the Dutch missed out on their place in the finals after defeat at home to Portugal and away to the Republic of Ireland. Portugal qualified top of the group, the Irish beating Iran over two legs in a play-off.

2002 FIFA WORLD CUP KOREA/JAPAN
31 MAY – 30 JUNE

Costa Rica were the big surprise package from the Central and North American region, finishing six points above Mexico and the USA, who qualified in second and third place. In the ten-team South American group, the first four teams qualified automatically. Argentina topped the table with 43 points from their 18 games, well clear of nearest rivals Ecuador, Brazil and Paraguay. Uruguay finished fifth but booked their place in the finals for the first time in 12 years by beating Australia 3-1 on aggregate in a play-off, despite losing the away leg 1-0. Australia could possibly feel slightly aggrieved. Having broken World Cup scoring records when beating American Samoa 31-0, not to mention the 22 goals they put past Tonga, they once again topped their group but had to face a play-off for a place in the finals. From the Asia group China and Saudi Arabia joined the two hosts in the finals, while four of the African qualifiers from 1998 – Cameroon, Nigeria, South Africa and Tunisia – qualified once again. They would be joined in the finals by World Cup debutantes Senegal, who would pull off one of the biggest surprises in World Cup history in the opening game.

Senegal's opponents were France, not only the holders but also undisputed favourites to retain their title. In a physical game, the Africans over-powered a jaded looking French team, who were clearly missing the talismanic presence of the injured Zinédine Zidane. A solitary goal by Pape Bouba Diop sent shockwaves around the world. The French team had won their last two tournaments – the World Cup and the European Championship – back to back, and now in Korea they were facing disaster. Playing against Uruguay in their next game, France could manage only a scoreless draw, playing for over an hour with just ten men after Thierry Henry's sending off. Coach Roger Lemerre brought back Zidane for their do-or-die game with Denmark, but lacking in match fitness there was little he could do to prevent a 2-0 defeat and the champions were on their way home, having failed to score a single goal in three group games. "We prepared for the game with everything we had and we did our best. The punishment of sport is here and we have to accept it," said Lemerre after the game. For French striker David Trezeguet, the defeat marked the passing of a glorious era for the French team: "The beautiful story, which started in 1996, has ended today."

Joint favourites Argentina also suffered the ignominy of elimination at the group stage. After a narrow win in their opening game against Nigeria, courtesy of a Gabriel Batistuta header, defeat to England and a draw with Sweden meant the hugely talented Argentine squad were to play no further part in the 2002 World Cup.

Sayonara: Even the skills of Hidetoshi Nakata were not able to prevent Japan losing to Turkey in the second round.

Their confrontation with England had been one of the most eagerly anticipated games of the competition, but David Beckham converted a match-winning penalty to gain revenge for his controversial red card in the quarter-final four years earlier. The Japanese in the crowd at the Sapporo Dome were delighted. They had turned out in force for all of England's group games, Japan's national obsession with their own star Hidetoshi Nakata was only matched by their complete fascination with David Beckham. Although out of form and performing well below his abilities as a result of rushing back from injury, he became the most talked about footballer at the World Cup.

The talented Portuguese side were the other high-profile casualties in the first stage of the tournament, losing to the USA and South Korea, who against all predictions topped their group despite having never before won a match at the finals in 48 years of trying. As with Beckham and Zidane, Portugal's biggest international star, Luis Figo, was not performing at the top of his game. Only two teams qualified with 100 per cent records: the impressive Brazil, looking more assured and confident with every game, and perennial under-achievers Spain. Slovenia, China and Saudi Arabia all went home without a point to their name, while Germany's 8-0 demolition of Saudi Arabia was, by quite a margin, the most one-sided of all the games of the tournament.

Despite the loss of influential captain Roy Keane, who walked out on the squad before they had even arrived at the World Cup, the Republic of Ireland increased in confidence as the competition progressed, battling through their three group games in Japan. They had stunned Germany with a last gasp Robbie Keane equaliser in the second minute of injury-time at Ibaraki's Kashima Stadium, and after beating Saudi Arabia 3-0 at International Stadium in Yokohama, they qualified for the second round in Korea. "I'll be sorry to see the back of Japan as we've enjoyed it, but you never know, we might be back," grinned Mick McCarthy, alluding to

Sweet revenge: David Beckham scores from the penalty spot to beat Argentina.

the final. "We came here to try and win it. Is that realistic? Who knows? But the French would swap with us right now, wouldn't they, and there will be 16 other teams wishing they were in our shoes."

Germany secured a routine win against Paraguay in the opening game of the second round, while England confidently cruised past Denmark with a 3-0 win at Niigata's Big Swan Stadium. First-half goals from Rio Ferdinand, Michael Owen and Emile Heskey sent the England fans ecstatic. The timid announcement that people should remain seated was a warning shot across the bows as fans from all areas of the arena dashed to join the dozens of concentric conga chains dancing around the stadium. While the English did the conga, the Brazilians took on Belgium with the samba, their fans turning Kobe's Wing Stadium yellow and green. Goals from Rivaldo and Ronaldo won the tie for Brazil. For all the optimism of the Irish, a last minute penalty scored by Robbie Keane only bought them an extra 30 minutes of play in their tightly fought second-round encounter with Spain, a penalty shoot-out eventually separating the two teams in favour of the Spanish. The USA, meanwhile, progressed with a win over Mexico, while Senegal continued their impressive run by defeating Sweden.

For the Japanese, the tournament had been a steep learning curve, but their team had risen to the challenge, the players becoming household names in the space of just two weeks. The more hysterical among their new supporters, brought to the football by the magic of the World Cup, were already imagining Tsuneyasu Miyamoto lifting the trophy, but a headed goal from Turkey's Umit Davala extinguished all hope for the hosts. "It's the end of an adventure," said their coach, Phillippe Troussier. "But we finished with a Japanese team which has a lot of spirit for the future. The team has proved they can play with the best." For Hidetoshi Nakata, he felt

Overleaf: David Seaman can only watch in horror as Ronaldinho's amazing free-kick hits the back of the net.

his team-mates had acquitted themselves well. "I hope that the world looks at Japan differently now," he said.

South Korea provided the major upset of the second round, but controversial refereeing decisions marred their 2-1 golden goal victory over the Italians. Francesco Totti was sent off for 'diving' and an apparently good Italy goal was ruled out. When Italy took to the field at the beginning of the game, they had been met with two huge banners intended to stir emotions: 'Again 1966' and 'Welcome To Azzuri's tomb'. In 1966 North Korea had inflicted a defeat on Italy that had psychologically scarred the national team's approach to the game for many years. Now neighbours South Korea had achieved the same feat.

In their three group games four Italian goals had been incorrectly disallowed for offside, but rather than examining the team's lacklustre performances, the Italian media seemed more intent on fanning the flames of the conspiracy theorists. Italy had gone into the tournament under the direction of the incredibly successful club manager, Giovanni Trapattoni, but *'Il Trap'* was a coach now past his best and many of his tactics were starting to look dated in the new millennium. As the World Cup progressed his behaviour had become increasingly erratic, screaming from the touchline through each game. Even in advance of the South Korean tie, Trapattoni and his players had been convinced that a conspiracy was in play. When the match was over, settled by a golden goal courtesy of Ahn, the only member of the Korean team playing in *Serie A*, the Italian players vented their fury at the refereeing decisions by trashing their dressing room. "It was a match full of emotions, a beautiful game and Korea played with their heart," said Trapattoni. "Korea definitely had a few advantages. I don't understand why we had to become a victim of bad decision-making. I think the winner should be Italy." Back home, Perugia president Luciano Gaucci promised that Ahn would never play for his club again and the media inquest into the conspiracy began, deflecting much of the blame from Trapattoni, who managed to keep his job.

'Again 1966': The South Koreans offer Italy a reminder of their World Cup defeat to North Korea in 1966.

If England's game with Argentina had been the tie of the first round, their clash with Brazil in the quarter-finals provided the most sought after ticket in the knockout stage. An opportunistic strike in the 23rd minute of the game at the Shizuoka Stadium gave England an early lead, Michael Owen latching on to the ball after a mistake by central-defender Lucio and firing home. After Rivaldo's equaliser, a freak long-range free-kick from Ronaldinho decided the tie in the 50th minute. Although Ronaldinho was sent off seven minutes later, England failed to find a final touch capable of beating ten-man Brazil.

Germany were fortunate to get past the USA 1-0 in their quarter-final in Ulsan, especially after Torsten Fring's goal-line handball had gone unnoticed. Oliver Kahn was again on such stupendous form that one German newspaper, *Süddeutsche Zeitung,* described Völler's tactics as "a flat back one". For fans back home, the German obsession with their team continued, one Berlin flag factory producing 10,000 flags a day, unable to keep up with the insatiable demand that World Cup fever had provoked. In Osaka, Turkey secured a golden goal victory over an unlucky Senegal, while South Korea continued their great run of good fortune with another act of giant-killing at the Gwangju World Cup Stadium. This time Guus Hiddink's superbly conditioned and well-drilled team got the better of Spain, but once more the victory was not without controversy. The Spanish side were angered to have two goals disallowed. "Everyone saw two

Opposite: The 2002 World Cup final. (top) Ronaldo puts the ball past Oliver Kahn. (bottom left) Brazil captain Cafu with the trophy. (centre) Rivaldo works his way past Carsten Ramelow and Bernd Schneider. (bottom right) Brazil lift the trophy. (right) Ronaldo celebrates his first goal.

怪物が暴れた！

Brazil 2 Germany 0

1:0 RONALDO (BRA) 67', RONALDO (BRA) 79'

perfectly good goals," said midfielder Ivan Helguera. "If Spain didn't win, it's because they didn't want us to win." The manner of the defeat caused Ángel Villar, the president of the Spanish football federation, to resign from his position on the international referee's committee, describing the handling of the match as a farce. It also sparked a diplomatic row between the two countries. The Spanish media, like the Italian press before them, focussed on conspiracy theories that suggested that the match had been fixed in favour of the hosts.

Overlooked amid the controversy was the fact that under the direction of the experienced Dutch coach Guus Hiddink, South Korea had proved a revelation. In preparation for the tournament Hiddink had persuaded the Korean football authorities to suspend their league championship in order to give him five months to transform the side in preparation for the World Cup. So grateful were the South Koreans for his services that immediately after the tournament the Gwangju World Cup Stadium was renamed the Guus Hiddink Stadium.

The established football powers finally started to assert their dominance in the semi-finals. South Korea's wonderful joyride came to an end, as Germany narrowly triumphed with a solitary goal from midfielder Michael Ballack, who would be suspended for the final after receiving a yellow card. Brazil eased past a spirited Turkey 1-0 with a memorable goal from a rejuvenated Ronaldo. One of the teams of the tournament, Turkey would go on to beat South Korea 3-2 in the third place play-off.

On Sunday June 30, 2002, in front of a crowd of 69,029 at the International Stadium, Yokohama, Brazil and Germany faced up to each other in the World Cup final. With the exception of 1978, one or other of them had appeared in every final since 1950, but despite sharing seven world titles between them, this was the first time they had met each other to decide the winner – indeed, it was the first time they had ever played each other in a World Cup. Brazilian confidence was high after several stirring displays in the early stages, and with goals coming from every area of the pitch they entered the game as favourites. Germany, on the other hand, were fortunate to reach the final, and had relied on three consecutive 1-0 wins to see them through the knockout stages. For the first time ever, the Germans had played a 4-4-2 formation through this tournament, their defence, superbly marshalled by goalkeeper Oliver Kahn, had conceded just one goal. Kahn's will to win was legendary. It has been said that he once agreed to take part in a fundraising penalty shoot-out against children – who would raise money by scoring against the German keeper – only to find Kahn incapable of letting the ball go past him, even for charity.

The final was a better game than could have been expected, the Germans playing their best football of the tournament. Brazilian midfielder Kleberson hit the bar, and a couple of half-chances fell to Ronaldo, while Oliver Neuville came close for Germany, Brazil keeper Marcos pushing his 35-yard free-kick on to the post. In the 67th minute, however, the tie was decided by a blunder from Oliver Kahn. The player who had done so much to get Germany to the final failed to hold Rivaldo's shot and Ronaldo pounced on the rebound to fire Brazil ahead. He was on the score sheet again 12 minutes later, curling the ball past Kahn to make it 2-0. It was Ronaldo's eighth goal of the tournament, earning him the coveted Golden Boot. Ronaldo celebrated at the final whistle, the misery of 1998 behind him, but a despondent Oliver Kahn slumped against his goalpost. Kahn was voted the tournament's best player and he was treated to a hero's welcome when the team arrived back at Frankfurt airport. But for a man so committed to winning it could have been of little consolation.

Brazil had entered the finals with what many critics regarded as their weakest team for years, but during the course of four weeks in Japan and Korea their players had grown in stature. In his third World Cup final, Cafu lifted the trophy to mark his country's wholly deserved fifth title. In the 52 years since defeat at the Maracanã had made such a devastating impact on the Brazilian national psyche, this passionate football nation had proved beyond all reasonable doubt that, when it came to the World Cup, nobody could perform at this level better than Brazil.

GROUP A

May 31: Seoul World Cup Stadium, Seoul
France **0 - 1** Senegal

June 1: Munsu Football Stadium, Ulsan
Uruguay **1 - 2** Denmark

June 6: Daegu World Cup Stadium, Daegu
Denmark **1 - 1** Senegal

June 6: Busan Asiad Main Stadium, Busan
France **0 - 0** Uruguay

June 11: Suwon World Cup Stadium, Suwon
Senegal **3 - 3** Uruguay

June 11: Incheon Munhak Stadium, Incheon
Denmark **2 - 0** France

	P	W	D	L	F	A	Pts
Denmark	3	2	1	0	5	2	7
Senegal	3	1	2	0	5	4	5
Uruguay	3	0	2	1	4	5	2
France	3	0	1	2	0	3	1

GROUP B

June 2: Busan Asiad Main Stadium, Busan
Paraguay **2 - 2** South Africa

June 2: Gwangju World Cup Stadium, Gwangju
Spain **3 - 1** Slovenia

June 7: Jeonju World Cup Stadium, Jeonju
Spain **3 - 1** Paraguay

June 8: Daegu World Cup Stadium, Daegu
South Africa **1 - 0** Slovenia

June 12: Daejeon World Cup Stadium, Daejeon
South Africa **2 - 3** Spain

June 12: Jeju World Cup Stadium, Seogwipo
Slovenia **1 - 3** Paraguay

	P	W	D	L	F	A	Pts
Spain	3	3	0	0	9	4	9
Paraguay	3	1	1	1	6	6	4
South Africa	3	1	1	1	5	5	4
Slovenia	3	0	0	3	2	7	0

GROUP C

June 3: Munsu Football Stadium, Ulsan
Brazil **2 - 1** Turkey

June 4: Gwangju World Cup Stadium, Gwangju
China **0 - 2** Costa Rica

June 8: Jeju World Cup Stadium, Seogwipo
Brazil **4 - 0** China

June 9: Incheon Munhak Stadium, Incheon
Costa Rica **1 - 1** Turkey

June 13: Suwon World Cup Stadium, Suwon
Costa Rica **2 - 5** Brazil

June 13: Seoul World Cup Stadium, Seoul
Turkey **3 - 0** China

	P	W	D	L	F	A	Pts
Brazil	3	3	0	0	11	3	9
Turkey	3	1	1	1	5	3	4
Costa Rica	3	1	1	1	5	6	4
China	3	0	0	3	0	9	0

GROUP D

June 4: Busan Asiad Main Stadium, Busan
South Korea **2 - 0** Poland

June 5: Suwon World Cup Stadium, Suwon
USA **3 - 2** Portugal

June 10: Daegu World Cup Stadium, Daegu
South Korea **1 - 1** USA

June 10: Jeonju World Cup Stadium, Jeonju
Portugal **4 - 0** Poland

June 14: Incheon Munhak Stadium, Incheon
Portugal **0 - 1** South Korea

June 14: Daejeon World Cup Stadium, Daejeon
Poland **3 - 1** USA

	P	W	D	L	F	A	Pts
South Korea	3	2	1	0	4	1	7
USA	3	1	1	1	5	6	4
Portugal	3	1	0	2	6	4	3
Poland	3	1	0	2	3	7	3

GROUP E

June 1: Niigata Stadium Big Swan, Niigata
Rep. Of Ireland **1 - 1** Cameroon

June 1: Sapporo Dome, Sapporo
Germany **8 - 0** Saudi Arabia

June 5: Kashima Stadium, Ibaraki
Germany **1 - 1** Rep. Of Ireland

June 6: Saitama Stadium 2002, Saitama
Cameroon **1 - 0** Saudi Arabia

June 11: Shizuoka Stadium Ecopa, Shizuoka
Cameroon **0 - 2** Germany

June 11: International Stadium, Yokohama
Saudi Arabia **0 - 3** Rep. Of Ireland

	P	W	D	L	F	A	Pts
Germany	3	2	1	0	11	1	7
Rep. Of Ireland	3	1	2	0	5	2	5
Cameroon	3	1	1	1	2	3	4
Saudi Arabia	3	0	0	3	0	12	0

THE FINAL

BRAZIL	**(0) 2**
GERMANY	**(0) 0**

DATE SUNDAY June 30, 2002
ATTENDANCE 69,029
VENUE International Stadium, Yokohama

Marcos	
Lucio Edmilson Roque Junior	
Cafu Kleberson Gilberto Roberto Carlos	
Ronaldinho	
Rivaldo Ronaldo	
Klose Neuville	
Bode Hamann Jeremies Schneider	
Metzelder Ramelow Linke Frings	
Kahn	

BRAZIL

COACH: LUIZ FELIPE SCOLARI

MARCOS
LUCIO
EDMILSON
ROQUE JUNIOR *Booked: 6 mins*
CAFU
KLEBERSON
GILBERTO SILVA
ROBERTO CARLOS
RONALDINHO *Subbed: 85 mins (Juninho)*
RIVALDO
RONALDO *Goal: 67 min, 79 min. Subbed: 90 mins (Denilson)*
sub: JUNINHO
sub: DENILSON

GERMANY

COACH: RUDI VÖLLER

KAHN
LINKE
RAMELOW
METZELDER
FRINGS
JEREMIES *Subbed: 77 mins (Asamoah)*
HAMANN
SCHNEIDER
BODE *Subbed: 84 mins (Ziege)*
NEUVILLE
KLOSE *Booked: 9 mins. Subbed: 74 mins (Bierhoff)*
sub: BIERHOFF
sub: ASAMOAH
sub: ZIEGE

REFEREE: Collina (Italy)

GROUP F

June 2: Kashima Stadium, Ibaraki
Argentina **1 - 0** Nigeria

June 2: Saitama Stadium 2002, Saitama
England **1 - 1** Sweden

June 7: Kobe Wing Stadium, Kobe
Sweden **2 - 1** Nigeria

June 7: Sapporo Dome, Sapporo
Argentina **0 - 1** England

June 12: Miyagi Stadium, Miyagi
Sweden **1 - 1** Argentina

June 12: Osaka Nagai Stadium, Osaka
Nigeria **0 - 0** England

	P	W	D	L	F	A	Pts
Sweden	3	1	2	0	4	3	5
England	3	1	2	0	2	1	5
Argentina	3	1	1	1	2	2	4
Nigeria	3	0	1	2	1	3	1

GROUP G

June 3: Niigata Stadium Big Swan, Niigata
Croatia **0 - 1** Mexico

June 3: Sapporo Dome, Sapporo
Italy **2 - 0** Ecuador

June 8: Kashima Stadium, Ibaraki
Italy **1 - 2** Croatia

June 9: Miyagi Stadium, Miyagi
Mexico **2 - 1** Ecuador

June 13: Oita Stadium Big Eye, Oita
Mexico **1 - 1** Italy

June 13: Niigata Stadium Big Swan, Niigata
Ecuador **1 - 0** Croatia

	P	W	D	L	F	A	Pts
Mexico	3	2	1	0	4	2	7
Italy	3	1	1	1	4	3	4
Croatia	3	1	0	2	2	3	3
Ecuador	3	1	0	2	2	4	3

GROUP H

June 4: Saitama Stadium 2002, Saitama
Japan **2 - 2** Belgium

June 5: Kobe Wing Stadium, Kobe
Russia **2 - 0** Tunisia

June 9: International Stadium, Yokohama
Japan **1 - 0** Russia

June 10: Oita Stadium Big Eye, Oita
Tunisia **1 - 1** Belgium

June 14: Osaka Nagai Stadium, Osaka
Tunisia **0 - 2** Japan

June 14: Shizuoka Stadium Ecopa, Shizuoka
Belgium **3 - 2** Russia

	P	W	D	L	F	A	Pts
Japan	3	2	1	0	5	2	7
Belgium	3	1	2	0	6	5	5
Russia	3	1	0	2	4	4	3
Tunisia	3	0	1	2	1	5	1

SECOND ROUND

June 15: Jeju World Cup Stadium, Seogwipo
Germany **1 - 0** Paraguay

June 15: Niigata Stadium Big Swan, Niigata
Denmark **0 - 3** England

June 16: Oita Stadium Big Eye, Oita
Sweden **1 - 2** Senegal
(aet)
Senegal won with golden goal

June 16: Suwon World Cup Stadium, Suwon
Spain **1 - 1** Rep. Of Ireland
(aet)
Spain won 3-2 on penalties

June 17: Jeonju World Cup Stadium, Jeonju
Mexico **0 - 2** USA

June 17: Kobe Wing Stadium, Kobe
Brazil **2 - 0** Belgium

June 18: Miyagi Stadium, Miyagi
Japan **0 - 1** Turkey

June 18: Daejeon World Cup Stadium, Daejeon
South Korea **2 - 1** Italy
(aet)
South Korea won with golden goal

QUARTER-FINALS

June 21: Shizuoka Stadium Ecopa, Shizuoka
England **1 - 2** Brazil

June 21: Munsu Football Stadium, Ulsan
Germany **1 - 0** USA

June 22: Gwangju World Cup Stadium, Gwangju
Spain **0 - 0** South Korea
(aet)
South Korea won 5-3 on penalties

June 22: Osaka Nagai Stadium, Osaka
Senegal **0 - 1** Turkey
(aet)
Turkey won with golden goal

SEMI-FINALS

June 25: Seoul World Cup Stadium, Seoul
Germany **1 - 0** South Korea

June 26: Saitama Stadium, Saitama
Brazil **1 - 0** Turkey

THIRD-PLACE PLAY-OFF

June 29: Daegu World Cup Stadium, Daegu
South Korea **2 - 3** Turkey

 TOP GOALSCORERS 8 goals: Ronaldo (Brazil) **5 goals:** Miroslav Klose (Germany); Rivaldo (Brazil)

FASTEST GOAL 10.8 seconds: Hakan Sükür (Turkey v South Korea)

TOTAL GOALS: 161 **AVERAGE GOALS** 2.51 per game:

INDEX

CHRIS HUNT: THE AUTHOR

Writer and broadcaster Chris Hunt has travelled the world covering football. A freelance editor and journalist, his travels around Japan for the World Cup in 2002 were documented in the BBC TV programme *Beckham For Breakfast*. The second edition of his definitive football encyclopedia, *The Complete Book Of Football*, will be published in 2006 by Harper Collins. For eight years he was Managing Editor of Britain's biggest-selling football magazine, *Match*. Now a regular contributor to *Four Four Two*, he has also worked as a broadcast journalist for BBC Radio 5, and more recently he was the Editor of many of the acclaimed special editions of *Mojo*, *Q*, *Uncut* and *NME*, covering subjects as diverse as The Beatles and punk rock. Although only three years old at the time of the 1966 World Cup final, he thanks his parents for making him watch it! He can be contacted through his website: *www.ChrisHunt.biz*

DAVID HOUGHTON: ART DIRECTOR

An experienced designer, David Houghton often specialises in football or music projects. Working with journalist Chris Hunt, as the design half of the 'Mile Away Club' magazine and book production team, David has been the Art Director of *Match*'s *Euro 2000 Guide, The Match Diary, The Complete Book Of Football* and *The Match Of The Day Annual 2006*. He has also worked as Art Director of monthly music magazine *Hip-Hop Connection*. Not only were his travels around Japan in 2002 with author Chris Hunt featured in the BBC TV programme *Beckham For Breakfast,* but he managed to come back from Tokyo with a wife, Ayumi. His photography of football fans has been published in *Four Four Two, Sport First, Football First* and *Match*. He has watched England play all over the world, and tries to live as near to the Cambridge United ground as possible.

BIBLIOGRAPHY

Many thanks to the authors, journalists and statisticians whose research on the World Cup has proved invaluable, many of whom were interviewed for the TV series on which this book is based.

BOOKS

100 Years Of Football by Pierre Lanfranchi, Christiane Eisenberg, Tony Mason, Alfred Wahl (W&N)

Ajax, Barcelona, Cruyff by Frits Barend & Henk Van Dorp (Bloomsbury)

Back Home: England And The 1970 World Cup by Jeff Dawson (Orion)

Brilliant Orange by David Winner (Bloomsbury)

Calcio: A History Of Italian Football by John Foot (Fourth Estate)

England: The Alf Ramsey Years by Graham McColl (Chameleon)

England v Germany by David Downing (Bloomsbury)

Football Against The Enemy by Simon Kuper (Orion)

Football And Fascism: The National Game Under Mussolini by Simon Martin (Berg)

Football In The Sun And Shadow by Eduardo Galeano (Fourth Estate)

Futebol: The Brazilian Way Of Life by Alex Bellos (Bloomsbury)

Goooal by Andréas Cantor (Simon & Schuster)

How Soccer Explains The World by Franklin Foer: (Harper Perennial)

Jack & Bobby by Leo McKinstry (Collins Willow)

Morbo: The Story Of Spanish Football by Philip Ball (WSC)

Sport In Latin American Society by JA Mangan & Lamartine P DaCosta (Frank Cass)

The Beautiful Team: In Search Of Pelé & The 1970 Brazilians by Garry Jenkins (Simon & Schuster)

The Complete Book Of The World Cup by Cris Freddi (Collins Willow)

The Boys Of 66 by David Miller (Pavilion)

The Story Of The World Cup by Brian Glanville (Faber)

They Think It's All Over by Kenneth Wolstenholme (Robson)

The World Cup: A Complete Record by Ian Morrison (Breedon)

The World Cup's Strangest Moments by Peter Seddon (Robson)

Three Lions On The Shirt: Playing For England by Dave Bowler (Victor Gollancz)

Tor! The Story Of German Football by Ulrich Hesse-Lichtenberger (WSC)

OTHER SOURCES

FIFA website: www.fifaworldcup.yahoo.com

Four Four Two magazine

Rec.Sport.Soccer Statistics Foundation: www.RSSSF.com

The Legend Of The FIFA World Cup DVD (20th Century Fox)

MANY THANKS

Hugh Sleight, Andy Winter, Steve Cresswell, James-Eastham, Mike Pattenden, John Plummer, Nick Gibbs, Alistair Phillips, Gary Tipp, Tim Hartley, Luke Nicoli.

Spoiler: Italy win